MINICOMPUTERS
FOR ENGINEERS
AND SCIENTISTS

MINICOMPUTERS FOR ENGINEERS AND SCIENTISTS

GRANINO A. KORN, Ph.D.

Professor of Electrical Engineering
University of Arizona
Tucson, Arizona

McGRAW-HILL BOOK COMPANY

New York   St. Louis   San Francisco   Düsseldorf   Johannesburg
Kuala Lumpur   London   Mexico   Montreal   New Delhi   Panama
Paris   São Paulo   Singapore   Sydney   Tokyo   Toronto

Library of Congress Cataloging in Publication Data

Korn, Granino Arthur
   Minicomputers for engineers and scientists.

   Includes bibliographies.
   1. Electronic digital computers.   I.   Title.
QA76.5.K67   001.6'4'044   72-10167
ISBN 0-07-035338-7

4 5 6 7 8 9 0   HDMM   7 6 5 4

The editors for this book were Tyler G. Hicks and
Stanley E. Redka, and its production was supervised
by George E. Oechsner.   It was set in Times New Roman.

It was printed by Halliday Lithograph Corporation and bound
by The Maple Press Company.

CONTENTS

Chapter 4. Minicomputer Programming with Assemblers and Macroassemblers . **98**

PREFACE

The new minicomputers represent a very remarkable achievement of engineering ingenuity and industrial know-how at their best. Quantity production with low-cost integrated circuits permits the use of inexpensive minicomputers as exceptionally versatile system components in an ever-increasing number of applications. Increasing sophistication of mini-computer instruction sets and programming systems often gives a small machine sufficient computing power to free researchers or engineers from bondage to a computing-center bureaucracy. This book attempts to introduce engineers and scientists to the principal features of minicomputers and minicomputation. I hope that it will help its readers to understand the manufacturer's literature better, to make intelligent choices of mini-computers, peripherals, and application areas, and thus to realize the exceptional possibilities of this novel tool.

The first chapter is a brief introduction to *the computer's role as a live mathematical model,* and to its *number systems, codes, logic,* and *principal arithmetic operations.* This chapter is intended to make the book self-sufficient, but even engineers familiar with digital computation will find the tabulated information on number systems, data word formats, and logic circuits useful for reference. *The presentation of these items in the form of boxed tables has made it possible to present a good deal of practical reference material in concise form without cluttering the text.*

Chapter 2 presents a thorough discussion of *the instruction sets, addressing schemes, and common options of single-address minicomputers.* Instruction execution is described from the minicomputer user's point of view; i.e., we emphasize its effect on programming rather than upon electronic or logic-circuit details. Such a view of instructions, addressing, and other minicomputer features is necessary if one is to make *intelligent choices among different minicomputer systems*, and it serves as an introduction to discussions of more advanced minicomputer systems in Chap. 6.

Chapter 3 introduces the user to the *operation of minicomputer front-panel controls, peripherals, and system software* and will serve as a helpful introduction to more detailed manufacturers' manuals on these subjects. I have emphasized the power of modern *disk-based operating systems* for general-purpose minicomputation and included discussions of *cassette-tape systems, cathode-ray-tube/keyboard terminals*, and *on-line editing*. Reference tables on minicomputer FORTRAN and the increasingly important BASIC interpreter language are included.

To get the most out of a minicomputer system, especially where high execution speeds and low costs are essential, some knowledge of *assembly-language programming* is required. Chapter 4 introduces *assembly language and assembler functions* and describes *the principles of programming and subroutine design for use with the simple instruction sets of typical minicomputers.* This should not be regarded as a formal text on assembly-language programming but rather as a discussion of the principal features of assemblers and instruction sets encountered in minicomputer systems; once again, this discussion will serve as a convenient—and unbiased—introduction to manufacturers' detailed manuals for specific machines. A number of sample minicomputer programs illustrate useful programming techniques. *With each computer instruction completely spelled out in special boldface type, there is no need to refer to special instruction mnemonics*, as in many texts.

Chapter 4 ends with a discussion of *macroassemblers and conditional assembly* and *emphasizes their extraordinary power in computation with small digital computers.* I believe that the exceptional capability of macroassemblers for enhancing the possibilities of small digital computers is not sufficiently understood and deserves added emphasis. *Emulation of one minicomputer's instruction set by another minicomputer and the writing of simple, homemade procedural languages* are presented as interesting examples.

The most important single feature of the new minicomputers is their ability to interact inexpensively with devices in the outside world. Chapter 5 presents what is probably the most extensive currently available description of *digital-computer interface systems*, including *programmed-instruction interfaces for synchronous and asynchronous transfers, interrupt systems, and direct memory access.* This chapter highlights the impressive simplicity of developing versatile minicomputer interfaces to external devices with off-the-shelf logic cards and simple hardware and discusses both low-cost and elaborate interrupt systems. The chapter closes with a discussion of *input/output software and the use of manufacturer-supplied device-driver routines.*

Chapter 6 discusses *trends in present and future minicomputer* architectures, again from the computer user's point of view. Descriptions of minicomputer systems include *sophisticated 8-bit machines, new multiregister computers* (including a complete subchapter on the new PDP-11/20 and PDP-11/45 systems), and *microprogrammed minicomputers.* A separate section describes *bus-connected accessory processors, special logic circuits connected as minicomputer peripheral devices,* and a complete two-address machine made up of bus-connected modules. Chapter 6 ends with *a checklist of important hardware and software features affecting the choice of a minicomputer system.*

Chapter 7 *surveys the principal minicomputer applications.* Included are minicomputer techniques for *graphic displays* and *plotters,* and instrumentation-*system control and data processing* (with FORTRAN, assembly-language, or interpreter-language programs); important applications to physics, biology/medicine, chemistry, and automated-test engineering are outlined and referenced. Introductions of *control-system supervision, communication-system applications, multiprocessor systems, and minicomputer time sharing* follow. Considering the fact that the need for a computer indicates a measure of sophistication in each minicomputer application, every one of the application fields listed could, surely, be the subject of an entire separate volume; I have tried, though, to point out essential features and possibilities and to give extensive literature references for further study.

The Appendix contains a set of useful reference tables on number systems and code conversion.

I am greatly indebted to my colleagues in the computer industry for supplying me with information and reference material for this book, which attempts to describe the astonishing success of *their* vision and *their* labor. I would, in particular, like to thank the following individuals and organizations:

Computer Operations, Inc.
  Beltsville, Maryland
                R. Bushnell

Data General Corporation   R. Brown
  Southboro, Massachusetts   E. DeCastro
                L. Seligman

Delta Data Systems   H. B. Maser
  Philadelphia, Pennsylvania

Digital Equipment Corporation R. Anundson
  Maynard, Massachusetts   B. Delagi
                E. Dow
                J. Gardiner
                W. Long
                J. Nelson
                J. Pitts
                R. Sumrall

Hewlett-Packard Corporation   R. Grimm
  Cupertino, California and   D. Harris
  Palo Alto, California   W. Hewlett

R. Moley
T. Perkins
R. Raecker
M. Spann
R. Storer
R. Toepfer

Honeywell Information Systems   R. Baron
Framingham, Massachusetts   W. Borgerding
J. Cashen
J. Doyle
R. Henzel
D. Strassbery
L. Templeton

Interdata   D. Ellis
Oceanport, New Jersey   A. Furman
S. Guty
J. Jones
J. Michels
D. Sinnott
V. Spencer

P. Stearns

Redcor Corporation   G. McCready
Woodland Hills, California
Tektronix, Inc.   D. P. Welch
Beaverton, Oregon
Varian Data Machines   A. McLagan
Irvine, California   J. Orris
G. Vosatka

I am also grateful to my colleagues and assistants at the Computer Science
Research Laboratory of the Electrical Engineering Department, the
University of Arizona, for their help:

H. Aus   J. Moore
M. Andrews   M. Naka
J. Belt   P. O'Grady
J. Ferguson   J. Puls
J. Goltz   S. Simons
R. Gonzalez   A. Trevor
W. Jensen   J. Wait
L. Kendrick   R. White
H. Kosako   C. Wiatrowski
T. Liebert   J. Wilkins
R. Martinez   A. Yagi
R. Miller

MINICOMPUTERS
FOR ENGINEERS
AND SCIENTISTS

CHAPTER 1

INTRODUCTION TO MINICOMPUTATION

A NEW TOOL OF EXTRAORDINARY POWER

1-1. Where Computers Fit. Scientists and engineers describe, measure, interpret, and predict the outside world in terms of idealized **mathematical models,** which relate numerical quantities and truth values through various mathematical operations. **Computers are physical systems designed to implement mathematical models** and to automate their manipulation. Professional workers are likely to meet computers in the following roles:

1. **Numerical problem solving and data processing:** This ranges from little slide-rule and calculator jobs to big number-crunching projects and includes design calculations, statistics, genetics calculations, bookkeeping, etc. The end product may be scientific or clerical *description,* but, in the long run, calculations usually serve for *making decisions.*
2. **Storing, retrieving, sorting, and updating data:** This is by no means restricted to numerical data only.
3. Computer **simulation:** We use the convenient, easy-to-change "live mathematical model" for *experiments* which might be slow, expensive, unsafe, or impossible with the real-world system or situation being simulated. Computer simulation serves the purposes of design, systems research, education, training, and play; simulation experiments or tests sometimes involve parts of real systems.
4. **"Real-time" or "on-line" computing devices** serve as components of control and instrumentation systems to:
   (*a*) Implement desired mathematical relations between physical variables (e.g., function generation, filtering, prediction, optimization)

1

(*b*) Control timing and logical sequencing of operations and experiments

The latter types of operations are often combined with on-line record keeping (data logging) and data processing.

5. Real-time timing, switching, coding, and data storage in **communication systems,** especially in communications between digital computers and/or computer terminals.

1-2. The Role of Small Computers. Conventional number-crunching calculations are traditionally performed by large digital computers operating in a **batch mode,** i.e., efficiently fed with a more or less continual and orderly sequence of things to do.   In this type of application, experience appears to indicate that "throughput" (defined as the number of computer operations, in some specified mix, per unit time) increases better than proportionally with computer cost (*Grosch's law*), so that large computer systems are economical.

Other computer applications involve several users who would not like to wait for batch-processed results but need quick *"conversational" input and output* from multiple computer terminals.   Again, *control and instrumentation work* is timed by the demands of real-world events.   Large digital machines subject to such random service requests cannot afford to wait idly until action is required: they must be *time-shared* among multiple programs. Time-sharing operations can utilize the resources of ever larger (and thus presumably more efficient) computer systems.   Time sharing also involves serious *overhead costs* resulting from communications with remote interfaces, from greatly complicated system programming, and from the many computer operations needed to swap and protect programs.   *We can, then, find applications where multiple small computers can neatly replace or complement large machines.*

We will (quite arbitrarily) define a **minicomputer** as a digital computer whose "minimum configuration" (4,000 words of memory, teletypewriter) costs under $20,000 and which usually employs short computer words (to 18 bits, Sec. 1-3) to represent data and computer instructions (see also Secs. 1-5 and 2-1); minicomputer cost is usually roughly proportional to word length.   As we shall see, 16 bits can represent numerical *data* with enough precision for many applications, but clever utilization of the short *instruction* words is the central problem of minicomputer system design (Sec. 2-5 and Chap. 6).   An *n*-bit instruction word can specify at most 2^n different instructions. $2^{16} = 65,536$ looks like a very large number of possible instructions, but many of these instructions must specify the source or destination of an operand in a computer memory having perhaps 8,000 locations.   This need for address specification greatly reduces the effective number of different one-word minicomputer instructions.

Nevertheless, even 8- and 12-bit minicomputers with fairly primitive instruction sets are very versatile, since multiple instructions can implement extremely complex operations. Such machines now replace hard-wired special-purpose logic in many real-time applications such as operation sequencing, timing, production testing, and data logging. **Custom-designed hardware is then replaced by the quantity-produced minicomputer, which can be programmed and reprogrammed for a huge variety of different applications and new conditions.**

Minicomputers are especially suitable for operations involving external real-world devices (Fig. 1-2 and Chap. 7) because:

1. Many jobs of this type do not require elaborate processor circuits.
2. We want no big expensive central processor standing idle during input/output operations.

For precisely the same reasons, **minicomputers can also relieve large digital computers of input/output and communications-handling chores.**

Many of the more recent small processors are in no sense primitive (Chaps. 2 and 6). **The truly revolutionary advance and acceptance of the newer minicomputers stems from the mass production of new integrated circuits, which have radically reduced processor and memory costs.** We actually have a twofold effect:

1. Medium-scale integration (MSI) of multiple logic functions on small silicon chips permits inexpensive construction of very fast and remarkably sophisticated miniprocessors (Fig. 1-1).
2. Inexpensive and much faster core and semiconductor memories make it less painful to use extra instruction words for improved instruction sets and addressing schemes (Sec. 2-7 and Chap. 6).

These two developments have given astonishing capabilities to the new small machines. While the majority of minicomputers continue to serve as *special-purpose* computers in control, instrumentation, and communications, an increasing proportion are employed in *general-purpose* computation and simulation. Minicomputers work especially well with conversational terminals, graphic displays, and all kinds of instruments. Operating inefficiencies can be tolerated; a small computer can "belong" to a small group of researchers or engineers rather than to a computer-center bureaucracy, and it is possible to modify programs (and even hardware!) without collapsing a large organization.

The situation is *not* one-sided. A reasonable end-user installation might require not only a $12,000 minicomputer but between $10,000 and $70,000 worth of computer *peripherals* (tape drives, disks, displays, printer, card reader—these are, unfortunately, not grown on monolithic silicon chips). Maintenance must be provided or paid for. Altogether, the economics of

(a)

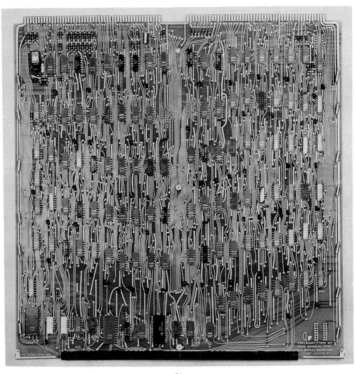

(b)

Fig. 1-1a to c. Figure 1-1a shows a complete 16-bit digital computer for desk-top or rack mounting. The entire central processor, built with medium-scale-integrated-circuit chips, fits a single etched-circuit board, and so does each 4K memory module (b and c). The small machine, which can control (or receive information from) hundreds of external devices, has an instruction-cycle time of 800 nsec with a core memory or 300 nsec with a semiconductor memory. (*Data General Corporation.*)

4

Fig. 1-1c.

Fig. 1-1d. With two accumulators, an index register, and one of the most comprehensive instruction sets available, the 16-bit Varian Data Machines 620L/100 costs only $5,400 for the basic processor and 4K words of 0.95-μsec memory; each additional 4K words costs $2,300. (*Varian Data Machines.*)

multiple minicomputers versus large time-shared multiprocessors are always good for an extended argument and depend on the specific utilization of specific installations. Even so, the question merits frequent reexamination since, while minicomputers and their peripherals are becoming cheaper and more powerful, the same is true for the new multiprocessor computer utilities and their formidable system software. Data communication, moreover, is sure to be improved over the pitiful telephone-based systems of the early 1970s.

In any case, the inexpensive, small, and light minicomputer, with its dramatic versatility, is surely the world's finest toy for innovators and experimenters. It opens unheard-of horizons in control and instrumentation. On experimenters' desks or wheeled carts, in large and small factories, and in ships or aerospace vehicles, minicomputers permit intelligent automation of all sorts of operation-sequencing and data-gathering operations and generate convenient displays for human operators. Physical interfacing of small digital computers and much real-world apparatus is quite easy (Chap. 5). The larger job of computer programming for a wide variety of applications is simplified by new system and application software (Chaps. 3 and 4).

DIGITAL-COMPUTER REPRESENTATION OF DATA AND TEXT

1-3. Binary and Digital Variables. While an **analog computer** represents problem variables by continuously variable physical quantities such as voltages or currents (Fig. 1-3a), a **digital computer** represents problem variables by physical quantities capable of taking only discrete and countable sets of values. Thus, the original "digital-computer user" long ago employed his fingers to count and add external objects, first up to five and then up to ten. The overwhelming majority of electronic digital computers, however, implements a **binary** representation in terms of basic variables which can take only **two** different states called (logical) 0 and 1. Most frequently, the state 1 is indicated by the presence of a voltage, usually 3 or 4 volts, on a line associated with a variable, while logical 0 is indicated by the absence of that voltage (Fig. 1-3b). Many other pairs of voltage levels, such as 0 and -3 volts or -1.75 and -0.5 volts, are also employed to represent 0 and 1.

Such binary variables, which involve only the presence or absence of a signal, are especially easy to generate, transmit, and store reliably. We pay for this great convenience, however: most problem situations or variables admit a much greater variety of possible states than just two and must, therefore, be labeled (represented) in terms of ordered *combinations* of binary variables. We must, then, develop **binary codes** which associate problem

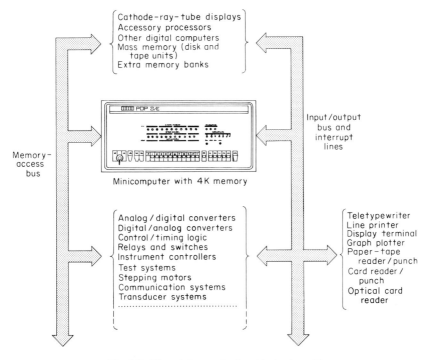

Fig. 1-2. The minicomputer input/output world.

states, messages, or numerical quantities with corresponding **digital words,** i.e., ordered sets of **binary variables.** Such codes may differ for different applications. In Fig. 1-3c, *four* binary variables specify which of four circuits is energized, while in Fig. 1-3d *two* binary variables control the same situation.

It is, of course, especially important to represent **real numbers** in terms of binary variables. In general, a real integer m will require at least $\log_2 m$

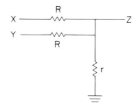

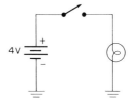

Fig. 1-3a. Simple analog computation. The summing network produces the output voltage $Z = \alpha(X + Y)$, where X and Y are input voltages and $\alpha = (R/r + 2)^{-1}$.

Fig. 1-3b. Logic states represented by voltage levels in an elementary digital circuit.

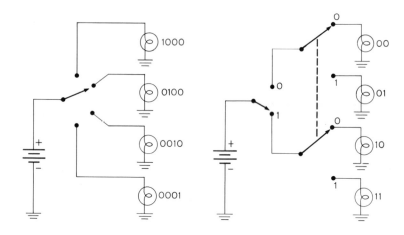

Fig. 1-3c and d. Two different binary representations of a switch setting energizing one of four circuits.

binary units of information or **bits,** plus a **sign bit** to tell whether the integer is positive or negative (Secs. 1-4 and 1-6).

It is common practice to designate an entire set of binary variables (which may or may not represent a numerical quantity) as a single **digital variable.** The different bits of such a digital variable may appear on parallel bus lines (**parallel representation**) and may be stored in a *register* like that of the toggle switches in Fig. 1-4a. The different bits of a digital variable could also follow each other in time as consecutive samples of a voltage waveform which can take the values corresponding to 0 or 1 (**serial representation,** Fig. 1-4b). Parallel representation, which can transmit all the bits of a word at the same time, is clearly faster and is most frequently employed in modern digital computers. Serial representation, on the other hand, simplifies long-distance data communication.

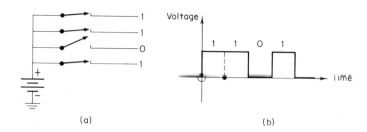

Fig. 1-4. Representation of the digital word 1101 by simultaneous levels on a parallel bus (a) and by timed serial pulses (b).

1-4. Digital-computer Representation of Numbers and Characters. (a) Binary Numbers. The n-bit binary word $(a_0, a_1, \ldots, a_{n-1})$, where a_k is either 0 or 1, can be interpreted as a one-to-one representation (**binary code**) for the nonnegative integers

$$X = 2^{n-1}a_0 + 2^{n-2}a_1 + \cdots + a_{n-1} \qquad 0 \leq X \leq 2^{n-1} - 1 \quad (1\text{-}1)$$

The integers [Eq. (1-1)], in turn, constitute a numerical code for the n-bit words $(a_0, a_1, a_2, \ldots, a_{n-1})$, whose original interpretation may not be numerical, e.g., a set of truth values. Table 1-1 and Sec. 1-9 further describe the n-bit binary codes for **negative integers** and for **fractions** most commonly employed in digital-computer arithmetic.

(b) Octal and Hexadecimal Numbers. Binary words are convenient for machines but not for people. To obtain a nice shorthand notation, we split a given binary word into *3-bit groups* (starting with a_{n-1}) and write the binary number corresponding to each group as an octal digit between 0 and 7:

$$
\begin{array}{llccccc}
& & a_0 & & & & a_{n-1} \\
& & \searrow & & & & \swarrow \\
\textbf{binary word} & & 11 & 111 & 001 & 000 & 010 \\
\textbf{octal word} & & 3 & 7 & 1 & 0 & 2 \\
& & \nearrow & & & & \nwarrow \\
& & A_0 & & & & A_{m-1}
\end{array}
$$

The resulting **octal word** $(A_0, A_1, A_2, \ldots, A_{m-1})$ represents the integer [Eq. (1-1)] in the form

$$X = 8^{m-1}A_0 + 8^{m-2}A_1 + \cdots + A_{m-1}$$

$$0 \leq X \leq 2^{n-1} - 1; \; m < \frac{n}{3} + 1 \quad (1\text{-}2)$$

The code we have just defined will describe every binary word as a *nonnegative octal integer* [Eq. (1-2)], even though the binary word may represent a negative number, a fraction, or a nonnumerical quantity such as a set of truth values or a text character. There is little need to learn octal *complement codes* for negative numbers since minicomputer assembly languages (Sec. 3-5) which accept negative octal integers automatically translate ordinary sign-and-magnitude notation, e.g.,

$$-400_8 = -256_{10}$$

into binary code (see also Sec. 4-2). Computer *output* is usually in decimal form, except for some debugging and troubleshooting programs (Sec. 3-17). It is, however, useful to know the octal code for *nonnegative pure fractions* encoded in binary forms as $(a_0, a_1, a_2, \ldots, a_{n-1})$ $(a_k = 0 \text{ or } 1)$, with a binary point implied ahead of the most significant bit a_0 (Table 1-2).

TABLE 1-1. **Binary Codes Representing Real Integers** X **by** n**-bit Words** $(a_0, a_1, a_2, \ldots, a_{n-1})$.

Each binary digit a_k is either 0 or 1. a_0 is the **most significant bit (MSB)**, and a_{n-1} is the **least significant bit (LSB)**.

---

1. Nonnegative Integers: $X = 2^{n-1}a_0 + 2^{n-2}a_1 + \cdots + a$ where $0 \le X \le 2^n - 1$.

    EXAMPLE (3 bits):

DECIMAL	BINARY	DECIMAL	BINARY
0	000	4	100
1	001	5	101
2	010	6	110
3	011	7	111

This is the conventional binary code used in most minicomputers. Many other codes exist. In particular, in the *Gray code* (Ref. 6) only one binary digit changes each time X is incremented; this is useful for encoding certain instrument outputs.

    Binary/decimal conversion is easiest with *decimal/octal tables* (Table A-3); or use the "doubling and dabbling" recursion (Ref. 4): $X = X_{n-1}$, where $X_0 = a_0$, $X_i = 2X_{i-1} + a_i$, and $i = 1, 2, \ldots, n - 1$; e.g.,

$$a_i \to 1 \quad 0 \quad 1 \quad 1$$

$$X_i \to 1 \quad 2 \quad 5 \quad 11 \qquad X = 11$$

2. Signed Integers (positive, negative, or zero). The **sign bit** a_0 is 0 for $X \ge 0$ and 1 for $X < 0$.

    (a) **Sign-and-magnitude Code:** $X = (-1)^{a_0}(2^{n-2}a_1 + 2^{n-3}a_2 + \cdots + a_{n-1})$, where $1 - 2^{n-1} \le X \le 2^{n-1} - 1$. There are *two* binary representations of 0: 000 ... and 100 .... This can cause complications, e.g., in statistical work. This code is often used in digital voltmeters.

    (b) **1s-complement Code:** $X = (1 - 2^{n-1})a_0 + 2^{n-2}a_1 + 2^{n-3}a_2 + \cdots + a_{n-1}$, where $1 - 2^{n-1} \le X \le 2^{n-1} - 1$. Negative integers X are coded into unsigned integers: $(2^n - 1) + X = (2^n + X) - 1$. There are *two* binary representations of 0: 000 ... and 111 .... *One obtains the code for* $-X$ *very simply by complementing each bit.* This code is used in a few arithmetic units.

    (c) **2s-complement Code:** $X = -2^{n-1}a_0 + 2^{n-2}a_1 + 2^{n-3}a_2 + \cdots + a_{n-1}$, where $-2^{n-1} \le X \le 2^{n-1} - 1$. Negative integers X are coded into unsigned integers $2^n + X$. It has a unique 0 and simple arithmetic. *To obtain code for* $-X$, *complement every bit and add 1 LSB.* It is used in binary counters and in almost all minicomputers.

    EXAMPLES (4-bit codes):

DECIMAL		SIGN-AND-MAGNITUDE			1S-COMPLEMENT			2S-COMPLEMENT		
+	7	0	1 1 1		0	1 1 1		0	1 1 1	
+	6	0	1 1 0		0	1 1 0		0	1 1 0	
+	.	.	. . .		.	. . .		.	. . .	
+	3	0	0 1 1		0	0 1 1		0	0 1 1	
+	2	0	0 1 0		0	0 1 0		0	0 1 0	
+	1	0	0 0 1		0	0 0 1		0	0 0 1	
+	0	0	0 0 0		0	0 0 0	} 0		0 0 0	
−	0	1	0 0 0		1	1 1 1				
−	1	1	0 0 1		1	1 1 0		1	1 1 1	
−	2	1	0 1 0		1	1 0 1		1	1 1 0	
−	3	1	0 1 1		1	1 0 0		1	1 0 1	
−	.	.	. . .		.	. . .		.	. . .	
−	6	1	1 1 0		1	0 0 1		1	0 1 0	
−	7	1	1 1 1		1	0 0 0		1	0 0 1	
−	8	−	—		−	—		1	0 0 0	

TABLE 1-2. Binary Codes Representing Real Fractions X by n-bit Words $(a_0, a_1, a_2, \ldots, a_{n-1})$.
Each binary digit a_k is either 0 or 1. a_0 is the **most significant bit (MSB)**, and a_{n-1} is the **least significant bit (LSB)**.

---

1. Nonnegative Fractions: $X = \dfrac{1}{2}a_0 + \dfrac{1}{2^2}a_1 + \cdots + \dfrac{1}{2^n}a_{n-1}$, where $0 \leq X \leq 1 - \dfrac{1}{2^n}$.

EXAMPLE (3 bits):

DECIMAL	BINARY	DECIMAL	BINARY
0.000	000	$\frac{4}{8} = 0.500$	100
$\frac{1}{8} = 0.125$	001	$\frac{5}{8} = 0.625$	101
$\frac{2}{8} = 0.250$	010	$\frac{6}{8} = 0.750$	110
$\frac{3}{8} = 0.375$	011	$\frac{7}{8} = 0.875$	111

2. Signed Fractions (positive, negative, or zero). The **sign bit** a_0 is 0 for $X \geq 0$ and 1 for $X < 0$.

(a) **Sign-and-magnitude Code:** $X = (-1)^{a_0}\left(\dfrac{1}{2}a_1 + \dfrac{1}{2^2}a_2 + \cdots + \dfrac{1}{2^{n-1}}a_{n-1}\right)$, where $\dfrac{1}{2^{n-1}} - 1 \leq X \leq 1 - \dfrac{1}{2^{n-1}}$. There are *two* binary representations of 0: 000 . . . and 100 . . . . This may cause complications, e.g., in statistical work.

(b) **1s-complement Code:**

$$X = \left(\frac{1}{2^{n-1}} - 1\right)a_0 + \frac{1}{2^2}a_2 + \cdots + \frac{1}{2^{n-1}}a_{n-1},$$

where $\dfrac{1}{2^{n-1}} - 1 \leq X \leq 1 - \dfrac{1}{2^{n-1}}$. There are *two* binary representations of 0: 000 . . . and 111 . . . . *One obtains the code for* $-X$ *very simply by complementing each bit.* This code is used in some arithmetic units.

(c) **2s-complement Code:**

$$X = -a_0 + \frac{1}{2}a_1 + \frac{1}{2^2}a_2 + \cdots + \frac{1}{2^{n-1}}a_{n-1},$$

where $-1 \leq X \leq 1 - \dfrac{1}{2^{n-1}}$. It has a unique 0 and simple arithmetic. *To obtain code for* $-X$, *complement every bit and add 1 LSB.* This code is used in almost all minicomputers.

EXAMPLES (4-bit codes):

DECIMAL	SIGN-AND-MAGNITUDE			1S-COMPLEMENT			2S-COMPLEMENT		
$+\frac{7}{8} = +0.875$	0	1 1 1		0	1 1 1		0	1 1 1	
$+\frac{6}{8} = +0.750$	0	1 1 0		0	1 1 0		0	1 1 0	
. . . .	.			. . . .			. . . .		
$+\frac{3}{8} = +0.375$	0	0 1 1		0	0 1 1		0	0 1 1	
$+\frac{2}{8} = +0.250$	0	0 1 0		0	0 1 0		0	0 1 0	
$+\frac{1}{8} = +0.125$	0	0 0 1		0	0 0 1		0	0 0 1	
$+0$	0	0 0 0		0	0 0 0		0	0 0 0	
-0	1	0 0 0		1	1 1 1				
$-\frac{1}{8} = -0.125$	1	0 0 1		1	1 1 0		1	1 1 1	
$-\frac{2}{8} = -0.250$	1	0 1 0		1	1 0 1		1	1 1 0	
$-\frac{3}{8} = -0.375$	1	0 1 1		1	1 0 0		1	1 0 1	
. . . .	.			. . . .			. . . .		
$-\frac{6}{8} = -0.750$	1	1 1 0		1	0 0 1		1	0 1 0	
$-\frac{7}{8} = -0.875$	1	1 1 1		1	0 0 0		1	0 0 1	
-1	—	—		—	—		1	0 0 0	

We again start 3-bit groups at the implied binary point, i.e., proceeding *to the right* from a_0:

$$a_0 \qquad\qquad\qquad\qquad\qquad a_{n-1}$$

binary word	.110	001	000	01	
octal word	. 6	1	0	2	

$$A_0 \qquad\qquad\qquad\qquad\qquad A_{m-1}$$

so that

$$X = \frac{1}{2} a_0 + \frac{1}{2^2} a_1 + \cdots + \frac{1}{2^n} a_{n-1}$$

$$= \frac{1}{8} A_0 + \frac{1}{8^2} A_1 + \cdots + \frac{1}{8^n} A_{m-1} \qquad 0 \le X \le 1 - \frac{1}{2^n}; \quad m \le \frac{n}{3} \quad (1\text{-}3)$$

Decimal-octal-decimal conversion is defined by Eqs. (1-2) and (1-3) but is usually done with the aid of *conversion tables* (Appendix). Octal-number representations work perfectly well even if the given word length n is not divisible by 3. Note, however, that the octal-*integer* code for nonnegative pure binary fractions is identical with the octal-*fraction* code if and only if the word size is divisible by 3. For this reason, our Appendix presents an octal-fraction conversion table as well as an octal-integer conversion table.

Hexadecimal notation similarly divides each binary word into *4-bit groups* labeled with hexadecimal digits (Table 1-3):

$$a_0 \rightarrow 1\ 0\quad 1\ 0\ 0\ 1\quad 1\ 1\ 1\ 0\quad 0\ 1\ 0\ 0\quad 0\ 0\ 1\ 0$$

2	9	E	4	2	(integer)

Octal-integer arithmetic, useful for "manual" work with binary operations (design, programming, see also Sec. 4-2) is easy to learn for those used to decimal arithmetic. We simply carry or borrow at 8 instead of 10 and learn a simple multiplication table. Especially for occasional use, octal numbers are probably easier to live with than hexadecimal numbers. But the latter are widely accepted in applications involving communications and/or IBM 360/370 computer systems. This is because representation of the 8-bit words or partial words (**bytes**) used for alphanumeric characters (Sec. 1-4d) requires *three* octal digits but only *two* hexadecimal digits:

$$10110010_2 = 262_8 = B2_{16}$$

Conversion and arithmetic tables for both systems will be found in the Appendix (Tables A-1 to A-6).

TABLE 1-3.   Hexadecimal Notation.

Hexadecimal	Binary	Decimal
0	0000	0
1	0001	1
2	0010	2
3	0011	3
4	0100	4
5	0101	5
6	0110	6
7	0111	7
8	1000	8
9	1001	9
A	1010	10
B	1011	11
C	1100	12
D	1101	13
E	1110	14
F	1111	15

(c) Parity Checking. In the course of a digital program, thousands or millions of digital words are transferred between the processor, the computer memory, and external devices. To improve reliability at the expense of some extra circuits, we can augment each n-bit word with an extra (redundant) **parity bit** which is made to equal 1 if and only if the number of 1s in the n information bits is odd. We can then check for **even parity** (even number of 1s) over all $n + 1$ bits to detect errors in 1, 3, 5, . . . bits (including the parity bit) and stop or repeat the operation as needed. Errors in 2, 4, . . . bits will remain undetected but are much less likely than 1-bit errors. Related checking methods apply to transfers of long lists of words (Sec. 3-10).

Parity checks for memory and interface transfers are recommended for critical applications, especially where a computer system is unattended. Note that simple parity checking does *not* check arithmetic or logic errors. Many end-user minicomputers operate satisfactorily without memory-transfer parity checks.

(d) Alphanumeric-character Codes. Computer input/output and digital data transmission, manipulation, and storage require binary coding of **alphanumeric-character strings** representing text, commands, numbers, and/or code groups. We use one binary word, or a byte, for each character. 4 bits ($2^4 = 16$) are enough to encode the 10 numerals 0 to 9 (*binary coding of decimal numbers*, Sec. 1-4e). The 26 letters of the alphabet (uppercase only) and the 10 numerals, plus some mathematical and punctuation symbols, can be squeezed into a **6-bit code** ($2^6 = 64$) if resources are scarce; Table A-11 shows an example of such a code. Most minicomputer applications will employ **a 7-bit code with an added 8th bit for parity checking** (Sec. 1-4c). Table A-9 shows the **ASCII code (American Standard Code for Information**

Interchange), which admits uppercase and lowercase letters, numerals, standard symbols, **control characters** for printers and communication links (tab, line feed, form feed, rubout, end-of-message, etc.) and still has room for extra agreed-on symbols and control characters ($2^7 = 128$). A similar 8-bit code is the EBCDIC code used by the IBM Corporation.

8- and 16-bit minicomputers neatly handle one or two ASCII-character bytes in a computer word. Perforated paper tape also has eight-hole columns fitting 8-bit bytes (Fig. 3-5a). 12- and 18-bit machines must pack successive 8-bit characters into multiple words through rather uncomfortable packing

TABLE 1-4.   Some BCD Codes.

(See Ref. 6 for special applications.)

Decimal	8, 4, 2, 1	Excess-3 (8, 4, 2, 1, code for $x + 3$)	2, 4, 2, 1
0	0000	0011	0000
1	0001	0100	0001
2	0010	0101	0010
3	0011	0110	0011
4	0100	0111	0100
5	0101	1000	1011
6	0110	1001	1100
7	0111	1010	1101
8	1000	1011	1110
9	1001	1100	1111

operations (Fig. 1-17d); 6-bit character sets are more convenient for such machines but may not have enough characters.

(e) Binary-coded-decimal (BCD) Numbers and Other Number Codes. Table 1-4 shows some **binary-coded-decimal (BCD) codes** which express numerical data in terms of strings of 4-bit character codes corresponding to decimal digits. As an example, the **8, 4, 2, 1 BCD code** encodes each decimal digit into the corresponding binary integer:

$$9 \quad 2 \quad 1 \quad 7 \quad 8 \quad 3$$
$$1001 \quad 0010 \quad 0001 \quad 0111 \quad 1000 \quad 0011$$

The numbers 8, 4, 2, 1 are the "weights" assigned to the binary bits defining each decimal digit. Some business-oriented computers employ BCD-coded arithmetic circuits, but this is not economical for general-purpose mini-computers (4 bits can specify 16 binary numbers, but only 10 BCD numbers). Thus, BCD circuits serve mainly in numerical displays, printers, and counters used directly by 10-fingered bipeds.

A large number of other number codes, both with and without redundant check bits, have been used. In particular, the *Gray code* (*reflected code*, Ref. 6) serves in some analog-to-digital converters (especially shaft encoders) where it is desirable to switch only 1 bit at a time during up or down counting operations.

Conversions between different coding schemes are important computer operations and are implemented both by hard-wired logic and by computer programs. **Coding schemes for punched cards and for punched tapes are illustrated in Fig. 3-5.**

1-5. Choice of Word Length and Data Format. (a) Word Length. Existing minicomputers are 8-bit, 12-bit, 16-bit, or 18-bit machines; we will arbitrarily eliminate 24-bit computers from the minicomputer classification. Intuitively, the number of bits quoted refers to the length of the most frequently used data word and thus to the number of bits in the main arithmetic registers. This interpretation has become somewhat blurred because software and/or microprogramming easily permits, say, an 8-bit computer to operate with composite 16-, 24-, or 32-bit words. Such an 8-bit machine may well have one or more 16-bit registers and can use single-word or multiple-word instructions. Again, modern 16-bit minicomputers can often address and fetch 8-bit half-words (bytes) as well as 16-bit words. We will speak of an n-bit computer if the *main data paths* (buses) connecting memory, processor circuits, and external devices are parallel n-bit paths (not counting extra bits used for parity checks and memory protection, Sec. 2-15). Advertising literature should be read somewhat critically in this respect.

Since computation with, say, a 4K memory can take 12 bits for addressing alone, most minicomputers with meaningful instruction sets require some double-word instructions, usually implied or disguised by indirect or relative addressing (Sec. 2-7). Depending on the application, longer word length may mean fewer double-word instructions and thus save memory and time. Clever design of short-word instruction sets is the central problem of mini-computer architecture and will be discussed in Chap. 6. We now consider the choice of *data-word* length.

In minicomputers serving largely as *logic controllers* rather than as arithmetic processors, word length need not be determined by numerical precision. Where speed is not important, any number of, say, relay closures can be controlled and/or sensed through *successive* 8-bit words. But there are also applications where an 18-bit word length (rather than 8, 12, or 16 bits) is just the thing to simplify control interface, program, and memory requirements.

In judging the data-word length to be used in **fixed-point numerical computation,** remember that **minicomputers do not perform a true roundoff to the least significant digit.** Instead, they effectively reduce the missing digit to a zero (they "chop" or "truncate" the missing digit), so that the resulting 2s-complement number *will never be larger than the correct quantity*. It follows that even with 18-bit data words, fixed-point sums of, say, 1,000 terms, such as are frequently encountered in numerical integration or statistical averaging, *must* be computed with *double-precision* arithmetic if we actually want 18-bit accuracy; up to 10 of the least significant bits might be meaningless.[1]

(b) 8-bit Machines. 8 bits (i.e., a resolution of 1 in 256) will not permit very accurate single-precision arithmetic, although very useful logic operations (say in industrial controllers) are possible. Multiword instructions and operations, however, permit powerful 16-, 24-, and even 32-bit computations (at reduced speed) with many 8-bit machines, especially with microprogramming (Sec. 6-13). Another very important application of 8-bit minicomputers is the manipulation, storage, recognition, and recoding of 8-*bit alphanumeric characters;* note that 8 bits are just right for an ASCII character with parity bit or for two BCD digits (Sec. 1-4).

(c) 12-bit Machines. 12-bit data words can accommodate the 1 in 4,000 resolution of medium-accuracy instruments (within 0.1 percent of half-scale and sign), although the results of 12-bit arithmetic will rarely have 12-bit accuracy.

As minimum-size data processors, 12-bit computers (more specifically the Digital Equipment Corporation's PDP-8 series) spearheaded the minicomputer revolution with enormous success at a time when the additional logic required for a 16-bit machine was still fairly expensive. The success of the PDP-8 has produced so much valuable software that new PDP-8-type 12-bit machines are produced not only by DEC but also by other manufacturers, with prices reduced to below $5,000 for the processor and a 4K-word memory.

(d) 16-bit Machines. Since the advent of low-cost integrated-circuit processor logic, 16-bit minicomputers have become the predominant type. Longer 16-bit instruction words permit the design of exceedingly sophisticated minicomputer architectures (Chap. 6). The second significant advantage is the ease with which two 8-bit ASCII bytes can be packed into a single 16-bit word; separate byte addressing and manipulation is possible in many 16-bit machines (Sec. 2-13).

(e) 18-bit Machines. The most successful 18-bit minicomputers have been the Digital Equipment Corporation's PDP-7/9/15 series, which have relatively simple instruction sets and employ the extra word length for direct addressing of as much as 8K of memory. Other computer designers prefer to use extra instruction bits for addressing multiple processor registers

---

[1] The situation is somewhat better in statistical averaging because we can subtract the expected value of the chopping error out of our result. Note, however, that the chopping-error *variance* still adds to the variance of our statistical estimate.

(Sec. 2-8). ASCII-character packing is either clumsy or wasteful with 18-bit words, but suitable packing and unpacking routines exist. Cathode-ray-tube or xy-recorder displays of fair resolution (512 by 512 points) can be very conveniently driven with 18-bit data words packed with 9-bit X and Y coordinate values; this arrangement halves both refresh memory and refresh time (Sec. 7-9).

(f) **Data Formats.** Figure 1-17 illustrates typical *data formats* used to code fixed-point binary numbers, floating-point numbers, and alphanumeric characters into 8-bit, 12-bit, 16-bit, and 18-bit words. *Instruction formats* are shown in Sec. 2-5 and in Chap. 6.

DIGITAL OPERATIONS: LOGIC AND ARITHMETIC

1-6. Logic Operations. The reasons for the explosive success of computers with binary variable representation are not only the ease of binary-data storage and transmission but also the remarkable simplicity, reliability, and

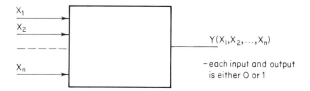

Fig. 1-5. Generation of a Boolean function Y of n inputs $X_1, X_2, \ldots, X_n$.

low cost of the basic *operations* on binary variables. Figure 1-5 shows a "black box" whose output Y is a **binary (Boolean) function** $F(X_1, X_2, \ldots, X_n)$ of n binary input variables $X_1, X_2, \ldots, X_n$. Since each input can take only two different values, *there are 2^{2^n} different Boolean functions of n inputs.* We can characterize each Boolean function by a simple table **(truth table)** showing the function values for all possible combinations of argument (input) values (Fig. 1-7).

We would like to implement many different operations like that of Fig. 1-5 with electrical circuits; inputs and outputs will be voltage levels corresponding to 0 and 1 (Sec. 1-1). Fortunately, *all Boolean functions can be obtained through combinations of simpler functions.* The simple one- and two-input functions of Fig. 1-6 will be more than sufficient, and all can be realized with readily available integrated circuits **(logic inverters** and **gates).**

The elementary Boolean operations of **complementation (inversion), logical addition (union, ORing),** and **logical multiplication (intersection, ANDing)** combine according to the rules of **Boolean algebra** listed in Table 1-5a. The table also illustrates how these rules are used to obtain useful

TABLE 1-5a. Very Little Logic Goes a Long Way: Gate Circuits (Combinatorial Logic).

1. Basic Gates and Truth Tables. The basic *logic gates* implement simple functions of binary variables. Each gate function is defined explicitly by a *truth table* listing the gate output for all combinations of inputs.

NAND and NOR gates also serve as *logic inverters* complementing a single input (1 becomes 0, and vice versa).

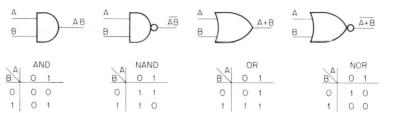

	AND	
B\ A	0	1
0	0	0
1	0	1

	NAND	
B\ A	0	1
0	1	1
1	1	0

	OR	
B\ A	0	1
0	0	1
1	1	1

	NOR	
B\ A	0	1
0	1	0
1	0	0

NOTE: In some types of logic, gate outputs can be ORed together.

2. Inverters. NAND and NOR gates also serve as **logic inverters** for **complementing** a single input. We use the following inverter symbols:

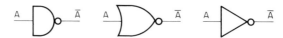

Some gates have *two complementary outputs*, and some logic modules provide gates with *inverting inputs*:

3. The Rules of Boolean Algebra. When we proceed to combine simple logic functions into more complicated functions of more variables, we find that the combinations satisfy the following *rules of Boolean algebra*. These rules are established by a simple combination of the basic truth tables. The rules may be applied to simplify logic circuits (logic optimization).

$$\left.\begin{array}{l} A + B = B + A \\ AB = BA \end{array}\right\} \quad \text{(COMMUTATIVE LAWS)}$$

$$\left.\begin{array}{l} A + (B + C) = (A + B) + C \\ A(BC) = (AB)C \end{array}\right\} \quad \text{(ASSOCIATIVE LAWS)}$$

$$\left.\begin{array}{l} A(B + C) = AB + AC \\ A + BC = (A + B)(A + C) \end{array}\right\} \quad \text{(DISTRIBUTIVE LAWS)}$$

$$A + A = AA = A \quad \text{(IDEMPOTENT PROPERTIES)}$$

$$A + B = B \text{ if and only if } AB = A \quad \text{(CONSISTENCY PROPERTY)}$$

$$A + 0 = A \qquad AI = A$$
$$A0 = 0 \qquad A + I = I$$

$$A(A + B) \equiv A + AB \equiv A \quad \text{(LAWS OF ABSORPTION)}$$

$$\left.\begin{array}{l} (\overline{A + B}) \equiv \bar{A}\bar{B} \\ (\overline{AB}) \equiv \bar{A} + \bar{B} \end{array}\right\} \quad \text{(DUALITY, OR DE MORGAN'S LAWS)}$$

$$\bar{\bar{A}} \equiv A \qquad \bar{I} = 0 \qquad \bar{0} = I$$

$$A + \bar{A}B \equiv A + B \qquad AB + AC + B\bar{C} \equiv AC + B\bar{C}$$

Every Boolean function is either identical to 0 or can be expressed as a unique sum of **minimal polynomials (canonical minterms)** $Z_1 Z_2 \cdots Z_n$, *where* Z_i *is either* X_i *or* $\overline{X}_i$ *(canonical form of a Boolean function).*

In view of de Morgan's laws, *every Boolean function not identically 0 can also be expressed as a unique product of* **canonical maxterms** $Z'_1 + Z'_2 + \cdots + Z'_n$, *where* Z_i *is either* X_i *or* $\overline{X}_i$. There are altogether 2^n minterms and 2^n maxterms.

These canonical forms show that *every* Boolean function can, in principle, be implemented with *two levels* of logic gates (either ORing of AND-gate outputs or ANDing of OR-gate outputs). But the number of gates and/or connections needed might be reduced decisively if we admit some intermediate levels at the expense of extra time delay.

4. Examples of Combinatorial Logic. *Combinatorial logic* involves only gates (including inverters), no memory or delays.

(a) NAND/NOR and NOR/AND Conversion (by de Morgan's theorem).

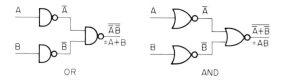

These conversion rules are useful when we have to work with specific commercially available components.

NOTE: *All* combinatorial logic *can* be implemented with NAND gates alone, or with NOR gates alone.

(b) Single-pole/Double-throw Switches.

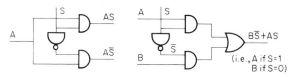

(c) EXCLUSIVE OR (XOR, Modulo-two Adder).

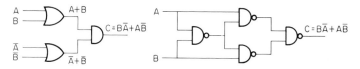

NOTE: $C = 0$ indicates that $A = B$ (coincidence detection).
Many other implementations exist.

(d) Recognition Gates (Decoding Gates) for selecting devices identified by a binary address code, for presetting counters, etc.

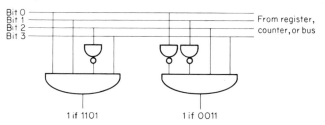

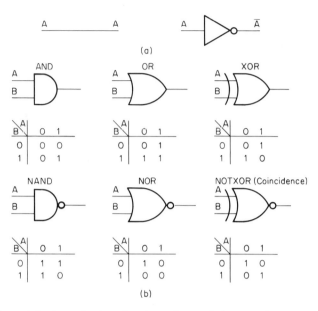

Fig. 1-6. Figure 1-6*a* shows Boolean functions of a *single* input. Figure 1-6*b* defines the most important functions of *two* inputs by simple truth tables and shows commonly used symbols for the corresponding logic gates.

Boolean functions with simple gates. In particular, AND gates and inverters alone, NAND gates alone, or NOR gates alone can perform *all* Boolean operations. This is of great practical importance because some types of solid-state logic make it easier to implement NAND gates, while others lead to a preference for OR and NOR gates. Many commercially available logic systems also offer logic gates with more than two inputs, which are often convenient (Fig. 1-7).

A **flip-flop** is a 1-*bit memory device* for storing a binary variable; **flip-flop registers** are ordered sets of flip-flops for storing digital words. Table 1-5*b* defines each of the most useful flip-flop types by the method of data entry and shows two important applications (see also Secs. 1-7 and 5-3). Figure 1-8 shows how appropriately timed control pulses are used to parallel-transfer the contents of a flip-flop register to other registers.

Digital-computer *arithmetic circuits* will be designed as logic circuits operating on the bits of binary-number inputs to produce desired binary output numbers, with inputs, outputs, and intermediate results stored in flip-flop registers (Sec. 1-9).

Techniques for simplifying logic circuits (i.e., minimizing the number of gates and flip-flops, gate inputs, interconnections, and/or crossovers) form the subject of **logic optimization** for digital-system design (Refs. 1 to 5). Optimization of a large digital system, such as a complete computer, is

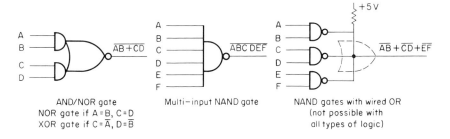

Fig. 1-7. Some multi-input gates available in integrated-circuit form.   Many other types exist.

often itself done with the help of a digital computer.   On the other hand, a researcher or engineer who merely wants to use a small digital computer, and to interface it to some real-world instruments and controls, will seldom require formal logic optimization.   *All we usually require is the material in Table 1-5, some reasonable common sense, and a nice collection of tried logic circuits we can adapt and modify.*   Manufacturers' catalogs and application

TABLE 1-5b.   Very Little Logic Goes a Long Way: Flip-flop Circuits.

---

1. Flip-flops. A **flip-flop,** like the familiar toggle switch, will stay in a given output state (0 or 1) even after inputs have been removed.   Flip-flops thus implement *memory* for binary variables and permit *data storage* and *automatic sequential operations.*   (That is, logic states can determine the sequence of future logic states, as in data transfers, counting, etc.)   Although a somewhat bewildering variety of different flip-flops are sold, all are derived from a few simple types.   Specifically, the basic **reset/set (RS) flip-flop** retains its output state through regenerative feedback until a new reversing input is applied.   Other types of flip-flops add different input-gating circuits.

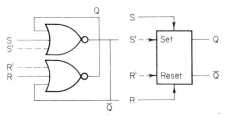

(*a*) **Reset/set (RS) flip-flop.** $R = 1$ (level or pulse) **resets (clears)** the flip-flop ($Q = 0$) until $S = 1$ **sets** the flip-flop ($Q = 1$). $R = S = 0$ leaves output *unchanged.* $R = S = 1$ is *illegal* (indefinite output), or $R = 1$ may *override* $S = 1$.   Multiple set inputs or multiple reset inputs are ORed together.

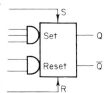

(*b*) **General-purpose flip-flop with enabling gates.**   Many different types exist.   Inputs may include inverting set and/or reset inputs, multiple gate inputs, etc.   Frequently, the lower reset input is designed to override all other inputs.

   In some general-purpose flip-flops (diode/transistor logic, DTL), gates have *ac-coupled inputs,* which set or reset the flip-flop when a voltage *step* (either up or down, depending on the type) is gated by a logic level.

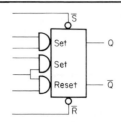

(*c*) **Another type of general-purpose flip-flop.** The two set-gate inputs are ORed together. The *inverted* set and reset inputs require $\bar{S} = 0$ to set and $\bar{R} = 0$ to reset.

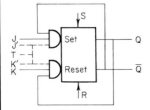

(*d*) **General-purpose flip-flop connected as a *JK* flip-flop,** which acts like an *RS* flip-flop except that $J = K = 1$ always reverses the output state. With J' and K' connected (dash lines), we have a *T*(**trigger) flip-flop**: For $J = K = 1$, output reverses whenever T goes to 1.

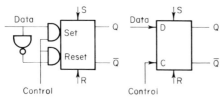

(*e*) **Data/control** (sometimes called **type D**) **flip-flop.** Output Q takes data-input value when control input goes to 1—it acts as a *binary sample-hold circuit*. It is important for jam transfer of data timed by control (strobe) pulses and in shift registers.

Dual-rank (master-slave) type D flip-flops are designed to establish a definite time interval between input and output steps.

Consult manufacturers' logic manuals for exact logic, fanout, logic-level tolerances, noise immunity, pulse duration, and step rise time required to trigger flip-flops, etc.

2. Important Flip-flop Circuits.

(*a*) **Simple shift registers.** Note the possibility of parallel input through extra set and reset terminals.

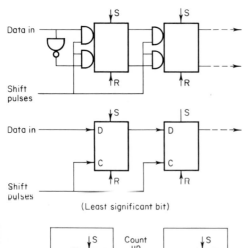

(*b*) **Simple binary counter.** Each counter flip-flop complements whenever its trigger T input changes to 1. Counter can be *preset* with S and R inputs.

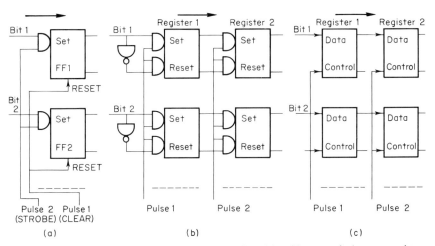

Fig. 1-8. Clear-and-strobe transfer into a flip-flop register (a) and jam transfer between registers (b) and (c). If the dual transfers in (b) or (c) are to take place simultaneously, we can use dual-rank flip-flops to make sure that the old output of the first register is transferred before it is updated.

notes should be consulted for special tricks and precautions applicable to specific types of commercially available logic. Digital-computer interface logic will be discussed in Chap. 5.

1-7. A General Finite-state Machine. If we agree to admit logic-state changes only at discrete clocked time intervals $0, \Delta t, 2\Delta t, \ldots$, then *every* sequential machine can be built from N type D flip-flops (Table 1-5b) plus combinatorial logic (e.g., AND gates, OR gates, and inverters; or NAND gates; or NOR gates), as shown in Fig. 1-9. Each flip-flop output equals its logic-level

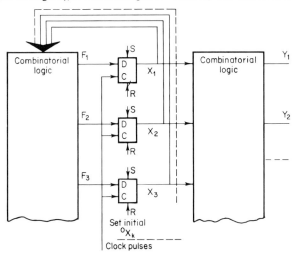

Fig. 1-9. A general clocked sequential machine. The given logic and the initial register contents ^0X determine all subsequent flip-flop states $^kX \equiv (^kX_1, {}^kX_2, \ldots)$ and outputs $^kY \equiv (^kY_1, {}^kY_2, \ldots) = Y(^kX, k)$ through the recursion relations

$$^{k+1}X = F(^kX, k) \qquad k = 0, 1, 2, \ldots$$

input at the time of the last clock-pulse upswing.   Thus the N flip-flop outputs

$$X_i = X_i(k \, \Delta t) \qquad i = 1, 2, \ldots, N$$

are **Boolean state variables** defining the state of our system during the kth clock interval.   Given the N initial values $X_i(0)$, *all future states are determined by the N recursion relations (Boolean difference equations, state equations)*,

$$X_i[(k + 1) \, \Delta t] = F_i[X_1(k \, \Delta t), X_2(k \, \Delta t), \ldots, X_N(k \, \Delta t); k] \qquad i = 1, 2, \ldots, N; k = 0, 1, 2, \ldots$$

where each F_i is a Boolean function of the X_i.   The M system outputs $Y_j(k \, \Delta t)$ are also Boolean functions of the state variables $X_i(k \, \Delta t)$ and may, like the F_i, depend explicitly on the time variable k.

In an actual digital computer, the state-determining flip-flops in Fig. 1-9 will be grouped into processor and memory registers containing numerical and control information.

1-8.   Fixed-point Arithmetic and Scaling.   Minicomputer data registers hold 8-bit, 12-bit, 16-bit, or 18-bit data words.   It is also possible to concatenate two or more such words for **double or higher precision** (Fig. 1-17). We have seen how a binary word can represent an integer (Table 1-1) or a fraction (Table 1-2).   In principle, a binary computer word $(a_0, a_1, a_2, \ldots, a_{n-1})$ could also represent a nonnegative binary number of the more general form

$$X = 2^r \left(\frac{1}{2} a_0 + \frac{1}{2^2} a_1 + \cdots + \frac{1}{2^n} a_{n-1} \right) \qquad 0 \le X \le 2^r - 2^{r-n} \quad (1\text{-}4)$$

with a **binary point** implied ahead of a_r (if $r < 0$, we imply 0 digits $a_r, a_{r+1}, \ldots, a_{-1}$ between the binary point and a_0, as in $X = 0.00101$).   An analogous generalization applies to signed (positive or negative) numbers.   With such representations, we must keep track of the exponent r determining the *binary-point location* throughout the computation; in particular, terms in a sum or difference must have the same r.   **Floating-point arithmetic** programs or circuits (Secs. 1-10 and 6-12) employ some or all the bits in an extra register to specify the exponent r and compute exponents separately at each step of the computation at considerable expense in either computing time or special hardware.

With fixed-point arithmetic, it is best to consider all numerical quantities in computer registers and memory as either integers or pure fractions (Tables 1-1 and 1-2).   **We propose to employ integers (which may be positive, negative, or zero) only to represent actual real integers used in counting, ordering, and addressing operations.   All other real numerical quantities X in the computer will be regarded as signed or unsigned pure fractions (-1 machine unit $< X < +1$ machine unit) proportional to corresponding quantities x occurring in the given problem:**

$$X = [a_x \quad x] \tag{1-5}$$

Each bracketed quantity $[a_x \quad x]$ is a **scaled machine variable** representing the corresponding problem variable x in the computer. *It is convenient to restrict the scale factors a_x to integral powers of* 2.

For best accuracy in fixed-point computations, we try to pick each scale factor a_x as the largest (positive, negative, or zero) integral power of 2 which will still keep the machine variable $[a_x \ \ x]$ between -1 and $+1$:

$$a_x = \frac{1}{2^r} < \frac{1}{\max |x|} \qquad (1\text{-}6)$$

Unfortunately, bounds for $\max |x|$ are not always known ahead of time, so that we may pick too small or too large scale factors. Too small scale factors waste computer precision. Too large scale factors cause **overflow** of the corresponding computer variables, **which makes the computation invalid.** Digital computers have flip-flops (flags) which set to indicate overflow in arithmetic operations. *These flags will not stop the computation by themselves but must be tested by programmed instructions* (Secs. 2-10 and 2-11).

To scale mathematical relations for any given problem, we simply express each problem variable x in terms of the corresponding scaled machine variable $[a_x \ \ x]$:

$$x = \frac{1}{a_x} [a_x \ \ x] \qquad (1\text{-}7)$$

Our scaling procedure is best exhibited through an example.

EXAMPLE: Scale

$$y = ax + bx^2$$

given $a = 10 \qquad b = 0.05 \qquad -7 \le x \le 19$

Since multiplication consumes more computer time than fixed-point addition, we rewrite

$$y = x(a + bx) = xz$$

We must scale the intermediate result $z = a + bx$ as well as y; substitution yields $|z| < 11 < 16$ and $|y| < 256$. Now we simply replace $a, b, x, z,$ and y by

$$16\left[\frac{a}{16}\right], \quad \frac{1}{16}[16b], \quad 32\left[\frac{x}{32}\right], \quad 16\left[\frac{z}{16}\right], \quad \text{and} \quad 256\left[\frac{y}{256}\right]$$

where the bracketed quantities are machine variables between -1 and $+1$. We thus find the scaled machine equation

$$\left[\frac{y}{256}\right] = 2\left[\frac{x}{32}\right]\left\{\left[\frac{a}{16}\right] + \frac{1}{8}[16b]\left[\frac{x}{32}\right]\right\}$$

which is easily checked against the given problem equation through cancellation of scale factors. Note that *our computation involves only scaled machine variables and multiplying factors 2^r ($r = 0, \pm 1, \pm 2, \ldots$) corresponding to simple signed-shift operations* (Sec. 1-9b).

Our scaling procedure, as it were, keeps track of the correct exponents r in Eq. (1-4) outside of the computer.

Although fixed-point computation requires us to *program* with scaled variables, *we may not have to bother with the job of scaling reams of machine input and/or output data.* Entering and printing arabic numerals requires some computation (translation to and from binary numbers) in any case, and it is usually readily possible to incorporate scaling operations in such input/output programs (Sec. 5-27).

1-9. Some Binary-arithmetic Operations. (a) Addition, Subtraction, and Overflow. As discussed in Sec. 1-8, *we will consider all fixed-point binary numbers as signed or unsigned integers and pure fractions;* 2s-complement coding is most common.

The **half-adder (modulo-2 adder)** of Fig. 1-10a is a logic circuit for adding *one-digit* binary numbers and is seen to involve an XOR circuit. For *multidigit* addition, e.g.,

$$
\begin{array}{r}
19 \\
09 \\
\hline
28
\end{array}
\qquad
\begin{array}{ccccc}
1 & 0 & 0 & 1 & 1 \\
0 & 1 & 0 & 0 & 1 \\
\hline
1 & 1 & 1 & 0 & 0
\end{array}
\quad \text{carries}
$$

each bit-by-bit addition can generate a carry bit, which must be added to the next-higher-order digit. This is accomplished by the **full-adder** scheme of Fig. 1-10b. Figure 1-10c shows a complete three-digit binary adder made up of three full-adders.

Such adders will produce correct results with **signed numbers** (2s- or 1s-complement code) if we follow these simple rules:

1. **With 2s-complement arithmetic, simply add as though words represented nonnegative numbers, and disregard sign-bit carries.**
2. *With 1s-complement arithmetic,* add the sign-bit carry (if any) to the least significant digit (*"end-around" carry*).

EXAMPLES:

DECIMAL (Integer)	2S-COMPLEMENT CODE				1S-COMPLEMENT CODE			
6	0	1	1	0	0	1	1	0
−7	1	0	0	1	1	0	0	0
−1	1	1	1	1	1	1	1	0
6	0	1	1	0	0	1	1	0
−4	1	1	0	0	1	0	1	1
2	← 0	0	1	0	0	0	1	0 ←

discarded carry   "end-around" carry

In simple adders like that of Fig. 1-10c, low-order carries must propagate ("ripple through") all the way to the highest-order bit before the sum output is complete. To save time, one could, in principle, compute the result bit of each given order as a Boolean function of all summand bits of the same and

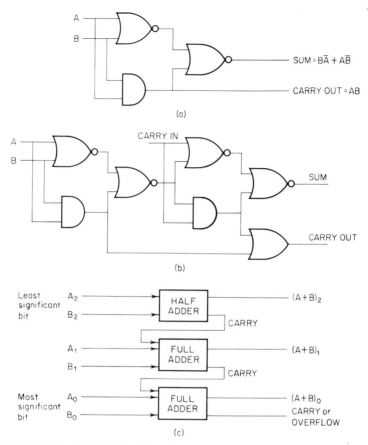

Fig. 1-10. Half-adder (a), full-adder (b), and a 3-bit adder with simple ripple-through carry propagation (c).

lower orders within two gate-delay times. Practical **carry-lookahead** circuits constitute various tradeoffs between circuit simplicity and speed (Refs. 1 and 3, and Fig. 1-11).

Minicomputer adders usually add a number in a processor arithmetic register (**accumulator**) to a number taken from memory (or from another register) and place the result into the accumulator (hence its name).

Fixed-point addition of two numbers produces **arithmetic overflow** if and only if:

1. Both terms of the sum have identical signs but the computed sum has a different sign.
2. Or, equivalently, addition produces a carry out of the sign bit *or* out of the most significant bit but *not both* (that is, the EXCLUSIVE OR of these carries is 1).

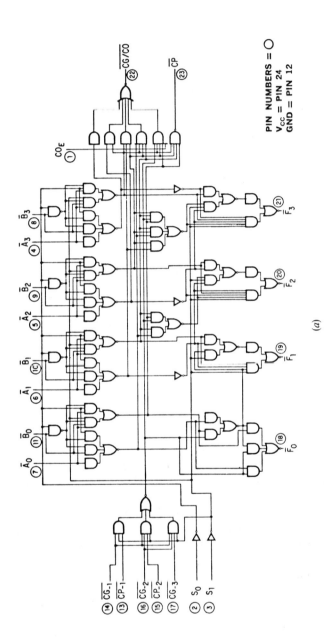

(a)

PIN NUMBERS = ○
V_{CC} = PIN 24
GND = PIN 12

28

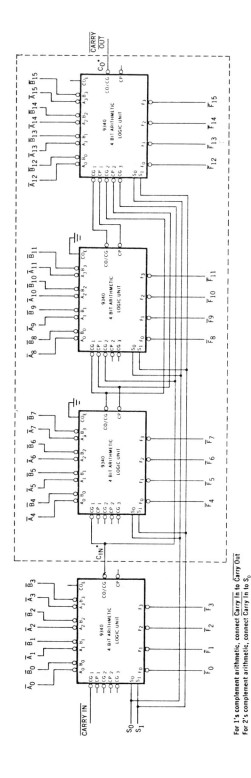

For 1's complement arithmetic, connect $\overline{\text{Carry In}}$ to $\overline{\text{Carry Out}}$
For 2's complement arithmetic, connect $\overline{\text{Carry In}}$ to S_0

(b)

Fig. 1-11. Complete 4-bit TTL arithmetic/logic unit on a single integrated-circuit chip (a) and a 16-bit minicomputer arithmetic/logic unit with group carry lookahead using four such chips (b). A 12-bit arithmetic/logic unit is also shown in dash lines. Bits marked $\overline{A}_i$, $\overline{B}_i$ on two input buses are combined to form output-bus bits $\overline{F}_i$. Two function-control bits S_0, S_1 determine the function:

00 SUBTRACT	01 XOR
10 ADD	11 AND

Maximum delay is 35 nsec for 4 bits, 49 nsec for 16 bits. Shifting would be done with register-gate circuits (*Fairchild Semiconductor.*)

29

The same reasoning applies to subtraction if we regard differences as sums of positive and/or negative numbers. Logic circuits can test summand and sum signs and set an **overflow-flag flip-flop.** Many minicomputers, however, do not have a true overflow flag but only a **carry flag (accumulator-extension** or **link flip-flop),** which is complemented by carries from the highest sum bit. Overflow tests for negative numbers then require several programmed instructions (Sec. 4-8c).

Binary **subtraction** can utilize modified adder circuits (*half-subtractors* and *full-subtractors* with *negative carries* or "*borrows,*" Ref. 1), or we may negate the subtrahend (Tables 1-1 and 1-2) and add.

Figure 1-11a illustrates the logic design of **a complete 4-bit arithmetic/logic unit,** which can implement the bit-by-bit **AND** and **XOR** functions as well as addition and subtraction. The entire circuit is a single integrated-circuit chip. Figure 1-11b shows how such circuits combine into 12-bit and 16-bit arithmetic/logic units.

(b) Shifting (see also Sec. 2-10b). The definition of binary-number codes (Tables 1-1 and 1-2) implies that *shifting each digit of an unsigned* 1*s-complement or* 2*s-complement number* 1 *bit to the right will multiply the number by* $\frac{1}{2}$, *provided that the new leftmost bit equals the old sign bit or is* 0 *for unsigned numbers.* The old least significant bit is lost (chopped rather than rounded off).

Conversely, *each* 1-*bit shift to the left will multiply the original number by* 2, *provided that the new rightmost bit is made* 0 *for unsigned and* 2*s-complement numbers and equals the original sign bit for* 1*s-complement numbers.* Such multiplication by 2 will produce *overflow* if and only if the most significant bit of the given number was 1 for positive numbers and 0 for negative numbers.

EXAMPLES (4-bit 2s-complement code):

$$0110 \text{ represents } +6 \text{ (or } +\tfrac{6}{8}) \qquad 1010 \text{ represents } -6 \text{ (or } -\tfrac{6}{8})$$
$$0011 \text{ represents } +3 \text{ (or } +\tfrac{3}{8}) \qquad 1101 \text{ represents } -3 \text{ (or } -\tfrac{3}{8})$$

0110 and 1010 cannot be shifted left without overflow in this code (sign bit and most significant bit differ).

Digital computers employ shift operations for multiplication by integral powers of 2, and also to move partial words (bytes) in character-handling operations. Shifting could be accomplished with a shift register (Table 1-5b), but in most computers gate circuits like those in Fig. 1 12 move each bit of a word "sideways" during parallel register-to-register transfers.

(c) Binary Multiplication. One ordinarily computes the product of two *n*-bit binary numbers *A* and *B* as a 2*n-bit number*, so that no information is lost. This works nicely for *unsigned* integers or fractions,

$$\left.\begin{array}{r} 3 \times 3 = 9 \\ \tfrac{3}{4} \times \tfrac{3}{4} = \tfrac{9}{16} \end{array}\right\} \text{ is represented by } 11 \times 11 = 1001$$

or

and also for *signed integers*, say in 2s-complement code:

$(-3) \times 3 = -9$ is represented by $101 \times 011 = 110111$
$(-4) \times (-4) = +16$ is represented by $100 \times 100 = 010000$

But if the *n*-bit multiplier inputs *A*, *B* and the 2*n*-bit multiplier output are interpreted as signed *fractions* (Table 1-2), *then the multiplier output is*

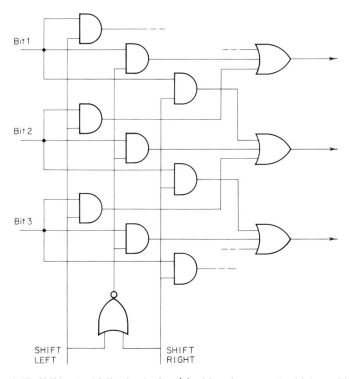

Fig. 1-12. Shifting (multiplication by 2 or $\frac{1}{2}$) with register gates (multiplexer chips).

$\frac{1}{2}AB$ (*not AB*).   Thus, in 2s-complement code:

$101 \times 011 \rightarrow 110111$ represents $\frac{1}{2}(-\frac{3}{4}) \times \frac{3}{4} = -\frac{9}{32}$
$100 \times 100 \rightarrow 010000$ represents $\frac{1}{2}(-1) \times (-1) = +\frac{1}{2}$

A fast multiplier for short words can use logic or table lookup to form product digits, but this is too expensive for minicomputer arithmetic. Instead, we proceed as in pencil-and-paper multiplication. We multiply the multiplicand by each multiplier digit in turn to form *partial products;* these are then multiplied by successive powers of 2 (i.e., shifted) and added.

For simplicity, let us consider multiplication of unsigned integers. Instead of shifting partial products, the computer adds the most significant partial product into a cleared 2*n*-bit register (actually two *n*-bit registers), shifts the register contents to the left, adds the next partial product, etc. With binary numbers, each multiplier bit is either 0 or 1, so that each partial product simply adds either 0 or the given multiplicand. These operations are accomplished either through successive computer instructions (multiplication subroutine, software multiplication) or more quickly by hard-wired logic.

EXAMPLE ($3 \times 5 = 15$):

$$
\begin{array}{r}
011 \times 101 \\
\hline
011 \\
000 \\
011 \\
\hline
001111
\end{array}
$$

(d) Division. Division subroutines or hardware employ a *double-length dividend* and a *one-word divisor*. The result will be a *one-word quotient* plus a *one-word remainder*.

We again consider only unsigned integers or unsigned fractions. We begin by comparing the divisor with the high-order half of the dividend: the division *overflows* (and is stopped as unsuccessful) unless the divisor is larger. No quotient bit is entered at this point.

The entire two-word dividend is next shifted 1 bit to the left, and the contents of the most significant register are again compared with the divisor. If it is still larger, we enter 0 as the most significant quotient bit and shift again; if not, we enter 1 and subtract the divisor into the most significant dividend register and shift. We continue in this way (much as in pencil-and-paper division) until all quotient bits are computed. At this point, *the most significant dividend register will contain the remainder; the least significant dividend register contains the (integral part of the) quotient.*

EXAMPLE ($15 \div 7 = 2\frac{1}{7}$, 3-bit words):

(a) 0 0 1 1 1 1	(b) 0 1 1 1 1 0	(c) 1 1 1 1 0 0
1 1 1	1 1 1	1 1 1
no overflow, shift	shift	subtract and shift

Quotient: 0 1 0   Remainder: 0 0 1

For division of *signed numbers*, consult your computer manual as to the specific format used. Most frequently, the correctly signed quotient is left in the least significant dividend register, while the remainder, again in the most significant dividend register, is an unsigned number preceded by the sign of the *dividend*.

To compute *scaled-fraction quotients* X/Y of N-bit scaled fractions X, Y (Sec. 1-8) or, for that matter, of N-bit integers X, Y with an N-bit computer, simply place X into the *most significant* dividend register and clear the least significant dividend register. The desired signed or unsigned fractional quotient will be correctly produced in the form $2^{-N}(2^N X/Y)$.

1-10. Floating-point Arithmetic.   (a) Floating-point Data Representation.
Binary **floating-point arithmetic** represents each real number X by *two* binary
numbers, an N-bit signed binary fraction (**mantissa**) A and an M-bit signed
binary integer (**exponent**) R so that

$$X = A \times 2^R \tag{1-8}$$

The mantissa is usually represented in sign-and-magnitude code (Table 1-2).
The exponent can be a 2s-complement integer (Table 1-1); some floating-
point number representations do not use the exponent R itself but employ,
instead, a nonnegative **biased exponent** or **characteristic**

$$R' = R + B \tag{1-9}$$

where B is an agreed-on positive integer.   Typical minicomputer floating-
point formats are shown in Fig. 1-17.

Floating-point number representation is not unique since, for instance,

$$0.10100_2 \times 2^9 = 0.01010_2 \times 2^{10} = 0.00101_2 \times 2^{11}$$

The first form, where the most significant binary digit of the (nonnegative)
mantissa is a 1, is often defined as the **normalized** form of the floating-point
number.   A number is also considered normalized if the exponent is as
small as possible and the absolute value of the mantissa is still less than $\frac{1}{2}$.

Some computer manufacturers (e.g., IBM, Interdata, Data General) use a
hexadecimal floating-point representation defined by

$$X = A \times 16^R \tag{1-10}$$

where A is a binary fraction and R is a binary integer (usually expressed in
hexadecimal code, Sec. 1-4b).   In this case, a properly normalized mantissa
will have at least the magnitude $\frac{1}{16}$; i.e., at least one of the four most
significant bits of the positive fraction is a 1.

Fortunately, most minicomputer users meet *binary* floating-point formats
only when troubleshooting.   Input/output is almost always in *decimal*
floating-point format, usually in the E format familiar to FORTRAN users:

$$0.2734\,\text{E} + 02 = 0.2734_{10} \times 10^2$$

The floating-point representation [Eq. (1-8)] covers the range

$$-2^{2^{M-1}-1} < X < 2^{2^{M-1}-1} \tag{1-11}$$

This range is usually so very large ($2^{2^{M-1}-1} > 10^{38}$ for $M = 8$, see also
Fig. 1-17) that *no scaling is necessary with most practical problems*.   This
truly dramatic advantage over fixed-point computation is paid for with
either extra computing time or more expensive hardware, and usually also
with *reduced precision* per bit used to represent X (M bits are used for
the exponent, which does not contribute "significant digits").   Roundoff

errors can be multiplied by large factors 2^R in some parts of a computation, so that a multidigit floating-point result may be less accurate than it looks. In particular, *minicomputer two-word floating-point formats have uncomfortably short mantissas*. Unless you know exactly what you are doing, we recommend *three- or four-word formats* with 16- and 18-bit machines (Fig. 1-17). This applies especially where many terms are added, as in numerical integration and averaging.

Overflow of the floating-point range [Eq. (1-11)] is possible, but rare. **Underflow** (normalized exponent R below $1 - 2^{M-1}$) will return $X = 0$ in most systems.

(b) Floating-point Operations. *Floating-point addition and subtraction* require the computer to perform the following—fairly involved—operations:

Compare exponents
Shift mantissa of smaller term so that both terms have equal exponents
Add (or subtract) mantissas
Normalize result; check for overflow, return 0 on underflow

With floating-point arithmetic, *multiplication and division* are rather simpler than addition and subtraction:

Enter with normalized data; multiply (or divide) mantissas—exit if 0
Add (or subtract) exponents; check for overflow, return 0 on underflow
Normalize result

All these operations must be implemented with software (subroutines), with a microprogram (Sec. 6-13), or with optional hardware (floating-point arithmetic unit). *We must also provide for the additional operations of "floating" fixed-point numbers and "fixing" floating-point numbers, and for decimal input/output.* Suitable assembly-language subroutines will be found in computer manufacturers' software listings; floating-point hardware is discussed in Refs. 1 and 6.

MEMORY AND COMPUTATION

1-11. Introduction. A **computer memory** is needed to store data and instruction sequences; in addition, a finite instruction set makes it necessary to compute and store intermediate results. In effect, each computer memory consists of a large number of binary storage registers (**memory locations**) each capable of storing a complete computer word, plus circuits to address a program-selected memory location for reading or writing a word.

To access a memory location, we place its number (**memory address**) in the **memory address register.** A "tree" of decoding gates (Table 1-5a) connected to the memory address register will then direct logic signals to read the selected memory word *into* the **memory data register (memory buffer**

register) or write a word *from* the memory data register into the selected memory location. The **access time** is the time needed to select and read. The **write time** required to select and write is often called **cycle time,** a **memory cycle** being the time required to read/erase *and* write/rewrite in a magnetic-core memory (Sec. 1-12).

The **main memory** of a minicomputer usually has between 1,000 and 32,768 words of magnetic-core, semiconductor, or plated-wire storage with effective cycle times between 250 and 8,000 nsec (Secs. 1-12 and 1-13). As a compromise, inexpensive 800- to 3,000-nsec main memories can be supplemented by very fast (50- to 200-nsec) *intermediate storage* (**scratchpad memories**) in the form of flip-flop-register or semiconductor memories. In addition, we often add slow but inexpensive *mass storage* in the form of magnetic disks, drums, and tape (Chap. 3). These can store large programs and data blocks (up to millions of words) which are (one hopes) not immediately needed at all times, but which can be transferred to and from the main memory as need arises. We thus have a *hierarchy of storage systems.*

1-12. Core Memories. Most minicomputer main memories are **core memories,** which store individual bits by magnetizing toroidal ferrite cores in the 1 or 0 direction through a write-current pulse (Fig. 1-13a). To read the information stored in such a core, one pulses the core in the 0 magnetization direction; if a 1 had been stored in the core, the resulting flux reversal would cause an output current pulse in a *sense wire* threaded through the core (Fig. 1-13b). To *select* only the cores associated with a specific word in the memory, we implement the read and write currents through superposition of select and inhibit currents in two or three wires threading each core (**coincident-current selection,** Figs. 1-13a and b). Figure 1-13c illustrates a typical core-memory word selection scheme (3D *scheme*), and Fig. 1-13d shows the wiring of a typical bit plane; the sense wire is threaded through all cores in the plane in a pattern designed to cancel the effects of the half-select current pulses associated with unselected cores. At the expense of a little extra switching logic, *the same bit-plane wire can be used for both inhibiting and sensing,* so that only *three* wires need to be threaded through each core. Reference 3 describes two different word/bit arrangements for core memories (2D and $2\frac{1}{2}$D).

Core storage is **nonvolatile;** i.e., the memory continues to store its contents even when computer power is off. Full-cycle times of typical minicomputer core memories are between 650 nsec and 8 μsec, half of which is the access time. As shown in Fig. 1-13b, **core-memory readout is destructive;** i.e., *reading clears the addressed memory location;* ordinarily, the word thus read into the memory data register is rewritten into core during the second half of the READ memory cycle. The cycle time of even a 650-nsec core memory is quite long compared to the 50- to 100-nsec clock-interval times

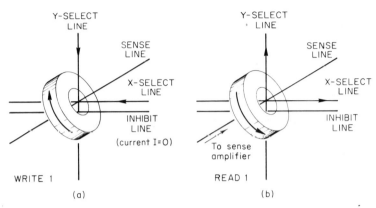

Fig. 1-13a and b. Coincident-current writing and reading/erasing in a typical minicomputer core memory. (a) WRITING: We start with all cores magnetized in the 0 direction. Writing a 1 into a given core (i.e., a given bit of a selected word) depends on *three* current pulses. Each of the two *select currents* X, Y must be one-half of the required magnetizing current (word selection), *and* the *inhibit current* I (which would oppose 1 magnetization) must be 0 (bit setting). The inhibit line, common to all *words*, belongs to a specific memory-data-register *bit*. (b) READING/ERASING: The X and Y select wires are both pulsed with current in the 0 magnetization direction. This produces no change if the core is already magnetized in the 0 direction. If a 1 was stored, it will be erased, and the flux reversal will cause a 1 pulse in the sense line. The latter, common to all *words*, sets a specific memory-data-register *bit* via a sense amplifier.

of integrated-circuit arithmetic units. In larger digital machines with multiple core-memory banks, one can partially circumvent core-access delays by taking successive memory words from *different* memory banks; this permits rewriting in one bank to be *overlapped* with logic operations and memory accesses to other banks. Such memory-bank overlapping is rarely used with minicomputers, which may have only a single memory bank altogether, but *the possibility should not be overlooked* (Sec. 6-9).

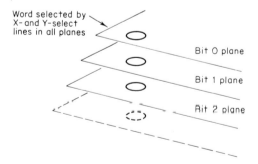

Fig. 1-13c. The cores belonging to a given *word* have the same X, Y position in each bit plane. Each plane has inhibit and sense lines associated with one memory-data-register *bit*.

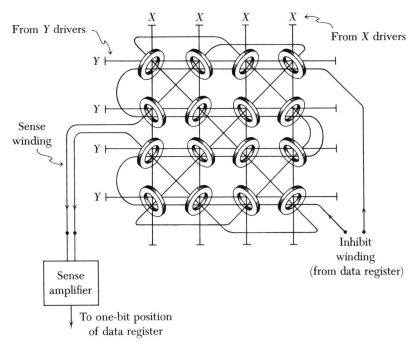

Fig. 1-13d. One bit plane of a 16-word 3D core-memory unit (*H. Hellerman, Digital Computer System Principles, McGraw-Hill, New York, 1967*).

Core-magnetization retention at temperatures much above 85°F requires either high-temperature core material or an automatic increase of core-driving currents with temperature. Typical minicomputer core memories can work at ambient temperatures up to 110 to 130°F; *you should check this specification carefully against your application requirements.*

With new monolithic sense and driver amplifiers and clever core-stringing techniques, core-memory manufacturers are still holding their own against the onslaught of new solid-state memories. Typical 16-bit 1-μsec minicomputer memories, including selection, driving, and sensing electronics, cost on the order of 2 to 5 cents/bit in 1K banks.

1-13. Semiconductor and Plated-wire Memories. With the advent of medium-scale and large-scale integrated circuits permitting fair manufacturing yields, all-electronic solid-state memories have become a reality. Semiconductor memories are smaller than equivalent core memories; they can be faster and consume less power; and, in the long run, semiconductor memories will probably be substantially cheaper (Ref. 23).

Bipolar-transistor static memories, which are essentially multiple flip-flop registers plus read/write/selection circuits, are directly compatible with transistor/transistor or emitter-coupled logic and are very fast: read and write times below 50 nsec are readily possible. No rewriting after reading is needed (**nondestructive readout, NDRO**). Bipolar memories are fairly complex integrated circuits and are still expensive (of the order of 20 cents/bit in 1K banks). They are, therefore, used mostly in small "scratchpad" memories. Prices are expected to decrease to below 2 cents/bit as integrated-circuit yields improve.

MOSFET (metal-oxide-silicon field-effect transistor) semiconductor memories involve simpler integrated-circuit patterns and are cheaper than bipolar memories. While older MOSFET circuits needed level-changing amplifiers to supply large logic-voltage swings, some newer MOSFET memories are TTL-compatible. MOSFET memories also come as **static** (flip-flop-register) memories but usually as **dynamic memories.** In a dynamic memory, each bit is stored in what amounts to a shift register whose output is fed back to the input through a clock-gated MOSFET *refresh amplifier*, so each stored bit is recirculated and regenerated, say, 1,000 times/sec (Fig. 1-14). The refresh amplifier can be time-shared among 16 to 32 memory cells. Simple silicon-substrate MOSFET memories are slower than bipolar memories (and slower than some core memories). Typical access times are between 300 nsec and 2 μsec with nondestructive readout. 1-μsec dynamic MOSFET memories cost about 1 to 3 cents/bit in quantities of 1,000, and prices can be expected to decrease to below 1 cent/bit.

The era of solid-state computer memories is still in its beginning. One may anticipate massive developments, both with respect to better yields (and thus much lower memory costs) and in the development of new integrated memory circuits. In particular, different types of MOSFET circuits (complementary MOSFETs, sapphire and garnet substrates) are under active development and can be expected to lead to substantially faster MOSFET memories. Compared to core memories, semiconductor memories have the advantage of *nondestructive readout*. On the other hand, semiconductor memories are **volatile;** i.e., memory contents are destroyed when computer power is turned off. In sufficiently critical applications, one must provide an emergency power source, such as a trickle-charged battery which, when a power failure is sensed, can take over memory operation for a time sufficient to transfer the entire contents of the memory onto an auxiliary magnetic storage medium (disk or tape).

Plated-wire memories are magnetic memories which utilize small zones of magnetizable thin films plated onto wires, rather than magnetic cores, for bit storage. Plated-wire memories permit fast access (access times as low as a few hundred nanoseconds) with nondestructive readout, are nonvolatile, and have been the subject of considerable hopes and expectations. In fact, excellent plated-wire memories are commercially available. But, although batch-production methods have been developed, quality control is not

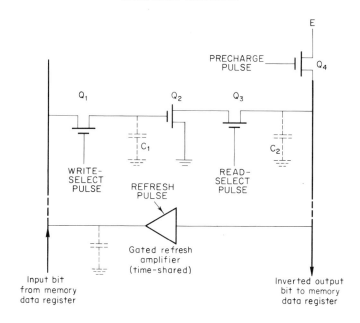

Fig. 1-14. A dynamic MOSFET memory, Q_1, Q_2, and Q_3 form a 1-bit memory cell. PRE-
CHARGE, WRITE-SELECT, READ-SELECT, and REFRESH pulses are associated with
consecutive phases of a four-phase clock. Each pulse, if enabled by the cell-selecting logic, will
transfer a bit from one parasitic capacitance to the next in a clockwise direction. PRE-
CHARGE charges C_2 by turning Q_4 ON and OFF. WRITE-SELECT turns Q_1 ON and OFF;
if a 1 is written, C_1 is charged. READ-SELECT turns Q_3 ON and OFF; if a 1 is stored, Q_2
turns ON and discharges C_2 so that the (inverted) output is 0. The gate refresh amplifier
(essentially another similar memory cell) inverts the selected output bit and transfers it back to
its cell input once every millisecond or so.

simple. As a result, plated-wire memories are not cheap (5 to 10 cents/bit)
and have been applied mostly in higher-priced digital computers (especially
in aerospace-vehicle computers); MOSFET memories seem to have over-
taken plated-wire circuits in the low-cost minicomputer field. This
situation may or may not be changed by future improvements in plated-
wire-memory fabrication.

1-14. Read-only Memories. Read-only memories (ROMs), whose contents
are usually checked out and written once and for all at the time of manufacture
and then cannot be overwritten, are used to store frequently reused program
sequences or bit patterns:

1. *Complete special-purpose programs*, especially in industrial logic-
   sequence controllers replacing old-fashioned relay-ladder logic
2. *Important library subroutines* for special arithmetic sequences, control
   or emergency routines, scale or format transformations, etc.

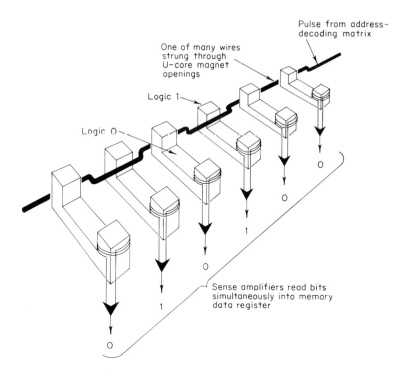

Fig. 1-15. Magnetic read-only memory (ROM) Each U core may be given a top to improve its magnetic circuit after the word wires have been strung.

3. *System programs* such as bootstrap loaders (Sec. 3-4*b*), input/output subroutines (Sec. 5-30), and even simple compilers
4. Special *directories* and *function tables*
5. *Microprograms* (firmware) for implementing or emulating special instructions or instruction sequences (Sec. 6-13)

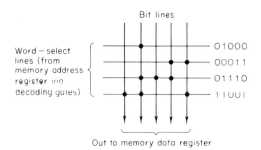

Fig. 1-16. Principle of a crossbar-matrix read-only memory. Each crosspoint connection is made through a diode or MOSFET gate.

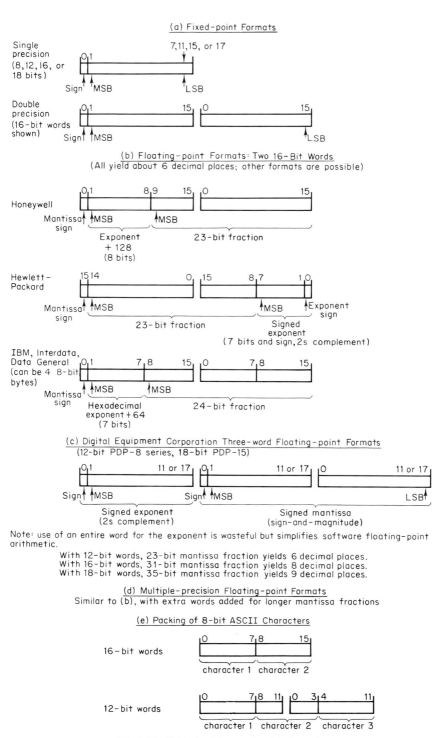

(a) Fixed-point Formats

Single precision (8,12,16, or 18 bits)

7,11,15, or 17

Sign | MSB | LSB

Double precision (16-bit words shown)

Sign | MSB | LSB

(b) Floating-point Formats: Two 16-Bit Words
(All yield about 6 decimal places; other formats are possible)

Honeywell

Mantissa sign | MSB | MSB

Exponent + 128 (8 bits)

23-bit fraction

Hewlett-Packard

Mantissa sign | MSB | MSB | Exponent sign

23-bit fraction

Signed exponent (7 bits and sign, 2s complement)

IBM, Interdata, Data General (can be 4 8-bit bytes)

Mantissa sign | MSB | MSB

Hexadecimal exponent + 64 (7 bits)

24-bit fraction

(c) Digital Equipment Corporation Three-word Floating-point Formats
(12-bit PDP-8 series, 18-bit PDP-15)

Sign | MSB | Sign | MSB | LSB

Signed exponent (2s complement)

Signed mantissa (sign-and-magnitude)

Note: use of an entire word for the exponent is wasteful but simplifies software floating-point arithmetic.

With 12-bit words, 23-bit mantissa fraction yields 6 decimal places.
With 16-bit words, 31-bit mantissa fraction yields 8 decimal places.
With 18-bit words, 35-bit mantissa fraction yields 9 decimal places.

(d) Multiple-precision Floating-point Formats
Similar to (b), with extra words added for longer mantissa fractions

(e) Packing of 8-bit ASCII Characters

16-bit words

character 1 character 2

12-bit words

character 1 character 2 character 3

Fig. 1-17. Typical minicomputer data formats.

6. *Bit-pattern generators* such as *character generators* for displays and *test-signal generators* (see also Sec. 7-10)

Users may value the ROM's reliability and assurance against accidental overwriting of important stored information. Another potential advantage is that nondestructive instruction readout from a ROM can be partially overlapped with instruction execution since no rewriting is necessary (Sec. 6-5). On the debit side, simple read-only memories do not make allowances for programming afterthoughts. Stored programs or data must be checked out very carefully through preliminary runs with an ordinary memory.

An important application of read-only memory is to logic design, for the ROM can produce complicated multi-input Boolean functions (Sec. 1-6) through simple table lookup. Such table-lookup functions can be used in the sequential-machine setup of Fig. 1-9 to generate complex sequential patterns (Ref. 22).

Figure 1-15 shows a **magnetic ("woven-wire") ROM.** Read-select logic pulses one of many word-wires strung inside and outside an n-bit array of U cores and causes an output pulse in those U-core windings wired for a 1. We see that memory contents are established by each word-wire stringing pattern. Access times of such magnetic ROMs vary between 300 and 2,000 nsec.

Semiconductor ROMs can use the dynamic-storage technique (Sec. 1-13), but most semiconductor ROMs are essentially **crossbar matrices** (Fig. 1-16), whose crosspoint connections are established by diode or MOSFET OR-gate connections. The storage pattern is established through selective erasure of crosspoint connections or semiconductors during manufacture or during installation ("field-programmable" ROMs). Typically, access times vary between 50 nsec and 1 μsec, and costs are decreasing from 2 cents/bit. Some semiconductor ROMs can be reprogrammed in the field through new metallic connections or even through electrical signals.

REFERENCES AND BIBLIOGRAPHY

1. Chu, Y.: *Digital-computer Design Fundamentals*, McGraw-Hill, New York, 1962.
2. ———: *Introduction to Computer Organization*, Prentice-Hall, Englewood Cliffs, N.J., 1970.
3. Hellerman, H.: *Digital-computer-system Principles*, McGraw-Hill, New York, 1967.
4. Baron, R. C., and A. T. Piccirilli: *Digital Logic and Computer Operations*, McGraw-Hill, New York, 1968.
5. Hill, F. J., and G. R. Peterson: *Introduction to Switching Theory and Logic Design*, Wiley, New York, 1968.
6. Huskey, H. D., and G. A. Korn: *Computer Handbook*, McGraw-Hill, New York, 1962.
7. Klerer, M., and G. A. Korn: *Digital Computer User's Handbook*, McGraw-Hill, New York, 1967.
8. Korn, G. A.: *Random-process Simulation and Measurements*, McGraw-Hill, New York, 1966.
9. ——— and T. M. Korn: *Mathematical Handbook for Scientists and Engineers*, 2d ed., McGraw-Hill, New York, 1968.

10. Korn, G. A., and T. M. Korn: *Electronic Analog and Hybrid Computers*, 2d ed., McGraw-Hill, New York, 1971.
11. *An Introduction to HP Computers*, Hewlett-Packard Corporation, Cupertino, Calif., 1970.
12. *Small Computer Handbook*, Digital Equipment Corporation, Maynard, Mass. (issued yearly).
13. Special Issue on Minicomputers, *IEEE Comput. Group News*, July–August 1970.
    Minicomputers: An Introduction, by T. Storer
    Minicomputer Architecture, by W. H. Roberts
    Minicomputer I/O and Peripherals, by E. Holland
    Small-computer Software, by H. W. Spencer et al.
14. Epstein, A., and D. Bessel: Minicomputers Are Made of This, *Comput. Decis.*, August 1970.
15. Federoff, A. M.: Minicomputers Are Used for This, *Comput. Decis.*, August 1970.
16. French, M.: Survey of Small Digital Computers, *EEE*, February 1970.

Semiconductor Memories

17. Semiconductor Memories Turn the Corner, *Electron. Des. News*, February 1970.
18. Selecting and Applying Semiconductor Memories, *EEE*, June, July, and August 1970.
19. Boysel, L., et al.: Random-access MOS Memory, *Electronics*, February 1970.
20. Boyle, A. J.: MOS Course: Read-only Memories, *Electr. Eng.*, July and September 1970.
21. Hoff, M. E.: MOS Memory and Its Applications, *Comput. Des.*, June 1970.
22. Kvamme, F.: Standard Read-only Memories Simplify Complex Logic Design, *Electronics*, January 1970.
23. Semiconductor Memory Survey, *Electronics*, August 23, 1972.

CHAPTER 2

"BASIC" MINICOMPUTERS AND INSTRUCTION SETS

INTRODUCTION AND SURVEY

This chapter outlines the design and operation of a "basic" minicomputer illustrating the common features of many small machines. The principal ingredients of such a system—memory, registers, buses, and arithmetic/logic unit—are introduced in Secs. 2-1 to 2-5. Sections 2-6 to 2-14 then list the most important machine instructions in the repertoire of a "basic" single-address minicomputer, discuss their implementation in terms of the system block diagram, and mention the most important applications of some instructions. Sections 2-13 to 2-15 describe useful options available with small digital computers. In Chap. 4, we will meet the basic computer instructions again; specifically, we will then see how they can be combined into practical assembly-language programs. Input/output will be further discussed in Chaps. 3 and 5. More advanced instruction sets and architectures for a new generation of minicomputers will be described in Chap. 6.

THE BASIC SINGLE-ADDRESS MACHINE

2-1. Instruction Sets and Stored Programs. From a very general point of view, *the essential objective of any digital computation is to obtain digital output words*

$$Y1 = F_1(X1, X2, \ldots)$$
$$Y2 = F_2(X1, X2, \ldots) \tag{2-1}$$

. . . .

from input words $X1, X2, \ldots$. Both input and output words will be ordered sets of 0s and 1s in suitably addressed computer registers and/or memory cells. Words may represent various types of numbers and alphanumeric-character strings or simply describe problem-logic states.

The desired relationships [Eq. (2-1)] may be numerous and enormously complicated. They must be broken down into elementary mathematical relations implemented by a (we hope small) set of **computer instructions.** It will, then, be necessary to supply additional registers or memory locations for storing intermediate results from elementary operations. The basic digital computer is, moreover, designed to perform all the various elementary arithmetic/logic operations *successively* with *the same* arithmetic/logic system (unlike, for instance, a conventional analog computer, which has separate adders, multipliers, etc., for separate operations). The resulting sequence of elementary instructions designed to implement a desired computation is called a **program.**

Short, simple, or repetitive digital programs can be implemented by hard-wired controllers (e.g., rotating-cam operation of control switches, read-only memories), by patch-cord systems, or by punched-tape or punched-card readers. Practical digital-computer programs, however, often require extremely large numbers (thousands and even millions) of instructions. It is also often desirable to change a digital-computer program very quickly and even to modify programs while they are being executed.

These considerations make it expedient **to code the instructions themselves into digital-computer words which, like the data words, are stored in sequences in the computer memory.** Operation of the resulting **stored-program digital computer** will now involve **alternate reading (fetching) of instruction words and execution of the corresponding instructions.**

The machine will most often read instructions in sequence, but is capable of *branching* to a different group of instructions as a result of decisions made in the course of the computation. The same group of instructions (subroutine, loop) may be traversed again and again for repeated and iterative operations.

Since the instruction words are, just like data words, simply sets of 0s and 1s to the computer, its arithmetic/logic circuits can, if we wish, *modify* instructions in accordance with intermediate results. The extraordinary power of the modern digital computer is not simply due to its speed and memory capacity but also to the flexibility of the stored-program concept: branching, looping, and instruction or data-address modification permit us to create dramatically complicated programs from very simple instruction sets.

2-2. Single-address Computers. Perhaps the most "natural" computer instruction might, say, add two numbers A and B taken from memory by specifying **ADD WORD** (addressed by) **A AND WORD** (addressed by) **B**; **PUT RESULT INTO MEMORY LOCATION** (addressed by) **C**. But specification of three separate addresses would make the instruction word too long (even for a large digital computer, not to speak of a minicomputer). We can, however, implement the above operation in terms of several simpler instructions each referencing only a single memory address:

> **LOAD INTO ACCUMULATOR** (the word addressed by) **A**
> **ADD INTO ACCUMULATOR** (the word addressed by) **B**
> **STORE ACCUMULATOR** (in memory location addressed by) **C**

The "basic" minicomputer discussed in this chapter, then, will be a **single-address machine** whose instructions move data between a single suitably addressed memory location and a specified processor register, or possibly between two such registers. There will also be some instructions which do not reference memory at all (e.g., **COMPLEMENT ACCUMULATOR**). We remark, however, that the possibility of using simplified two-address instructions and zero-address (stack) instructions in minicomputers is of the greatest interest and will be discussed in connection with more advanced designs in Chap. 6.

2-3. The "Basic" Minicomputer. Figure 2-1 illustrates the typical organization of a small digital computer. The machine has all the ingredients of Secs. 1-6 to 1-13, viz.,

1. A core or semiconductor **memory,** which will store instructions and data
2. A set of **processor registers** (flip-flop registers), viz.,
   - (*a*) **Memory buffer register (memory data register):** contains the instruction or data word currently leaving or entering the memory
   - (*b*) **Memory address register:** contains the address of the currently addressed memory location
   - (*c*) **Program counter:** contains the address of the instruction to be executed
   - (*d*) **Instruction register:** contains the current instruction
   - (*e*) **General-purpose register (accumulator, arithmetic register) or registers;** and, possibly, an **index register** (Sec. 2-7)
   - (*f*) **One-bit registers ("flags"):** indicates **overflow, carry, sign bit,** etc., resulting from past or current operations
3. An **arithmetic/logic unit:** logic circuits to combine words from two registers by addition, subtraction, bit-by-bit ANDing, etc., and to complement, shift, etc., single words
4. **Control logic:** decodes the 0s and 1s of the instruction currently in the instruction register to generate logic levels and time pulses, which:
   - (*a*) **Gate (steer) words between processor registers**
   - (*b*) **Determine the function of the arithmetic/logic circuits**

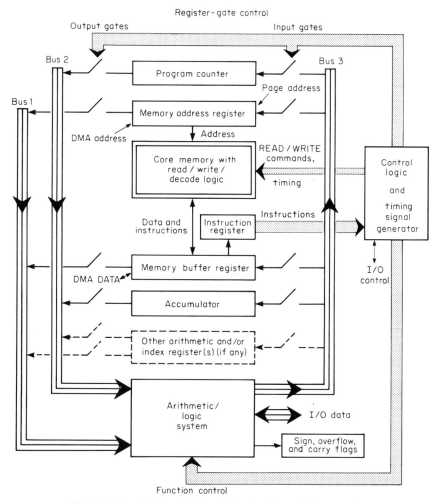

Fig. 2-1. Organization of a "basic" single-address minicomputer.

In Fig. 2-1, there are three **buses** for transfers between registers, always via the arithmetic/logic unit. This is a practical compromise: some extra register-to-register paths would permit more concurrent register transfers and speed computation, but we would pay for more complex interconnections and logic.

Finally, we must have **input/output connections** through the arithmetic/logic unit or through register gates.

2-4. Processor Operation. (a) Instruction Fetching. If we assume that a suitable program and data are in memory, processor operation proceeds in clock-timed steps (**microoperations**):

1. The *program counter*, which we assume to be preset to the address of the first instruction (manually as in Sec. 3-4 or by a preceding computer program), transfers this address to the *memory address register*.
2. The instruction word thus addressed is read into the *memory buffer register* and from there into the *instruction register*.

These instruction-fetch microoperations require one memory half-cycle (READ half-cycle, Sec. 1-12). A *core* memory must next restore the instruction word while its address is still in the memory address register (RESTORE half-cycle). Even with a core memory, operations which do not involve the memory can "overlap" the restoring operation. Hence most non-memory-reference instructions can be executed in a single memory cycle, which is commonly referred to as the **FETCH cycle.**

(b) **Instruction Execution.** As soon as the instruction word is in the instruction register, its 0s and 1s are decoded to control processor operations on register and memory words and input/output operations.

When each instruction is completed, the program counter must contain the address of the next instruction in the program. Most instructions simply *increment* the program counter to produce the next instruction address, while *branching* instructions load the program counter with a nonconsecutive address (Sec. 2-9). The computer (unless halted) then proceeds with a new FETCH phase.

2-5. Instruction Sets. The timing-and-control block in Fig. 2-1 produces a sequence of timed pulses available for jam transfers, sensing, and clearing of words in registers, memory, and arithmetic circuits (see also Table 1-5b and Sec. 1-6). In a conventional n-bit computer, the instruction register has at most n bits, which can be decoded to furnish up to 2^n gate-level combinations for steering pulses and/or words. We can, thus, have up to 2^n different one-word instructions (including input/output instructions). Unfortunately, each instruction referencing an operand or result in memory (**memory-reference instructions,** e.g., LOAD ACCUMULATOR, STORE ACCUMULATOR, JUMP, etc.) must address one of, say, 8,000 memory locations, and this *alone* requires 13 bits. To have a meaningful variety of instructions, even 18-bit machines do not use more than 13 bits for direct addressing, and most minicomputers use only 7 or 8 bits. It follows that *every minicomputer must sometimes and somehow employ multi-word instructions;* the extra word or words may be implied by an effective-address computation (Sec. 2-7). It is of at least academic interest that any and all digital-computer programs can be implemented with very small instruction sets, but this requires many more instructions, which are costly in terms of memory, time, and programming effort. Altogether, **mini-computer design depends crucially on elegant compromises in coding broadly useful instruction sets into short instruction words** (see also Chap. 6).

Table 2-1 lists the most common instructions used with minicomputers of the "basic" type shown in Fig. 2-1. Figure 2-2 illustrates **instruction-word formats** for such machines.

WHAT INSTRUCTIONS DO

2-6. Register-storing Instructions. Referring to Fig. 2-1, an instruction

STORE ACCUMULATOR IN	(effective address)
STORE ACCUMULATOR NO. 2 IN	(effective address)
STORE INDEX REGISTER NO. 2 IN	(effective address)

transfers the contents of the specified processor register to the memory data register via buses 2 and 3. Concurrently, the effective memory address implied by the instruction word is determined (Sec. 2-7) and loaded into the memory address register. The machine then deposits the register word into the effectively addressed memory location, whose previous contents are *lost*. The contents of the source register are *unchanged*.

The arithmetic/logic unit (Fig. 2-1) acts simply as a data-transfer path joining buses 2 and 3. Since both instruction fetching *and* execution require memory read/write operations, register-storing instructions require *two memory cycles*.

2-7. Addressing Modes and Index Registers (see also Sec. 4-9). **(a) Direct, Relative, and Indexed Addressing.** Memory-reference instructions like the register-storing instructions of Sec. 2-6 may have to address 4,000, 8,000, and even as many as 64,000 memory locations. But the minicomputer memory-reference-instruction formats of Fig. 2-2 have only 7 to 13 bits available for addressing since we need some **operation-code** bits to distinguish different memory-reference instructions. It is, therefore, necessary to *compute* an **effective address** by combining the instruction-word address bits with another digital word previously loaded into another processor register or memory location. This means, of course, that we may need two or more words to specify the memory-reference instruction completely. Every minicomputer employs two or more of the following **addressing modes**:

1. **Direct addressing on "page 0":** m address bits in the instruction word directly address memory locations 0 through $2^m - 1$.

With, say, $m = 8$, the resulting 256-word **page** does not go far, but we often use memory locations on page 0 for special purposes (interrupt trap locations, autoindex locations, etc.).

TABLE 2-1. Basic Instructions for Single-address Computers.

The most frequently supplied instructions are shown in fat print (see also Secs. 2-6 to 2-12).

	Memory-reference Instructions (they may be indexed; most need two processor cycles, more with indirect address)	Non-memory-reference Instructions (one processor cycle)	Programmed Input/Output (to or from addressed device, two to four processor cycles)
Move word	**LOAD** } (word or byte; specify register) **STORE** } STORE ZERO	**MOVE** (register-to-register) LOAD IMMEDIATE	**READ** (device-to-register) **WRITE** (register-to-device)
Arithmetic (with overflow and/or carry flag)	**ADD SUBTRACT** MULTIPLY } (usually optional) DIVIDE }	INVERT ADD CARRY INCREMENT SUBTRACT CARRY ROTATE/SHIFT* SWAP BYTES ADD } (register-to-register) SUBTRACT }	—
Logic (bit-by-bit)	**AND OR** XOR	CLEAR REGISTER* CLEAR BYTE SET REGISTER COMPLEMENT REGISTER*	issue logic levels and/or timed pulses
Program control (changes program counter): **unconditional branch**	EXECUTE } (need one cycle only) **JUMP** } **JUMP AND SAVE**	HALT NO OPERATION SKIP*	
branch on condition (register contents = 0, ≠ 0, < 0, ≤ 0, > 0, ≥ 0, overflow, and/or carry)	EXECUTE ON CONDITION JUMP ON CONDITION JUMP AND SAVE ON CONDITION	SKIP ON CONDITION*	SKIP ON FLAG (sense line)
compare word	**SKIP IF REGISTER DIFFERS** SKIP IF BYTE DIFFERS	—	
loop indexing	**INCREMENT MEMORY, SKIP IF ZERO** DECREMENT MEMORY, SKIP IF ZERO	INCREMENT REGISTER } and set flag DECREMENT REGISTER } or skip if 0	
clear/set condition (e.g., to prepare for branch test)	—	CLEAR* register, half register, sign bit, SET* overflow flag, and/or carry flag COMPLEMENT FLAG	CLEAR FLAG CLEAR ALL FLAGS CHANGE INTERRUPT PRIORITIES

* Some of these instructions can often be combined.

50

2. **Direct addressing with a page register:** A processor **page register** loaded by an *extra instruction* adds enough high-order bits to the instruction address bits to address all of memory in terms of 2^m-word pages.

3. **Double-word direct addressing:** The second of *two consecutive instruction words* is or contains the address. 16-bit machines can address all of memory in this way. 8-bit minicomputers always use double-word addressing, but will still need paging and/or relative addressing, or more words.

4. **Direct addressing on the current page:** The m address bits (*page address*) are *augmented by the high-order bits of the current program-counter reading*, which constitute the *current page number*.

5. **Addressing relative to the program counter (relative addressing):** The instruction-word address bits are interpreted as a signed integer, which is *added to the current program-counter reading* to determine the effective address.

Current-page and relative addressing require no page-setting instruction, and experience indicates that many programs mostly reference memory locations close to the current program-counter reading. *Relative addressing simplifies program relocation* (Sec. 4-18).

6. **Addressing relative to an index register:** The instruction-word address bits are interpreted as a signed or unsigned integer, which is *added to the contents of a specified* **index register** to determine the effective address.

Index registers are extra processor registers holding a full computer word ("base address"). They can be cleared, loaded, incremented and/or decremented by special instructions (Sec. 2-10). Index addition takes no extra time or, at most, a fraction of a memory cycle. Index modification is, therefore, a good way to address different elements of *data structures* (Secs. 4-9 to 4-11). Index registers can also be used as temporary storage registers and may or may not serve as accumulators as well.

Most minicomputer indexing operations involve only one index register at a time.

(b) Indirect Addressing, Preindexing, and Postindexing. Indirect addressing, specified by an instruction-word bit, means that the address found by paged, double-word, relative, or indexed addressing does not itself contain the desired operand but rather its effective address in memory. Our memory-reference instruction, then, addresses a memory location whose contents serve as a *pointer* to the desired operand.

Some minicomputers permit **multilevel indirect addressing;** i.e., an indirect-address bit in the pointer indicates that it points not to the final operand but to yet another pointer.

Indirect addressing is the key to vitally important programming techniques. Since an indirectly addressed operand is **a function of its pointer,** we can implement *table lookup* (function and directory tables) and modify pointers to access different elements of *data structures* (Secs. 4-9 to 4-11). Indirect addressing can be combined with indexing:

1. **Preindexing:** The instruction-word address bits, interpreted as a signed or unsigned integer, are added to the contents of a specified index register to determine the *pointer address.*
2. **Postindexing:** The indirect address contains an index bit or bits specifying an index register. *The contents of this index register are added to the indirect address to form the effective address.* The pointer stays in memory without change.

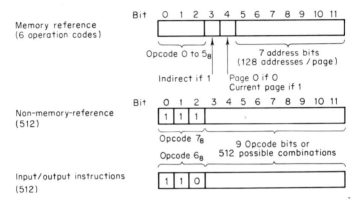

Fig. 2-2a. Instruction formats for a simple 12-bit minicomputer (PDP-8 series).

(c) **Autoindexing.** Some minicomputers have 8 to 16 special memory locations on page 0 called **autoindex registers.** **When one of these autoindex registers is indirectly addressed, it produces the effective address by auto-matically incrementing or decrementing its contents.** Autoincrementing or autodecrementing is a cheap way to address successive elements of arrays (Sec. 4-9); no index register needs to be loaded, and the only price paid is the extra memory cycle required for indirect addressing. Note also that no instruction-word bit is needed to produce autoindexing, but the autoindex-register locations cannot be used for ordinary indirect addressing. As an alternative, an extra instruction-code bit can be used to specify incrementing or decrementing of *any* indirect address.

(d) **Microoperations Determining the Effective Address.** We have already noted that minicomputers always offer a *choice* of several addressing modes. **Opcode bits in the memory-reference-instruction words are used to select the addressing mode** (*direct/indirect, return to page* 0, *relative,* and/or *choice of index register*). Figure 2-2 shows typical instruction formats. Good assemblers may accept instructions like **STORE ACCUMULATOR IN A** and automatically effect paged, relative, indirect, or double-word addressing to get around page boundaries (Sec. 4-2).

Referring to Fig. 2-1, a *direct-address instruction* transfers its address bits from the memory data register to the memory address register during the EXECUTE phase of the first instruction cycle by way of bus 1, the arithmetic/logic unit, and bus 3.   Program-counter bits (for current-page addressing) or page-register bits are transferred at the same time.   *Relative-address and index instructions* employ the arithmetic/logic unit to add program-counter or index-register contents via bus 2.   Larger computers may have a separate adder for address computations.   *Double-word and indirect-address instructions* use an extra memory cycle to transfer the pointer from

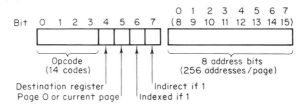

Fig. 2-2b. This could be a one-word memory-reference instruction for a 16-bit minicomputer or a two-word memory-reference instruction for an 8-bit machine (see also Fig. 6-8).

memory into the memory data register and then to the memory address register (with postindexing, if any).   *Autoindexing* requires no more time than ordinary indirect addressing but needs some extra logic.

NOTE: Double-word instructions must increment the program counter *twice*. Also, in 8-bit minicomputers, indirect addresses can be double 8-bit words, so that indirect addressing can take *two* extra memory cycles.

(e) **Immediate Addressing.**   One-word immediate-addressing instructions are not really memory-reference instructions, although instruction formats are similar.   In each immediate-address instruction, e.g.,

LOAD ACCUMULATOR IMMEDIATE   (integer)
ADD INTO ACCUMULATOR NO. 2 IMMEDIATE   (integer)

what looks like the address bits is interpreted as a signed or unsigned integer **operand.**   One-word immediate-address instructions are completed in a single memory cycle and are, therefore, handy for setting up index registers, counters, etc.   Some minicomputers admit **two-word two-cycle immediate-address instructions** with the operand stored as the second of two instruction words.

2-8.   Memory-to-register Operations.   (a) How They Work.   Such operations are fundamental to single-address arithmetic.   Referring to Fig. 2-1, each of these instructions will fetch the contents of a suitably addressed memory location into the memory data register and then via bus 1 to the arithmetic/logic system.   With appropriate bus gating, the arithmetic/logic unit can now combine the memory word with a word fetched from a processor register (accumulator or index register specified by the instruction) via bus 2. The result is loaded into *the same* processor register via bus 3.   The original register contents are lost.

Since both instruction fetching *and* execution require memory read/write operations, each of these instructions typically takes *two memory cycles*.   If a memory-to-register instruction reads from a core memory, the original word is immediately rewritten (Sec. 1-12) so that *memory contents are unchanged.* Memory contents are obviously also unchanged in memories with non-destructive readout (read-only magnetic memories, semiconductor memories).

(b) Register Loading.   The simplest memory-to-register instructions merely *load* a specified register with a word taken from memory:

LOAD (INTO) ACCUMULATOR   (effective memory address)
LOAD (INTO) ACCUMULATOR NO. 1   (effective memory address)
LOAD (INTO) INDEX REGISTER NO. 2   (effective memory address)

Effective addresses are specified as in Sec. 2-6.

Some minicomputers (e.g., PDP-8) omit the LOAD instruction and load the accumulator by adding or ORing into it after first clearing the register.   A few minicomputers also have the useful two-cycle instruction INTERCHANGE ACCUMULATOR AND MEMORY.

(c) Memory-to-register Arithmetic: Overflow and Carry Flags (see also Sec. 2-10).   The most important (and often the only) memory-to-register arithmetic operation is *addition:*

ADD INTO ACCUMULATOR NO. 2   (effective memory address)

The sum will **overflow** if and only if both terms have identical signs *and* the sign of the sum turns out to be different.   We can detect 2s-complement overflow by combining the carries from the sign bit and the most significant bit in an XOR gate: overflow occurs if there is a carry from one of the two but not both.

2s-complement arithmetic (Sec. 1-9) is usually implied, but consult your manual.   PDP-15, for instance, has *both* 1s-complement *and* 2s-complement addition (ADD and TAD).

Some minicomputers permit *subtraction of a memory word from the contents of a register:*

SUBTRACT INTO ACCUMULATOR NO. 1   (effective memory address)

and a few have *inverse subtraction:*

SUBTRACT INTO ACCUMULATOR—THEN INVERT RESULT
                                                (effective memory address)

(That is, multiply the original difference by -1.)   2s-complement arithmetic is implied.

After an addition or subtraction, the processor sets special flip-flops ("flags")

1. If *arithmetic overflow* (Sec. 1-9*a*) occurs (**overflow flag**), and/or
2. If there is a carry out of the most significant (sign) bit in the register (**carry flag, extend flip-flop, link**)

Carry flags are useful in positive-integer arithmetic, 1s-complement arithmetic, and double-precision arithmetic (Secs. 2-14 and 4-11).

Check your computer manual carefully: Some minicomputers have only an overflow flag or only a carry flag (PDP-8 series).   PDP-15 indicates carries and 1s-complement overflow with the same flag, but has no 2s-complement overflow flag.   In any case, note that *minicomputer overload flags will not by themselves halt or change the computer program.*   It is up to the programmer to "test" the flag with suitable skip or branch instructions; the programmer must also be sure to *clear* overload and carry flags before they are needed.

Memory-to-register *multiplication* and *division* require multiple (extended) arithmetic registers.   Most minicomputer manufacturers sell hardware for these operations as special *options*, which will be described in Sec. 2-14.   The "bare" processor can perform multiplication and division as subroutines involving addition and shifting.

(d) Memory-to-register Logic.   The *memory-to-register logic instructions*

AND INTO ACCUMULATOR	(effective memory address)
OR INTO ACCUMULATOR NO. 1	(effective memory address)
XOR INTO ACCUMULATOR NO. 1	(effective memory address)

perform the indicated operations *bit by bit* on corresponding pairs of bits from register and memory, with the result left in the register.   Thus, if an 8-bit accumulator and the effectively addressed 8-bit memory word contain

$$01110101$$
and
$$11110001$$

respectively, then

AND produces the accumulator contents	01110001
OR produces the accumulator contents	11110101
XOR produces the accumulator contents	10000100

(See also Sec. 1-6.)   In practice, **AND** is used to replace selected bits of a register word with 0s set up in a *mask* word in memory.   **OR** will similarly replace selected bits with 1s.   **XOR** produces 0 bits wherever the two original words agree (coincidence check).   Some applications will be discussed in Sec. 4-11.

2-9. Operations on Words in Memory.   The two-cycle instruction

STORE ZERO IN   (effective address)

clears the effectively addressed memory location *without* affecting the contents of any accumulator.   Minicomputers without a **STORE ZERO** instruction must clear and deposit an accumulator.

The two-cycle instruction[1]

INCREMENT, SKIP IF ZERO   (effective address)

(ISZ) moves the contents of the effectively addressed memory location into the arithmetic/logic unit via the memory data register.   The number is incremented and returned to its memory location (again via the memory data register).   If the incremented result is 0 (i.e., if incrementing causes a carry), then the program counter is made to skip (i.e., it is incremented by 2 rather than by 1).   *This conditional skip lets the program branch in the manner of Sec. 2-11c.*

The **STORE ZERO** and **INCREMENT, SKIP IF ZERO** instructions are used to clear and increment a counter in the effectively addressed memory location.   To implement a counter preset to a count of N, we store $-N$ in a memory location and then **ISZ** until the program branches after N **ISZ**s (Sec. 4-9).   Some computers have a similar **DECREMENT, SKIP IF ZERO** instruction.

2-10. Operations on Register Words and Flag Bits.   (a) Register Arithmetic/Logic.   Instructions like

CLEAR ACCUMULATOR
COMPLEMENT ACCUMULATOR NO. 2
INCREMENT INDEX REGISTER

move the contents of a specified register into the arithmetic/logic unit and back again to perform the indicated operation in one memory cycle (FETCH cycle, Sec. 2-4*a*.   See also Fig. 2-1).   **COMPLEMENT ACCUMULATOR** produces the **1s-complement negative** of a signed number in the register. **INVERT ACCUMULATOR** is the same as **NEGATE ACCUMULATOR** or **COMPLEMENT AND INCREMENT ACCUMULATOR** and produces the **2s-complement negative** (see also Tables 1-1 and 1-2).

Most minicomputers have an instruction or instructions like

MOVE ACCUMULATOR NO. 2 TO ACCUMULATOR NO. 1
MOVE ACCUMULATOR TO INDEX REGISTER

which move (transfer) register contents in one cycle via buses 2 and 3 (Fig.

---

[1] Three cycles are required in some machines.

2-1); the contents of the source register remain unchanged. Most mini-computers do not permit register-to-register addition or subtraction. Some machines have a one-cycle instruction to INTERCHANGE ACCUMULATOR CONTENTS.

The LOAD IMMEDIATE operation, which loads the instruction address bits into a specified register, was already discussed in Sec. 2-7e. Similar addition, subtraction, AND, and OR operations may also be implemented.

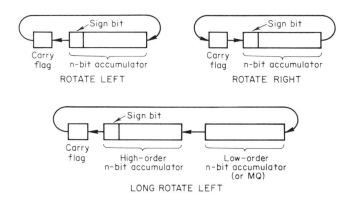

Fig. 2-3. ROTATE/SHIFT operations. The carry-flag flip-flop can be set, reset, or equated to the sign bit before each 1-bit rotation.

(b) Rotate/Shift Operations. One-cycle instructions like

ROTATE ACCUMULATOR LEFT
ROTATE ACCUMULATOR NO. 1 RIGHT

rotate (circulate) the contents of the specified register **and the carry bit** by 1 bit, as shown in Fig. 2-3. Some minicomputers also admit 2-bit rotations. Physically, the register bits go to the arithmetic/logic unit via bus 2, are "shifted sideways" by means of gates (Sec. 1-9b), and return to the register via bus 3.

Rotation has three important applications:

1. **Individual bits of a register word** (which might indicate the logical states in some external device, Sec. 5-8) **can be rotated into the sign-bit and/or carry-bit position for tests and branching** (Sec. 2-11).

2. **Partial words or bytes can be moved, packed, and unpacked** in connection with input/output operations (see also Sec. 4-11).

3. **With the carry bit appropriately cleared or set, rotations act as arithmetic shifts implementing multiplication or division by 2** (Sec. 1-9 and Tables 1-1 and 1-2).

Specifically, **an unsigned binary number (no sign bit) is multiplied or divided by 2 if we first clear the carry flag and then rotate, respectively, left or right.** Such an operation is called an **unsigned shift.** After multiplication by 2, a 1 in the carry flag indicates **overflow.**

A signed 1s-complement number is multiplied or divided by 2 if we first make the carry bit equal to the sign bit and then rotate. Such an operation is a **signed shift.**

A signed 2s-complement number is multiplied by 2 through an unsigned left shift but divided by 2 through a signed right shift.

Overflow of any such multiplication by 2 is indicated if the sign and carry bits differ. Each division by 2 will "chop" rather than round the result to the given number of bits; i.e., the result is always less than or equal to the correct result.

Some minicomputers have explicit **SIGNED SHIFT** and **UNSIGNED SHIFT** instructions. Some machines can also rotate a register *without* the carry flag (see also Secs. 2-11, 2-12, and 2-14).

(c) **Operations on Flag Bits.** A number of one-cycle instructions permit the program to **clear, set,** and **complement specified processor flip-flops** such as carry and overflow flags, e.g.,

CLEAR CARRY FLAG

This may be done in preparation for conditional branching (Sec. 2-11c), to store 1-bit decisions for later use, or in connection with arithmetic shifts (Sec. 2-10b). Bit operations are often combined with rotation and/or conditional skips (Sec. 2-11d). **ADD CARRY** and **SUBTRACT CARRY** (into accumulator; and clear carry flag) are useful for double-precision operations (see also Sec. 2-14).

2-11. Instructions Controlling Program Execution and Branching. (a) **NO OPERATION and HALT.** The one-cycle instruction **NO OPERATION** does nothing except advance the program counter to the following instruction and serves as a time delay or as a "spacer" for later insertion of another instruction or data word. **HALT** advances the program counter and stops processor operation to give the operator a chance to examine or change registers, switch settings, and/or peripheral-device operation.

(b) **Unconditional Branching.** The one-cycle instructions **SKIP** and

JUMP TO (effective address)

are employed for **program branching** (Secs. 4-8 and 4-9) and also to "jump around" memory locations used to store data between instructions (Secs. 4-5 and 4-14). **SKIP** simply increments the program counter twice to jump over one memory location. **JUMP** resets the program counter to the effective-address value; the old program-counter setting is *lost*. By contrast, the two-cycle instruction

JUMP AND SAVE (effective address)

resets the program counter (and thus causes a jump) to the effective address plus 1 or 2 and **saves the (incremented) old program-counter setting** at the effective-address location. **JUMP AND SAVE** permits one to **return to the original program after a subroutine** (Sec. 4-14) and is, therefore, often referred to as **JUMP TO SUBROUTINE**.

In some machines, **JUMP AND SAVE** automatically saves not only the return address but also the page register and/or carry, overflow, etc., flags (combined at the effective address plus 1). More sophisticated minicomputers also automatically increment a *stack pointer* to keep track of reentrant-subroutine nesting (Secs. 4-16 and 6-10). More advanced computers can have a **JUMP AND SAVE IN INDEX** instruction, which stores the return address in an *index register* rather than in memory. This speeds up subroutine processing by avoiding memory references (Secs. 4-14 and 6-10).

The one-cycle instruction

EXECUTE (effective address)

causes execution of an instruction stored at the effectively addressed memory location and then continues with the program—this amounts to the execution of a one-instruction subroutine.

(c) Conditional Branching. Each one-cycle instruction

SKIP ON CONDITION

causes a skip subject to a condition or conditions specified by instruction-code bits, e.g.,

ACCUMULATOR = 0	**CARRY FLAG = 0**
ACCUMULATOR NO. 2 < 0	**CARRY FLAG = 1**
INDEX REGISTER > 0	**OVERFLOW FLAG = 1**

Different instruction-bit combinations can produce logical ORing or ANDing of such conditions, e.g., **ACCUMULATOR** ≥ 0 (see also Sec. 2-11d).

There are also two types of *two-cycle* conditional-skip instructions which reference memory. **INCREMENT** (or **DECREMENT**), **SKIP IF ZERO** was introduced in Sec. 2-9. The second type is exemplified by

SKIP IF ACCUMULATOR DIFFERS FROM (effective address)
SKIP IF ACCUMULATOR NO. 2 EQUALS (effective address)

SKIP ON CONDITION instructions are the (only) way most minicomputers implement **conditional branching,** e.g.,

SKIP ON CONDITION	/Condition true?
JUMP TO (effective address)	/No, go to branch 2
(next instruction)	/Yes, continue on branch 1
. . .	

(Sec. 4-8). Only a few minicomputers have "direct" conditional-branching instructions, i.e., JUMP ON CONDITION, JUMP AND SAVE ON CONDITION, and EXECUTE ON CONDITION.

(d) **Combined Register/Flag Operations, Rotations, and Tests.** Most computers can implement certain *combinations* of register/flag clearing, setting, or complementing, a rotation, and/or a skip test through single one-cycle instructions. Appropriate instruction-code bits will call for the individual operations, and the *programmer must be sure to understand their relative order of execution.* For instance, to multiply an unsigned number in a register by 2, one must *first* clear the carry flag, *then* rotate left, and *then* test for a carry indicating overflow (Sec. 2-10b). **Check the reference manual and also the assembler manual for your specific computer.**

An especially useful one-cycle combination instruction is INCREMENT (or DECREMENT) INDEX REGISTER, SKIP IF ZERO, which is used to implement and terminate program loops (Sec. 4-9).

2-12. Input/Output-related Instructions. Each minicomputer instruction set must reserve a respectably large number of different instruction-code-bit combinations for input/output instructions intended to select and operate external devices (Secs. 5-2 to 5-8, Table 5-1). For example, the Hewlett-Packard 2115A, which is a typical "basic" 16-bit minicomputer, admits $2^{12} = 4,096$ different one-word input/output instructions, and the 12-bit PDP-8 series admit $2^9 = 512$ such instructions. In addition, each minicomputer has some instructions for controlling its interrupt system, such as INTERRUPT ON and INTERRUPT OFF (Secs. 5-9 to 5-15).

SPECIAL FEATURES, INSTRUCTIONS, AND OPTIONS

2-13. Byte Manipulation. 8-bit minicomputers naturally handle 8-bit **bytes** holding an ASCII character plus parity or two BCD digits. A 16-bit word holds two such bytes. Most 16-bit minicomputers have at least one or two one-cycle **byte-manipulation instructions**

CLEAR LEFT (or RIGHT) ACCUMULATOR BYTE
INTERCHANGE ACCUMULATOR BYTES
INTERCHANGE AND CLEAR LEFT (or RIGHT) ACCUMULATOR BYTE

Such instructions replace multiple ROTATEs and ANDing with mask words and can save much time and memory in character-handling programs (e.g., text editing, communications).

Some 16-bit machines permit **byte addressing** of LOAD and STORE ACCUMULATOR instructions. Byte addressing is specified by an opcode bit or by a status register set through a special instruction (BYTE mode).

We load or store accumulator bits 8 through 15, while bits 0 through 7 remain unaffected. The effective address refers to individual bytes in memory, so an extra address bit will be needed to specify even or odd bytes. Another type of byte-addressed instruction is

SKIP IF ACCUMULATOR BYTE DIFFERS   (effective address)

which is useful for detecting special characters in text strings.

2-14. Arithmetic Options.   (a) Double Store, Load, Add/Subtract, and Rotate/Shift Operations. To simplify double-precision operations, some minicomputers can store the contents of two accumulators in successive memory locations through a single (usually three-cycle) instruction

DOUBLE STORE   (effective address)

DOUBLE LOAD similarly loads two accumulators from successive memory locations.   More extensive facilities for double-precision operations usually come only as part of extra-cost hardware multiply/divide options.   The Honeywell 316/516 high-speed arithmetic option, for instance, has DOUBLE ADD and DOUBLE SUBTRACT, with an automatic carry from the low-order accumulator to the high-order accumulator.   To accommodate so many extra memory-reference instructions, the 316/516 must first set a status register to DOUBLE PRECISION through a separate instruction.   The *sign bit* of the double-precision number is usually bit 0 of the high-order accumulator (Fig. 1-17).

Two accumulators can be similarly concatenated (together with the carry flag) for double-precision LONG ROTATE, LONG UNSIGNED SHIFT, and LONG SIGNED SHIFT operations (see also Sec. 2-10*b*).   Most extended-arithmetic options have instructions for multiple shifts; the number of bits shifted is determined by an extra processor register, the **shift counter.**

With a binary fraction in the double accumulator, the instruction NORMALIZE will shift the double fraction left until its most significant bit differs from the sign bit (see also Sec. 1-10).   Some computers use ordinary long shifts and test the result with a special instruction SKIP IF ACCUMULATOR IS NORMALIZED.

(b) Hardware Multiply/Divide Options (see also Sec. 1-9).   Multiply/divide hardware always requires two arithmetic registers to hold a double-precision product or dividend.   It is best if these registers are general-purpose accumulators accessible through DOUBLE STORE and DOUBLE LOAD instructions (Sec. 2-14*a*; e.g., Hewlett-Packard and Honeywell mini-computers).   A less desirable arrangement adds a special multiplier/quotient (MQ) register, which is harder to access (PDP-8 series, PDP-9/15).

The better hardware multiply/divide options place no restrictions on

operand signs, employ 2s-complement arithmetic, and have simple instructions

MULTIPLY	(effective address)
DIVIDE	(effective address)

It is most convenient to interpret operands and the result either as *signed binary integers* or as *signed binary fractions* (Tables 1-1 and 1-2 and Sec. 1-9).

NOTE: Many popular minicomputers (PDP-8 series, NOVA/SUPERNOVA) implement *unsigned* multiplication/division (unsigned, nonnegative operands and result). This produces some extra precision since no bits are needed as sign bits; but signed multiplication/division then requires cumbersome multiple-instruction sequences, which waste time and memory. PDP-9/15 has basically unsigned multiplication/division with some special extra instructions attempting to simplify signed operations which are, however, still inconvenient.

The multiplication $A \times B = C$ starts with A (single-precision) in an accumulator and B (also single-precision) in the effectively addressed memory location. The double-precision result C appears in a pair of accumulators (or, less desirably, in an accumulator plus index register or MQ register).

The division $C \div B = A$ starts with the double-precision dividend C in the two registers and B (single-precision) in the effectively addressed memory location. The **quotient** A will appear in the high-order register (accumulator), while the **remainder** will be left in the low-order register. Unlike multiplication, division can cause **overflow,** which should be detectable by a flag test; **consult your minicomputer manual.**

In some minicomputer multiply/divide units (PDP-9/15, PDP-8 series except for PDP-8e), the operand B cannot be taken from an arbitrary memory location but must be placed into the location following the MULTIPLY or DIVIDE instruction.

Typical hardware multiply/divide times are between 5 and 35 machine cycles. This compares with between 70 and 300 cycles required for non-hardware multiply/divide subroutines.

2-15. Miscellaneous Options. The following useful options are offered by many minicomputer manufacturers:

1. **Extra memory** may simply require extra plug-in modules, or one may have to add a page register or extended memory address register to the processor. **Read-only memory** (ROM, Sec. 1-14), often interchangeable with ordinary memory-bank modules, stores important programs or routines "firmly" ("firmware"). Some minicomputers yield faster cycle times for instructions read from ROM (Sec. 6-5).

2. **Parity-check interrupt** (Sec. 1-4c) on all word or byte transfers to and from memory requires an extra bit per memory word, plus parity logic. This option may be useful, e.g., in critical process-control applications. It is not really needed in most end-user installations.

3. **Memory protection,** which usually also requires an extra bit per memory word, protects preselected areas of memory from unauthorized users. This is done to protect system programs from overwriting and to protect time-sharing users from each other. Either all instructions referencing unauthorized memory locations, or STORE instructions only, cause interrupts which usually return control to an executive program (Sec. 3-11). Memory-protection hardware is operated by a set of special instructions, which permit the system programmer to "tag" selected memory areas for protection. The computer user is not directly concerned with these instructions.

4. **Power-failure protection/restart:** Low power-supply voltage causes an interrupt, and a service routine stores all processor registers safely in core memory before the power-supply capacitors can discharge. A restart routine makes it easy to restore the registers. With semi-conductor memories, a trickle-charged battery keeps the computer working while memory as well as register contents are saved on a disk or on tape.

5. **Extra interrupts** and/or **more sophisticated interrupt logic** (Secs. 5-9 to 5-16).

6. **Hardware floating-point arithmetic** is often a small accessory processor; it is still fairly expensive but is potentially very useful (Secs. 6-12 and 6-13).

7. **Automatic bootstrap loader** is a hard-wired program to load system programs from paper tape or magnetic tape (Sec. 3-4b).

8. **Indicator-light test switch:** This small feature avoids surprises due to panel-light failures.

Other options will deal with **improved or additional input/output circuits** (Chap. 5), **peripheral equipment,** and **software.**

REFERENCES AND BIBLIOGRAPHY

Consult the minicomputer reference manuals of various manufacturers for specific detailed instruction lists, execution times, and other hardware features. See also the bibliographies of Chaps. 1 and 6.

CHAPTER 3

MINICOMPUTER OPERATION AND SOME PROGRAMMING, WITHOUT ASSEMBLY LANGUAGE

INTRODUCTION AND SURVEY

In this chapter, we describe the *front-panel operation of small digital computers*, including the most common procedures for *loading, translating, and executing computer programs* (Secs. 3-1 to 3-6). To squeeze the last bit of efficiency from the minicomputer hardware, we will have to learn some assembly language (Chap. 4), but many small computers do remarkably well with FORTRAN and BASIC, which are more convenient for general problem solving (Secs. 3-7 and 3-8). To make a general-purpose minicomputer center truly powerful and convenient, we must get away from paper-tape operation. The remainder of this chapter deals with the hardware (*small disks, tape units, cathode-ray-tube/keyboard terminals*) and software (*executive systems or monitors*) which make comfortable minicomputation possible; a discussion of *on-line editing* is included.

CONTROL PANEL AND PAPER-TAPE OPERATION

3-1. The Operator's Control Panel. A typical minicomputer **control panel** (Fig. 3-1) will have the following controls and indicators:

1. A **key-operated main power switch** with three positions: ON, OFF, and LOCK PANEL. In the latter position, power is ON, but all front-

panel controls are ineffective—this keeps visitors from ruining computations by playing with the controls.

2. **Indicator-light fields,** which display the contents of the principal processor registers for examination. Smaller machines may have only one indicator field, which can display different processor registers selected by a REGISTER SELECTOR switch.

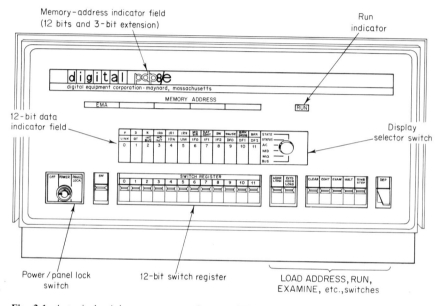

Fig. 3-1. A typical minicomputer control panel (Digital Equipment Corporation PDP-8/e. a 12-bit machine). Individual indicator fields display memory address and data; a selector switch connects various processor registers, or a set of status indicators, for display in the data field. Indicator fields and switch register are arranged in 3-bit groups to simplify octal-number interpretation.

3. A **switch register or registers** for entering binary numbers bit by bit into a processor register selected by a REGISTER SELECTOR switch or by the LOAD ADDRESS and DEPOSIT switches.
4. Various switches.
    (*a*) A **REGISTER SELECTOR switch** selects the processor register connected to indicator and/or switch registers.
    (*b*) A **LOAD ADDRESS switch** loads the memory address register (in some machines also the program counter) with the number set into the switch register.
    (*c*) A **DEPOSIT switch** loads the currently addressed memory location with switch-register contents.

5. An **EXAMINE (FETCH) switch** fetches the contents of the currently addressed memory location into the memory data register for front-panel display.

6. **Controls for starting, stopping, and stepping processor operation.**

   (*a*) The **START (RUN)/STOP switch** starts the program with the current register contents.

   (*b*) **SINGLE INSTRUCTION** and **SINGLE CYCLE switches** for "stepping" the program one instruction or one processor cycle at a time; they are used for troubleshooting hardware or programs.

Additional controls and indicators may be provided.   Some minicomputers have a **READ IN switch** for starting a paper-tape reader or even for automatic loading (Sec. 3-4).   **Sense switches** on the front panel may permit the operator to modify a program while it is running (Sec. 5-8; in other machines, sense lines are available only in peripheral devices).   As further aids in troubleshooting, there may be **indicators for the current processor status,** e.g., INSTRUCTION FETCH, EXECUTE, INPUT/OUTPUT, INTERRUPT, etc.

Some minicomputers have a front-panel **CLEAR switch,** which clears a selected processor register or registers and which may also send a clear pulse to the computer peripheral devices for clearing appropriate flags and/or registers.

Some machines (PDP-15) have an I/O instruction to read their front-panel switch register during computation.

The operator's control panel is used mainly for starting programs and for troubleshooting through examination of register contents and stepwise program execution.   Original equipment manufacturers (OEMs) using minicomputers with little reprogramming may wish to purchase machines without elaborate control panels; service technicians can then carry *plug-in control panels* for start-up and diagnostic work.

3-2.   Typical Control-panel Operations.   Please be sure to note that specific front-panel controls and their operation will vary somewhat for different computers—you must consult the operator's manual for your own machine.   The following operations are typical:

1. With the computer halted by the START/STOP switch, we can examine and change the contents of registers and memory locations.   **To examine a memory location,** we set its address into the switch register and press the LOAD ADDRESS switch.   The EXAMINE switch will now bring the contents of the addressed location into the memory data register for display.

2. **To load a memory location manually,** we set its address into the switch register and press LOAD ADDRESS.   Then we set the desired binary number into the switch register and press DEPOSIT.

3. It will be useful to examine or load *successive* memory locations.   For

this purpose, we must increment the memory address register between successive EXAMINE or DEPOSIT operations. Different mini-computers do this in different ways, e.g.,

(*a*) In the PDP-8I, LOAD ADDRESS sets the address into the program counter as well as in the memory address register. Program counter and memory address are incremented after *every* EXAMINE or DEPOSIT operation.

Fig. 3-2a. ASR-33 teletypewriter console. The paper-tape reader/punch is on the left.

(*b*) The more elaborate PDP-9 has *special switch positions* (EXAMINE NEXT, DEPOSIT NEXT) which step the memory address before fetching or depositing.

(*c*) In the PDP-11, *repeated* operation of the EXAMINE or DEPOSIT switch steps the memory address register.

3-3. The Console Typewriter. Most minicomputers are furnished with an ASR-33, ASR-35, KSR-33, or KSR-35 **printer/keyboard (teletypewriter)** manufactured by the Teletype® Corporation (Fig. 3-2).[1] With the OFF/LINE/LOCAL switch in the LOCAL position, the teletypewriter is disconnected from the computer and acts like a typewriter with the special character set shown in Fig. 3-2b. In the LINE position, the keyboard

---

[1] ASR stands for Automatic Send/Receive, while KSR stands for Keyboard Send/Receive. ASR-37 has both uppercase and lowercase characters and permits 15 character/sec operations, but it is substantially more expensive.

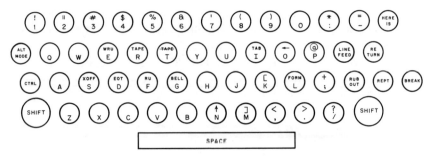

Fig. 3-2b. ASR-33 teletypewriter keyboard.   Note the following:

RETURN returns printer to start of current line.
LINE FEED advances printer one line (without return, unless RETURN is also depressed).
FORM FEED advances printer to the top of a new page (without return).

The nomenclature on the extra keys is intended for communications applications, not for computing, but the extra keys are useful.

transmits 8-bit ASCII character sequences (Table A-9) to the computer, and the printer can accept and output ASCII characters.   These machines can print up to 10 characters/sec.   They produce only capital letters but do have two shift keys (SHIFT and CTRL), which produce special characters or control functions when depressed simultaneously with other keys (see also Fig. 3-2b).   Some of these special functions will depend on specific computer programs; conventional interpretations are listed in Table A-7.

The ASR models have a slow (10 character/sec) **paper-tape punch** and **reader**; in the LOCAL mode, we can punch the tape from the keyboard or get printed output through the paper-tape reader.   In the LINE mode, we can read paper tape into the computer or let the computer punch paper tapes.   Program preparation with the console typewriter will be further discussed in Sec. 3-16.

ASR-33 and KSR-33 are designed "for intermittent light duty," and this means exactly what it says.   Teletypewriters will not last long if you use them as line printers for long listings.   Even the "continuous-duty" ASR-35 and the KSR-35 teletypewriters are really designed for use in communications offices, where they are rebuilt on a regular schedule.   Altogether, tele-typewriters are the most frequent source of minicomputer troubles, and repairs are not cheap.   To save your teleprinter, we suggest substitution of a cathode-ray-tube/keyboard terminal for conversational input/output; this is also much faster and more pleasant to operate.   Use the printer only when you really need hard copy, and keep the printer motor turned off as much as possible.   If you require much hard-copy output, get a small line printer.   The Digital Equipment Corporation DECwriter (Fig. 3-3), which costs about as much as a KSR-35 and is faster and also mechanically simpler, is another useful alternative.   An IBM Selectric typewriter with an adapter base plate for computer control is another possibility.

3-4.   Loading and Running Simple Programs with Paper Tape.   (a) Manual Loading.   An **executable program** (which may or may not have some data attached to it) is, as we have seen, a sequence of multibit computer words. We might have such a program in binary form (or in the more convenient octal form, Sec. 1-4*b*) on a sheet of paper; **we must enter the program words into appropriate (usually consecutive) memory locations in the computer.**   A simple-minded way to *load the program* is to use the front-panel controls:

1. Select a memory location for the first program word (which could be an instruction or a data word) via the switch register and the LOAD ADDRESS switch.
2. Load successive program words into consecutive memory locations with the aid of the switch register and the DEPOSIT switch, as shown in Sec. 3-2.
3. Set the actual starting address (address of the first instruction) into the program counter via switch register and selector or DEPOSIT switch.

The program is now ready to run if we press the RUN switch.   As the program runs, it will *output data* via the teletypewriter, paper-tape punch, or other peripherals.   The program may also *read input data* (or additional input data) from the teletypewriter, paper-tape reader, measuring instruments, etc.

(b) Paper-tape Systems and Bootstrap Loaders.   Practical programs can have hundreds or thousands of words.   Manual loading is clearly impractical, and programs are prepared (and stored for repeated use) on a **computer-readable storage medium,** usually punched cards, punched paper tape, or magnetic tape.   These media are compared in Table 3-3.   Most mini-computers are available with paper tape because this requires minimal

Fig. 3-3. The $2,500 type LA30 DECwriter employs seven solenoid-driven printing wires to form different character sets from a five by seven dot matrix.   There are relatively few moving parts, and printing speed is 30 characters/sec.   (*Digital Equipment Corporation.*)

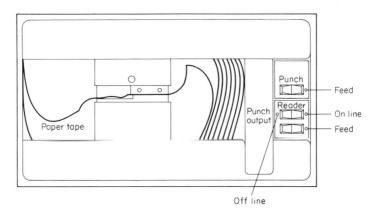

Fig. 3-4. Medium-speed reader/punch for fanfold paper tape. Read at 300 characters/sec; punch at 50 characters/sec. (*Digital Equipment Corporation.*)

peripheral equipment. The ASR-33 and ASR-35 teletypewriters, for instance, have built-in 10 character/sec tape punches and readers. These will do for loading (binary) program tapes and for infrequent problem preparation in applications requiring few such operations (e.g., special-purpose-system start-up, interpreter systems). For faster work, *one usually buys a* 300 *character/sec reader and a* 50 *character/sec punch* (Fig. 3-4), *both for fanfold paper tape, which does not require rewinding* (see also Table 3-3 and Sec. 3-9). *Faster reel-type readers* serve in special applications with long program or data tapes.

The operations needed to load words from paper tape into the computer memory will themselves constitute a computer program (**paper-tape loader**).

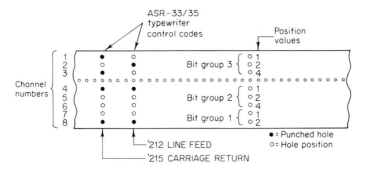

Fig. 3-5a. Paper tape with eight-channel ASCII code. This format is commonly employed for *source-program* tapes. *Binary object programs* are punched in different formats depending on the minicomputer word length. 12-bit words, for instance, can be coded into two paper-tape frames with channel 8 blank, while channel 7 indicates whether the word is meant to be a memory word or its *address*. The most economical object-tape codes contain only the starting addresses for recorded blocks of consecutive memory words, while others alternate words and their storage addresses. (*Honeywell Computer Control Division.*)

This is usually supplied on a short paper tape: The loader will read and load its own tape as soon as the first few instructions are in memory and is therefore called a **bootstrap loader.** The initial loading instructions can be loaded manually; some computers protect them from overwriting with a special front-panel switch. We set the program counter to the first loading-instruction address (usually printed on the loader tape) and press READ IN (or RUN, depending on the computer) to load the loader. As a desirable option, some minicomputers have the entire paper-tape-loader program permanently in read-only memory.

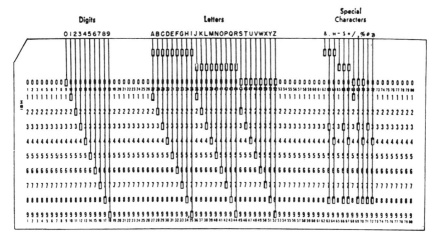

Fig. 3-5b. International Business Machines Corporation 80-column punched-card code.

Once the loader is in memory, we can load any program or data tape directly behind the loader program:

1. Place the tape in the reader (consult your manual).
2. Set the program counter to the first loading-instruction address.
3. Press READ IN, or RUN (consult your manual).

An executable program thus loaded can now be started as soon as we set the program counter to the appropriate starting address. Some programs include a jump to the starting address as the last instruction loaded, so we can simply press RUN and go.

MINICOMPUTATION: SOURCE-PROGRAM TRANSLATION

3-5. Programming and Program Translation. In Sec. 3-4, we did *not* discuss preparation of new programs but only the loading and running of executable machine-language programs.   Indeed, *with many special-purpose computer systems we may never have to prepare a program,* for the system may come with "canned" programs on tapes, kindly furnished by the computer manufacturer or by a software house, for a variety of jobs.   All we do is supply the data inputs, load, and run.

Less specialized applications require us to create our own programs.   It would be a cruel job to write programs in binary or even octal machine language, so we type and/or punch a **source program** in a **programming language** admitting a restricted set of stylized English and mathematical statements.   A **translator program** then employs the computer itself to read the source-program character code and to translate our source-program statements into machine-language instructions and data words of an executable **object program.**

Translators will be rather formidable system programs supplied (one hopes) by the computer manufacturer.   There are three types of translators:

1. An **assembler** translates an **assembly language,** most of whose statements correspond to machine-language instructions on a one-to-one basis (e.g., **LOAD ACCUMULATOR WITH CONTENTS OF MEMORY LOCATION A,** or **LAC A**).

2. A **compiler** translates a **compiler language,** which is closer to English-cum-mathematics and can include statements (e.g., formulas) which will each be translated into *many* machine-language instructions (e.g., FORTRAN, ALGOL, Sec. 3-7).

Each new computer type needs a new assembly language, and relatively simple mathematical and input/output operations can require substantial numbers of assembly-language instructions.   But **assembly-language programming** (Chap. 4) **can take the most efficient advantage of minicomputer hardware to save memory and time during execution.**   By contrast, some minicomputer compilers generate slow-executing code because both compiler and object programs are compromised by the small amount of memory available.

After an assembler or compiler is loaded, we load the source program (Fig. 3-6).   The machine then produces either the object program (say on paper tape) in one pass, or the same or an intermediate tape is processed in a second pass (**two-pass assembler or compiler**).   A third pass can produce a teletypewriter **listing** of both source program and machine code.

If we have made a mistake in our source-language syntax, exceeded the available memory storage, used too large numbers, etc., the translator program will notify us of this fact by stopping and printing an appropriate **error message** on the teletypewriter.   At this point, we will have the pleasure of doing the job over.   If the program works correctly, however, we will have a storable **"binary" object tape,** which can be used again and again with new data, without any need for translation.

Punching intermediate paper tapes consumes time (more time than tape reading with most tape reader/punches). For this reason:

All modern two-pass *assemblers* are designed to read the original source tape a second time after the first pass, without any need for an intermediate tape.
Some minicomputers (e.g., Raytheon 700 series) have a "conversational" FORTRAN compiler which can compile (somewhat restricted) FORTRAN directly into the memory; object-tape punching is optional.

A number of minicomputer manufacturers also furnish assemblers and/or compilers which can be run on a large batch-processing digital computer. The resulting minicomputer object programs will still be on paper tape, or possibly on cards.

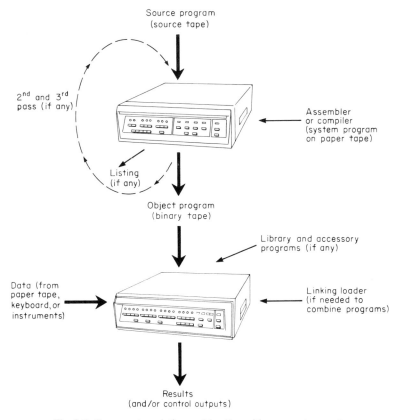

Fig. 3-6. Program translation and loading with a paper-tape system.

Assemblers and compilers generate complete object programs ·for execution. Our third translation scheme works differently:

3. An **interpreter** translates one source-language statement at a time, executes the resulting machine instruction or instructions at once, translates the next statement, etc.

Interpreter translation is inefficient for "production programs" which are to be executed many times, since each execution will be slowed by translation. This is not objectionable in **on-line conversational computing,** where interpreter systems translate compiler-type source languages like BASIC and FOCAL (Secs. 3-8 and 7-3). Interpreters can also implement step-by-step emulation of computer instructions by the instruction set of a different computer.

3-6. Loading and Combining (Linking) Binary Object Programs. An independent binary object program loaded into core with our paper-tape loader should be ready to execute. *Data* for such a program may have been loaded together with the program, or the program contains instructions to get its data from peripheral devices, e.g., from typed input, from another paper tape placed in the paper-tape reader, or from instruments such as analog-to-digital converters. Program output will be obtained on the teleprinter, display, tape punch, etc., as specified by the program itself. Very often, though, *we should like to combine a binary object program with other such programs.* These may be user programs, perhaps modules of a larger program, or **library subroutines** supplied by the computer manufacturer (e.g., floating-point arithmetic routines, sine/cosine generators, input/output routines). With a paper-tape operating system, all these programs and subroutine libraries will be on various pieces of paper tape; we would like to load them for combined execution. This will practically always impose two requirements:

1. We must **relocate** binary programs so that they can be loaded into successive core-memory areas. This will mean *changing both instruction addresses and memory-reference addresses.*
2. Since the combined programs will refer to one another (by supplying data and/or through jump instructions), we must find all such **external references** and provide them with the correct memory addresses.

To satisfy the first requirement, the object programs to be relocated must have been prepared by an assembler or compiler which generates **relocatable code.** That is, all memory references to addresses needing relocation are either specially marked—say with an extra word—or they are relative to the current program-counter reading; see also Sec. 4-18. To satisfy the second requirement, **each program segment must list all its external references according to a specified convention.**

To combine program segments satisfying these requirements, we first load a new system program called a **linking loader** and then the various object tapes. **The linking loader will note the final address of each program segment, relocate the succeeding program, and supply the necessary linkage references.** The combined program will be left in core ready for execution. Options, usually selected by front-panel register or sense switches, will run the combined program as soon as it is loaded ("load and go") and/or punch a binary tape for the combined object program. The linking loader will also type out *error messages* if it is prevented from doing its job by user errors such as faulty or missing external references; consult your minicomputer manual.

3-7. FORTRAN Computations and Related Topics. Many engineers and scientists will be familiar with FORTRAN programming (or, especially if they live in Europe, with ALGOL; minicomputer operation will be quite similar). The principal features of the FORTRAN language are outlined in Table 3-1. Note that minicomputer compilers may implement only a subset or restricted version of the FORTRAN language available with larger machines; **consult your minicomputer manual.** But many minicomputers have remarkably comprehensive versions of FORTRAN. Minicomputer FORTRAN compilers are usually designed to minimize the core storage required for the compiler and for the compiled program at some expense in execution speed.

Normally, you will need a linking loader (Sec. 3-6) to load a compiled FORTRAN program or program segments with the computer manufacturer's "math library" of floating-point-arithmetic and function-generator routines; the linking loader will load only those routines actually called by your program. I/O routines are usually supplied by the compiler or by the compiler together with an executive program (Sec. 3-13).

Other compiler languages available with minicomputers (ALGOL, subsets of COBOL) are dealt with quite similarly.

3-8. Conversational Computing with Interpreter Programs. Conversational interpreter systems (Sec. 3-5) **are especially easy to use with paper-tape-loaded minicomputers: Only the interpreter tape must be loaded, for the program itself will be supplied by the user on the teletypewriter or on a cathode-ray-tube/ keyboard terminal.**

The most popular conversational-interpreter language is BASIC, which is widely used in time-sharing systems. BASIC interpreters are available for many minicomputers. The Digital Equipment Corporation has developed another rather similar system called FOCAL (but DEC machines all come with BASIC interpreters as well). Both BASIC and FOCAL can be learned rapidly; both allow you to employ a minicomputer as a very versatile desk calculator and for real stored-program computation with loops, subroutines, etc. Such interpreters permit floating-point computation but usually only with six-decimal-digit precision (this is less than that available from most desk calculators). BASIC and FOCAL interpreters supply their own utility routines (e.g., for trigonometric functions). BASIC, unlike FORTRAN, permits operations with matrices. Both BASIC and

TABLE 3-1.   Minicomputer FORTRAN Check List.

In FORTRAN:

1. **Specification statements** *define the properties of, and allocate storage to,* **named variables, functions,** and **arrays.**
2. **Arithmetic statements** define computing operations which assign the value of an·expression to a variable, e.g.,

$$VAR = B + 0.1$$

3. **Control statements** determine the sequence of operations in a program,* e.g.,

$$GO\ TO\ 17$$

4. **Input/output statements** specify input/output operations.

FORTRAN is "portable"; i.e., the language is to a large extent independent of the processor and compiler used.   Most minicomputer FORTRAN systems are subsets of USASI FORTRAN IV.   But different minicomputers (and even the same minicomputers with different amounts of core) implement more or less complete FORTRAN systems.   It will be necessary to check precisely on your particular minicomputer:

1. Are **logical** and/or **complex** type quantities admissible?
2. **Representation of Real Constants:** How many digits are accommodated?   Are all possible formats, for example,

$$5E\text{-}02 \quad\quad 0.05$$

$$0.5E\text{-}01 \quad\quad 0.5E\text{-}1$$

$$5.0E\text{-}02$$

admissible?   The same questions should be answered for **double-precision** quantities.
3. **Logical constants** are **.TRUE** and **.FALSE**.   If no logical variables and operations are available, you can still employ the arithmetic IF statement.
4. Check on **specification statements** for declaring variables as real, logical, etc.   In general, **integer** names begin with I, J, K, L, M, or N.
5. Check on the extent to which expressions can be used as subscripts for **subscripted variables.**
6. **Relational Operators:** **.LT.**, **.LE.**, **.EQ.**, **.NE.**, **.GT.**, **.GE.**.   Are all admissible?   Are **logical expressions** admitted?
7. Check on the availability of each of the following **control statements:**
   (*a*) **Assigned** GO TO: ASSIGN 18 TO K
         GO TO K, (3, 4, 18, 21)

   (*b*) **Computed** GO TO: I = 2
         GO TO (3, 18, 21), I

   The examples in (*a*) and (*b*) are equivalent to the *unconditional* GO TO 18.
   (*c*) **Arithmetic** IF: IF (arithmetic expression) n_1, n_2, n_3
         Program goes to statement number $n_1, n_2,$ or n_3 if the specified expression is, respectively, less than, equal to, or greater than zero.
   (*d*) **Logical** IF: IF (logical expression) (statement)
         The specified statement, which must be executable and neither a DO nor a logical IF statement, is executed if the logical expression is true; otherwise, control transfers to the following statement.   The logical expression might be a hardware sense line or switch output:

         IF (SENSE SWITCH 3)   (statement)

   (*e*) DO n INDEX = m_1, m_2, m_3
         n is a statement number; m_1 and m_2 are the *initial* and *final values* of the integer INDEX, and m_3 is the *increment* of INDEX.   If $m_3 = 1$, one may write

         DO n INDEX = m_1, m_2

* *PDP-9 FORTRAN IV Manual,* Digital Equipment Corporation, Maynard, Mass., 1968.

TABLE 3-1.   Minicomputer FORTRAN Check List (*Continued*).

(*f*) CONTINUE   STOP   PAUSE n

     PAUSE   END   STOP n

8. Check on the interpretation of READ and WRITE statements and device numbers; mini-computer peripheral devices may differ from those used with batch-processed FORTRAN systems on large digital computers.
9. Check on the **library subroutines** and **special functions** available with your FORTRAN system.
10. **Can FORTRAN programs be linked to assembly-language programs** (Secs. 4-20 and 5-28)?
11. Can FORTRAN be used for interrupt servicing (Secs. 4-16 and 5-16)?

FOCAL permit graphic output from cathode-ray-tube displays and digital plotters.   Table 3-2 outlines the main features of the BASIC language; many good texts on BASIC programming are available (Refs. 8 to 11).

Some of the most useful minicomputer applications employ BASIC or FOCAL interpreters extended to incorporate input/output commands for operating measuring instruments, test-voltage sources, and process-control equipment (Secs. 7-3 and 7-5).

TABLE 3-2.   A Quick Reference Guide to BASIC.

This table was prepared by the software staff of the Hewlett-Packard Corporation for their 2000B (time-shared) version of BASIC (Refs. 9 and 10).   The complete BASIC system illustrated here is more than a simple algebraic-interpreter language; it permits array and matrix manipulation, limited string manipulation, some editing, file manipulation, and chaining (overlays) of program segments.   Hewlett-Packard BASIC has also been extended to operate with *displays* and *instruments* (Sec. 7-3b).   Nevertheless, completely untrained operators can use BASIC as a very simple "conversational calculator" by typing statements like

LET V1 = 7.5

LET B   = V1 + 2.1

as commands, i.e., *without statement numbers*, and to obtain answers by typing, say

PRINT B, V1

OPERATORS

Operators are used in the statements of a program.

Sample Statement	Purpose/Meaning/Type
100 A = B = C = 0	Assignment operator; assigns a value to a variable.
110 LET A = 0	May also be used without LET.
120 Z = X↑2	Exponentiate (as in X^2).
130 LET C5 = (A∗B)∗N2	Multiply.
140 IF T5/4 = 3 THEN 200	Divide.
150 LET P = R1 + 10	Add.
160 X3 = R3 − P	Subtract.

NOTE: The numeric values used in logical evaluation are: "true" = any nonzero number; "false" = 0.

170 IF D = E THEN 600	*Expression* "equals" *expression*.

TABLE 3-2. A Quick Reference Guide to BASIC (*Continued*).

Example	Purpose
18Ø IF (D + E) ≠ (2∗D) THEN 71Ø	*Expression* "does not equal" *expression.*
18Ø IF (D + E) < > (2∗D) THEN 7ØØ	*Expression* "does not equal" *expression.*
19Ø IF X > 1Ø THEN 62Ø	*Expression* "is greater than" *expression.*
2ØØ IF R8 < P7 THEN 64Ø	*Expression* "is less than" *expression.*
21Ø IF R8 > = P7 THEN 81Ø	*Expression* "is greater than or equal to" *expression.*
22Ø IF X2 < = 1Ø THEN 65Ø	*Expression* "is less than or equal to" *expression.*
23Ø IF G2 AND H5 THEN 9ØØ	*Expression* 1 AND *expression* 2 must both be "true" for composite to be "true."
24Ø IF G2 OR H5 THEN 91Ø	If either *expression* 1 OR *expression* 2 is "true," composite is "true."
25Ø IF NOT G5 THEN 95Ø	Total expression NOT G5 is "true" when *expression* G5 is "false."
26Ø LET B = A2 MAX C3	Evaluates for the larger of the two expressions.
27Ø LET B1 = A7 MIN A9	Evaluates for the smaller of the two expressions.

STATEMENTS

Programs consist of numbered statements. The statements are ordered by number.

Example	Purpose
3ØØ CHAIN PROG	GETs and RUNs the program specified. The current
31Ø CHAIN $LIBR	program is destroyed, except for COMmon variables.
32Ø COM A,B1,C(2Ø),C$(72)	Declares variables to be in COMmon; they can then be accessed by other programs. Must be lowest numbered statements.
36Ø DATA 99, 1Ø6.7, "HI!"	Specifies data; read from left to right.
31Ø DIM A(72)	Defines maximum size of a string or matrix.
4ØØ END	Terminates the program; must be last statement in a program.
375 ENTER #T	Fills the first variable #T with the user terminal number
38Ø ENTER A,B,C	and/or allows the user a specified number of seconds to
39Ø ENTER T,A,B,C$	reply (A), returns the actual response time B, and returns the value entered C,C$. On time out, the response time is set to −256. On illegal input type, the response time is negated.
4ØØ FOR J = 1 TO N STEP 3	Executes the statements between FOR and NEXT a
5ØØ NEXT J	specified number of times, incrementing the variable by a STEP number (or by 1 if STEP is not given).
33Ø GO TO 9ØØ	Transfers control (jumps) to specified statement number.
412 GO TO N OF 1ØØ,1Ø,2Ø	Transfers control to the Nth statement of the statements listed after "OF."
42Ø GOSUB 8ØØ	Begins executing the subroutine at specified statement. (See RETURN.)
415 GOSUB N OF 1ØØ,1Ø,2Ø	Begins executing the subroutine N of the subroutines listed after "OF." (See RETURN.)
34Ø IF A ≠ 1Ø THEN 35Ø	Logical test; transfers control to statement number if "true."
39Ø INPUT X$,Y2,B4	Allows data to be entered from terminal while a program is running.
3ØØ LET A = B = C = Ø	Assigns a value to a variable; LET is optional.
31Ø A1 = 6.35	
36Ø READ A,B,C	Reads information from DATA statement.
35Ø READ #3;A	See "Files."

TABLE 3-2. A Quick Reference Guide to BASIC (*Continued*).

Example	Purpose
320 REM--ANY TEXT**!!	Inserts nonexecutable remarks in a program.
356 PRINT A,B,C$	Prints the specified values; 5 fields per line when commas are used as separators, 12 when semicolons are used.
358 PRINT	Causes the teleprinter to advance one line.
395 PRINT #3;A	See "Files."
380 RESTORE	Permits rereading data without rerunning the program.
385 RESTORE N	Permits data to be reread, beginning in statement N.
850 RETURN	Subroutine exit: transfers control to the statement following the matching GOSUB.
410 STOP	Terminates the program; may be used anywhere in program.

STRINGS

1. A string is 1 to 72 teleprinter characters enclosed in quotes; it may be assigned to a string variable (an A to Z letter followed by a $).
2. Each string variable used in a program must be dimensioned (with a DIM or COM statement) if it has a length of more than one character. The DIM sets the physical or maximum length of a string.
3. Substrings are described by subscripted string variables. For example, if A$ = "ABCDEF," then A$ (2,2) = B, and A$ (1,4) = "ABCD."
4. The LEN function returns the current string length, for example: 100 PRINT LEN (A$). This length is the logical length.

Example	Purpose
10 DIM A$ (27)	Declares the maximum string length in characters.
20 LET A$ = "**TEXT 1"	Assigns the character string in quotes to a string variable.
30 PRINT LEN (B$)	Gives the current length of the specified string.
105 IF A$=C$ THEN 600	String operators. They allow comparison of
110 IF B$≠X$ THEN 650	strings, and substrings, and transfer to a
115 IF N$(2,2)>B$(3,3) THEN 10	specified statement. Comparison is made in
120 IF N$<B$ THEN 999	ASCII codes, character by character, left to
125 IF P$ (5,8)> =Y$(4,7) THEN 10	right until a difference is found. If the strings
130 IF X$< =Z$ THEN 999	are of unequal length, the shorter string is considered smaller if it is identical to the initial substring of the longer.
205 INPUT N$	Accepts as many characters as the string can hold (followed by a *return*). The characters need not be in quotation marks if only one string is input.
210 INPUT N$,X$,Y$	Inputs the specified strings; input must be in quotes, separated by commas.
215 READ P$	Reads a string from a DATA statement; string must be enclosed in quotes.
220 READ #5; A$,B$	Reads strings from the specified file.
310 PRINT #2; A$,C$	Prints strings on a file.

FUNCTIONS

Functions return a numeric result; they may be used as expressions or parts of expressions. PRINT is used for examples only; other statement types may be used.

TABLE 3-2. A Quick Reference Guide to BASIC (*Continued*).

Example	Purpose
3ØØ DEF FNA (X)=(M*X)+B	Allows the programmer to define functions; the function label A must be a letter from A to Z.
31Ø PRINT ABS (X)	Gives the absolute value of the expression X.
32Ø PRINT EXP (X)	Gives the constant e raised to the power of the expression value X; in this example, $e+X$.
33Ø PRINT INT (X)	Gives the largest integer $\leq$ the expression X.
34Ø PRINT LOG (X)	Gives the natural logarithm of an expression; expression must have a positive value.
35Ø PRINT RND (X)	Generates a random number greater than or equal to Ø and less than 1; the argument X may have any value.
36Ø PRINT SQR (X)	Gives the square root of the expression X; expression must have a positive value.
37Ø PRINT SIN (X)	Gives the sine of the expression X; X is real and in radians.
38Ø PRINT COS (X)	Gives the cosine of the expression X; X is real and in radians.
39Ø PRINT TAN (X)	Gives the tangent of the expression X; X is real and in radians.
4ØØ PRINT ATN (X)	Gives the arctangent of the expression X; X is real, result is in radians.
41Ø PRINT LEN (A$)	Gives the current length of a string A$, i.e., number of characters.
42Ø PRINT SGN (X)	Gives: 1 if X>Ø, Ø if X=Ø, −1 if X<Ø.
43Ø PRINT TAB (X);A	Tabs to the specified position X, then prints the specified value A. Used for plotting.
44Ø PRINT TIM(X)	Gives current minute (X=Ø), hour (X=1), day (X=2), or year of century (X=3).
45Ø PRINT TYP (X);	If argument X is negative, gives the type of data in a file as: 1 = number, 2 = string, 3 = "end of file," 4 = "end of record"; or if argument X is positive, gives the type of data in a file as: 1 = number, 2 = string, 3 = "end of file." (For sequential access to files— skips over "end of records.") If argument X = Ø, gives the type of data in a DATA statement as: 1 = number, 2 = string, 3 = "out of data."

MATRICES

Absolute maximum matrix size is 2,500 elements. Matrix variables must be a single letter from A to Z.

Sample Statement	Purpose
1Ø DIM A (1Ø, 2Ø)	Allocates space for a matrix of the specified dimensions.
15 MAT X = IDN (M,M)	Establishes an identity matrix (with all 1s down the diagonal). A new working size (M,M) can be specified.
2Ø MAT B = ZER	Sets all elements of the specified matrix equal to Ø.
25 MAT D = ZER (M,N)	A new working size (M,N) may be specified after ZER.
3Ø MAT C – CON	Sets all elements of the specified matrix equal to 1.
35 MAT E = CON (M,N)	A new working size (M,N) may be specified after CON.
4Ø INPUT A(5,5)	Allows input from the teleprinter of a single specified matrix element.
45 MAT INPUT A(4,7)	Allows input of an entire matrix from the teleprinter; a new working size can be specified.
5Ø MAT PRINT A;	Prints the specified matrix on the teleprinter.

TABLE 3-2.   A Quick Reference Guide to BASIC (*Continued*).

Sample Statement	*Purpose*
55 PRINT A(X,Y)	Prints the specified element of a matrix on the teleprinter; element specifications X and Y can be any expression.
60 PRINT #2; A(1,5)	Prints matrix element on the specified file.
65 MAT PRINT #2,3;A	Prints matrix on a specified file and record.
70 MAT READ A	Reads matrix from DATA statements.
75 MAT READ A(5,5)	Reads matrix of specified size from DATA statements.
80 READ A(X,Y)	Reads the specified matrix element from a DATA statement.
85 MAT READ #3; A(I,J)	Reads matrix from the specified file; new working size can be specified.
90 MAT READ #3,5; A	Reads matrix from the specified record of a file.
100 MAT C = A + B	Matrix addition; A and B must be the same size.
110 MAT C = A − B	Matrix subtraction; A, B, and C must be the same size.
120 MAT C = A ∗ B	Matrix multiplication; number of columns in A must equal number of rows in B.
130 MAT A = B	Establishes equality of two matrices; assigns values of B to A.
140 MAT B = TRN (A)	Transposes an *m* by *n* matrix to an *n* by *m* matrix.
150 MAT C = INV (B)	Inverts a square matrix into a square matrix of the same size; matrix can be inverted into itself.

FILES

A FILE = a named storage area of from 1 to 128 records.   Maximum size varies
with systems.
A RECORD = 64 words of memory.
A NUMBER = a data item using 2 words of memory.
A STRING = a data item using about ½ word of memory per character.

Example	*Purpose*
OPE-MYFILE,80	Opens a file with a specified name and size.
KIL-MYFILE	Removes the specified file.
10 FILES BUG,GANG	Declares which files will be used in a program. Up to 4 FILES statements with a total of 16 files per program. Files must be OPEned first.
20 PRINT #N A,B	Prints the specified values A,B on a specified file at the current position. Files are numbered from 1 as they appear in the FILES statements.
30 PRINT #X,Y A,B,C$	Prints the specified values on a specified record Y of a file X.
40 PRINT 3,5	Erases the specified record of a file.
70 READ #1 A,B2	Reads the next values of a specified file into the specified variables.
80 READ #2,3 A,B	Reads values from the beginning of a specified record of a file into specified variables.
185 READ #3,5	Resets the pointer for a file to a specified record.
190 IF END #N THEN 800	Transfers control to a specified statement if an end-of-file occurs on a specified file.

COMMANDS

Commands are executed immediately; they do not have statement numbers.

Example	*Purpose*
APP-PROGI	Appends the named program to the current program.
BYE	Logs the user off his terminal.

TABLE 3-2.   A Quick Reference Guide to BASIC (*Continued*).

Example	*Purpose*
CAT	Lists the names and lengths of user library programs.
CSA	Saves the current program in semicompiled form.
DEL-1∅∅	Deletes all statements after and including the specified ones.
DEL-1∅∅,2∅∅	Deletes all statements between and including the specified ones.
ECH-OFF	Permits use of half-duplex coupler.
ECH-ON	Returns user to full-duplex mode.
GET-SAMPLE	Retrieves the program from the user's library and makes it the current program.
GET-$PROG	Retrieves the program from the system library.
HEL-D∅∅7,B^{c}G^c	Logs the user onto his terminal. User must give I.D. code and password.
KEY	Returns terminal to keyboard entry after TAPE command.
KIL-SAMPLE	Deletes the specified program from the user's library (does not modify the current program).
LEN	Lists the current program length in words.
LIB	Lists the names and lengths of system library programs.
LIS LIS-15∅ LIS-1∅∅,2∅∅	Lists the current program, optionally starting at a specified statement number and stopping at a specified statement.
NAM-SAMPLE	Assigns the name to the current program; name may consist of one to six printing characters.
PUN PUN-5∅ PUN-1∅∅,2∅∅	Punches the current program to paper tape, optionally starting at a specified statement number and optionally stopping at a specified statement.
REN REN-5∅ REN-5∅,2∅	Renumbers the current program from 1∅ (optionally from a specified statement number) in multiples of 1∅ (optionally in multiples of a specified number).
RUN RUN-5∅	Starts executing the current program, optionally starting at a specified statement number.
SAV	Saves the current program in the user's library.
SCR	Erases the current program (but not the program name).
TAP	Informs system that input will now be from paper tape.
TIM	Lists terminal and account time.

EXAMPLE: A Complete BASIC Program

```
Program    1∅ LET X = 1
           2∅ FOR Y = 1.1 TO 3.1 STEP .5
           3∅ LET H = SQR(X↑2 + Y↑2)
           4∅ PRINT "WHEN (X,Y) =" X;Y; "THE HYPOTENUSE IS" II
           5∅ NEXT Y
           6∅ END
           RUN
Results    WHEN (X,Y) =    1   1.1   THE HYPOTENUSE IS 1.48661
           WHEN (X,Y) =    1   1.6   THE HYPOTENUSE IS 1.8868
           WHEN (X,Y) =    1   2.1   THE HYPOTENUSE IS 2.32594
           WHEN (X,Y) =    1   2.6   THE HYPOTENUSE IS 2.78568
           WHEN (X,Y) =    1   3.1   THE HYPOTENUSE IS 3.2573
           DONE
```

CONVENIENT VERSUS INCONVENIENT OPERATING SYSTEMS

3-9. Introduction. Paper-tape operation, as described in Secs. 3-4 to 3-6, is a reasonable way to operate minicomputer systems dedicated to a single task or to only a few different tasks. But for general-purpose computation requiring frequent creation, translation, loading, correction, and modification of different programs, paper-tape operation presents an untenable situation, even with high-speed paper-tape readers and punches. Loading and compilation with an ASR teletypewriter *alone* can take hours even for relatively small FORTRAN programs. We will need a system which can quickly read, store, and retrieve system programs (loaders, assembler, compiler), source programs, and object programs without so many repeated manual loading operations. Above all, **we should like to load, combine, and execute programs automatically or on typed commands.** This is made possible by an **executive program** (sometimes called a **monitor system**) in conjunction with **magnetic disk, drum, or tape storage of system and library programs, user files, and intermediate translator outputs.** In addition, it will be a good idea to supplement the failure-prone, slow, and noisy teletypewriter with an inexpensive **cathode-ray-tube/keyboard terminal.**

3-10. Magnetic Disk, Drum, and Tape Storage. (a) **Storage Requirements and Operations.** Minicomputer system programs, such as assemblers and compilers, typically require several thousand words each. Additional thousands of words will be required for library programs (frequently used arithmetic, function-generator, and input/output routines), stored user programs, and user programs in the intermediate stages of a translation process. For general-purpose computation on minicomputers with 8K to 32K of core memory we will, moreover, "chain" successive segments of longer user programs stored on a disk or tape: We load and execute the first program segment, keep some intermediate results in core, load and execute a second program segment, etc.; such program segments are known as successive *core overlays.* Many applications also involve creation of permanent or intermediate **text or data files** with many thousands of words. Altogether, general-purpose minicomputation will require between 30K and several million words of mass storage, which should be accessible without manual loading operations. Since mass *core* storage is too expensive for minicomputers (of the order of $0.30 per 16-bit word), disk, drum, and/or magnetic-tape storage is used.

Magnetic mass-storage systems are compared in Table 3-3. Fixed-head rotating disks and drums have the highest *data-transfer rates* and, since they can access any storage location within one revolution, also the shortest *access times.* Disks are, therefore, best for storing system programs and intermediate output. Small disks are, moreover, inexpensive (about $6,000

TABLE 3-3. Comparison of Minicomputer Input/Output Storage Media and Peripherals.

	PAPER TAPE		MAGNETIC TAPE Synchronous (continuous) operation			FIXED-HEAD DISKS AND DRUMS
	ASR-33 tele-typewriter	Medium-speed reader/punch	Cassette/ Cartridge	DECtape	Standard (IBM-compatible) tape	
8-bit characters/sec	10	300 READ 50 PUNCH	500– 5,000	10,000	6,000– 60,000	40,000– 360,000
16-bit words/sec	5	150 READ 25 PUNCH	250– 2,500	7,500 (12-bit words) 5,000 (18-bit words)	3,000– 30,000	20,000– 180,000
Time to read 1,000 16-bit words (object programs)	200 sec	7 sec	0.4– 4 sec	133 msec (12-bit words) 200 msec (18-bit words)	30– 300 msec	6– 50 msec
Time to read 1,000 typical 20-character lines (source programs for assembly or compilation)	2,000 sec (over 30 min)	70 sec	4– 40 sec	2 sec	0.3– 3 sec	60– 500 msec
Access time	—	—	12– 150 sec	up to 100 sec	up to 240 sec	8– 17 msec
Total storage (16-bit words in one unit)	—	—	50K– 250K	100K 18-bit words or 150K 12-bit words	200K– 2M	30K– 600K
Typical price (combined input/output unit and interface)	$300 more than KSR-33	$3,000	$300– $3,000	$3,400– $9,700*	$5,000– $13,000	$6,000– $30,000

* One $7,400 interface can serve up to eight transports.

for 30K words), but magnetic tape on removable reels is cheaper for larger amounts of storage. Small and larger disks are often combined with magnetic tape so that different programs or data can be loaded from removable tape reels. There are also disk systems with removable disks or disk cartridges and combinations of fixed and removable disks.

Disk, drum, and magnetic-tape interface hardware and operations are described in Table 5-2. Blocks of computer words are almost always transferred directly from or to the computer core (or semiconductor) memory. Input/output programs are fairly involved, but they are usually supplied by the computer manufacturers. The user/programmer simply sees **buffer areas in the computer memory**, i.e., blocks of memory locations whose contents will be transferred to or from mass storage. Each buffer is identified by its *starting address* and *size* (*word count*); *header words* in each storage block may identify the block by a name and specify word count and addresses of succeeding or preceding blocks. To safeguard the large amounts of information handled, mass-storage systems usually employ parity checks (Sec. 1-4c) on each partial word (byte) transferred *and* an additional parity check for each multiword block.

(b) Disk and Drum Systems (see Fig. 3-7). Disk and drum systems record data words in *serial* form; i.e., successive bits are recorded or read as

Fig. 3-7. A complete minicomputer system with a 500 character/sec paper-tape reader, disk memory (top right), and a 16,700 character/sec magnetic-tape transport. A card reader is seen on the table at left. (*Hewlett-Packard*, 2100A computer.)

the magnetic film passes under a record/read head (see also Sec. 1-3). Magnetic drums, and most small disks, have *fixed heads* for individual data tracks. *Moving-head disks* require fewer heads, but they must be positioned quickly and accurately by expensive mechanisms. Storage addresses on disks and drums refer to the track and to timing marks on special timing tracks. The program usually establishes a *directory table* which produces the specific timing-track readings corresponding to the starting words of named blocks.

(c) Magnetic-tape Systems. Unlike disks and drums, magnetic-tape systems store several bits of a partial word (byte) *in parallel* across the tape. Parity can be checked across the tape (*transverse parity*) and for blocks of data along the tape (*longitudinal parity*). **Formatted tape** employs a **pre-recorded timing track or tracks** to find blocks of data by reference to a directory table, just like a disk. **Unformatted tape** has no timing track, and the header word of a desired block must be found by scanning the tape. **Incremental-tape** systems start and stop the tape for individual words, but most magnetic-tape units stop only at *record gaps* between blocks of words. Start and stop times are between 1 and 20 msec. The better tape transports can read or write backward as well as forward. The beginning and end of each tape are usually marked by reflective markers sensed by tape-transport hardware.

Blocks of data on tape can be of fixed or variable length. To **update** a block of data on tape will require *two* tape transports unless one is sure that the new data will fit the old block.

Fig. 3-8. 4-in reels of this type CO-600A LINCtape system hold about 100,000 16- or 18-bit words; prerecorded timing tracks address blocks of data. Transfer rate is 4,200 words/sec at 60 in/sec, with 30 sec maximum access time. A thin Mylar layer over the tape oxide protects both oxide and heads. Phase recording on nonadjacent duplicate data and timing tracks and capstan-less simplicity make such systems very reliable. (*Computer Operations, Inc., Beltsville, Maryland.* Digital Equipment Corporation DECtape is similar.)

Small capstan-less formatted-tape units like that shown in Fig. 3-8 (see also Table 3-3) employ duplicate data tracks for redundancy checks, have very handy small reels, and are reliable and inexpensive, an excellent choice for minicomputers. **Standard unformatted-tape (IBM-compatible) systems** are somewhat faster and can store more data, but they are also more complicated and expensive; we would use them with a minicomputer only *if tapes must be transferred from or to a larger digital computer* (Fig. 3-7).

Unformatted-tape systems record either 9 or 7 bits across the tape (1 bit will be a parity bit). Figure 3-9 shows a typical arrangement of data blocks, record gaps, and longitudinal check characters.

(d) Tape Cassette/Cartridge Systems. **Tape cassette/cartridge units** (Fig. 3-10) are slower than other tape systems but are so convenient to mount and change that they should be an excellent replacement for punched paper tape

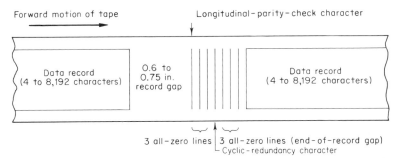

Fig. 3-9. Arrangement of data on nine-track tape. Tape *records*, corresponding to core buffers accommodating some reasonable amount of information (teletypewriter line), have between 4 and 8,192 eight-bit *characters;* each character comes with a ninth bit (transverse-parity bit). Each record is terminated by three all-zero lines (*end-of-record* gap), a cyclic redundancy character, three more zero lines, and a longitudinal-parity-check character. This is followed by a *record* gap at least 0.6 in long. A *file* is a group of records terminated by a 3-in gap followed by a *file mark* comprising an *end-of-file character* and a longitudinal-parity-check character.

in many computer systems. Since the small reels have limited storage, and also to speed access, one usually employs multiple cassette drives. Both formatted and unformatted tape are used, and a wide variety of systems exists (Table 3-3). Access times are a little slow for serious operating systems. Cassettes might be replaced by simple "flexible" disks.

3-11. Keyboard Operating Systems with Mass Storage. With a mass-storage system (we hope it is a disk), we are ready for respectable general-purpose computation. We initially use paper tape or magnetic tape to load

Fig. 3-10. Minicomputer with dual tape-cassette units. Each unit stores 250,000 eight-bit bytes on 300 ft of formatted tape at an 800 bit/in density. Transfer rate is 300 bytes/sec at 3 in/sec tape speed; fast-rewind speed is 90 in/sec. (*Interdata, Inc.*, Model 1 computer.)

an **executive program** (sometimes called a **monitor system;** different manufacturers employ different terms). This is a system program which announces its presence by typing EXEC or MONITOR on a teletypewriter or display and then waits for *keyboard commands.* The executive program responds to an interrupt (Sec. 5-9) when a key is struck, reads keyboard commands, and branches to an appropriate subroutine for loading and/or executing programs stored in core or in mass storage. To save core storage, only the portion of the executive needed to recognize keyboard commands is permanently stored in core (**resident executive, resident monitor**) and serves to call the various loading and service subroutines of the executive program from the system disk or tape. The minicomputer user does not need to study the detailed operation of the executive program; he need only consult the computer manufacturer's manual for the available list of keyboard commands and options.

Suppose that we have an edited FORTRAN source program stored on the system disk under the file name MYFILE. **We want to compile this program, combine it with a binary object program available on paper tape, load, and execute.** We will assume that the necessary system programs (compiler and linking loader) are available on our system disk; with small disk systems, assemblers might have to be loaded from paper tape or magnetic tape as needed. **The following conversational-programming sequence will exhibit typical features of minicomputer keyboard-executive operation.** Please note that specific features, codes, and rules will differ from system to system; consult your minicomputer manual.

1. When the executive is loaded and ready, it types out

EXEC

We now type

FORTRAN

to call the *FORTRAN compiler* from the system disk.
2. The executive loads the compiler and responds with

FORTRAN LOADED.   OUTPUT?

We want to give the compiler output the file name CPUT for reference and store it on the system disk for loading and execution; we type

DISK 1/CPUT

We could also have saved CPUT on a library tape (Sec. 3-12) by typing, say, TAPE 3/CPUT. Paper-tape output could also be specified, but is usually a compiler option (see below).

3. The system next asks

INPUT?

We specify the compiler input by typing

DISK 1/MYFILE

4. The system now asks us to specify *compiler options:*

FORTRAN-OPTIONS?

We type an option code (if any), and then a carriage return to start compilation.

Compiler options could include *preparation of a binary object-program paper tape, printing a symbol table,* and/or *printing a listing.* The compiler will use the system disk for quick storage and retrieval of intermediate output.

5. The system completes compilation and saves the output (CPUT) or, if compilation is unsuccessful, prints *error diagnostics.* Return to executive control is announced with

EXEC

We call the *linking loader* by typing

LOADER

6. The system loads the linking loader and asks for input:

LOADER-INPUT?

We specify

DISK 1/CPUT; READER

and place our second object program (which was on paper tape) in the paper-tape reader, pushing an appropriate button to clear the reader interface (Table 5-2).

7. The system asks

LOADER-OPTIONS?

We type an option code asking for a *combined object tape,* a *memory-map printout,* and/or **LOAD AND GO** to execute the combined program (we could also start execution with the computer front-panel switch or by typing **RUN**).

8. After execution, the system returns to monitor control and types

EXEC

We can, if we wish, *save the combined program* by giving it a *file name*, say **NUFILE**, and typing

SAVE TAPE 1/NUFILE

If we no longer need our source program **MYFILE** we can *delete* it by typing

DELETE DISK 1/MYFILE

To *save* **MYFILE** *on a library tape*, however, most operating systems require us to call another system program (**copying program, peripheral-interchange program**) specifically designed *to copy files from one peripheral device onto another.* Such a copying program must be given *format information* (binary, ASCII on paper tape, etc.). Other service programs callable from the system disk or from a library tape include *listing programs, editors, debugging programs, extra assemblers and compilers,* etc. (see also Secs. 3-12, 3-16, and 3-17). *Hardware-diagnostics programs* are usually loaded separately from paper tape, not through the executive.

The better executive programs can also be called from user programs, which may request loading and saving of specified files. This permits, in particular, **successive core overlays of chained-program segments.** Each program segment can call other overlays by simple external references (such as **CALL SEGMENT 3** in FORTRAN), whereupon the resident executive causes loading of the desired segment. Such systems will, in general, include a special linking loader ("chain loader"), which loads all program segments (and all required library routines) of a chained program together as one big file onto a disk or tape prior to execution.

3-12. More Operating-system Features. (a) **Input/Output Control System and Device Assignment** (see also Secs. 5-27 to 5-32). Since the executive program will, in any case, comprise many input/output routines, most software systems incorporate their entire library of standard I/O routines (**device drivers** or **device handlers** for the most frequently used peripheral devices) with the executive program. All user-program requests for these device drivers take the form of system macros (like FORTRAN **READ** and **WRITE** statements) or subroutine calls linked through a portion of the executive program usually called the **input/output control system (IOCS)**. *The user need not write or know any details of I/O programs but only the simple calls on IOCS* (Secs. 4-20 and 5-31).

In our description of keyboard-executive operation (Sec. 3-11), we referred to I/O devices for the executive, compiler, and loader by actual *device names,* such as **DISK 1, TAPE 3,** etc. In a more elaborate system, it is preferable for system and user programs to employ **logical device numbers.** Thus, in the FORTRAN statement

READ (2, 12)

the device number 2 could be made to refer to the paper-tape reader or to a selected magnetic-tape transport by a **device-assignment command** in the executive program *without any change in the user program* (**device-independent I/O programming**).   Similarly, any tape transport could be substituted for the system disk, magnetic tapes could be loaded on any one of several tape transports, etc.   Device assignments can be changed by new entries in a **device-assignment table** in the executive program; there may be different device assignments for different system and user programs.

Users can ascertain the current device assignments for, say, the FORTRAN compiler by typing a request like

REQUEST FORTRAN ASSIGNMENTS

(this might be contracted into an abbreviated code).   The system will answer by typing out device assignments, say

SYSTEM	DISK 1 (intermediate-pass storage)
INPUT	TAPE 3
OUTPUT	PAPER-TAPE PUNCH
2	PAPER-TAPE READER

The user may then *change device assignments* by a typed command like

ASSIGN TAPE 4 TO INPUT

for use in his compilation, but the standard device assignments will be restored the next time the compiler is loaded (see also Sec. 5-31d).

   (b) System Generation.   A minicomputer system with an executive program will need a special system program called a **system generator,** which tailors the executive program to a specific minicomputer configuration at the time the system is installed or modified.   The system generator (supplied by the manufacturer on paper tape or magnetic tape) loads the skeleton executive program and completes it through a conversational sequence in which the user is asked to type in his memory size, his interrupt-system options, and a list of his peripheral devices.   This procedure generates a *system tape* (paper tape or magnetic tape), which is saved and serves to refresh the system disk (if any).

   (c) File Manipulation.   Our example of executive-program operation included several instances where a program was saved on (or retrieved from) a "file-oriented" mass-storage device (disk or magnetic tape).   A **file** is a block of instructions and/or data on a disk or tape usually ending with an **end-of-file code** and starting with a **file header,** which is a set of words comprising the file name and various information about the file.   Each tape or disk will have a **directory table** listing all files stored (and, on disks and formatted tapes, also their addresses).   One file can contain several pro-grams or sets of data, but these will not be listed separately in the directory table; they must be found by scanning the file for record-header words.

The executive program has **file-manipulation commands,** such as

FIND	DELETE
SAVE	RENAME
LOAD	READ HEADER

each followed by a device number (or name) and a file name.   Note that SAVE, DELETE, and RENAME involve operations on the directory table as well as on the file.   A keyboard command such as

DIRECTORY   (device number or name)

will cause typing or CRT display of the directory table for the named device. *Copying or updating a file* involves *two* files and is usually accomplished by a copying program (peripheral interchange program) called by the executive.

Other file-manipulation operations include *saving and retrieving specified core areas* and *protection of specified files against deletion or overwriting.* Assembly-language operations or named files (or named blocks in a file) are done with the aid of READ and WRITE IOCS subroutines or macros (Secs. 4-20 and 5-31).   The first READ or WRITE must be preceded by an OPEN FILE (device, file name) subroutine or macro, which reserves a core buffer for communication with the file and may initialize some I/O operations.   After the user's program is finished with the file, a CLOSE FILE (device, file name) subroutine or macro dismisses the buffer and enters the file name, if it is new, into the device directory.

3-13.   Real-time Executives and Batch-processing Monitors.   The executive program described in Secs. 3-11 and 3-12 was specifically designed for *keyboard-controlled general-purpose computation.*   In review, we see that the executive's main task is to call specified stored programs and data in response to interrupt-service requests from the keyboard.   With the addition of IOCS to the executive, it also handles *user-program requests for routine I/O service.*

In many important applications, minicomputer systems must execute program sequences for reading instruments, processing data, or implementing control actions in response to interrupt requests from real-time clocks, sensors, or control logic as well as in response to keyboard commands. An executive program extended to handle such real-time service requests is known as a **real-time executive** (or **real-time monitor**).   The real-time executive will again comprise IOCS, plus *skeleton interrupt-service subroutines* with entry points for user-written service programs.   The user will write his service programs and label them for reference by the executive program, *which adds the tedious routines of the skeleton interrupt-service programs,* such as saving and restoring registers, I/O drivers, formatting, etc. (Secs. 5-27 to 5-32).   The executive program will assign initial interrupt-service priorities, which can be changed by certain user programs (Sec. 5-14).

An example would be executive-program control of a minicomputer system which must (1) perform routine data logging at clock-determined times, (2) compute some statistics from the data, (3) control valves or power-supply voltages supervised by temperature or voltage sensors, and (4) respond to overload alarms.

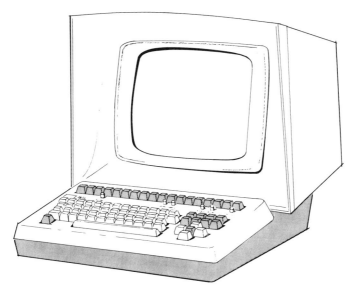

Fig. 3-11. A cathode-ray-tube/keyboard terminal for alphanumeric input/output. (*Delta Data Systems, Inc.*)

Another type of executive program (needed less frequently with mini-computers than with large digital computers) is a **batch-processing monitor.** Batch processing involves execution of multiple programs transcribed onto magnetic tape or a disk from punched cards or paper tape.   Each program will have a *priority code* determined by the arrival time, urgency, and pro-gram length.   The batch-processing monitor must load and execute the various programs, together with any needed library routines and data files, according to some priority-sequence strategy; the monitor must also make a record of the time and resources spent on each program.

3-14.   Cathode-ray-tube/Keyboard Terminals and Other Peripheral Devices. The convenience of a keyboard operating system is greatly enhanced if we use the slow, noisy, and trouble-prone teletypewriter only when hard copy is really wanted and employ a **cathode-ray-tube/keyboard terminal** (Fig. 3-11) for communicating with the computer (and for program preparation and debugging, Secs. 3-16 and 3-17).

Typical CRT/keyboard terminals display 40 to 48 forty-character lines on a standard television monitor. This is inexpensive and quite satisfactory for most assembly-language and FORTRAN programming. If much text or tabular material is to be displayed or if the system handles programs prepared by or for a larger digital computer, then 80-character lines are preferable. An 80-character line can display a complete 80-column punched-card image or a complete 72-character teletypewriter line.

The pattern for each ASCII character is generated by table lookup in a MOSFET read-only memory (Sec. 1-14). The display character sequence is periodically refreshed by a serial (MOSFET-shift-register) memory. Most such terminals are *teletypewriter-compatible;* i.e., they connect to the serial teletypewriter interface on a minicomputer or communication system. It is usually possible to speed up the shift-pulse rate of such an interface when the much faster CRT/keyboard unit is substituted for a teletypewriter.

CRT/keyboard control keys are similar to those on teletypewriters but can have more pleasing and convenient arrangements. A blinking cursor, which can be moved up, down, left, or right by control keys, indicates the current point for character entry.

Other minicomputer peripherals include small *line printers, card readers,* and *pencil-mark readers. Graphic CRT displays* and *graphic plotters* will be discussed in Secs. 7-8 to 7-12.

3-15. A First Look at Minicomputer Time Sharing. Hands-on on-line computer operation, especially with CRT/keyboard terminals, is a tremendously effective way of working for *people* It is also a very inefficient operation for the *computer*, which tends to be mostly idle while the operator thinks about the next step, scratches himself, or interprets results. It is surely one of the finer features of the inexpensive minicomputer that it still permits this type of operation to be cost effective (conversational computation on a larger machine *must* be time-shared). Nevertheless, especially in a research organization, a good on-line computing facility creates its own scarcity. Given a chance for creative "play" with the on-line computer, research workers may feel constrained not so much about cost but by the nagging feeling: "I am depriving Joseph Blow of computer time." For this reason, some sort of time sharing is psychologically as well as economically indicated. Time sharing may also be attractive where a minicomputer supervises a relatively slow-moving experiment or process and is largely idle between operations.

Executive programs like those described in Secs. 3-11 and 3-13 can be readily extended to provide **foreground/background programming.** This is the simplest way to time-share the computer between two programs. The lower-priority *background program* is interrupted by keyboard, clock, or other device requests for the *foreground program*, which is entirely interrupt-driven. To prevent either program from overwriting the other, it is best to establish memory boundaries with memory-protection hardware (Sec. 2-15), which interrupts the guilty program before any harm is done. In any case, serious program changes must usually wait until both programs are finished. Some types of programs can coexist nicely (Ref. 11). More ambitious multiuser time sharing requires *program swapping from a disk*, which is usually controlled by a second minicomputer (Sec. 7-13).

PROGRAM PREPARATION, EDITING, AND DEBUGGING

3-16.   Program Preparation and Editing.   (a) Off-line Paper-tape and Card Punching. The most primitive way to prepare a FORTRAN or assembly-language program for a minicomputer is with the built-in punch of an

ASR-type teletypewriter. An advantage of this procedure is that it can be done *off-line* if a second teletypewriter is available for the computer itself. Limited editing can be done with the aid of the teletypewriter RUBOUT key. The result is, generally speaking, a mess, although the computer can retype a clean copy of the program later; it is very hard to keep track of successive program corrections. Patching paper tapes for corrections is, essentially, impractical.

Conventional punched-card program preparation is preferable to such tele-typewriter operation, assuming that a card punch and reader are available. The advantage of punched-card operation is that *individual cards can be corrected.* Punched-card operation is also employed where assembly or compilation of minicomputer programs is done with a larger digital computer.

(b) Editor Programs. Most minicomputer program preparation is done with the aid of **editor programs** loaded from paper tape, from magnetic tape, or from the system disk. The text to be edited (program or data, usually in ASCII-character format) comes from a teletypewriter, CRT keyboard, or paper-tape reader, or from an *unedited file* on a magnetic tape or disk. The editor program moves this text to an *edited file* or output device by way of a **working area** (variable-length text buffer) in core. The text in the working area is printed out by a teletypewriter or (preferably) displayed by a CRT/keyboard terminal and can be modified, deleted, or added to by means of the teletypewriter or CRT keyboard. This is very convenient but, unfortunately, ties up the computer itself for on-line editing.

In the **input mode** (text mode) of a typical editor program (Ref. 12), the user can type on the current text line and delete individual characters, or the entire line, with control keys. The working area to be edited may be the last line typed or a block of lines. Text may be output from the working area line by line (after each line-feed/return), or an entire block may be output on command.

A control key switches the editor program between input mode and **command mode.** In *command mode*, the user may type *editor commands*, such as:

TOP   Moves the current line to the first line of the input file (if any).

NEXT   Moves the current line to the start of the next block or display page.

BOTTOM   Moves the current line to the last line of the input file.

GET N LINES FROM DEVICE   Adds *N* lines from a subsidiary input device after the current line.

LOCATE (character string)   Moves the current line to the first occurrence of the quoted string. It is used, for example, to change a variable name each time it occurs.

CLOSE (file name)   Outputs the remainder of the input file, edited or not, and closes the output file at the end of an editing job.

When a teletypewriter is used, most actual editing (text modification) is done in *command mode;* the user types commands underneath the current line, e.g.,

INSERT (string)   The string just typed is inserted after the current line.
REPLACE (old string/new string)   The old string in the current line is replaced with the new string (which can be longer).

The editor can also be commanded to *retype* some or all the text or to prepare *paper-tape output.*

Editing with a CRT/keyboard terminal is by far more convenient.   The user can *type over the displayed text, insert characters or lines with the aid of control keys,* and *delete characters or lines.*   All these changes are automatically applied to the text buffer.

NOTE: Editing programs can be very useful for editing *general text* (e.g., reports) as well as computer programs and data.

3-17.   On-line Debugging (Ref. 13).   A good **program-debugging system** works with both FORTRAN and assembly-language programs.   The debugger is loaded with the linking loader, which loads the user's programs; as a rule, the debugger disables all interrupts, so interrupt-service routines must be tested separately.   The debugger can:

1. Insert **breakpoints** at specified memory locations.   When started, the program will run and stop at the next breakpoint to permit examination of register and memory contents.
2. Remove one breakpoint or all breakpoints.
3. Start or restart the program at a specified location, e.g., after a breakpoint.
4. Display the contents of a symbolically addressed memory location on the teletypewriter or CRT terminal, step the displayed-location address up or down, or display the contents of the memory location indirectly addressed by a desired symbol.
5. Modify the contents of memory locations addressed as above.
6. Search a specified area in memory for the location addressed by a specified symbolic expression or for specified symbolic contents.
7. Output modified or corrected program sections onto a named file; the new program sections can contain newly defined symbols.

Less elaborate debugging programs permit only octal (rather than symbolic) address references (**octal debuggers**).   Reference 12 contains a short example of a debugging session; see also Ref. 13.

REFERENCES AND BIBLIOGRAPHY

(Refer also to manufacturers' manuals for computers and peripheral devices.)

Minicomputer Peripheral Devices

1. Rexroad, W. T.: *Teletypewriter Fundamentals Handbook*, Computer Design Publishing Corporation, West Concord, Mass., 1970.
2. Murphy, W. J.: Cassette-Cartridge Transports, *Mod. Data*, August 1970.
3. Kashman, M. J.: Computer Peripherals Buyer's Guide, *Control Eng.*, February 1970.
4. French, M.: Digital Cassette and Cartridge Recorders, *EEE*, May 1970.
5. Sykes, J. R.: Design Approach for a Digital Cassette Recording System, *Comput. Des.*, October 1970.
6. Brick, D. B., and E. N. Chase: Interactive CRT Terminals, *Mod. Data*, May–July 1970.
7. Murphy, W. J.: Medium and Small-scale Disk and Drum Drives, *Mod. Data*, March 1971.

BASIC Programming

Many minicomputer manufacturers supply BASIC manuals. Among the best ones are:

8. *Programming Languages* (PDP-8 Handbook Series), Digital Equipment Corporation, Maynard, Mass. (current year).
This reference also describes FOCAL.

9. 2000*B: A Guide to Time-shared BASIC*, Hewlett-Packard Corporation, Cupertino, Calif. (current year).
There are many books on BASIC. The classic text is that by BASIC's originators:

10. Kemeny, J. G., and T. E. Kurtz: *BASIC Programming*, Wiley, New York, 1967.

Miscellaneous

11. Puls, J. H.: A Simple Method of Multiprogramming the PDP-9 Computer, *CSRL Rept.* 207, Electrical Engineering Department, University of Arizona, 1970; see also *Proc. Fall DECUS Symp.*, Digital Equipment Corporation, Maynard, Mass., 1970.
12. *Introduction to Programming*, PDP-8 Handbook Series, Digital Equipment Corporation, Maynard, Mass. (current issue).
13. Evans, T. G., and D. L. Durley: On-line Debugging Techniques: A Survey, *Proc. FJCC*, 1966 (contains further bibliography on debugging).

CHAPTER 4

MINICOMPUTER PROGRAMMING WITH ASSEMBLERS AND MACROASSEMBLERS

INTRODUCTION AND SURVEY

Assembly-language programming will enable us to obtain the greatest possible effort from a digital computer, i.e., to optimize computing speed and/or memory requirements. This is because assembly-language instructions correspond, more or less, to the actual hardware operations possible with a specific machine and permit us to exploit its features cleverly. This advantage of assembly-language programming is especially pronounced for small digital computers, whose algebraic compilers (which must fit into 4K to 8K words of memory) may not produce very efficient code.

Modern symbolic assemblers not only *translate instruction mnemonics into machine code* but also permit *symbolic memory references* by assigning binary location numbers to symbols (Sec. 4-2). The better symbolic assemblers can also *compute addresses by evaluating symbolic expressions* (Sec. 4-3), can *reserve blocks of storage locations* (as well as single storage locations) for data or instructions, and can arrange for storage and formatting of decimal, double-precision, and floating-point data (Sec. 4-5). Good general-purpose assemblers further free the programmer from assigning program pages and work with a companion linking-loader program to facilitate *relocation and linkage of multiple program segments* (Sec. 4-17; see also Sec. 3-6). Finally, *macroassemblers* can generate useful multi-instruction sequences from one-line commands (Sec. 4-21) and, together with *conditional assembly* (Sec. 4-23), can combine some of the programming simplicity of a compiler language with assembly-language efficiency.

With a suitable operating system, assembly-language program segments can be neatly combined with FORTRAN programs (Sec. 4-20) so that even a little knowledge of assembly language can be used to improve important or frequently used routines.

ASSEMBLY LANGUAGES, ASSEMBLERS, AND SOME OF THEIR FEATURES

4-1. Machine Language and Primitive Assembly Language. A typical program sequence for a 12-bit minicomputer, say

2	5
3	. . .
4	LOAD INTO ACCUMULATOR (the contents of) 2
5	INVERT ACCUMULATOR
6	STORE ACCUMULATOR IN 3

specifies the contents of successive memory locations 2, 3, 4, 5, *and* 6. Location 2 contains a *data word* (5) given by our program, but location 3 is only *reserved* for an as yet unspecified data word to be stored there by the program. The program proper (i.e., the first instruction) starts at location 4. *The program counter will be initially set to* 4 and will step to 5, 6, and on to 7 as each instruction is executed.

Such a program is actually entered into the computer in **binary machine language,** viz.,

000	000	000	010	000	000	000	101
000	000	000	011	. . .	. . .	. . .	. . .
000	000	000	100	001	000	000	010
000	000	000	101	111	000	100	001
000	000	000	110	011	000	000	011

perhaps from a binary paper tape or from front-panel toggle switches. The first 12-bit word on each line is the memory address of the second word. The first line again locates the data word (5). The second line reserves location 3 for a data word which is not supplied by the program, but will be stored there at run time by our last instruction; some assemblers would deposit 0 in such a location for the time being.

The first word of the third line is, again, the address of the second word. This time, this stored-program word represents an *instruction code* and, since this is a memory-reference instruction, some address bits needed to determine an effective memory address. In our simple example, the five leading instruction-code bits 001 00 signify LOAD INTO ACCUMULATOR with the "page 0" direct-addressing mode (Sec. 2-7). In this case, the remaining seven address bits 0 000 010 directly represent the binary address. The remaining two instructions are similarly translated.

To work with long programs in this machine-language form would be decidedly uncomfortable even if we make the program easier to read and write by using *octal code* (Sec. 1-4*b*)

0002	0005
0003	....
0004	1002
0005	7041
0006	3003

which the machine could decode quite readily from typed input.   We have actually seen people program in octal code to avoid paper-tape assembly! In practice, even the simplest minicomputers have assembler programs which translate programs written in terms of **mnemonic instruction codes,** e.g.,

0002	0005	
0003	...	
0004	LDA	002
0005	NEG	
0006	STO	003

Mnemonics like LDA, NEG, and STO approximate English words; the assembler program translates mnemonics into binary code by table lookup. We have supplied addresses and address bits in octal form, just as in octal machine language.

To improve our primitive assembly language, it would be convenient if we could specify the actual 12-bit *effective address* of each memory-reference instruction, say

0006	STO	0003

Note that now the assembler must not only translate STO by table lookup, but it must also *compute* the correct address bits determined by the addressing mode (implicit in STO without extra character codes) together with the effective address.   If the desired address cannot be reached by direct current-page or relative addressing, the assembler will either stop and print an error message, or (preferably) it will automatically substitute indirect or two-word addressing (see also Sec. 2-7).

4-2.   Symbolic Assembly Language.   Most practical assemblers are **symbolic assemblers,** which permit the user to refer to instruction and operand addresses in terms of symbols.   In a **symbolic assembly language,** the sample program segment of Sec. 4-1 might look like Fig. 4-1.   **Each symbol (a string of up to 5 or 6 alphanumeric characters) represents a location (symbolic memory address).**   The word in the **location-tag field (label field)** of a line represents the location of the corresponding instruction or data word.

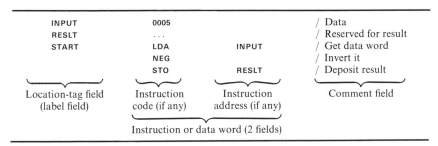

Fig. 4-1. The program segment of Sec. 4-1 written in symbolic assembly language. Note that each line (assembly-language statement) has four fields, all but one of which could be empty. When such statements are typed or punched (one to a teletypewriter line or punched card), the fields must be separated by spaces, teletypewriter tabs, or other *field delimiters* (colons, slashes, etc.) so that the assembler can recognize the end of each field.

Unless the contrary is specified, consecutive lines still represent consecutive program words. Therefore, if INPUT represents location 2, RESLT *must* represent location 3, START *must* represent location 4, and the last two instruction words *must* go into locations 5 and 6, *although we omitted their location tags in Fig.* 4-1.

The first pass of a symbolic assembler scans the user's source program and creates a **symbol table** which lists all user symbols defined as location tags together with their location numbers relative to a starting address. Symbolic instruction addresses as well as mnemonic instruction codes can then be translated by table-lookup operations. Taking due account of each addressing mode used, the assembler still has to compute the address bits for each memory-reference instruction. Good symbolic assemblers will automatically introduce indirect or two-word addressing when a symbolic address is not within reach of one-word paged or relative addressing (Sec. 2-7).

Multiply defined symbols will stop the assembly process and/or produce an error printout (Fig. 4-3). Some assemblers also indicate an error if a symbolic address has no location-tag counterpart (*undefined symbol*). A

PROGRAMMER			DATE		PAGE	
PROGRAM					CHARGE	
LOCATION Ⓣ	OPERATION Ⓣ	ADDRESS, X		Ⓣ COMMENTS		Ⓒᴿ
1 4	6 10	12		30		72 7
S T R T	L D A	C∅NS		L∅AD C∅NSTANT		

Fig. 4-2. Some people like to use *coding forms* similar to the one shown for assembly-language programming. The column numbers indicated on the form are for punched cards. In teletypewriter-prepared programs, the fields are delimited by tabs, colons, slashes, etc. (*Honeywell Information Systems.*)

good assembler, though, may automatically supply each undefined symbolic address with a corresponding storage location at the end of the program so that the programmer is relieved of this task. You can see that a good symbolic assembler is a fairly complex system program.

NOTE: Precisely, **A** represents the assembler-determined **address** of the memory location whose **contents** (A) at run time will be the **value** of a constant A or **values** of a variable A.

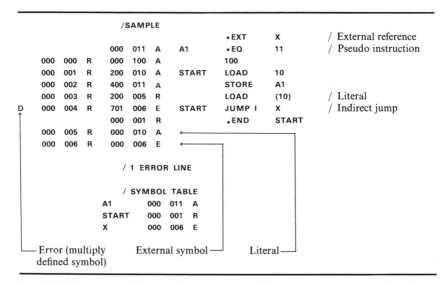

Fig. 4-3. Listing produced by a symbolic assembler. The assembler has started at location 0 and has marked each location and address as absolute A, relocatable R, or external E for the linking loader (Sec. 4-19). Words which do not contain addresses are marked absolute (their *locations* may be relocatable). An *error line* has been found and marked with an error code by the assembler.

If requested by a front-panel switch setting or typed command, the assembler will print an **assembly listing** in an extra pass. The listing shows *the user's symbolic source program and the resulting octal machine code side by side* with some extra annotations (Fig. 4-3; see also Sec. 4-2). The assembler can also produce a **symbol-table printout** for reference (either in alphabetical or numerical order). You should consult your minicomputer manual for the *maximum number of symbols* and the *maximum number of program lines* which can be handled with a given computer memory.

4-3. Symbolic Expressions and Current-location References. Since correct addressing requires computations at assembly time in any case, many symbolic assemblers improve programming convenience further by permitting **symbolic expressions** in address fields.   For example,

```
03       ADD INTO ACCUMULATOR          SYM          / Adds 000 173
         STORE ACCUMULATOR IN          LEAP-HOP+2/ Address is 06
HOP      JUMP TO                       SYM + 2      / Address is 11₈
         000 000
SYM      000 173
         101 201
LEAP  JUMP IF ACCUMULATOR NEGATIVE SYM-4        / Address is 03
```

Note carefully that each expression involves **addresses** and **not** data. Integers will be interpreted as *octal* unless the contrary is stated (Sec. 4-5c). Such more elaborate assemblers usually make *two* passes through the source program, plus an optional listing pass.

Some assemblers also admit *multiplication and division* in address expressions, but these operations may not have the customary precedence, and no parentheses may be allowed. Thus, A + B * C *may* be interpreted as (A + B) * C in an address expression; *consult your assembler manual.* Some assemblers also permit bit-by-bit **AND, OR,** and **XOR** operations with symbolic-address words.

NOTE: Numerical values of symbols and expressions are necessarily fixed at assembly time.   The program can only change the *contents* of symbolically addressed locations at run time.

As a further convenience, it is usually possible to **reference the location of the current instruction,** say as **.** , so that

```
03       LOAD ACCUMULATOR              . + 3     / Address is 06
BOUND    JUMP IF ACCUMULATOR ZERO      . - 1     / Address is 03
         JUMP                          . + A - 1/ Address is A + 4
```

NOTE: To establish addresses like SYM − 4 or . + 3 in our examples, we have treated each source-program instruction as *one word* in memory.   In general, two-word instructions (Sec. 2-7) will count as *two* locations.   *Check your assembler manual on this point and on the manner of counting byte locations (if any).*

4-4.   Immediate Addressing and Literals.   Some minicomputers permit you to specify the *operand* (rather than the address) of a memory-reference instruction through *immediate addressing* (Sec. 2-7e), e.g.,

> **LOAD ACCUMULATOR, IMMEDIATE   010   711**

where 010 711₈ is the actual number loaded, *not* an address.   Similarly, **LOAD ACCUMULATOR, IMMEDIATE SYMBL + 2** loads the *numerical value* of the symbolic address **SYMBL + 2**, *not* its contents.

For computers without true hardware immediate addressing, a symbolic assembler may implement memory-reference operations on **literals** like

(010 711) or (SYMBL + 2), which are defined as follows:

(010 711) is a symbolic memory location *which contains* 010 711.

(SYMBL + 2) is a symbolic memory location *which contains the numerical value of* SYMBL + 2.

The assembler automatically assembles memory locations containing each literal value at the end of the program (Fig. 4-3). It follows that

> LOAD ACCUMULATOR   (010 711)

actually loads 010 711. Note also that

> LOAD ACCUMULATOR, INDIRECT VIA   (010 711)

produces the same result in the accumulator as

> LOAD ACCUMULATOR   010 711

4-5. Pseudo Instructions. (a) Introduction. The assembler can perform still more operations to improve programming convenience. To request **operations to be done at assembly time,** we enter **pseudo instructions** into the source program. To distinguish pseudo instructions from true instructions (which directly correspond to operations at *run time*), we will write a word in each pseudo instruction with a preceding dot (.). The remainder of this section will help you to interpret advertised lists of assembler features.

(b) Pseudo Instructions for Defining and Redefining Symbols. As we have seen, one can *define* a symbol (i e., give it a numerical value) by using it as a location tag (label). Another way to define a symbol is through the pseudo instruction

> . DEFINE ADDRESS   SYMBL

which assigns SYMBL the value of the current location, just like

> SYMBL   . . .   . . .

As it stands, either statement leaves the *contents* of SYMBL unspecified. *With computers permitting repeated indirect addressing and/or post-indexing, however, the .DEFINE ADDRESS pseudo instruction can be used with indirect or indexed addressing to set the indirect or index bits of the specified location.* For example,

> . DEFINE ADDRESS, INDEXED   SYMBL
> STORE ACCUMULATOR, INDIRECT   SYMBL

would produce an effective storage address equal to the sum of the contents of SYMBL and the contents of the index register.

The pseudo instruction (assignment statement)

> SYMBL1   .EQ   SYMBL2 + SYMBL3 − 1

assigns the value of the expression on the right to **SYMBL1** in the *following* program statements. Such assignment can be used to define or redefine a symbol before or after it is used as a label or address. Note, however, that with the usual two-pass assembler

```
SYMBL1    .EQ    7
SYMBL2    .EQ    SYMBL1-2
```

is legal, but

```
SYMBL2    .EQ    SYMBL1-2
SYMBL1    .EQ    7
```

will cause an error message ("UNDEFINED SYMBOL") unless **SYMBL1** was defined (as a label, by a **.DEFINE ADDRESS** statement, or by another assignment statement) earlier in the program.

  (c) Pseudo Instructions Defining Data Types. Most minicomputer assemblers normally interpret integers in source-program addresses, expressions, or data as **single-precision octal integers,** so a statement like

```
ALFA        017002
```

reserves *one* memory location. Some assemblers can define **double-precision quantities** (still in **octal** code) by pseudo instructions like **.DOUBLE**, so

```
BETA     .DOUBLE     7173514
```

generates *two* words (in locations **BETA** and **BETA + 1**).

  The pseudo instruction **.DECIMAL** permits you to enter **decimal** integer constants in your source program; thus

```
GAMMA    .DECIMAL    1982
```

will generate the correct one-word binary number.

  Some assemblers will correctly assemble binary **floating-point numbers** when **.DECIMAL** is followed by a real number containing a *decimal point*. (Either **10.73** or **0.1073 E + 02** will work.) Other assemblers require a separate pseudo instruction, such as **.FLOAT**. It is similarly possible to declare **double-precision floating-point data;** the assembler will correctly assign *three or more* words for each data entry.

  Some assemblers also accept **hexadecimal integers** following the pseudo instruction **.HEX**.

  The pseudo instruction **.ASCII** followed by alphanumeric text (usually delimited by quotation marks) causes ASCII characters to be packed into successive computer words, where they can be accessed, for example, by output routines for printing error messages, for example,

```
.ASCII    'BOOBOO IN LINE 12'
```

NOTE: In some assemblers, a pseudo instruction like .DECIMAL remains valid for subsequent words until it is revoked by another data-defining pseudo instruction, such as .OCTAL.

(d) Pseudo Instructions for Reserving Storage Blocks.   A pseudo instruction like

SYMBL   .BLOCK   N

where N is a positive integer, **reserves N storage locations, starting with the location SYMBL**, for data or instruction words.   N can be a symbol or, in fact, an expression; the block size is, in any case, given its numerical value at assembly time.   Some assemblers automatically reset all reserved locations to 0 if their contents are not specified.   Some assemblers can also reserve blocks *ending* at a specified location.

NOTE: Locations reserved for noninstruction words *must be situated at the beginning of a program, at its end, or immediately following an unconditional-jump instruction.*   Otherwise, the machine might execute a noninstruction as the program counter advances, with regrettable results!

(e) Pseudo Instructions for Controlling the Assembly Process.   The pseudo instruction

.ORIGIN   (address)

causes the subsequent program to start (or continue) from the specified address (which can be relocatable, Sec. 4-18).

Every assembly-language source program *must* terminate with the pseudo instruction

.END   (starting address of program)

to tell the assembler that no more program statements follow.   The assembler may then add extra words for literals and for previously undefined symbolic addresses if it has these features.   The *starting address* is the address of the first *instruction* to be executed and is usually appended to the .END pseudo instruction, so that a loader program (Sec. 4-19) can insert a jump to the starting address and a   HALT   for convenient restarting. With simpler operating systems, absolute starting addresses are set up with front-panel switches (Sec. 3-4).

NOTE: The *pseudo instruction* .END signifies the end of *assembly*.   *Program* execution may end with the *instruction* HALT or with a jump to an executive program.

(f) Other Pseudo Instructions.   Additional types of pseudo instructions are used to *link programs* (Secs. 4-17 and 4-19) and to define *macros* (Sec. 4-21) and *conditional assembly* (Sec. 4-23).   Some assemblers also have pseudo instructions *to control or format listings*, but it is probably more convenient to do this with front-panel switches or, preferably, with keyboard-executive commands (Sec. 3-11).

4-6. The .REPEAT **Pseudo Instruction.**   The pseudo instruction .REPEAT is a program-writing convenience.   The statement

.REPEAT   m,n

where the **count** m is a positive integer and the **increment** n is a signed integer (positive, negative, or zero), causes the immediately following program word (instruction or data word) to be repeated m times with $0, n, 2n, \ldots, (m-1)n$ added to successive words.   For example,

```
          .REPEAT    3,2
          0001
          .REPEAT    2,-1
          0002
```

generates

```
              0001
              0003
              0005
              0002
              0001
```

Note that addresses as well as data can be incremented.   Some assemblers have more elaborate .REPEAT pseudo operations capable of repeating *groups* of words.

INTRODUCTION TO PROGRAMMING

4-7.   Program Documentation: Use of Comments.   Unless you intersperse your program statements with plenty of explanatory comments, not even you yourself (and surely no one else) will be able to understand your program one month later.   This is true for FORTRAN programs and any other programs as well as for assembly-language programs.

Comments are not restricted to the comments fields of assembly-language statements; the assembler will recognize any line preceded by / (or similar delimiters such as ; , * , etc.) as a comment line, say

/ THIS IS A COMMENT LINE

Such comment lines can also be used for *program titles*.   Comments will not cause any program words to be assembled, but comments will be reproduced in the assembler listing for future reference.

4-8.   Branching and Flow Charts.   Many minicomputers do not have conditional-jump instructions but combine unconditional jumps with conditional skips (which fit better into short instruction words):

```
/ THE FOLLOWING COMPARISON OF THE CONTENTS OF
/ LOCATIONS A AND B IS AN EXAMPLE OF A
/ THREE-WAY DECISION USING CONDITIONAL SKIPS
```
TEST   LOAD ACCUMULATOR   A

          SUBTRACT INTO ACCUMULATOR   B / $A - B$ in accumulator

          SKIP IF ACCUMULATOR POSITIVE   / $A > B$?

          SKIP   / No, test for $A = B$

          JUMP TO   POS / Yes, branch to POS

          SKIP IF ACCUMULATOR   ZERO   / $A = B$?

          JUMP TO   NEG / No, branch to NEG

ZERO   (program continues)   / Yes, go on

In general, specific operation-code bits of conditional-skip instructions correspond to conditions such as $<$, $>$, $=$, carry, and overflow. Such conditions can then be ORed together to form *combined conditions* such as $\leq$ (see also Secs. 2-11, 6-1, and 6-5).

Figure 4-4 is a **flow chart** for our program-branching example. Such flow charts are helpful when there are many complicated decisions and

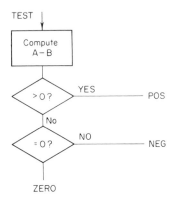

Fig. 4-4. Flow chart for the example of Sec. 4-8.

especially when there are program loops (Sec. 4-9 and Fig. 4-5). A flow chart is a topological model of the actual paths traced through the computer memory as the program executes instructions along different branches. The source program itself, on the other hand, is a *one-dimensional* rendering of each path in turn, together with listings of memory locations reserved for data and addresses (these do *not* appear on flow charts). It can be helpful to supplement your flow chart with a **memory map** listing data-storage locations.

4-9. Simple Arrays, Loops, and Iteration. A one-dimensional array of, say, 1,000 variables $A1, A2, \ldots, A1000$ will be stored in the computer memory as an example of a **data structure** arranged to simplify access to the data during common operations with this type of data. For our one-dimensional array, we simply reserve 1,000 consecutive memory locations with

```
            . DECIMAL
    A1      . BLOCK      1000
```

or (in octal code)

```
    N .EQ 1750          / Permits N to
    A1      . BLOCK   N  /    be changed at assembly
```

(Sec. 4-5). You should always check carefully whether the starting value of the array **index** I in AI is $I = 1$ or $I = 0$. This is a frequent source of errors.

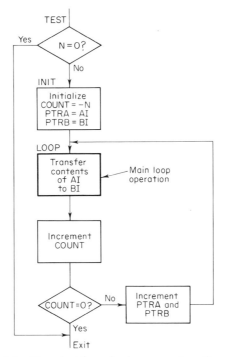

Fig. 4-5a. Flow chart for a simple program loop (Sec. 4-9).

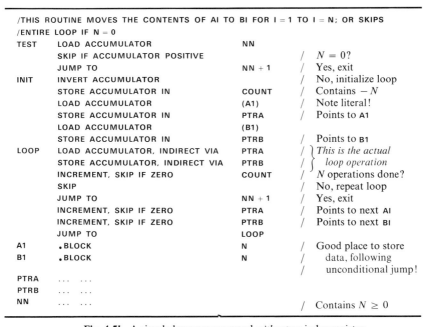

Fig. 4-5b. A simple loop programmed *without* an index register.

```
/ THIS ROUTINE MOVES THE CONTENTS OF AI TO BI FOR I = 1 TO I = N, USING INDEX
/ REGISTER; OR SKIPS ENTIRE LOOP IF N = 0
 TEST    LOAD INDEX REGISTER              NN
         SKIP IF INDEX POSITIVE                    / N = 0?
         JUMP TO                          NN + 1   / Yes, exit
 LOOP    LOAD ACCUMULATOR, INDEXED        A1 – 1   / Loads AN first
         STORE ACCUMULATOR, INDEXED       B1 – 1   / Stores BN first
         DECREMENT INDEX, SKIP IF ZERO             / N operations done?
         JUMP TO                          LOOP     / No, repeat loop
         JUMP TO                          NN + 1   / Yes, exit
 A1      .BLOCK                           N        / Good place to
 B1      .BLOCK                           N        /    store data!
 NN      ...   ...                                 / Contains N ≥ 0
```

Fig. 4-5c. The same simple loop programmed *with* an index register.

Programs for typical array operations, e.g., moving the contents of **AI** to **BI**, or

$$CI = AI + BI \qquad I = 1, 2, \ldots, N$$

$$S = \sum_{I=1}^{N} (AI)(BI)$$

require execution of a number of instructions proportional to N. Since memory capacity is limited, it is not just convenient but quite necessary to use **program loops,** which repeat the same instructions with successively incremented addresses **AI**, **BI**, and/or **CI**; a *counting operation* will be set up to advise us when the loop has run N times (Fig. 4-5).

Figure 4-5a shows how a simple loop can be programmed for a primitive minicomputer *without index registers.* Some minicomputers (PDP-8 series) would simplify the incrementation of **PTRA** and **PTRB** by *autoindexing* (Sec. 2-7c); the **ISZ** instruction would still be needed to increment **COUNT** since it is necessary to sense when N operations have been completed. But *by far more efficient loop operations are possible with an index register.* Figure 4-5b shows how *a single index register is used to step two data addresses as well as the loop count.* Many minicomputers, though, will require separate instructions for stepping an index register and testing it for 0.

We have stepped the loop index *after* each actual loop operation. We could do this *before* the loop operation instead. Note also:

1. The loop index (or **COUNT**, **PTRA**, and **PTRB** in Fig. 4-5a) must be *initialized* before the actual loop processing begins. While assembly-language statements like

   COUNT   000   000

   would initialize the loop before it runs *for the first time* after assembly, subsequent runs would *not* be initialized!

2. Since a loop may be traversed many times, *it is uneconomical to include unnecessary operations in the loop.* For instance, in the computation of

$$\sum_{i=1}^{n} ab_i = a \sum_{i=1}^{n} b_i$$

the multiplication by a is common to all terms and should *not* be included in the loop. The same is, of course, true in FORTRAN or BASIC programming.

An array may well contain two-word or multiword items, such as multiple-precision or floating-point data. In such situations, index-register incrementing becomes only a little more complicated. To access, say, every fourth word of an array *without index registers,* however, is a more cumbersome (but still straightforward) operation.

Every loop must contain a test to branch out of the loop when a desired condition is met. In our simple example, this condition was the completion of exactly N elementary operations, but a loop could be determined before N operations, e.g., when a sum exceeds a specified value or when an error becomes small enough.

In fact, *the loop technique is in no way restricted to operations* with elements of stored arrays; array elements could be *generated* by the loop. This is the case for *iterative-approximation operations.*

4-10. More Data Structures. (a) Two-dimensional Arrays. Two-dimensional arrays, like

A11	A12	...	A1N
A21	A22	...	A2N
...	...	...	...
AM1	AM2	...	AMN

($M \times N$ array), are usually stored in the computer memory as one-dimensional arrays, say *by rows,* as

$$A1, A2, \ldots, A(MN)$$

where the single subscript J in AJ is related to the subscripts I and K of AIK by

$$J = (K - 1)N + I \qquad I = 1, 2, \ldots, N; K = 1, 2, \ldots, M \qquad (4\text{-}1)$$

To access the location **AIK** of the array element AIK, the computer will have to add $J - 1$ to the address **A11** (starting address), i.e.,

$$\text{AIK} = \text{A11} + (K - 1)N + I - 1$$

$$I = 1, 2, \ldots, N; K = 1, 2, \ldots, M \qquad (4\text{-}2)$$

Larger digital computers permit computation of such addresses by *double indexing* (adding contents of two index registers), but this is *not* possible with most minicomputers even if two index registers are available. Accessing of the individual array elements *AIK* (as in matrix computations) will, therefore, be somewhat cumbersome unless *postindexing* (Sec. 2-7) is available (as in the Honeywell 316/516 and the Varian Data Systems 620/f).

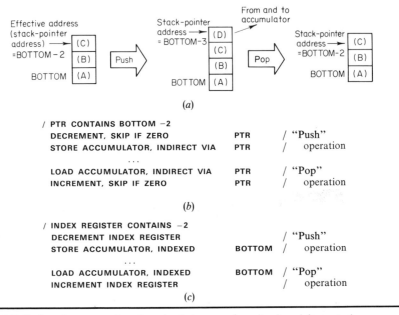

Fig. 4-6. Push and pop operations in a simple (one word per item) pushdown stack: memory map (*a*) and programming without an index register (*b*) and with an index register (*c*). Addresses *increase* toward the bottom of the stack in this example; the contrary could be true.

In that case, $(K - 1)N$ can be generated in the index register by successive additions of N, while $A11 + I - 1$ will appear in an indirectly addressed memory location which is incremented to advance I.

NOTE: As with one-dimensional arrays, you should make sure that row and column subscripts of given arrays really start with 1 and not with 0.

(b) Stacks (Pushdown Lists). A practically important class of data structures are **stacks**, i.e., arrays permitting words or subarrays (**items**) to be adjoined, removed, or accessed from the top of the stack *on a last-in–first-out basis*. Such stacks are also known as **pushdown lists** or **LIFO (last-in–first-out) lists**. Stacks are especially useful for orderly intermediate-result storage and for various systems-programming applications (Fig. 4-6; see also Secs. 4-16, 6-8, and 6-10).

(c) Other Data Structures (see Refs. 1 to 4). Structures of multiple (and possibly variable-length) subarrays which can be *created* and *deleted* in the course of computation are often organized as various types of **(linked) lists,** rather than as multidimensional arrays, which might waste permanently assigned storage space. A **(linked) list** or **chain** is an ordered set of word arrays **(items),** *each comprising a pointer to the next item in the list or to a directory array of item starting addresses.* Individual item arrays can be located *wherever memory space is available.* One usually keeps a separate **list of available space;** an item is deleted from this available-space list whenever an item is added to another list, and vice versa.

List structures are used to store and access program lines (character strings) in editing programs, catalog and inventory items, bibliographical references, graphic-display items (Sec. 7-11), and rows or columns of sparse matrices (i.e., matrices with many 0 elements—this would make simple two-dimensional-array storage uneconomical). List items can also contain *backward pointers* to preceding items, pointers to subitems, and/or counters indicating sizes of item arrays. Reference 4 is a good introduction to your study of list processing, which has opened up many interesting new programming techniques.

4-11. Miscellaneous Programming Techniques. (a) Table-lookup Operations. Section 4-8 illustrates a *triple* branch implemented with conditional skip-jump instructions. When a decision has more than a few possible outcomes, though, it may be best to store the jump-destination addresses in an array **(table)** addressed in the manner of Sec. 4-9. The result of each decision will correspond to the value of an **array index** I placed in an index register or address pointer to access an address in the array. If the decision depends on more than one factor, we can use a multidimensional-table array with an index computation like the one in Sec. 4-10a.

Such table-lookup operations are, of course, precisely those needed to look up values of tabulated numerical functions. To reduce the size of the function table needed to compute a continuously differentiable function with suitable accuracy, we can *combine table lookup and interpolation.*

Figure 4-7 illustrates a high-speed method for **fixed-point table-lookup/ interpolation approximation** of a function $Y = F(X)$ in the form

$$Y \approx (Y_{i+1} - Y_i)\frac{X - X_i}{X_{i+1} - X_i} + Y_i \tag{4-3}$$

where scaled function values $Y_i = F(X_i)$ are tabulated for $2^N + 1$ uniformly spaced breakpoint abscissas

$$X_i = 2^{1-N}i - 1 \qquad i = 0, 1, 2, \ldots, 2^N \tag{4-4}$$

between $X_0 = -1$ and $X_{2^N} = 1$ (Fig. 4-7a). The program of Fig. 4-7b begins with the n-bit 2s-complement fraction

$$X = X_i + (X - X_i)$$

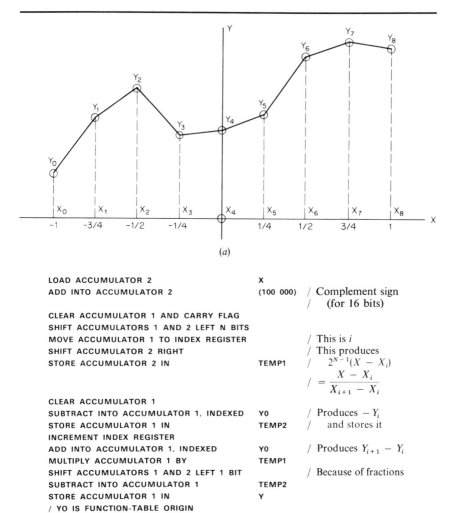

Fig. 4-7. Table-lookup/interpolation approximation of a function $Y = F(X)$ with 2^N equal breakpoint intervals (Sec. 4-11b).

in the form

Sign	$(N - 1)$ bits	$(n - N)$ bits

represents X_i represents $X - X_i$

Note that the right-hand $(n - N)$ bits represent the nonnegative difference $X - X_i$ needed for interpolation; *we shift them into a second accumulator*

(accumulator extension, MQ register, Sec. 2-10) and save them for multiplication. The sign bit of X_i is complemented to form the breakpoint index i, which is added to the table origin **Y0** (location of Y_0) to produce a pointer to Y_i. The entire operation requires under 40 memory cycles (typically less than 40 μsec) and can be generalized for nonuniform breakpoint spacing and functions of two or more variables (Ref. 10).

(b) Program Switches. A **program switch** stores the result of a binary or multiple branching decision to implement the actual branching *later on* in another part or parts of the program. An example is precomputation and storage of decisions for use inside loops (Ref. 3) to free the latter of repeated decision making. The decision result can be stored in a memory location, in a processor flag (if it is not otherwise in use), or, if possible, in an index register.

EXAMPLE:

```
LOAD ACCUMULATOR                     A1
ADD INTO ACCUMULATOR                 A2
ADD INTO ACCUMULATOR                 A3
SUBTRACT                             B
CLEAR INDEX REGISTER
SKIP IF ACCUMULATOR NOT POSITIVE
INCREMENT INDEX REGISTER                 / Positive
SKIP IF ACCUMULATOR NOT ZERO
INCREMENT INDEX REGISTER                 / Positive or zero
```

The index register now reads 0, 1, or 2 if **A1** + **A2** + **A3** – **B** was negative, zero, or positive, respectively. The desired three-way branch can be obtained now or later with

JUMP, INDEXED, INDIRECT VIA   PTR

The program will jump via **PTR, PTR** +1, or **PTR** + 2.

(c) Miscellaneous Examples. The program segments of Fig. 4-8 illustrate useful programming techniques possible with typical minicomputer instruction sets (see also Chap. 6).

```
LOAD ACCUMULATOR            A
SHIFT LEFT, UNSIGNED
STORE ACCUMULATOR IN        TEMP
LOAD ACCUMULATOR            B
SHIFT LEFT, UNSIGNED
CLEAR CARRY FLAG
ADD INTO ACCUMULATOR        TEMP
LOAD ACCUMULATOR            A
ADD INTO ACCUMULATOR        B
SKIP ON CARRY FLAG CLEAR
JUMP TO                     OFLO     / Overflow-error routine
STORE ACCUMULATOR IN        C
```

Fig. 4-8a. Overflow check for 2s-complement addition ($A + B = C$) on a machine having a carry flag but no true overflow flag. Carries from the most significant bit and from the sign bit are both allowed to complement the carry flag in turn, so that they are effectively XORed (see also Secs. 1-9a and 2-10a).

```
      CLEAR CARRY FLAG
      LOAD ACCUMULATOR          A2
      ADD INTO ACCUMULATOR      B2
      STORE ACCUMULATOR IN      A2
      LOAD ACCUMULATOR          A1
      SKIP IF NO CARRY               / Used instead of
      INCREMENT ACCUMULATOR          /   ADD CARRY instruction
      ADD INTO ACCUMULATOR      B1
      STORE ACCUMULATOR IN      A1
```

Fig. 4-8b. Double-precision addition on a minicomputer without DOUBLE ADD or ADD CARRY instructions. A double-precision number is added from B1, B2 into A1, A2. A1 and B1 hold signs and most significant bits. No overflow check is included.

```
/ ONE-ACCUMULATOR MACHINE        / TWO-ACCUMULATOR MACHINE
/ NEEDS 12 CYCLES                / NEEDS 8 CYCLES
  LOAD ACCUMULATOR        A         LOAD ACCUMULATOR   1     A
  STORE ACCUMULATOR IN   TEMP       LOAD ACCUMULATOR   2     B
  LOAD ACCUMULATOR        B         STORE ACCUMULATOR 1 IN   B
  STORE ACCUMULATOR IN    A         STORE ACCUMULATOR 2 IN   A
  LOAD ACCUMULATOR       TEMP
  STORE ACCUMULATOR IN    B
```

Fig. 4-8c. Multiple accumulators can often save time-consuming memory references by serving as quickly accessible temporary-storage locations. As an example, the Data General NOVA/SUPERNOVA manual compares routines for interchanging the contents of two memory locations A, B (e.g., in sorting operations).

```
  LOAD ACCUMULATOR, IMMEDIATE    777000   / Load mask
  AND INTO ACCUMULATOR           Y        / Mask 9 low-order bits
  STORE ACCUMULATOR IN           TEMP     / Save result
  LOAD ACCUMULATOR               X
  SHIFT RIGHT 9 BITS, UNSIGNED            / Shift right
  ADD INTO ACCUMULATOR           TEMP     / Combine with Y
```

(Store in array, or output and display packed word)

Fig. 4-8d. This routine truncates two 18-bit numbers X, Y to 9 bits and packs the truncated words into one 18-bit word for a cathode-ray-tube display (Sec. 7-9). Y is truncated by masking, and X is truncated by shifting.

SUBROUTINES AND CALLING SEQUENCES

4-12.   Introduction: Subroutines without Direct Data Transfer.   In many applications, a reasonably involved program section is used over and over again in the course of a computation.   We may then save a great deal of memory if we store such a **subroutine** only once, jump to its tagged starting location whenever the subroutine is needed, and make a return jump to the calling program when the subroutine is finished.   Besides saving memory, the use of subroutines can give our programs a more easily understood "modular" structure, but subroutines will *not* save time compared to straight-line programming.   They will (at the least) add extra jump instructions as "overhead" and can provide excellent chances for making programming errors, especially when subroutines must call one another.

The simplest subroutines do *not* process data passed to them directly by the various subroutine-calling sections of the main program.   A good example is a subroutine which, at several points of a data-processing program, transfers the words of the same buffer area in memory to a line printer, perhaps doing some reformatting and checking on the way.   This can be a rather long subroutine (100 or more instructions, see also Sec. 5-27). It will be a real relief to store it only once in memory and to have to write it only once in our program.   Calling this particular subroutine is simple, for the calling program need not tell the subroutine what data to process: the subroutine always operates on the same buffer.

When we jump to the subroutine, we must *save the return address* for our later return to the calling program.   Most minicomputers do this with the instruction

JUMP AND SAVE   (effective address)

which will store the correct return address (incremented program-counter contents) at the effective address, say **SUBR**, which precedes that of the first subroutine instruction.

After our subroutine is finished, an indirect jump via the location **SUBR** (where the return address is stored) will return us to the calling program (Fig. 4-9).

The instruction JUMP AND SAVE can also be used with indirect addressing.

NOTE: Contents of processor registers (accumulators, index registers, processor flags, page register, interrupt mask) needed later by the calling program may have to be saved in memory before we call a subroutine which uses these registers.   In some computers, the JUMP AND SAVE instruction automatically saves processor flags and the page register in an extra location following the return address.

4-13.   Argument and Result Transfer through Processor Registers.   Many subroutines will process **arguments (parameters)** passed to them by each program section which calls the subroutine.   Arguments can be data words

```
011 (last instruction of calling program)
012 JUMP AND SAVE                          SUBR ───────────────┐
┌──→013 (calling program continues)                            │
│                           .                                  │
│                           .                                  │
│                           .                                  │
│   SUBR (013 will be stored here for this subroutine call)    │ / jump address ←──┘
│        (body of subroutine)
└─────── JUMP INDIRECT VIA              SUBR          / return jump
```

Fig. 4-9. Simple subroutine call and return. No special provisions are made to transfer arguments or results.

but may also be symbolic addresses. Subroutines will also have to return **results** to calling programs. Quite often, only one argument and/or result or only a few arguments and/or results must be passed, as in a function-generating subroutine (e.g., square root, table-lookup function). Note that while the code for the subroutine remains the same for each call, argument(s) and/or result(s) will differ. A simple way to pass one data word is to place it into an accumulator or index register during the subroutine jump or return jump; several words can be passed if several registers are available.

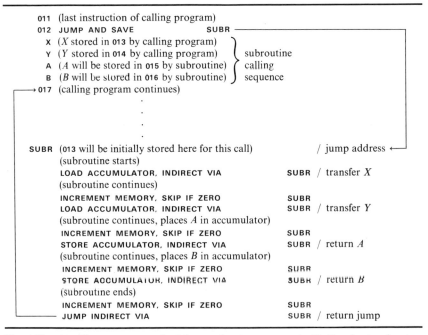

Fig. 4-10a. A calling-sequence method for passing two arguments X, Y and returning two results A, B. A computer permitting autoincrementing or postindexing of the indirect-address pointer SUBR would make this program simpler and faster.

4-14.   Argument and Result Transfer through a Calling Sequence.   Use of an Index Register.   Quite often, we must pass more subroutine arguments and/or results than we have processor registers, or our registers are otherwise occupied.   In such cases, we can employ a **subroutine calling sequence.** In Fig. 4-10a, the calling program reserves locations for the arguments, say X, Y, and for the results, say A, B, immediately following the subroutine jump.   The subroutine can then access X, Y, A, and B in turn by indirect addressing and successive incrementation of the jump address SUBR. The last incrementation produces the correct return address.

A few minicomputers can avoid the repeated ISZ instructions in Fig. 4-10a by **postindexing the indirect address** or by supplying an **autoincrement addressing mode,** which increments indirectly addressed memory locations when a special operation-code bit is set (Secs. 2-7 and 6-7c).   **Other minicomputers use an index register to store the return address** (or the first calling-sequence address) through the instruction JUMP AND SAVE IN INDEX (Secs. 2-11b and 6-10).   In this case, we can access the subroutine arguments and transfer results more rapidly through indexed addressing.   It also becomes much easier to deal with arguments and results *in random order* rather than strictly consecutively (Fig. 4-10b).

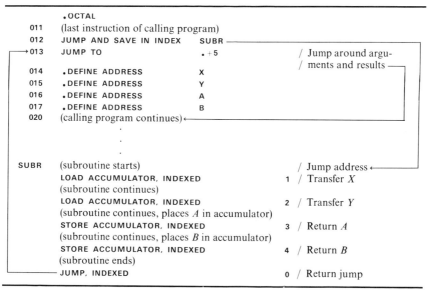

Fig. 4-10b.   Subroutine and calling sequence employing the JUMP AND SAVE IN INDEX instruction.   Note that arguments and results could be just as easily accessed in any other order.   The return jump was made to location 013 (immediately following the subroutine jump) with an extra jump around the calling-sequence items.   This is a convention expected of subroutines called by system programs in some computer systems.   Otherwise, a return jump through JUMP, INDEXED 5 would be simpler and faster.

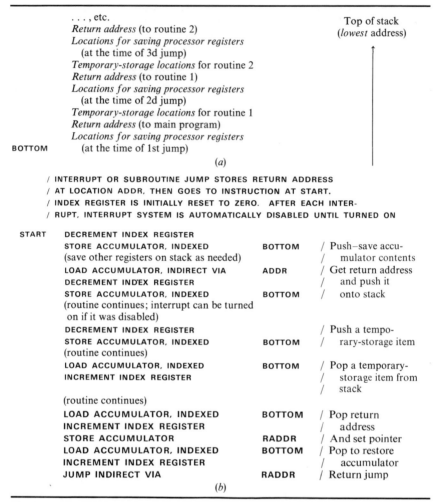

. . . , etc.   Top of stack
Return address (to routine 2)   (*lowest* address)
Locations for saving processor registers
   (at the time of 3d jump)
Temporary-storage locations for routine 2
Return address (to routine 1)
Locations for saving processor registers
   (at the time of 2d jump)
Temporary-storage locations for routine 1
Return address (to main program)
Locations for saving processor registers
BOTTOM   (at the time of 1st jump)

(*a*)

```
/ INTERRUPT OR SUBROUTINE JUMP STORES RETURN ADDRESS
/ AT LOCATION ADDR, THEN GOES TO INSTRUCTION AT START.
/ INDEX REGISTER IS INITIALLY RESET TO ZERO.  AFTER EACH INTER-
/ RUPT, INTERRUPT SYSTEM IS AUTOMATICALLY DISABLED UNTIL TURNED ON

START   DECREMENT INDEX REGISTER
        STORE ACCUMULATOR, INDEXED          BOTTOM    / Push–save accu-
        (save other registers on stack as needed)    /   mulator contents
        LOAD ACCUMULATOR, INDIRECT VIA      ADDR      / Get return address
        DECREMENT INDEX REGISTER                      /   and push it
        STORE ACCUMULATOR, INDEXED          BOTTOM    /   onto stack
        (routine continues; interrupt can be turned
        on if it was disabled)
        DECREMENT INDEX REGISTER                      / Push a tempo-
        STORE ACCUMULATOR, INDEXED          BOTTOM    /   rary-storage item
        (routine continues)
        LOAD ACCUMULATOR, INDEXED           BOTTOM    / Pop a temporary-
        INCREMENT INDEX REGISTER                      /   storage item from
                                                      /   stack
        (routine continues)
        LOAD ACCUMULATOR, INDEXED           BOTTOM    / Pop return
        INCREMENT INDEX REGISTER                      /   address
        STORE ACCUMULATOR                   RADDR     / And set pointer
        LOAD ACCUMULATOR, INDEXED           BOTTOM    / Pop to restore
        INCREMENT INDEX REGISTER                      /   accumulator
        JUMP INDIRECT VIA                   RADDR     / Return jump
```

(*b*)

Fig. 4-11. A pushdown stack for saving return addresses, processor-register contents, and temporary-storage items for reentrant nested subroutines and/or interrupt-service routines (*a*) and typical programming (*b*). An index register is used to produce the effective stack-pointer address, but an indirect-address pointer can be used if no index register is free (see also Fig. 4-6). A few minicomputers have special *stack-pointer registers*, which are automatically decremented and incremented when an interrupt-service routine starts or is completed (see also Sec. 6-10). Note that some register contents and/or temporary-storage items may not get stored before the next interrupt occurs.

4-15. Subroutines Calling Other Subroutines. If, as is frequently the case, a subroutine calls another subroutine (**nesting** of subroutines), then the following points may require attention:

1. If the computer stores subroutine return addresses and/or computer status words in special registers (e.g., an index register) or in fixed

memory locations, then their contents must be saved prior to the subroutine call. It will be necessary to establish an orderly procedure for saving and restoring these items with each new subroutine call.

2. A special problem arises if a subroutine calls itself (**recursive** subroutine call, Ref. 3).

4-16. Interrupt-service Routines and Reentrant Subroutines. An **interrupt-service routine** is a subroutine called into action by a signal (**interrupt request**) from outside the computer or because of an alarm condition in the computer (power-supply failure, violation of memory protection), rather than by a computer-program call. Interrupt-system hardware and programming will be discussed in some detail in Chap. 5, but it will be useful to see right here how interrupt-service programming differs from ordinary subroutine programming.

The essential point is this: We *know* where in our program a subroutine will be called, and we can prepare data, save registers, etc., beforehand. But we do *not* in general know where an interrupt request will cause our program to jump to an interrupt-service routine (at best, we can *suppress* interrupts during critical program phases, Chap. 5). Hence interrupt-service routines cannot employ calling sequences, and they must do any saving and restoring of return addresses, register contents, and status words themselves without any help from the main program.

A special program arises when a subroutine (say a library routine for computing the square root) is interrupted, and the interrupt-service program calls *the same* subroutine. The original subroutine call may cause intermediate-result storage in temporary-storage locations, say TEMP1 and TEMP2. Unless special precautions are taken, intermediate results from the second subroutine call can *overwrite* TEMP1 and TEMP2 so that the program will fail upon return from interrupt. *The library subroutines of most FORTRAN systems fail in this manner.*

Subroutines designed to work properly when they are interrupted and recalled for interrupt service are called **reentrant.** Since "real-time" computations involving many interrupt-driven program segments are important minicomputer applications, reentrant programming is often desirable. A good way to obtain reentrant subroutines, as well as assured saving of return addresses, register contents, etc., is to store all temporary-storage and saved items in a stack (Sec. 4-10*b*); a stack pointer is advanced and retracted as the subroutine is called and completed (Fig. 4-11; see also Secs. 5-16 and 6-10).

RELOCATION AND THE LINKING LOADER

4-17. Problem Statement (see also Sec. 3-6). Minicomputers loading mainly single special-purpose programs or interpreter programs (such as BASIC, Sec. 3-8) will not require program **relocation.** For general-purpose computation, though, *one will want to combine different program segments and library subroutines,* so it must be possible to *relocate programs* anywhere in the computer memory. Program segments will, moreover, want to call other program segments as subroutines, and it will be necessary to pass arguments and results between programs. This requires techniques for **program linkage,** i.e., for associating the proper relocated addresses with symbolic names of **external references.** Programming systems permitting relocation and linkage will require:

1. An assembler (or compiler) *specifically designed* to permit relocation and linkage
2. A **relocating/linking loader program,** which supplies the correct addresses and cross references at load time

4-18.   Relocation.   An assembler (or compiler) designed to produce relocatable code creates a preliminary version of the object program, with addresses and program-counter readings normally referred to location **0** as a fictitious origin.   The assembler (or compiler) will, moreover, **mark** every word, address, and symbol to be relocated with a **relocation bit, byte, or word** so that the loader will know which words and addresses to modify. These words and addresses usually appear marked with an **R** in the assembler listing (Fig. 4-3) and include:

1. Most of the normal *instruction and data words* of the program, with the exception of special pointers on page 0
2. Symbolic and numerical *addresses* in the program, again with the exception of special references to page 0

The nonrelocatable addresses are known as **absolute** addresses (see also Fig. 4-3).

The relocating/linking loader will complete the assembly (or compilation) process to produce the actual executable object program.   The loader determines the true relative origin (relocation base) for each program segment, normally the first free location following the instructions and data of a preceding program.   **This relocation base is then added to each address marked as relocatable by the assembler.**

Special problems may arise with the relocation of addresses specified as *symbolic expressions* (Sec. 4-3).   While an expression like A + 2 will be relocated correctly if we simply add the relocation base to A, A + B + 3 will cause trouble if *both* A *and* B are relocatable addresses; the assembler may mark the line containing A + B + 3 as a "possible relocation error."   The expression A – B, on the other hand, defines an *absolute* address if both A and B are relocatable.

Note also that minicomputers making extensive use of *relative addressing* (Sec. 2-7) will require fewer computations in the relocation process.

4-19.   Linking External References.   Assemblers intended for use with a linking loader usually require the user *to list all external references* (and frequently all symbols to be used as external references by other program segments) somewhere in the program, thus,

.EXT   A1, ARG, SYMB

Note that these "global" symbols must be uniquely defined, while symbols not used as external references can be used with different meanings in different program segments without causing any trouble.

A typical linking loader for a minicomputer operates much like another assembler.   It creates a **loader symbol table** which includes the global symbols identified in each program segment, and then supplies the correct addresses after the relocation base for each program has been established. The loader symbol table is then used much like an assembler symbol table for the loader's "reassembly" job.

When a linking loader is given a library tape containing a set of utility programs (such as arithmetic or input/output routines), it will usually load only those routines which are actually requested by other programs.

4-20. Combination of Assembly-language Programs and FORTRAN Programs. Combinations of assembly-language and FORTRAN program segments are of substantial practical importance because:

1. FORTRAN **READ**, **WRITE**, and **FORMAT** statements are often the most convenient way to call the complicated formatting and I/O routines required to deal with numerical data on standard peripherals such as card readers and line printers. This is true even for minicomputers with relatively convenient input/output macros (see also Secs. 5-27 to 5-32).

2. Frequently used or special-purpose program segments may be written in assembly language for efficient execution and called as subroutines or functions by FORTRAN programs. Again, input/output routines, this time for nonstandard peripherals, are good examples.

In general, the FORTRAN compiler for a given minicomputer will expand a call to an assembly-language subroutine, say

$$\text{CALL} \qquad \text{SUBR (I,K)}$$

into code corresponding to a standardized assembly-language calling sequence specified in the computer reference manual, e.g.,

.EXT	**SUBR** /	External reference
JUMP AND SAVE INDIRECT VIA	**SUBR** /	Subroutine jump
JUMP	**.+ 3** /	Jump around arguments
	/	after return
.DEFINE ADDRESS	**I**	
.DEFINE ADDRESS	**K**	

and the assembly-language subroutine must access **I** and **K** accordingly (Sec. 4-14). The FORTRAN compiler will expect a similar calling sequence when an assembly-language program calls a FORTRAN subroutine **SUBR (I,K)**. Refer to your minicomputer manual for the specific conventions used to access floating-point or double-precision data.

MACROS AND CONDITIONAL ASSEMBLY

4-21. Macros. (a) Macro Definitions and Macro Calls. A **macroassembler** allows the user to define an entire sequence of assembly-language statements as a **macro instruction (macro)** called by a symbolic name. Each macro is created by a *macro definition*, e.g.,

```
.MACRO      SUM      Z,X,Y
LOAD ACCUMULATOR              X
ADD INTO ACCUMULATOR         Y
STORE ACCUMULATOR IN         Z
.ENDMACRO
```

The pseudo-instruction words **.MACRO** and **.ENDMACRO** delimit the macro definition; **SUM** is the **macro name,** and **Z, X, Y** are **dummy arguments.** Once the macro is defined (which could be anywhere in a program), the user can employ a one-line **macro call** to generate the entire code sequence with new arguments as often as desired. Thus, the user-program sequence

```
START    SUM      A,A1,A2
         SUM      B,B1,B2
```

will produce code (and, if desired, a listing) corresponding to

```
START    LOAD ACCUMULATOR         A1      Expansion
         ADD INTO ACCUMULATOR     A2      of
         STORE ACCUMULATOR IN     A       SUM A,A1,A2
         LOAD ACCUMULATOR         B1      Expansion
         ADD INTO ACCUMULATOR     B2      of
         STORE ACCUMULATOR IN     B       SUM B,B1,B2
```

Note that the label **START** was not part of the macro-call expansion.

A macro may or may not have arguments. Arguments can be symbols, expressions, numbers, or literal constants and can appear as location tags as well as addresses. The better macroassemblers permit calls to other macros within a macro definition (see Sec. 4-22*b* for an example).

Calls to *the same* macro (**recursive** macro calls) lead to complications but can produce interesting program sequences when used in conjunction with conditional assembly (Sec 4-23; see also Ref. 9).

Beware of unintentionally using symbols other than arguments in macro definitions; they will stay the same in different macro-call expansions and may cause overwriting. Thus, if a sequence like

```
TEST    SKIP IF ACCUMULATOR POSITIVE
        JUMP TO                 ACT
        JUMP TO                 ACT +2
ACT     INVERT ACCUMULATOR
```

appears in a macro definition, *it should be replaced with*

SKIP IF ACCUMULATOR POSITIVE
JUMP TO   **.+2**
JUMP TO   **.+3**
INVERT ACCUMULATOR

Some macroassemblers have the facility of automatically "creating" new symbolic labels in such situations when the macro is called more than once, but the necessary procedures rather complicate programming.

(b) Importance of Macros. Macros are not simply a programming convenience or shorthand notation: their power in enlarging the scope of assembly-language programming can hardly be overemphasized. A macroassembler permits you to create and use entire classes of new computer operations, which can *simplify programming* and/or *help with applications-related modeling.*

(c) Macros and Subroutines. As we saw in Sec. 4-14, functional program modules can also be called as *subroutines*, with arguments and results in appropriate calling sequences. It is important to distinguish between subroutines and macros. Each macro call will generate *new in-line code* so that long macros will *not* save memory like long subroutines. Short macros can be more economical than short subroutines because of the overhead associated with subroutine jumps, calling sequence, and data transfers; in any case, macros will execute more quickly.

Macro calls with multiple arguments are more "natural" for most programmers than subroutine calling sequences. Hence it is convenient to define the complete data-transfer and calling sequences of frequently used subroutines as **subroutine-calling macros.** This technique is used, in particular, to define *system macros calling input/output subroutines* (Sec. 5-31).

4-22. Two Interesting Applications. (a) Computer Emulation. To emulate the operation (instruction set) of a different digital computer on an existing "host" computer, we can write a macro for each computer instruction to be simulated. If we can take care of input/output, our "host" computer should then be able to run any assembly-language program written for the emulated "target" computer.

EXAMPLE: Emulation of indexed addition on a single-accumulator minicomputer. The memory location INDEX simulates a single index register in the "target" computer.

```
.MACRO    ADDX    A
STORE ACCUMULATOR IN     SAVAC / Save accumulator
LOAD ACCUMULATOR         (A)   / Compute
ADD INTO ACCUMULATOR     INDEX /    indexed
STORE ACCUMULATOR IN     ADDR  /    address
LOAD ACCUMULATOR         SAVAC / Restore accumulator
ADD INDIRECT VIA         ADDR  / Perform addition
.ENDMACRO
```

Note that in this example the temporary-storage symbols SAVAC and ADDR will *not* cause trouble in later macro calls.

See also Sec. 6-13 for other computer-emulation techniques (micro-programming).

(b) Writing Simple Procedural Languages. Macros make it possible to write application programs solely in terms of operations directly related to the user's application. Once the macros have been written (perhaps by a professional programmer), the lucky user will be able to write his application programs using only a few simple rules (syntax) *without knowing any assembly*

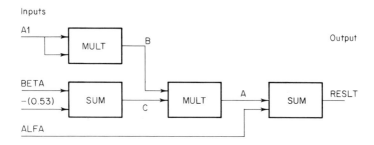

Fig. 4-12. A block diagram producing
$$RESLT = A1^2(BETA - 0.53) + ALFA$$

language at all. As a generally applicable example, we shall develop a block-diagram language suitable for doing any sort of arithmetic and/or function generation with fixed-point numbers (integers and scaled fractions, Sec. 1-8). The user need not know assembly language; the block-diagram language will actually be a simple substitute for a compiler language and will generate remarkably efficient code.

Scaled-fraction *inputs* $X1, X2, \ldots$ and *outputs* $Y1, Y2, \ldots$ will be referred to as symbolic locations, whose contents can be accessed by input/output routines (which can also be called in macro form) as needed. We now define a set of macros for *algebraic-operation blocks* (Table 4-1), plus extra blocks for function generation (sine, cosine, table-lookup functions) if we need them. *We can now combine such blocks to compute any reasonable scaled expression,* say

$$RESLT = A1^2(BETA - 0.53) + ALFA$$

in terms of a corresponding *block diagram*, much like an analog-computer block diagram (Fig. 4-12). We can then write an assembly-language routine producing the desired expression by simply listing the block macros

TABLE 4-1. Macros for a Simple Block-diagram Language (Sec. 4-22*b*).

Extra blocks, such as function-generator blocks (sine, cosine, table-lookup functions) can be added at will.   *X*, *Y*, and *Z* are scaled fractions.

.MACRO SUM Z, X, Y		/ $Z = X + Y$
LOAD ACCUMULATOR	X	
CLEAR OVERFLOW FLAG		
ADD INTO ACCUMULATOR	Y	
OTEST	Z	/ Overflow-test macro, see below
STORE ACCUMULATOR IN	Z	
.ENDMACRO		
.MACRO NEGATE Z,X		/ $Z = -X$
LOAD ACCUMULATOR	X	
INVERT ACCUMULATOR		
STORE ACCUMULATOR IN	Z	
.ENDMACRO		
.MACRO SCALE Z, X, M		/ $Z = 2^M X$, where M is a positive integer
LOAD ACCUMULATOR	X	
CLEAR OVERFLOW FLAG		
LONG SIGNED SHIFT LEFT, M BITS		
OTEST	Z	
STORE ACCUMULATOR IN	Z	
.ENDMACRO		
.MACRO MULT Z, X, Y		/ $Z = XY$
LOAD ACCUMULATOR	X	
MULTIPLY BY	Y	/ $XY/2$ in accumulator (Sec. 1-9)
LONG SIGNED SHIFT LEFT, 1 BIT		/ XY in accumulator
STORE ACCUMULATOR IN	Z	
.ENDMACRO		
.MACRO DIV Z, X, Y		/ $Z = X/Y$
LOAD ACCUMULATOR	X	
CLEAR OVERFLOW FLAG		
DIVIDE BY	Y	
OTEST	Z	
MOVE MQ TO ACCUMULATOR		
STORE ACCUMULATOR IN	Z	
.ENDMACRO		
.MACRO OTEST	Z	/ Test for overflow of fraction
SKIP ON OVERFLOW FLAG		/ Overflow?
JUMP TO	. + 3	/ No, go on
LOAD ACCUMULATOR	(Z)	/ Identifies guilty variable for error-message routine
JUMP TO	ERROR	/ Error-message routine
.ENDMACRO		

with their input and output variables:

```
        .DECIMAL
START   MULT    B, A1, A1
        SUM     C, BETA, (−0.53)
        MULT    A, B, C
        SUM     RESLT, A, ALFA
```

As in any procedural language, *we have taken care to write any intermediate result* A, B, C, *as well as the result* RESLT *only if it has been computed* (*as a block output*) *in a preceding line.* Such a program is most easily written when we start with the *last* block: Our simple scheme is, in fact, simulating the reverse Polish string generated by an algebraic compiler! After some practice, we may not even have to draw the block diagram.

Our simple block-diagram language generates quite efficient code (probably better than most minicomputer FORTRAN). It includes an error-message routine (not shown in Table 4-1) which will print out the symbol-table number of any block-output variable which overflows because of faulty scaling. A similar set of blocks could readily be written for floating-point arithmetic.

Expansion of our macro blocks shows that almost all block macros end with STORE ACCUMULATOR IN Q, which is often followed by LOAD ACCUMULATOR Q in the next macro. Such store/fetch pairs are redundant; each wastes four memory cycles. Our block-diagram language can be modified (or reprocessed) to cancel redundant store/fetch pairs (Refs. 9 and 10); the resulting code can be as efficient as that written by a good assembly-language programmer.

4-23. Conditional Assembly. **Conditional assembly** directs the assembler *to suppress specified sections of code unless stated conditions are met by the program at assembly time.* Conditional assembly is available with some ordinary assemblers but is most useful with macroassemblers. One can, in particular, modify the definitions of user-defined or system macros if named symbols do or do not appear in the program or if certain symbolic variables are zero, positive, or negative at *assembly time.*

Specifically, all statements (instructions and/or data) between the pseudo instructions .IFDEF X and .ENDCOND will be assembled if and only if the named symbol X is defined anywhere in the program. Other conditions are similarly employed by the pseudo instructions .IFUNDEF, .IFZERO, .IFNONZR, .IFPOS, .IFNEG. Note that the condition expressed by

$$.\text{IFZERO} \quad A - B$$

means that the symbols A and B reference the same variable or memory location.

As a very simple example, consider a multi-input summer block for the simple algebraic block-diagram language of Sec. 4-22*b*. We will write a macro to add a maximum of four inputs, $X1$, $X2$, $X3$, and $X4$, to produce an output Z:

```
.MACRO      SUMR           Z, X1, X2, X3, X4
   LOAD ACCUMULATOR        X1
   CLEAR OVERFLOW FLAG
   ADD INTO ACCUMULATOR    X2
.IFDEF                      X3
   ADD INTO ACCUMULATOR    X3
.ENDCOND
.IFDEF                      X4
   ADD INTO ACCUMULATOR    X4
.ENDCOND
   OTEST
   STORE ACCUMULATOR IN    Z
.ENDMACRO
```

We now see the beauty of the conditional-assembly feature. If our four-input summer is given only *three* inputs, say **X1**, **X2**, and **X4**, with **X3** undefined in our program, then the assembler will omit the unneeded **ADD INTO ACCUMULATOR X3**; this saves memory and execution time. We could similarly omit **X4** or both **X3** and **X4**.

4-24. Nested Macro Definitions. We mentioned in Sec. 4-21 that macro definitions may contain macro *calls* (see also Table 4-1). A macro definition which contains another macro *definition*, as in

```
.MACRO      MAC1           Z, X
   LOAD ACCUMULATOR        X
   STORE ACCUMULATOR IN    Z
.MACRO      MAC2           U, V
   XOR INTO ACCUMULATOR    V
   STORE ACCUMULATOR IN    U
.ENDMACRO
   ROTATE ACCUMULATOR LEFT
.ENDMACRO
```

(nested definitions), is a different situation. The assembler regards **MAC2** as *undefined* in the part of our program preceding the first call for **MAC1**, say

```
MAC1     P, Q
```

This results in the expansion

```
LOAD ACCUMULATOR              Q
STORE ACCUMULATOR IN          P
ROTATE ACCUMULATOR LEFT
```

Note that *no code due to* **MAC2** *is generated this time*, but **MAC2** is now defined and can be called either alone or through the next call to **MAC1**. Multiple nesting of definitions is possible. We have here another means of turning assembly of a section of code off and on.

REFERENCES AND BIBLIOGRAPHY

1. Flores, I.: *Computer Programming*, Prentice-Hall, Englewood Cliffs, N.J., 1966.
2. ———: *Computer Software*, Prentice-Hall, Englewood Cliffs, N.J., 1965.
3. Gear, C. W.: *Computer Organization and Programming*, McGraw-Hill, New York, 1969.
4. Maurer, W. D.: *Programming: An Introduction to Computer Languages and Techniques*, Academic Press, New York, 1969.
5. *Introduction to Programming*, PDP-8 Handbook Series, Digital Equipment Corporation, Maynard, Mass. (current edition).
6. *Programming Languages*, PDP-8 Handbook Series, Digital Equipment Corporation, Maynard, Mass. (current edition).
7. *MACRO-15 Manual*, Digital Equipment Corporation, Maynard, Mass. (current edition).
8. *DAP/15 Mod 2 Assembler Manual*, Honeywell Information Systems, Framingham, Mass. (current edition).
9. McIlroy, M. D.: Macro-instruction Extensions of Compiler Languages, *Comm. ACM*, April 1960.
10. Liebert, T. A.: "The DARE II Simulation System," Ph.D. thesis, University of Arizona, 1970.

CHAPTER 5

INTERFACING THE MINICOMPUTER
WITH THE OUTSIDE WORLD

INTRODUCTION AND SURVEY

The exceptional power of the small digital computer is substantially based on its ready interaction with real-world devices—analog-to-digital converters (ADCs), digital-to-analog converters (DACs), transducers, displays, logic controllers, alarm systems—in addition to the usual card readers, line printers, and tape drives. To the outside world, the minicomputer presents a relatively small number (30 to 80) of bus-line terminations. These lines transmit and receive digital data words together with a few command pulses and control levels, which select devices and functions or alert the computer, in turn, to new real-world situations.

This chapter introduces the basic logic and programming principles for such interfaces. With inexpensive, off-the-shelf digital and analog system components widely and readily available, a little knowledge of interfacing principles can produce dramatically effective new systems and also surprising cost savings. A handful of integrated circuits, cards, and connectors, which you can wire-wrap yourself for a total cost of $500, quite easily gets to be a $3,000 subsystem if you purchase it from an instrument manufacturer.

Sections 5-1 through 5-8 deal with *program-controlled input/output and sensing operations*. Sections 5-9 to 5-16 describe minicomputer *interrupt systems*—the basic means for time-sharing the small computers between different time-critical tasks. Sections 5-17 to 5-23 deal with *direct memory access* and *automatic block transfers*, which permit not only remarkable time savings but also more manageable input/output programming. The remainder of the chapter adds a little *hardware know-how* and discusses the elements of *input/output programming*. Additional applications and examples will be given in Chap. 7.

PROGRAMMED I/O OPERATIONS

5-1. The Party-line I/O Bus. Minicomputers usually transmit digital data on **parallel 8- to 18-bit buses;** i.e., all data bits are transmitted simultaneously in the interest of processing speed. Serial data transmission is usually restricted to communication links.

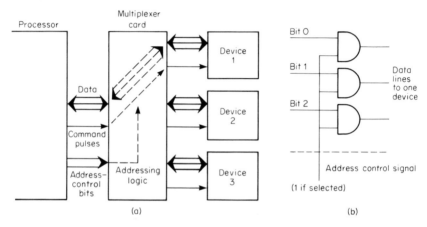

Fig. 5-1. Simple switching (multiplexing) of multiple bus lines with a multiplexer card in the processor cabinet (*a*) and switching circuits for one set of processor output data lines (*b*). In this arrangement, bus-driving circuits are loaded only by one processor-to-device bus at a time, and no device addresses need be transmitted over the bus. But multiple-line switching becomes cumbersome if there are more than a few devices.

The 8- to 18-data-bit lines can be **bidirectional** (this takes extra logic at each device, Fig. 5-19*c*), or we can have separate **input and output buses.** (This takes less logic but more interconnections, Fig. 5-19*b*.) In addition to the data lines, we will need a comparable number of **interface-control-logic lines.**

If the computer must service only a few external devices, processor instructions can select individual buses for each device through multiplexing gates (Fig. 5-1). But the circuits needed to multiplex data and control lines for more than 4 (and perhaps as many as 1,000) devices could compromise the processor design. Thus, most interface systems employ a **party-line I/O bus** of the general type illustrated in Fig. 5-2. Here, *all* "devices" (printers, displays, ADCs, DACs, etc.) intended to receive or transmit data words are wired to a parallel I/O data bus connected to a processor register via suitable logic. Additional party-line wires carry control-logic signals for selecting a specific device and its function (e.g., transmission or reception) and synchronize data transfers with the digital-computer operating cycle.

5-2.   Program-controlled Device Selection and Operation.   For a minimum of linkage hardware, interfaces work with programmed digital-computer instructions (**input/output instructions, I/O instructions**; refer to Sec. 5-17 for

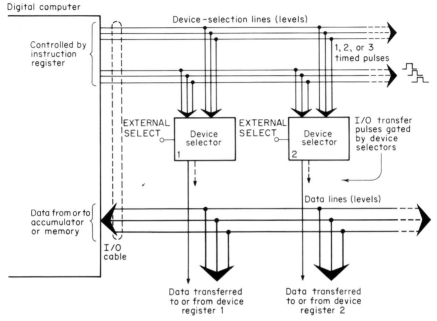

Fig. 5-2. Programmed control of multiple devices by a minicomputer with a party-line I/O bus. An I/O instruction addressed to a specific device is recognized by a device selector, which gates data-transfer or command pulses to the device in question (*based on Ref.* 6).

direct-memory-access operation).   **Figure 5-3 shows how the individual bits of an input/output instruction word in a typical processor determine device-selection and control-line signals on a party-line I/O bus:**

1. Bits 0 to 4 tell the processor that an I/O instruction is wanted.   One of these bits can select a READ or WRITE operation, or this decision may be left to a logic input from the device.
2. Bits 5 to 10 (**device-address bits**) place logic levels (0 or 1) on **device-selection lines** parallel-connected to all devices on the I/O bus.   When these lines carry the **device-selection code** assigned to a specific device, its **device selector** (decoding AND gate) accepts (and regenerates) a set of one, two, or three successive command pulses (IO pulses) used to effect data transfers and other operations in the selected device as determined by instruction bits 13 to 15.

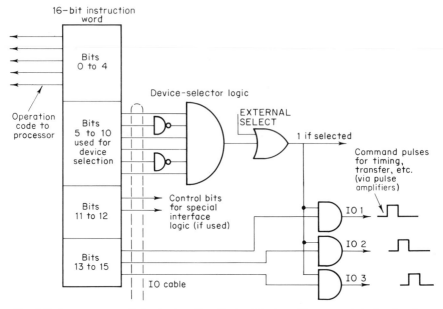

Fig. 5-3. Program-controlled selection (decoding) of device addresses and device functions (*based on Ref. 6*).

3. Bits 11 and 12 (**control bits, select bits,** or **subdevice bits**) determine levels on two control lines. These can be used to select additional devices or different functions to be performed by a given device.

4. Bits 13, 14, and 15, respectively, produce successive timed **command pulses** IO1, IO2, and IO3 on three separate control lines. A pulse occurs if the corresponding bit is 1.

With the arrangement of Fig. 5-3, a 16-bit I/O instruction can select one of $2^{11} = 2,048$ possible devices and/or device functions through different combinations of device-address bits, control bits, and command pulses. This particular system requires four complete digital-computer memory cycles for each I/O operation, one to fetch the instruction, and one for each IO pulse. Many modifications of our basic programmed-I/O scheme are possible, e.g.,

1. Different numbers of processor-code bits, device-selection bits, control bits, and IO pulses may be used.

2. IO pulses can be simultaneous (on different lines), rather than successive, to save execution time.

Some more incisive modifications will be described in Secs. 5-6, 5-7, and 6-9.

5-3. Programmed Data Transfers. The most common application of the device-selector-gated command pulses is **data transfer to and from the**

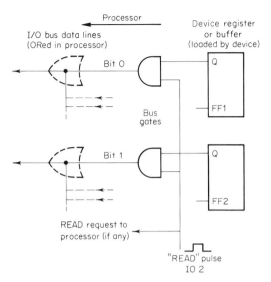

Fig. 5-4a. Programmed transfer of data into the processor.

processor. In our basic programmed-I/O scheme, the IO pulses are synchronized with the processor operation cycle, and thus with the computer's ability to accept or transmit data.

In Fig. 5-4*a*, the correctly timed IO2 pulse gates data **from an external device** (e.g., an ADC) **into a processor register (accumulator)** via the I/O-bus data lines.

Figure 5-4*b* illustrates **clear-and-strobe data transfer** from the I/O data lines into the flip-flops of a device register. Each flip-flop is first cleared by

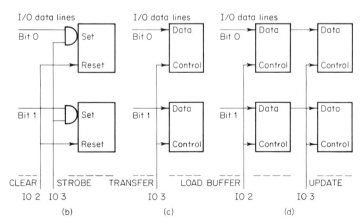

Fig. 5-4b to d. Programmed data transfer into device registers: clear-and-strobe (*b*) jam transfer (*c*) and transfer through a device buffer register, as in a double-buffered digital-to-analog converter (*d*).

IO2; then IO3 strobes the 1s on the data bus into the flip-flop register. Figure 5-4c shows **jam transfer** of bus data into a device register (see also Sec. 1-6). Jam transfers require only a single transfer pulse and must be employed whenever clearing and strobing operations would disturb device functions. This is true, for instance, with DACs required to switch through successive voltage levels without returning to 0 in between.

Figure 5-4d illustrates a **double-buffered-register data transfer.** Data are first transferred into the buffer register and then into the device register proper. In an analog/hybrid computer or display system, for instance, one can load a set of DAC buffer registers in turn and then "update" all DAC registers simultaneously with another I/O instruction or with a clock pulse.

5-4. Device Control Registers. Many peripheral devices have more different functions or operating modes than we can control with a few control bits or IO-pulse bits in a single I/O instruction. Such devices can be designed to accept, store, and execute multibit "device instructions" loaded into a **device control register** or registers via the I/O-bus data lines (just like into a data register). In general, control registers will require jam transfers or double-buffered transfers (Fig. 5-4b and c). An important example of a control register is the multiplexer control register for selecting different multiplexer input channels for an ADC. Control registers may permit incrementation; i.e., the control register can be a counter set to a given initial count by an I/O instruction and then incremented by I/O pulses as needed; the variety of possible arrangements is endless. Control registers of many old-fashioned process controllers simply operate *electromechanical relays.*

Typical examples of more complex devices whose status and function are established by computer-controlled registers are process controllers, cathode-ray-tube displays (Sec. 7-9), automatic data channels (Sec. 5-19), analog/hybrid computers (Sec. 7-18), and other digital computers.

5-5. Interfacing with Incremental and Serial Data Representations. Device-selector-gated command pulses (IO pulses) are not used only to transfer data and control-register settings. Command pulses can also **set, reset, or complement special flip-flops** and **increment or decrement counters** in device interfaces (Fig. 5-5).

Computer-read digital counters can also accumulate external **incremental data** (variables proportional to pulse rates) into parallel digital words. Incremental data representation is employed in control and navigation systems based on *digital-differential-analyzer (DDA) integrators* (Ref. 19).

Digital communication systems, teletypewriter keyboard/printers, and disk or drum storage systems employ **serial data representation** (Sec. 1-3). **Parallel-to-serial** and **serial-to-parallel conversion** is accomplished by either

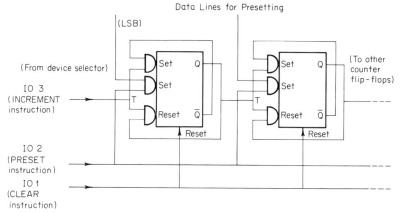

Fig. 5-5. Three different processor instructions employ one of three successive command pulses from the same device selector to clear, strobe, or increment a binary counter. A fourth instruction combines IO1 and IO2 for clear-and-strobe presetting (see also Table 1-5*b*).

of two methods:

1. Serial *n*-bit data words (usually 8-bit bytes) are shifted in or out of a **shift register** in the interface by shift pulses from a clock oscillator, which is stopped by a control counter after *n*, *n* + 1, or *n* + 2 shift pulses. The extra shift pulses transmit or receive start and stop bits marking spaces between serial words in some systems. The shift register is parallel-loaded or read by the digital computer like any other device register.

2. Shift pulses cause interrupt-activated processor instructions for shifting data words bit by bit into or out of an accumulator carry bit.

5-6. Timing Considerations: Synchronous and Asynchronous I/O Operations. Programmed data-transfer operations with processor-timed command pulses require that an external device accept or transmit data levels within the allotted instruction time. More specifically, timing diagrams like Fig. 5-6, supplied in every minicomputer interface manual, show (perhaps obviously) that *a set of data-bit levels must be established when the processor issues the data-transfer command pulse (IO pulse)*.

We will assume here that our device (say an ADC) is already *prepared* to transfer data in the sense that an ADC conversion has been completed; we can, and should, make sure of this through a sense instruction (Sec. 5-8) or interrupt operation (Sec. 5-9). What we *are* concerned with here is that data levels may not be established *soon enough* or *long enough* to complete a data transfer, allowing for cable-transmission and logic delays and rise times. Cable delays are, at best, about 1.5 nsec/ft; programmed-I/O instruction timing usually allows for up to 50 ft of I/O bus cable.

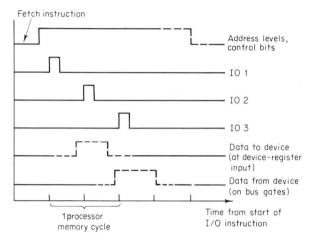

Fig. 5-6. Typical timing for processor-synchronized programmed data transfers. Data levels must be ready for the bus when transfer pulses occur.

When cable and/or logic delays become critical, we can escape the tyranny of the processor clock through **asynchronous ("hand-shaking") I/O operations.** An asynchronous data-transfer instruction addresses an external device with address levels, as in Sec. 5-3. But the processor does not issue an automatically timed IO pulse. Instead, it waits until the device-selector-gate output has set an ADDRESS ACTIVE flip-flop in the addressed device (Fig. 5-7). The resulting voltage step returns to the processor over a special interface line; *only then* will the processor issue the appropriate IO pulse or pulses. The processor may now continue with the next instruction after a

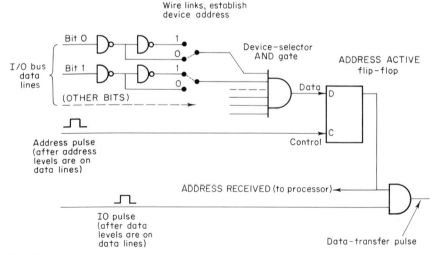

Fig. 5-7. An ADDRESS ACTIVE flip-flop (type D flip-flop, Table 1-5b) indicates reception of the device address and also stores the device-selector output when the address levels are no longer on the bus. Note that all ADDRESS ACTIVE flip-flops which are *not* addressed will be reset by the "ADDRESS" pulse. Wire links are used to set up each device address.

decent interval.   If we wish to be even more careful, the processor may not continue its operation until the data-transfer pulse actuates another device-response signal signifying that the IO pulse has been received and that the data transfer is complete.

5-7.   Minicomputers Using Data Lines for Device Addressing.   To save interconnections at the expense of time and interface hardware, some minicomputer I/O systems transmit the device address over the *data lines*. After the address levels are on the bus, an ADDRESS control level or pulse from the processor sets an ADDRESS ACTIVE flip-flop in the addressed device and resets all other ADDRESS ACTIVE flip-flops (Fig. 5-7).   The output of the ADDRESS ACTIVE flip-flop substitutes for the simple device-selector output of Fig. 5-3; it can activate non-data-transfer operations immediately, or *it can gate data transfers from and to the bus after the address has been removed from the data lines.*   There are two main types of such systems:

1. In the Varian Data Systems 620i and 620f, the successive addressing and data-transfer operations form part of *the same* 16-bit I/O instruction; the address bits come from the processor *instruction* register, as in Sec. 5-2.
2. In the 8-bit Interdata Model 1, we must first load the desired device address into the *accumulator*.   Then *a separate addressing instruction* places the address bits from the accumulator on the data line to activate the selected device.   Data-transfer operations (to or from the accumu-lator) follow; note that one addressing operation may do for several data transfers from and/or to the same device.

5-8.   Sense-line Operation and Status Registers.   The IO pulses implement program-controlled operations at times determined by the digital-computer program.   But a device thus addressed might not be ready; an important example is an ADC which has not completed a conversion.   In such cases, program-controlled data or control-logic transfers may be preceded by a **sense-line interrogation or flag test.**   The device status is indicated by a **flag** (logic level, usually a flip-flop output).   A special instruction addressed to the associated device selector gates one of the command pulses (IO1 in Fig. 5-8) into a **sense gate** and, if the flag level (sense line) is up, onto the **skip bus** in the interface cable.   The pulse on the skip bus then increments the processor instruction counter, which thus skips the next instruction to produce a program branch.   An example would be

SKIP IF ADC FLAG IS UP
REPEAT LAST INSTRUCTION
READ ADC

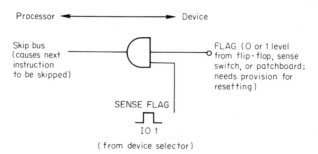

Fig. 5-8. Sense-line operation using a device selector, sensing gate, and common skip bus.

The program will cycle until the device flag is up, at which time the program continues, usually with a data-transfer instruction. The ADC flag must be *reset* by the **READ ADC** instruction and/or by the **START CONVERSION** instruction or timing pulse.

Other sense-line systems exist. Many computers do away with device-selector addressing of sense gates by simply accepting flag levels on **multiple sense lines,** which are interrogated with processor instructions like **SKIP IF SENSE LINE 5 IS UP.**

Flag logic levels controlled by manually operated **sense switches** permit a human operator to control program branching during computation.

Instead of interrogating multiple sense lines in turn, we can treat several flag flip-flops (which may or may not be associated with the same peripheral device) as a **device status register.** The processor can read this register (**READ FLAGS** or **READ STATUS** instruction) via the data bus. The resulting "status word" in the processor accumulator can then be logically interpreted by the computer program; in particular, the status word may serve as an indirect address for the next instruction and thus permit multiple branching.

Sense/skip instructions can be profitably combined with data-transfer operations. Thus, the single instruction **SKIP AND READ ADC IF ADC FLAG IS UP** combines two instructions by using the IO1 pulse to test the flag and the IO3 pulse to transfer data; the flag level itself is employed to gate IO3 off if the ADC is not ready.

I/O systems with *asynchronous data transfer* (Sec. 5-6) do not need a sense/skip loop to wait for device readiness. The device-flag level can simply operate a gate which keeps the ADDRESS RECEIVED signal in Fig. 5-7 from returning to the processor until the device is ready for the data transfer.

Sense lines are inexpensive, but even small digital computers can rarely afford the time for "idle" sense/skip loops such as the simple ADC example shown above. Sense lines are, therefore, used mainly for decisions between device-dependent program branches which do *not* cause idling. Otherwise we require *program interrupts*.

INTERRUPT SYSTEMS

5-9. Simple Interrupt-system Operations. In an **interrupt system,** a device-flag level (INTERRUPT REQUEST) **interrupts the computer program on completion of the current instruction. Processor hardware then causes a subroutine jump** (Sec. 4-12):

1. Contents of the incremented program counter and of other selected processor registers (if any) are automatically saved in specific memory locations or in spare registers.
2. The program counter is reset to start a new instruction sequence (**interrupt-service subroutine**) from a specific memory location ("trap location") associated with the interrupt. The interrupt thus acted upon is *disabled* so that it cannot interrupt its own service routine.

Minicomputer interrupt-service routines must usually first *save the contents of processor registers (such as accumulators) which are needed by the main program, but which are not saved automatically by the hardware.* We might also have to save (and later restore) some peripheral-device control registers. Only then can the actual interrupt service proceed: the service routine can transfer data after an ADC-conversion-completed interrupt, implement emergency-shutdown procedures after a power-supply failure, etc. Either the service routine or the interrupt-system hardware must then *clear the interrupt-causing flag* to prepare it for new interrupts. The service routine ends by *restoring registers and program counter to return to the original program*, like any subroutine (Sec. 4-12). As the service routine completes its job, it must also *reenable the interrupt*.

EXAMPLE: Consider a simple minicomputer which stores only the program counter automatically after an interrupt. The interrupt-service routine is to read an ADC after its conversion-complete interrupt.

Location	Label	Instruction or Word Data		Comments
		(main program)		
.		.		
.		.		
.		.		
1713		current instruction		/ Interrupt occurs here
0000		1714		/ Incremented program
				/ counter (1714) will be
				/ stored here by hard-
				/ ware
0001		JUMP TO SRVICE		/ Trap location, contains
				/ jump to relocatable
3600	SRVICE	STORE ACCUMULATOR IN	SAVAC	/ service routine

3600	SRVICE	STORE ACCUMULATOR IN	SAVAC	/ Save accumulator
3601		READ ADC		/ Read ADC into
				/ accumulator and
				/ clear ADC flag
3602		STORE ACCUMULATOR IN	X	/ Store ADC reading
3603		LOAD ACCUMULATOR	SAVAC	/ Restore accumulator
3604		INTERRUPT ON		/ Turn interrupt back on
3605		JUMP INDIRECT VIA	0000	/ Return jump
1714		(main program)		/ Interrupted program
.		.		/ continues
.		.		
.		.		

NOTE: Interrupts do not work when the computer is HALTed, so *we cannot test interrupts when stepping a program manually.*

5-10. Multiple Interrupts.   Interrupt-system operation would be simple if there were only one possible source of interrupts, but this is practically never true. Even a stand-alone digital computer usually has several interrupts corresponding to peripheral malfunctions (tape unit out of tape, printer out of paper), and flight simulators, space-vehicle controllers, and process-control systems may have *hundreds* of different interrupts.

A practical **multiple-interrupt system** will have to:

1. **"Trap" the program to different memory locations** corresponding to specific individual interrupts
2. Assign **priorities** to simultaneous or successive interrupts
3. **Store lower-priority interrupt requests** to be serviced after higher-priority routines are completed
4. **Permit higher-priority interrupts to interrupt lower-priority service routines** as soon as the return address and any automatically saved registers are safely stored

Note that programs and/or hardware must carefully **save successive levels of program-counter and register contents,** which will have to be recovered as needed. Interrupt-system programming will be further discussed in Sec. 5-16.

More sophisticated systems will be able to *reassign new priorities through programmed instructions* as the needs of a process or program change (see also Secs. 5-12, 5-14, and 5-16).

5-11. Skip-chain Identification of Interrupts.   The most primitive multiple-interrupt systems simply OR all interrupt flags onto *a single interrupt line. The interrupt-service routine then employs sense/skip instructions* (Sec. 5-8) *to test successive device flags in order of descending priority.*

Suppose that the simple interrupt system discussed in Sec. 5-9 was connected not only to the ADC requesting service but also to "emergency" interrupts from a fire alarm and from the computer power supply (Sec. 2-15). A skip-chain service routine with appropriate branches for fire alarm, emergency shutdown, and ADC might look like this (only the ADC service routine is actually shown):

SRVICE	SKIP IF FIRE-ALARM FLAG LOW		/ Fire alarm?
	JUMP TO FIRE		/ Yes, go to service / routine
	SKIP IF POWER FLAG LOW		/ No; power-supply / trouble?
	JUMP TO LOWPWR		/ Yes, go to service / routine
	SKIP IF ADC DONE FLAG LOW		/ No; ADC service / request?
	JUMP TO ADC		/ Yes, service it
	JUMP TO ERROR		/ No; spurious / interrupt—print / error message
ADC	STORE ACCUMULATOR IN SAVAC		/ ADC service routine
	READ ADC		
	STORE ACCUMULATOR IN X		
	LOAD ACCUMULATOR	SAVAC	/ Restore accumulator
	INTERRUPT ON		/ Turn interrupts back / on
	JUMP INDIRECT VIA	0000	/ Return jump

The skip-chain system requires only simple electronics and disposes of the priority problem, but the flag-sensing program is time-consuming. (n devices may require $\log_2 n$ successive decisions even if the flag sensing is done by successive binary decisions). A somewhat faster method is to employ a *flag status word* (Sec. 5-8), which can be tested bit by bit or used for indirect addressing of different service routines (Sec. 4-11a).

Note also that our primitive ORed-interrupt system must automatically disable *all* interrupts as soon and as long as any interrupt is recognized. We cannot interrupt even low-priority interrupt-service routines.

5-12. Program-controlled Interrupt Masking. It is often useful to enable (**arm**) or disable (**disarm**) individual interrupts under program control to meet special conditions. Improved multiple-interrupt systems gate individual interrupt-request lines with **mask flip-flops** which can be set and reset by programmed instructions. The ordered set of mask flip-flops is usually treated as a control register (**interrupt mask register**) which is loaded with appropriate 0s and 1s from an accumulator through a programmed I/O instruction.   Groups of interrupts quite often have a common mask flip-flop (see also Sec. 5-14).

A very important application of programmed masking instructions is to give selected portions of main programs (as well as interrupt-service routines) greater or lesser protection from interrupts.

Note that we will have to restore the mask register on returning from any interrupt-service routine which has changed the mask, so program or hardware must keep track of mask changes.   We must also still provide programmed instructions to enable and disable the entire interrupt system without changing the mask.

EXAMPLE: *A skip-chain system with mask flip-flops.*   Addition of mask flip-flops to our simple skip-chain interrupt system (Fig. 5-9) makes it practical to interrupt lower-priority service routines.   *Each such routine must now have its own memory location to save the program counter*, and the mask must be restored before the interrupt is dismissed.   The ADC service routine of Sec. 5-11 is modified as follows (all interrupts are initially disabled):

ADC	STORE ACCUMULATOR IN	SAVAC	
	LOAD ACCUMULATOR	0000	/ Save program
	STORE ACCUMULATOR IN	SAVPC	/ counter
	LOAD ACCUMULATOR	MASK	/ Save
	STORE ACCUMULATOR IN	SVMSK	/ current mask
	LOAD ACCUMULATOR	MASK 1	/ Arm higher-
	LOAD MASK REGISTER		/ priority interrupts
	INTERRUPT ON		/ Enable interrupt system
	READ ADC		
	STORE ACCUMULATOR IN	X	
	INTERRUPT OFF		
	LOAD ACCUMULATOR	SVMSK	/ Restore
	LOAD MASK REGISTER		/ previous
	STORE ACCUMULATOR	MASK	/ mask, and
	LOAD ACCUMULATOR	SAVAC	/ restore accumulator
	INTERRUPT ON		
	JUMP INDIRECT VIA	SVPC	/ Return jump

Since most minicomputer mask registers cannot be read by the program, the mask setting is duplicated in the memory location **MASK**.   Some minicomputers (e.g., PDP-9, PDP-15, Raytheon 706) allow only a restricted set of masks and provide special instructions which simplify mask saving and restoring (see also Sec. 5-15).   Machines having two or more accumulators can reserve one of them to store the mask and thus save memory references.

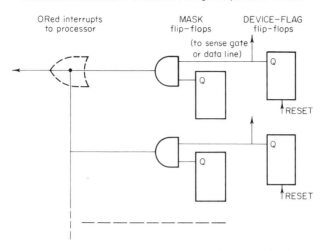

Fig. 5-9. Interrupt masking.   The mask flip-flops are treated as a control register (*mask register*), which can be cleared and loaded by I/O instructions.

5-13.   Priority-interrupt Systems: Request/Grant Logic.   We could replace the skip-chain system of Sec. 5-11 with *hardware* for polling successive interrupt lines in order of descending priority, but this is still relatively slow if there are many interrupts.   We prefer the priority-request logic of Figs. 5-10 or 5-11, which can be located in the processor, on special interface cards, and/or on individual device-controller cards.

Refer to Fig. 5-10a.   If the interrupt is not disabled by the mask flip-flop or by the PRIORITY IN line, a **service request** (device-flag level) will set the **REQUEST flip-flop,** which is clocked by periodic processor pulses (I/O SYNC) to fit the processor cycle and to time the priority decision.   The resulting timed PRIORITY REQUEST step has *three* jobs:

1. It preenables the **"ACTIVE" flip-flop** belonging to the same interrupt circuit.
2. It blocks lower-priority interrupts.
3. It informs the processor that an interrupt is wanted.

If the interrupt system is on (and if there are no direct-memory-access requests pending, Sec. 5-17), the processor answers with an **INTERRUPT ACKNOWLEDGE pulse** just before the current instruction is completed (Fig. 5-13).   This sets the preenabled "ACTIVE" flip-flop, which now gates the correct trap address onto a set of bus lines—the interrupt is **active.** INTERRUPT ACKNOWLEDGE also resets *all* REQUEST flip-flops to ready them for repeated or new priority requests.

Each interrupt has three states: **inactive, waiting** (device-flag flip-flop set), and **active.**   Waiting interrupts will be serviced as soon as possible.   Unless reset by program or hardware, the device flag maintains the "waiting" state

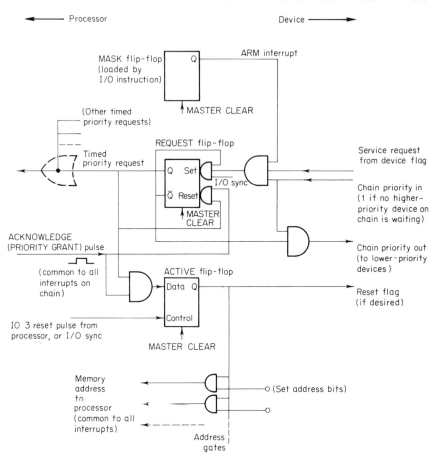

Fig. 5-10a. Priority-chain timing/queuing logic for one device (see also the timing diagram of Fig. 5-12). The ACKNOWLEDGE line is common to all interrupts on the chain. Note how the flip-flops are timed by the processor-supplied I/O SYNC pulses. MASTER CLEAR is issued by the processor whenever power is turned on, and through a console pushbutton, to reset flip-flops initially. Many different modifications of this circuit exist (see also Fig. 5-11). Similar logic is used for direct-memory-access requests.

while higher-priority service routines run and even while its interrupt is disarmed or while the entire interrupt system is turned off.

5-14. Priority Propagation and Priority Changes. There are two basic methods for suppressing lower-priority interrupts. The first is the **wired-priority-chain** method illustrated in Fig. 5-10. Referring to Fig. 5-10a, the PRIORITY IN terminal of the lowest-priority device is wired to the PRIORITY OUT terminal of the device with the next-higher priority, and so on. Thus the timed requests from higher-priority devices block lower-priority requests. The PRIORITY IN terminal of the highest-priority

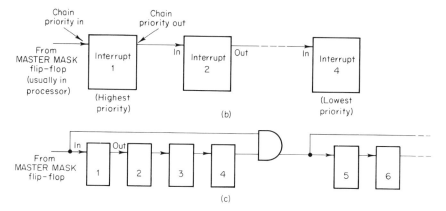

Fig. 5-10b and c. Wired-chain priority-propagation circuits. Since each subsystem (and its associated wiring) delays the propagated REQUEST flip-flop steps (Fig. 5-10a) by 10 to 30 nsec, the simple chain of Fig. 5-10b should not have more than four to six links; the circuit of Fig. 5-10c bypasses priority-inhibiting steps for faster propagation (*based on Ref.* 10).

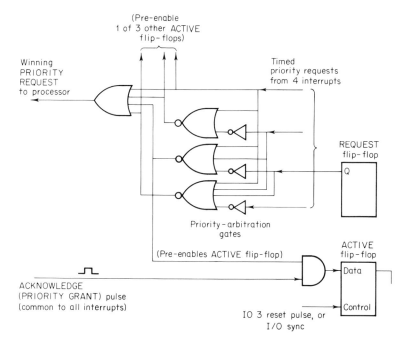

Fig. 5-11. This modified version of the priority-interrupt logic in Fig. 5-10a has priority-propagation gates at the output rather than at the input of the REQUEST flip-flop. Again, many similar circuits exist.

device (usually a power-failure, parity-error, or real-time-clock interrupt in the processor itself) connects to a processor flip-flop ("master-mask" flip-flop), which can thus arm or disarm the entire chain (Fig. 5-10*b* and *c*).

The computer program can load mask-register flip-flops (Fig. 5-10*a*) to *disarm* selected interrupts in such a wired chain, but the relative priorities of all armed interrupts are determined by their positions in the chain. It is possible, though, to assign two or more different priorities to a given device flag: we connect it to two or more separate priority circuits in the chain and arm one of them under program or device control.

Figure 5-11 illustrates the second type of priority-propagation logic, which permits every armed interrupt to set its REQUEST flip-flop. The timed PRIORITY REQUEST steps from different interrupts are combined in a **"priority-arbitration" gate circuit,** which lets only the highest-priority REQUEST step pass to preenable its "ACTIVE" flip-flop. Some larger digital computers implement dynamic priority reallocation by modifying their priority-arbitration logic under program control, but most mini-computers are content with programmed masking.

The two priority-propagation schemes can be *combined*. Several mini-computer systems (e.g., PDP-9, PDP-15) employ four separate wired-priority chains, each armed or disarmed by a common "master-mask" flip-flop in the processor. Interrupts from the four chains are combined through a priority-arbitration network which, together with the program-controlled "master-mask" flip-flops, establishes the relative priorities of the four chains.

5-15. Complete Priority-interrupt Systems. **(a) Program-controlled Address Transfer.** The "ACTIVE" flip-flop in Fig. 5-10*a* or 5-11 places the starting address of the correct interrupt-service routine on a set of address lines common to all interrupts. Automatic or "hardware" priority-interrupt systems will then immediately trap to the desired address (Sec. 5-15*b*). But in many small computers (e.g., PDP-8 series, SUPERNOVA), the priority logic is only an add-on card for a basic single-level (ORed) interrupt system. Such systems cannot access different trap addresses directly. With the interrupt system on, *every* PRIORITY REQUEST disables further interrupts and causes the program to trap to *the same* memory location, say 0000, and to store the program counter, just as in Sec. 5-9. The trap location contains a jump to the service routine

```
SRVICE    STORE ACCUMULATOR IN      SAVAC    / Unless we have
                                             /   a spare
                                             /   accumulator

          READ INTERRUPT ADDRESS
          STORE ACCUMULATOR IN      PTR
          JUMP INDIRECT VIA         PTR
```

READ INTERRUPT ADDRESS is an ordinary I/O instruction, which employs a device selector to read the interrupt-address lines into the accumulator (Sec. 5-9). The IO2 pulse from the device selector can serve as the ACKNOWLEDGE pulse in Fig. 5-10a or 5-11 (in fact, the "ACTIVE" flip-flop can be omitted in this simple system). The program then transfers the address word to a pointer location **PTR** in memory, and an indirect jump lands us where we want to be.

Unfortunately, the service routine for each individual device, say for an ADC, must save and restore program counter, mask, *and* accumulator (see also Sec. 5-12):

```
ADC   LOAD ACCUMULATOR            0000
      STORE ACCUMULATOR IN        SAVPC
      LOAD ACCUMULATOR            SAVAC
      STORE ACCUMULATOR IN        SAVAC2
      LOAD ACCUMULATOR            MASK
      STORE ACCUMULATOR IN        SVMSK
      LOAD ACCUMULATOR            MASK 1
      STORE ACCUMULATOR           MASK
      LOAD MASK REGISTER
      INTERRUPT ON
      READ ADC                                / Useful work
      STORE ACCUMULATOR IN        X           /   done only here!
      INTERRUPT OFF
      LOAD ACCUMULATOR            SVMSK
      STORE ACCUMULATOR           MASK
      LOAD MASK REGISTER
      LOAD ACCUMULATOR            SAVAC 2
      INTERRUPT ON
      JUMP INDIRECT VIA           SAVPC
```

Note that most of the time and memory used up by this routine is **overhead** devoted to storing and saving registers.

(b) A Fully Automatic ("Hardware") Priority-interrupt System. In an **automatic** or **"hardware" priority-interrupt system,** the "ACTIVE" flip-flop in Fig. 5-10a or 5-11 gates the trap address of the active interrupt into the processor memory address register as soon as the current instruction is completed (Fig. 5-12). This requires special **address lines** in the input/output bus and a little extra processor logic. This hardware buys improved response time and simplifies programming:

1. **The program traps immediately to a different trap location for each interrupt;** there is no need for the program to identify the interrupt.
2. There is no need to save program counter and registers twice as in Secs. 5-11, 5-12, and 5-15a.

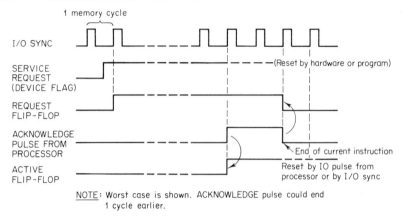

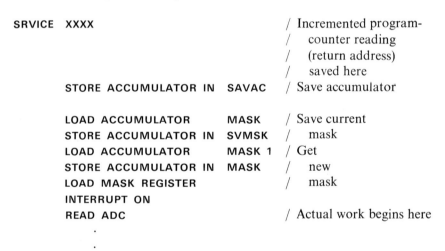

Fig. 5-12. Timing diagram for the priority-interrupt logic of Figs. 5-10 and 5-11. The ACKNOWLEDGE pulse remains ON until the trap address is transferred (either immediately over special address lines or by a programmed instruction).

In a typical system, each hardware-designated trap location is loaded with a modified **JUMP AND SAVE** instruction (Sec. 2-11). Its effective address, say **SRVICE**, will store the interrupt return address (plus some status bits); this is followed by the interrupt-service routine, which can be relocatable:

```
SRVICE  XXXX                              / Incremented program-
                                          /     counter reading
                                          /     (return address)
                                          /     saved here
        STORE ACCUMULATOR IN  SAVAC       / Save accumulator

        LOAD ACCUMULATOR      MASK        / Save current
        STORE ACCUMULATOR IN  SVMSK       /     mask
        LOAD ACCUMULATOR      MASK 1      / Get
        STORE ACCUMULATOR IN  MASK        /     new
        LOAD MASK REGISTER                /     mask
        INTERRUPT ON
        READ ADC                          / Actual work begins here
            .
            .
            .
```

Saving (and later restoring) the interrupt mask in this program is the same as in Secs. 5-12 and 5-15a and is seen to be quite a cumbersome operation. A little extra processor hardware can simplify this job:

1. We can combine the **LOAD MASK REGISTER** and **INTERRUPTION** instructions into a single I/O instruction.

2. We can use only masks disarming *all* interrupts with priorities *below* level 1, 2, 3, ... Such simple masks are easier to store automatically.

In the more sophisticated interrupt systems, the interrupt return-jump instruction is replaced by a special instruction (**RETURN FROM INTERRUPT**), which automatically restores the program-counter reading and all automatically saved registers. Be sure to consult the interface manual for your own minicomputer to determine which hardware features and software techniques are available.

5-16. Discussion of Interrupt-system Features and Applications. Interrupts are the basic mechanism for sharing a digital computer between different, often time-critical, tasks. The practical effectiveness of a minicomputer interrupt system will depend on:

1. **The time needed to service possibly critical situations**
2. **The total time and program overhead** imposed by saving, restoring, and masking operations associated with interrupts
3. The number of priority levels needed versus the number which can be readily implemented
4. Programming flexibility and convenience

The minimum time needed to obtain service will include:

1. The "raw" **latency time,** i.e., the time needed to complete the longest possible processor instruction (including any indirect addressing); most minicomputers are also designed so that the processor will always execute the instruction following any **I/O READ** or **SENSE/ SKIP** instruction. We are sure you will be able to tell why! **Check your interface manual.**
2. The time needed for any necessary saving and/or masking operation.

A look at the interrupt-service programs of Secs. 5-11, 5-12, 5-15*a*, and 5-15*b* will illustrate how successively more sophisticated priority-interrupt systems provide faster service with less overhead. You should, however, take a hard-nosed attitude to establish whether you really need the more advanced features in your specific application.

It is useful at this point to list the principal applications of interrupts. Many interrupts are associated with I/O routines for relatively slow devices such as teletypewriters and tape reader/punches, and thousands of minicomputers service these happily with simple skip-chain systems. Things become more critical in instrumentation and control systems, which must not miss real-time-clock interrupts intended to log time, to read instruments, or to perform control operations. Time-critical jobs require *fast responses*. If there are many time-critical operations or any time-sharing computations, *the computing time wasted in overhead operations* becomes interesting. Some real-time systems may have periods of peak loads when it becomes actually impossible to service *all* interrupt requests.   At this point, the designer must decide whether to buy an improved system or which interrupt requests are at least temporarily expendable.   It is in the latter connection that *dynamic priority allocation* becomes useful: it may, for instance, be expedient *to mask certain interrupts during peak-load periods.*   In other situations we might, instead, *lower the relative priority of the main computer program by unmasking additional interrupts during peak real-time loads.*

If two or more interrupt-service routines employ the same library sub-routine, we are faced, as in Sec. 4-16, with the problem of *reentrant programming.*   Temporary-storage locations used by the common sub-routine may be wiped out unless we either duplicate the subroutine program in memory for each interrupt or unless we provide true reentrant subroutines. This is not usually the case for FORTRAN-compiler-supplied library routines.   Only a few minicomputer manufacturers and software houses provide reentrant FORTRAN (sometimes called "real-time" FORTRAN). The best way to store saved registers and temporary intermediate results is in a stack (Sec. 4-16); a stack pointer is advanced whenever a new interrupt is recognized and retracted when an interrupt is dismissed.   *The best mini-computer interrupt systems have hardware for automatically advancing and retracting such a stack pointer* (Sec. 6-10).

If very fast interrupt service is not a paramount consideration, *we can get around reentrant coding by programming interrupt masks which simply prevent interruption of critical service routines.*

In conclusion, remember that the chief purpose of interrupt systems is to initiate computer operations more complicated than simple data transfers. The best method for time-critical reading and writing as such is not through interrupt-service routines with their awkward programming overhead but with a *direct-memory-access system,* which has no such problems at all.

DIRECT MEMORY ACCESS AND AUTOMATIC BLOCK TRANSFERS

5-17. Cycle Stealing.   Step-by-step program-controlled data transfers limit data-transmission rates and use valuable processor time for alternate instruction fetches and execution; programming is also tedious.   It is often preferable to use additional hardware for interfacing a parallel data bus directly with the digital-computer memory data register and to request and grant 1-cycle pauses in processor operation for **direct transfer of data to or from memory** (**interlace** or **cycle-stealing** operation).   In larger digital machines, and optionally in a few minicomputers (PDP-15), a data bus can even access one memory bank without stopping processor interaction with other memory banks at all.

Note that **cycle stealing in no way disturbs the program sequence.**   Even though smaller digital computers must stop computation during memory transfers, the program simply skips a cycle at the end of the current memory cycle (no need to complete the current *instruction*) and later resumes just where it left off.   One does not have to save register contents or other information, as with program interrupts.

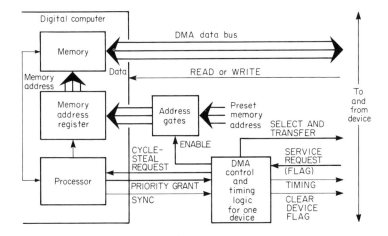

Fig. 5-13. A direct-memory-access (DMA) interface.

5-18.   DMA Interface Logic.   To make **direct memory access (DMA)** practical, the interface must be able to:

1.   **Address desired locations in memory**
2.   Synchronize cycle stealing with processor operation
3.   **Initiate transfers** by device requests (this includes clock-timed transfers) or by the computer program
4.   Deal with **priorities** and queuing of service requests if two or more devices request data transfers

DMA priority/queuing logic is essentially the same as the priority-interrupt logic of Figs. 5-10 and 5-11; indeed, identical logic cards often serve both purposes.   **DMA service requests are always given priority over concurrent** *interrupt requests.*

Just as in Fig. 5-11, a **DMA service request** (caused by a device-flag level) produces a **cycle-steal request** unless it is inhibited by a higher-priority request; the processor answers with an **acknowledge (priority-grant) pulse.** This signal then sets a processor-clocked "ACTIVE" flip-flop, which strobes a suitable **memory address** into the processor memory address register and then causes memory and device logic to transfer data from or to the DMA data bus (Fig. 5-13).

In some computer systems (e.g., Digital Equipment Corporation PDP-15), the DMA data lines are identical with the programmed-transfer data lines. This simplifies interconnections at the expense of processor hardware. In other systems, the DMA data lines are also used to transmit the DMA address to the processor before data are transferred. This further reduces the number of bus lines, but complicates hardware and timing.

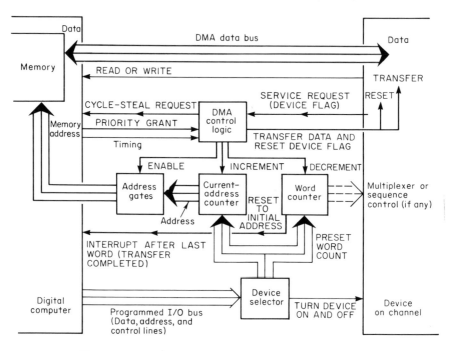

Fig. 5-14. A simple data channel for automatic block transfers.

5-19. Automatic Block Transfers. As we described it, the DMA data transfer is *device*-initiated. A *program-dependent* decision to transfer data, even directly from or to memory, still requires a programmed instruction to cause a DMA service request. This is hardly worth the trouble for a *single-word* transfer. Most DMA transfers, whether device or program initiated, involve not single words but **blocks** of tens, hundreds, or even thousands of data words.

Figure 5-14 shows how the simple DMA system of Fig. 5-13 may be expanded into an **automatic data channel** for block transfers. Data for a block can arrive or depart asynchronously, and the DMA controller will steal cycles as needed and permit the program to go on between cycles. A block of words to be transferred will, in general, occupy a corresponding block of adjacent memory registers. Successive memory addresses can be gated into the memory address registered by a counter, the **current-address counter.** Before any data transfer takes place, a programmed instruction sets the current-address counter to the desired initial address; the desired number of words **(block length)** is set into a second counter, the **word counter,** which will count down with each data transfer until 0 is reached after the desired number of transfers. As service requests arrive from, say, an analog-to-digital converter or data link, the DMA control logic implements successive cycle-steal requests and gates successive current addresses into the memory address register as the current-address counter counts up (see also Fig. 5-5a).

The word counter is similarly decremented once per data word. When a block transfer is completed, the word counter can stop the device from requesting further data transfers. The word-counter carry pulse can also cause an *interrupt* so that a new block of data can be processed. The word counter may, if desired, also serve for sequencing device functions (e.g., for selecting successive ADC multiplexer addresses).

Some computers replace the word counter with a program-loaded **final-address register,** whose contents are compared with the current-address counter to determine the end of the block.

A DMA system often involves several data channels, each with a DMA control, address gates, a current-address counter, and a word counter, with different priorities assigned to different channels. For efficient handling of randomly timed requests from multiple devices (and to prevent loss of data words), data-channel systems may incorporate buffer registers in the interface or in devices such as ADCs or DACs.

5-20. Advantages of DMA Systems (see Ref. 6). Direct-memory-access systems can transfer data blocks at very high rates (10^6 words/sec is readily possible) without elaborate I/O programming. The processor essentially deals mainly with buffer areas in its own memory, and only a few I/O instructions are needed to initialize or reinitialize transfers.

Automatic data channels are especially suitable for servicing peripherals with high data rates, such as disks, drums, and fast ADCs and DACs. But fast data transfer with minimal program overhead is extremely valuable in many other applications, especially if there are many devices to be serviced. To indicate the remarkable efficiency of cycle-stealing direct memory access with multiple block-transfer data channels, consider the operation of a training-type digital flight simulator, which solves aircraft and engine equations and services an elaborate cockpit mock-up with many controls and instrument displays. During each 160-msec time increment, the interface not only performs 174 analog-to-digital conversions requiring a total conversion time of 7.7 msec but also 430 digital-to-analog conversions, and handles 540 eight-bit bytes of discrete control information. The actual

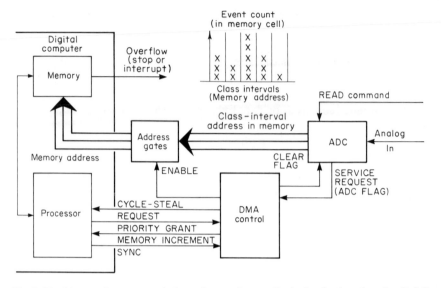

Fig. 5-15a. Memory-increment technique of measuring amplitude distributions (*based on Ref.* 6).

time required to transfer all this information in and out of the data channels is 143 msec per time increment, but because of the fast direct memory transfers, cycle-stealing subtracts only 3.2 msec for each 160 msec of processor time (Ref. 2).

5-21. Memory-increment Technique for Amplitude-distribution Measurements. In many minicomputers, a special pulse input will *increment* the contents of a memory location addressed by the DMA address lines; an interrupt can be generated when one of the memory cells is full. When ADC outputs representing successive samples of a random voltage are applied to the DMA address lines, **the memory-increment feature will effectively generate a model of the input-voltage amplitude distribution in the computer**

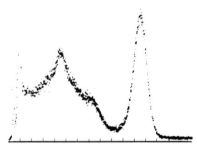

Fig. 5-15b. An amplitude-distribution display obtained by the method of Fig. 5-15a. (*Digital Equipment Corporation.*)

memory: Each memory address corresponds to a voltage class interval, and the contents of the memory register represent the number of samples falling into that class interval. Data taking is terminated after a preset number of samples or when the first memory register overloads (Fig. 5-15a). The empirical amplitude distribution thus created in memory may be displayed or plotted by a display routine (Fig. 5-15b), and statistics such as

$$\overline{X} = \frac{1}{n} \sum_{k=1}^{n} X_k \qquad \overline{X^2} = \frac{1}{n} \sum_{k=1}^{n} X_k^2 \qquad \cdots$$

are readily computed after the distribution is complete. This technique has been extensively applied to the analysis of pulse-energy spectra from nuclear-physics experiments.

Joint distributions of two random variables X, Y can be similarly compiled. It is only necessary to apply, say, a 12-bit word X, Y composed of two 6-bit bytes corresponding to two ADC outputs X and Y to the memory address register. Now each addressed memory location will correspond to the region $X_i \leq X < X_{i+1}$, $Y_k \leq Y < Y_{k+1}$ in XY space.

5-22. Add-to-memory Technique of Signal Averaging. Another command-pulse input to some DMA interfaces will *add* a data word on the I/O-bus data lines to the memory location addressed by the DMA address lines without ever bothering the digital-computer arithmetic unit or the program. This "add-to-memory" feature permits useful linear operations on data obtained from various instruments; the only application well known at this time is in **data averaging.**

Figure 5-16a and b illustrates an especially interesting application of data averaging, which has been very fruitful in biological-data reduction (e.g., electroencephalogram analysis). Periodically applied stimuli produce the same system response after each stimulus so that one obtains an analog waveform periodic with the period T of the applied stimuli. To pull the desired function $X(t)$ out of additive zero-mean random noise, one adds $X(t)$, $X(t + T)$, $X(t + 2T)$, . . . during successive periods to enhance the signal, while the noise will tend to average out. Figure 5-16c shows the extraction of a signal from additive noise in successive data-averaging runs.

5-23. Implementing Current-address and Word Counters in the Processor Memory. Some minicomputers (in particular, PDP-9, PDP-15, and the PDP-8 series) have, in addition to their regular DMA facilities, a set of fixed core-memory locations to be used as data-channel address and word counters. Ordinary processor instructions (not I/O instructions) load these locations, respectively, with the block starting address and with minus the block count. The data-channel interface card (Fig. 5-17) supplies the address of one of the four to eight address-counter locations available in the processor; the word counter is the location following the address counter.

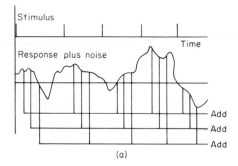

(a)

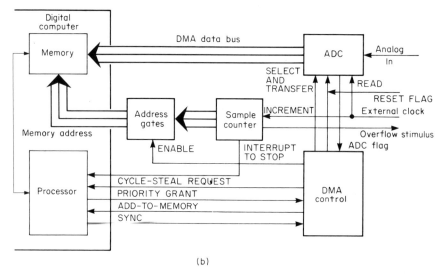

(b)

Fig. 5-16a and b. Signal enhancement by periodic averaging (*a*) and add-to-memory technique for signal averaging (*b*) (*based on Ref. 6*).

Now, successive service requests steal not one but three or four cycles since the processor must increment the two counter locations, and they then transfer data to or from successive memory cells indirectly addressed via the address counter. When the word counter reaches 0 (from its negative initial setting), the processor issues a special signal which is used to stop further service requests and usually to interrupt the processor (Fig. 5-17).

Some memory-implemented data channels will also permit add-to-memory operation (PDP-9, PDP-15). The Honeywell 316/516 machines implement a final-address register in memory rather than a word counter (Sec. 5-19) and permit automatic alternation of data transfers to or from two blocks of memory locations (*swinging buffers*).

Memory-implemented data channels permit automatic block transfers with a minimum of interface hardware since they eliminate the two external counter/ registers plus the circuits needed to preset them. On the other hand, **logic**

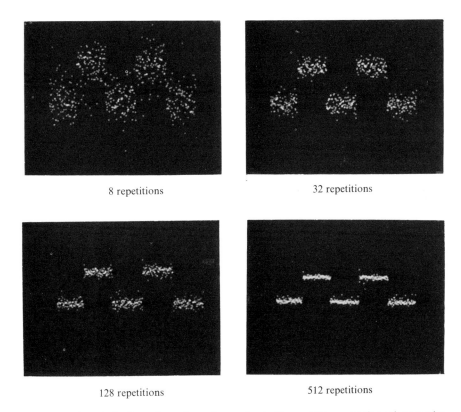

8 repetitions   32 repetitions

128 repetitions   512 repetitions

Fig. 5-16c. A periodically retriggered waveform extracted from additive noise through successive signal-averaging runs. The display is self-scaling; i.e., ordinate words are shifted right by 1 bit after $2, 4, 8, \ldots$ repetitions to divide accumulated sums by the number of repetitions. (*University of Arizona, PDP-9 data taken by H. M. Aus.*)

circuits are becoming more and more inexpensive, and true data channels steal only one-third to one-fourth as much processor time as memory-implemented channels.

SOME INTERFACE-HARDWARE CONSIDERATIONS

5-24. From Ready-made to Do-it-yourself Interfaces. Device controllers for typical peripheral devices have many common features, so several minicomputer manufacturers sell standard **interface cards.** Typical device-controller cards implement a device selector, bus gates, a register, and/or some device-flag flip-flops and sense gates. The same card or a second card may comprise interrupt logic or a data-channel controller. Some minicomputer main-frames (e.g., Hewlett-Packard, Data General) have

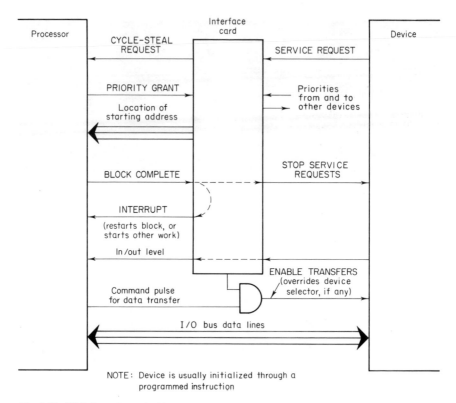

Fig. 5-17. With data-channel address and word counters implemented in the processor memory, data-channel operation requires only a simple interface card containing priority/queuing and address logic like that in Fig. 5-10, but each data transfer steals three or four processor cycles, not just one cycle.

special slots for interface cards.   In other systems, a substantial portion of the interface logic is physically associated with each device.

Interface logic, all the way from simple data-transfer and sensing logic to new and special controllers, displays, and accessory arithmetic units, is remarkably easy to make from commerically available logic cards and/or socket-mounted integrated circuits.   Several manufacturers sell logic and related analog/digital circuit cards (ADCs, DACs, electronic switches, amplifiers, power supplies), plus very convenient mounting hardware, enclosures, panel switches, indicators, etc. (Fig. 5-18).   Transistor/transistor logic (TTL) interfaces naturally with most minicomputers, but *high-noise-immunity logic* (Motorola HTL, Digital Equipment Corporation K-series cards) should be considered for high-noise environments; these circuits have larger logic-level swings and are intentionally slower to reduce the possibility of random-noise triggering.

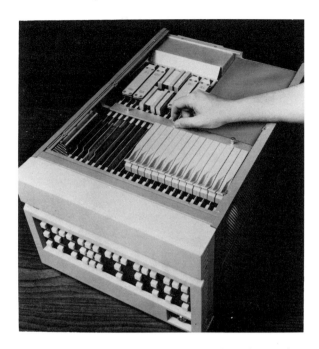

Fig. 5-18a. Much of the interface logic in this Hewlett-Packard 2100A system is on manufacturer-supplied interface cards plugged into the processor chassis. (*Hewlett-Packard Corporation.*)

We recommend wire wrapping with a simple "squeeze gun" (Fig. 5-18c), rather than soldering, for convenient and reliable connections except for fast emitter-coupled logic (ECL) and radio-frequency circuits.   A very little knowledge of digital-logic design goes a long way (Table 1-5), but if you have problems, we suggest that you hire a graduate student from the nearest electrical engineering department part time.

5-25. I/O-bus Lines and Signals. Party-line I/O buses (Sec. 5-1) are usually "daisy-chained" from device to device through male/female connector pairs, with a suitable line termination plugged into the last female connector.

Figure 5-19 shows some typical bus circuits.   Most minicomputer TTL interfaces employ open-collector integrated circuits (gates or amplifiers) as line drivers (Fig. 5-19a).   Off-the-shelf ICs not specifically designed as line drivers may require testing for voltage levels and rise times.   Ordinary gates used as line receivers may also have to be tested for safe logic-level thresholds.   It is surely best to employ special drivers and receivers (perhaps even push-pull drivers and receivers, Sec. 5-26), but this may not be necessary for short buses.   If in doubt, use special cards supplied by the computer manufacturer.

(b)

(c)

Fig. 5-18*b* and *c*. Logic cards, receptacles, and a Gardner-Denver wire-wrap tool for assembling homemade minicomputer interface systems.   (*Digital Equipment Corporation.*)

With wiring delays (at least 1.5 nsec/ft) of the same order as logic rise times, transmission-line reflections must be considered (Fig. 5-20).   **If the power to each device on a daisy-chained bus can be turned off separately, the interface designer must make sure that this will not affect proper operation of other devices** (see also Figs. 5-19 and 5-20).

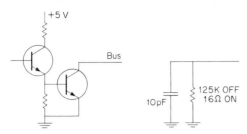

Fig. 5-19a. Output stages of an open-collector, inverting TTL bus driver and its equivalent source impedance.

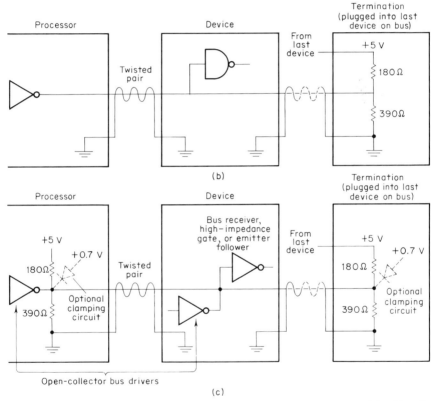

Fig. 5-19b and c. A *unidirectional processor-to-device bus* (b) and a *bidirectional bus* (c) each without differential line receivers. *Unidirectional device-to-processor* bus lines would also be terminated at both ends as in Fig. 5-19c.

Use lines whose characteristic impedance Z_0 is at least 90 ohms (93-ohm coax or 100-ohm No. 26 or 28 twisted pair, about 30 turns/ft), with ground return. Flat cable, with signal conductors separated by ground returns, and possibly with a shielding backplane, is very convenient, especially for short (below 1 to 3 ft) cable runs. A diode or Schottky-diode reverse termination at the output end will limit negative overshoot; follow the

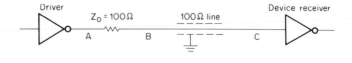

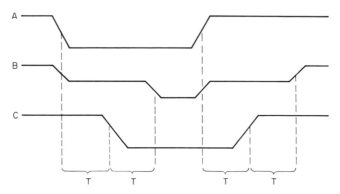

Fig. 5-20. A series-terminated transmission line. The effect on the driving circuit does not change when the receiver power supply is turned off. T is the line-propagation delay.

computer manufacturer's recommendations. Do *not* use flip-flops as line drivers.

I/O-bus logic levels are *not* usually the same as standard logic levels but will depend on the bus system and loading. Note in particular that many minicomputer I/O buses are driven by amplifiers or gates which **invert logic levels** (e.g., Fig. 5-19*a*), i.e., bus signals corresponding to logical 1 may be LOW voltage ("ACTIVE LOW" signals). **Check your interface manual,** which will also specify the load each bus line can drive under various conditions.

5-26. Noise, Interconnections, and Ground Systems. Digital-computer interfaces are very often connected to sensitive and accurate analog instrumentation and computing circuits. **Digital-system noise,** especially high-frequency spikes and pulse ringing, can cause very objectionable noise in analog circuits via ground currents and radiation. This can be true even though the digital circuits themselves work well within their noise-immunity limits. Transistor/transistor logic (TTL) and diode/transistor logic (DTL), with their harsh ground current transients and relatively high output impedances, are bad offenders in this respect. Emitter-coupled logic (ECL) has near-constant ground current, low logic levels, and low output impedances, and it is a good choice for critical wide-band analog/digital circuits. Digitally controlled analog switching circuits (digital-to-analog converters, sample-hold circuits, multiplexers) should be designed to minimize impedances common to digital and analog signals.

Ground-system noise and **common ground impedances** can cause serious problems.   A good earth ground is not always easy to come by, and the power-line "industrial" ground should be used for ac return only.   To minimize common ground impedances within a cabinet or subsystem, it is best to select a single **common ground point** and to return all signal, power, and chassis grounds separately to this point, which is also connected to earth ground.

Unfortunately, this simple technique may not work when we must ground widely separated subsystems interconnected by signal lines (e.g., a digital

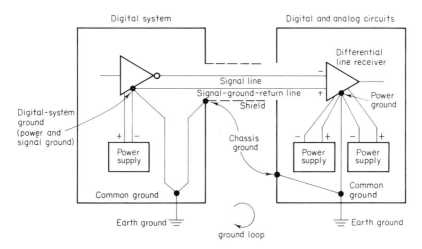

Fig. 5-21. Interconnection and grounding of two typical subsystems.   Differential line receivers cancel common-mode ground-loop and other disturbances.   An even better method is to use push-pull line receivers and line drivers without any ground return between subsystems. Radiation from digital circuits is still a problem (see also Table 5-2).   Earth-ground connections, required for electrical safety, may need shielding.   Power-supply ac inputs may need radio-frequency filters, and power transformers may need electrostatic shields.

computer and an analog subsystem 40 ft away).   We will then give each subsystem a common ground point and try to keep all power-supply loops within each subsystem.   But if each subsystem has an earth ground (often required for electrical safety), then we have a **ground loop** enclosed by the ground connections and each signal wire.   Such inductive loops will pick up and/or radiate noise (Fig. 5-21).   The best way to fix this is to use differential (push-pull) signal transmission or at least **differential signal receivers,** which will cancel ground-loop noise and other disturbances common to both differential inputs (Fig. 5-21; see also Table 5-1).

If electrical safety is no problem, we may omit one earth ground and interconnect the subsystem grounds through a ground return line in the signal cable.   Signal-cable shields must *never* carry ground currents; they ordinarily connect to chassis ground at the source end.   Even so, we may still have a ground loop formed through leakage resistances and capacitances.

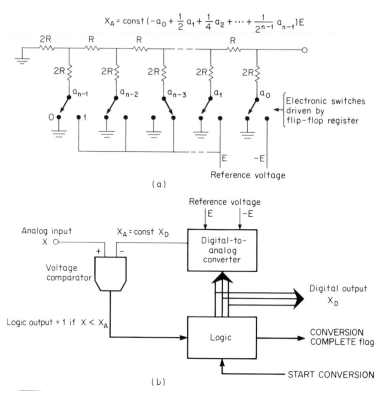

$$X_A = \text{const} \left(-a_0 + \frac{1}{2}a_1 + \frac{1}{4}a_2 + \cdots + \frac{1}{2^{n-1}}a_{n-1}\right)E$$

(a)

(b)

Fig. 5-22. Ladder-network digital-to-analog converter for converting 2s-complement binary numbers (a) and a feedback-type analog-to-digital converter (b). (*Based on G. A. Korn and T. M. Korn, Electronic Analog and Hybrid Computers, 2d ed., McGraw-Hill, New York, 1972.*)

Table 5-1 summarizes **general rules for minimizing digital-circuit noise in analog subsystems.**

You must consult the interface manual for your specific minicomputer in every case to check on:

The specific interface-logic scheme employed and details of its operation and timing

Special I/O instructions used

Tolerances on logic levels, rise times, pulse-timing permissible circuit loads (fanout), total bus length, etc.

Integrated-circuit modules recommended for interfacing

Whether the power to individual devices can be turned off without affecting the rest of the system

Different manufacturers employ terms like *multiplexer channel*, *data channel*, and *selector bus* with completely different meanings. Each of these terms

TABLE 5-1. Checklist for Minimizing Digital-noise Effects in Combined Analog/ Digital Systems (based on Refs. 18 and 21).

1. *To reduce the digital noise at its source,* avoid long lines which are not carefully terminated and/or clamped to prevent ringing. Consult the applications manual for the type of logic circuits used. Wires from each circuit should fan out, not continue from point to point.
2. *It is important to keep as much of the digital noise as possible within the digital-circuit cards and out of power-supply and ground circuits, and to keep the remainder out of the analog circuits as best possible.* For this reason, every digital and analog circuit card should have a *decoupling circuit* on each power-supply line. A *ground plane* ought to be used on each card, not so much for electrostatic shielding as to reduce the areas of inductive loops. *Laminated power-supply buses* also help with decoupling.
3. Digital ground returns (which act as transmitting antennas!) should be kept separate and well away from analog ground leads. It is, in fact, a good idea to keep digital and analog circuits in separate shielded enclosures and to operate their power supplies from different phases of the three-phase line, with RF filters in each ac lead.
4. *Where a digital computer is connected to a linkage or analog subsystem, we must avoid returning any digital signals through the common ground.* It is best to use *push-pull line drivers* with twisted and shielded lines into *differential line receivers,* or at least differential line receivers fed with the digital signal and digital ground-return lines. Balun transformers have also been successfully used to replace actual differential lines. Slow logic signals (below 20 to 100 kHz) can be isolated by light-coupled semiconductor switches.
5. Finally, make sure that all operational amplifiers and other analog feedback circuits are equalized so as to avoid high-frequency peaks (which cause ringing when excited by digital noise).

With all these precautions, it is possible to keep digital noise on analog circuits below 5 to 10 mv peak to peak.

could refer to a multiplexed I/O bus (Sec. 5-1), a party-line I/O bus (Sec. 5-1), or a direct-memory-access interface (Sec. 5-19).

ELEMENTS OF INPUT/OUTPUT SOFTWARE

5-27. I/O-software Requirements. We have already exhibited some simple I/O routines in Secs. 5-8 to 5-15 (see also Table 5-1). Most practical applications will involve *multiple* data transfers: a program may need an *array* of 1,000 ADC readings in memory, or one may want to print a 72-*character line* taken from a list of two-character 16-bit words. Storage areas for arrays thus intended for I/O are known as **buffers.**

Since external devices usually process data at rates different from that of the program, we may have to provide intermediate storage in the form of *two or more* buffers in memory so that, for instance, ADC readings can be recorded in one array while the program operates on earlier readings in a second buffer. We can then *interchange buffers* (by changing pointer addresses) when the processor or the ADC is finished with one array; if necessary, three or more such buffers may have to be provided.

We can now discern requirements typical of input/output programming:

1. Practically all input/output routines require **careful programming of interrupt service,** i.e., of priorities, masking, register saving and restoring,

etc. (even DMA block transfers are usually terminated and reinitiated by interrupts).

2. These interrupt-service programs must also **manage assignment and reassignment of buffer areas** so as to avoid interference between data-processing and I/O operations.

3. Numerical-character I/O for numerical computations is necessarily associated with **formatting routines** relating numerical input or output data to binary fixed-point or floating-point number representations used in the computer. **Character packing/unpacking** (Sec. 4-11) is in a similar category. Formatting and packing/unpacking are not themselves I/O operations but are often combined with I/O.

4. In addition to this, input/output programs often include **error routines** which advise the programmer of incorrect I/O requests (e.g., calls to devices which do not exist or are assigned to other jobs), parity errors, etc.

As a result of these requirements, input/output programming always involves an ugly amount of tedious (but important) detail, which has little to do with the computer application as such. To relieve the computer user (who would like to concentrate on his applications programs), computer manufacturers furnish "canned" I/O and formatting routines and special system programs which make it easy to call I/O-related routines from user programs.

5-28. Use of FORTRAN Formatting and I/O. Most readers will be familiar with FORTRAN formatting and I/O statements like

> 12   FORMAT   (E 10.4)
>   READ   (2, 12)   X

where E 10.4 calls for a floating-point conversion, 2 is the number of the peripheral device to be read, and 12 refers to the associated FORMAT statement. *Unformatted* READ or WRITE statements like

> WRITE (7) X, Y, Z

call for input or output of the listed quantities in *binary* form (e.g., for ADCs and DACs).

Minicomputer FORTRAN compilers recognize such statements and automatically generate the appropriate formatting and I/O routines without further effort on the part of the programmer. With programs written in *assembly language*, the easiest way to produce formatted numerical input/output is still to link the assembly-language program to a short FORTRAN program for FORTRAN I/O (Sec. 4-20). The time consumed by the (unseen, but quite formidable) FORTRAN-generated formatting and I/O routines will rarely bother you with slow keyboard/printer I/O, although you might notice the time lost with alphanumeric cathode-ray-tube displays supervising real-time computations.

5-29. Interpreter-program Formatting and I/O. Interpreter systems (e.g., BASIC and FOCAL, Sec. 3-8) include formatting and I/O commands used much like the corresponding FORTRAN statements, plus special commands for simple cathode-ray-tube and plotter graphics output. Several mini-computer manufacturers supply special versions of interpreter systems such as BASIC with greatly enhanced I/O capabilities for "conversational" programming of instruments, test systems, and process controllers (Sec. 7-3). Such systems are extra convenient, but their range of applications may be restricted. Interpreters do not generate relocatable code which can be combined with other programs, and execution may be slow.

5-30. I/O at the Assembly-language Level: Device Drivers. At the assembly-language level, a complete I/O operation is called as a subroutine known as a **device driver** or **device handler.** The most important drivers implement block transfers, and any one device driver can involve all or most of the I/O-related jobs listed in Sec. 5-27, including formatting. The same peripheral device (a paper-tape punch, say) could have two, three, or more associated drivers for different jobs or formats (e.g., binary and ASCII output).

Most device drivers involve interrupt service and can, therefore, be separated into two sections. The **initiator** subroutine reserves buffer space in memory through pseudo instructions like

BUFFR .BLOCK SIZE / Saves **SIZE** locations
/ starting at **BUFFR**

initializes buffer pointers, and prepares a peripheral device by clearing flags, setting control registers, and checking status.

The **continuator** section of the device driver typically initiates data transfer (e.g., **START ADC CONVERSION** or **ENABLE DATA CHANNEL**) and returns to the main program to wait for an interrupt. The continuator section of the device driver also comprises the interrupt-service routine(s) needed for data transfer and/or its termination (as in DMA block transfers, Sec. 5-19). Both initiator and continuator routines will, in general, have exits to the main computer program and to *error printout or display subroutines* (in case we have called for a nonexistent, illegal, or unready device; if there is no buffer space left; etc.).

Frequently needed device drivers (e.g., for reading and printing a line of text, reading and writing ASCII and binary tape records, etc.) are practically always furnished by the computer manufacturer as library routines. Complete device drivers for specific systems, including some DMA drivers, will be found in each minicomputer manual. They can often be used as

TABLE 5-2.   **Typical Minicomputer Peripheral Devices and I/O Instructions** (see also Secs. 3-10, 3-14, and 7-9).

A. PAPER-TAPE READER, PAPER-TAPE PUNCH, KEYBOARD, TELEPRINTER

Each of these electromechanical character-handling devices has an **8-bit device register (character buffer),** which can be read or loaded by a processor I/O instruction.   But each such data transfer must wait until completion of a relatively slow electromechanical reading, punching, or printing operation is signaled by a **device flag** (flip-flop) via a sense or interrupt line. Typical instructions are:

1. CLEAR DEVICE FLAG/OPERATOR ON NEXT CHARACTER: clears the flag and permits the device register to receive or transmit a new character through electromechanical operations (shift 8 bits into device register from keyboard *if a key is struck*, read and advance tape, punch, print).
2. READ (LOAD) DEVICE REGISTER: a fast, all-electrical data transfer to or from a processor accumulator.
3. SKIP ON DEVICE FLAG: used to implement a skip loop as in Sec. 5-8 for noninterrupt operation.
4. *Two or all three of these instructions can be combined into a single I/O instruction* employing two or three IO pulses (Sec. 5-3).

Special control characters control special teleprinter operations (tab, line feed, form feed, etc.).

B. MAGNETIC-TAPE TRANSPORTS (see also Sec. 3-10)

Tape-transport-controller logic "repacks" 8- to 18-bit computer words into 7-bit or 9-bit tape words, adding extra parity bits as needed.   Binary or character formats can be selected through processor instructions.

Data transfers to and from magnetic tape are usually direct-memory-access block transfers, so the controller has a *current-address counter* and a *word counter* (Sec. 5-19), which can be preset by processor instructions.   Since tape keeps moving once a transfer is initiated and may transfer as many as 50,000 bytes/sec, the tape-transport controller employs double buffering (Fig. 5-4d) between tape and memory.   Only one transport at a time transfers data, but others can wind or rewind at the same time.

The controller has a *control register* (Sec. 5-4) whose control bits are set by processor instructions which implement (and possibly combine) functions like:

Select one of 4 to 16 transports	Write (read) forward
Select binary or character format	Write (read) backward
Select tape speed	Rewind
Select record density	Backspace
Write end of file	Advance to end of file

The current-address counter and the status of the control register can also be *read* by processor instructions.   In addition, tape-transport flag flip-flops can be sensed or cause interrupts to detect conditions such as:

Transport not ready (no power, no tape)	End (or beginning) of tape
Transport busy	Parity or check-sum error
Word-counter overflow	

Magnetic-tape driver routines are usually supplied as part of system programs (Secs. 3-12 and 5-31) and can be quite complicated since hardware and program will, respectively, check lateral and longitudinal parity (Sec. 3-10).   The controller can "retry" reading or writing when a parity error occurs.

C. FIXED-HEAD DISKS AND DRUMS

A disk or drum rotates continuously.   Each computer word (plus a parity bit and word-delimiting guard bits) is recorded *serially* along numbered tracks, with one read/write head to each track.   Each memory location on a disk system (*disk address*) is specified by its *disk*

TABLE 5-2. Typical Minicomputer Peripheral Devices and I/O Instructions (see also Secs. 3-10, 3-14, and 7-9). (*Continued*)

---

number, track number, and *segment address.* Segment addresses are prerecorded on an *address track;* each segment address is read before the corresponding words pass under the read/write heads.

Data transfers (typically 50,000 to 180,000 words/sec) are DMA block transfers via a *disk buffer register,* which buffers a *shift register* implementing the parallel/serial or serial/parallel conversion. The controller has a *current-address counter* and a *word counter,* which can be preset by processor instructions (Sec. 5-19). DMA word-transfer request pulses synchronized with the disk rotation are derived from another prerecorded track. All prerecorded tracks are duplicated in case one gets damaged.

A typical disk may have 128 data tracks, with 2,048 word locations and an end-of-track gap on each track. Word sequences can be written or read consecutively along a track, switching to the next track when the end-of-track gap is reached ("spiral" writing or reading). If a slower data-transfer rate is desirable, the controller can also read every other word, or every fourth word, along each track, so that words are effectively interleaved.

To initiate a data transfer, programmed instructions set a *disk control register* to WRITE or READ and preset the *current-address register,* the *word counter,* and the *disk address register.* The latter (which may be a two-word register) specifies the disk, track, and segment address for the first word of a data block. When the segment address matches that read on the address track, the disk controller initiates the block transfer, which stops when the word counter runs out; this will also cause a program interrupt (Sec. 5-19).

Besides WRITE and READ, disk systems have a CHECK (COMPARE, SEARCH) mode which *compares* a word set into the disk buffer register with the word currently read from the disk into the shift register, and which sets an interrupt flag when the words agree. This mode is used for checking purposes, and can also find words on the disk.

Other interrupt flags detect *parity errors, missing prerecorded-track bits,* illegal addresses, etc. Front-panel *write-lock switches* can protect selected tracks from overwriting, e.g., to protect system programs.

D. REAL-TIME CLOCKS

Timing pulses needed to relate computer operations to real time are derived either from the 60-Hz line frequency (50 Hz in Europe) or from a 10-Hz to 1-MHz crystal oscillator (*clock oscillator*); counter flip-flops yield submultiples of the clock frequency, as desired. Timing pulses can be started by an external gate signal or by a programmed instruction setting a control-register bit (Sec. 5-4), or the clock may run free.

Timing pulses are counted by a *clock counter.* If the clock counter is initially reset to 0 by a programmed I/O instruction, the count will be proportional to *elapsed time* and can be read by the computer program when desired. *To mark a preset time interval,* we preset the clock-counter recognition gate (NAND gate, see also Table 1-5a), which detects when the counter reaches 0 after N clock pulses. The gate output then interrupts the processor (*clock interrupt*). The ensuing interrupt-service routine performs whatever timed operation is wanted and can reset the clock counter to *repeat periodic cycles.*

In many minicomputers, the clock counter is not a flip-flop register but an *incrementable memory location* (memory-increment technique, Sec. 5-21).

E. DIGITAL-TO-ANALOG CONVERTERS

The most commonly used *digital-to-analog converters* (*DACs*) are resistance networks whose output voltage or current is determined by an analog input (*reference voltage*) and a digital number set into the DAC flip-flop register. Each register bit controls one of the electronic switches (*bit switches*), which together determine the correct output. As a typical example, the *ladder-network DAC* of Fig. 5-22a is designed to convert 2s-complement-coded binary numbers (Tables 1-1 and 1-2) into positive and negative analog output. Converters for many other codes (e.g., BCD, Table 1-4) exist (Ref. 18).

If two or more DACs must be updated simultaneously (as in cathode-ray-tube displays, Sec.

TABLE 5-2.   Typical Minicomputer Peripheral Devices and I/O Instructions (see also Secs. 3-10, 3-14, and 7-9).   *(Continued)*

7-9, or analog/hybrid computers), the *double-buffering* scheme of Fig. 5-4*d* permits individual loading of DAC buffer registers.   All DACs can then be updated simultaneously through a programmed instruction producing a common transfer pulse.   If one must service more DACs than there are readily available I/O addresses, DAC addresses can be entered as data words into a control register (*DAC address register*).

F.   ANALOG-TO-DIGITAL CONVERTERS

Analog-to-digital converters (ADCs) are discussed in detail in Ref. 18.   There are two principal types.   Many digital voltmeters employ *analog-to-time conversion;* i.e., the START CONVERSION command causes a binary or decimal counter to count clock pulses while an analog sweep voltage varies between a reference voltage level and a voltage level proportional to the unknown input (or, in the more accurate *integrating converters*, to a time average of the input).   See Ref. 18.   The count then terminates, and the CONVERSION COMPLETE flag level goes up; the counter can now be read by the digital computer.   8- to 14-bit precision is possible, with conversion times between 0.5 and 500 msec.

Faster binary ADCs employ the *feedback principle* illustrated in Fig. 5-22*b*.   After the START CONVERSION signal, *digital logic tries to set a DAC register so that the DAC output approximates the unknown analog input* as *closely as possible*.   A *voltage comparator* (basically a high-gain amplifier) produces logic 1 output if the comparison DAC output is too large, and 0 otherwise.   The most commonly used ADC feedback logic successively tries the sign bit (with all other DAC bits at 0), then the most significant bit, etc. (*successive-approximation ADC*).   This requires n voltage comparisons for n bits.   The CONVERSION COMPLETE flag goes up, and the ADC output can be read from the DAC register when the comparison voltage equals the unknown input within one-half of the voltage step determined by the least significant bit.   Up to 15-bit precision is possible, but that may require 30 to 50 μsec; 1 to 20 μsec is typical for 8- to 12-bit precision.

The ADC flag is reset (cleared) by the READ ADC instruction and/or by the START CONVERSION instruction or timing pulse.

An ADC often serves multiple analog channels through an analog-switching scheme (relay or electronic *analog multiplexer*).   The multiplexer address is determined by a control register (*multiplexer address register*), which may be set by the digital computer or can be incremented to scan successive input channels.

Because of the finite ADC conversion time, accurately timed sampling of time-variable analog signals may require an analog *sample-hold circuit*, which holds the desired analog voltage sample long enough for conversion (Ref. 18).

NOTE: Other important and interesting peripheral-interface systems discussed in this book are *cathode-ray-tube displays* (Sec. 7-8) and *communication-system interfaces* (Sec. 7-14).

models for new or modified drivers.   References 10 and 11 give detailed instructions for writing drivers fitted to Hewlett-Packard computers and operating systems.

5-31.   Input/Output Control Systems (IOCS).   (a) Subroutine Calls for Device Drivers.   The subroutine calling sequence for a device-driver initiator (which may also pass parameters to its continuator) must transfer device number and function, buffer location(s) and size(s), and pointers to error routines.   To simplify and standardize calls for I/O operations and to simplify assignment of devices to different tasks (Sec. 5-30), the better minicomputer systems incorporate their device-driver libraries into a special system program, the **input/output control system (IOCS),** which is usually furnished as part of a monitor or executive system (Sec. 3-12).

With IOCS, the device drivers in the IOCS library are never called *directly*. Instead, **user programs requesting I/O call on a single master subroutine, IOCS,** whose four-word to eight-word calling sequence specifies device, functions, formatting (if any), buffer(s), and error exit:

> JUMP AND SAVE   IOCS
> (device/function/format/code)
> (address of error routine)
> (buffer starting address)
> (buffer size)

The proper codes to be used will be found in your minicomputer manual. The IOCS subroutine passes the information in the calling sequence to the appropriate device driver, calls its initiator routine, and returns control to the calling program. Interrupts which occur during or on termination of the transfer are processed entirely by the system; *no interrupt-handling subroutines are required in the user's program* (Ref. 10).

With such a system, the user program requires only a single **.EXTERNAL** reference (Sec. 4-19) to IOCS for any and all drivers. Some operating systems, however, save core space by requiring a list of the devices or drivers actually used, e.g.,

> .EXTERNAL   IOCS   3, 4, 7

so that the loader need only load the device drivers which are actually used.

NOTE: To make IOCS practical, the assembler used must permit *external linkage to* IOCS, or else the IOCS subroutine and the associated device drivers must be supplied by the assembler itself; just as some FORTRAN compilers supply their own I/O programming system.

(b) Buffer-status Management. In connection with appropriate device handlers, an input/output control system also maintains *status words* which can specify not only device status but also the buffer(s) currently kept busy by program or devices. Special IOCS-subroutine calling sequences or IOCS macros can read these status words for use by the user program. We may also have special IOCS subroutines or macros (e.g., **.WAIT** m, n) which *stop the user program until a required buffer is free* (this is analogous to, but *not* the same as, a skip loop waiting for device readiness). More elaborate device handlers may do such buffer management automatically.

(c) IOCS Macros (see also Sec. 4-21). As a further convenience, the larger minicomputer input/output control systems replace each IOCS subroutine call and its elaborate calling sequence by an **IOCS macro,** such as

> .WRITE a, b, c, d
> .READ a, b, c, d

where the arguments a, b, c, d specify device, function, format, buffer, and error exit. Assembly-language I/O programming then approaches the simplicity of FORTRAN I/O, with various optional tradeoffs between programming flexibility and simplicity. It is, for instance, possible to standardize buffer sizes so that they need not be included as parameters.

(d) **Device-independent IOCS** (see also Sec. 3-12). Good input/output control systems permit **device-independent programming**; i.e., user programs refer to each peripheral device by the **logical device number** to which a physical device (identified by a **physical device number,** name, or code) is attached through program statements. Device-independent IOCS will, of course, let us reassign multiple similar peripherals such as tape drivers, but it does more. Through simple device-number reassignment, an otherwise unchanged program can, for instance, either process real data from a communications interface or be tested with analogous data from cards or tape; or a compiler can accept source programs from paper tape, magnetic tape, or a disk.

Device-independent IOCS subroutines or macros do not call device drivers directly but reference a **device-assignment table** which assigns a *physical* device number to each *logical* device number. The user sets up his own "normal" device assignments for system programs (monitor, assembler, compiler, debugging program, etc.) when the computer system is first put together; most computers have a special conversational program ("system generator") for this purpose. The "normal" device assignments are reestablished whenever a system program is first loaded, but the user can change device assignments through special commands like

.ASSIGN TTYO   3 / Teleprinter becomes
            /   logical device 3

The user can also request printout or display of the current device assignment table.

5-32. Discussion. A convenient input/output control system permits the user to concentrate on his applications program without having to bother with the massive detail involved in I/O, buffer management, formatting, and packing/unpacking operations. IOCS is an indispensable part of modern operating systems which make it simple to store, retrieve, load, combine, and execute modular programs. The elaborate device drivers and multiple subroutine calls of an IOCS system do exact a price in computing time. In the most time-critical applications, users may have to write simplified device drivers and insert them into their own programs.

REFERENCES AND BIBLIOGRAPHY

Interface Design

(Refer also to the interface manuals of various digital-computer manufacturers.)

1. Borger, E. R.: Characteristics of Priority Interrupts, *Datamation*, June 1965.
2. Andelman, S. J.: Real-time I/O Techniques, *Comput. Des.*, May 1966.
3. Klerer, M., and G. A. Korn: *Digital Computer User's Handbook*, McGraw-Hill, New York, 1967.
4. Schmidt, W. E.: Methods for Priority Interrupts and Their Implication for Hybrid Programs, *Simulation*, July 1967.
5. Marston, G. P.: A Medium-scale Hybrid Interface, *Simulation*, May 1968.
6. Korn, G. A.: Digital-computer Interface Systems, *Simulation*, December 1968.
7. ——— et al.: A New Graphic-display/Plotter for Small Digital Computers, *Proc. SJCC*, 1969.
8. Wilkins, J.: "The PDP-9/LOCUST Interface," M.S. thesis, University of Arizona, 1969.
9. Van Gelder, M. K., and A. W. England: A Primer on Priority-interrupt Systems, *Control Eng.*, March 1969.
10. *A Pocket Guide to Interfacing HP Computers*, Hewlett-Packard Corporation, Cupertino, Calif., 1969.
11. *Driver Manual*, Hewlett-Packard Corporation, Palo Alto, Calif., 1969.
12. Flores, I.: *Computer Organization*, chaps. 2 and 3, Prentice-Hall, Englewood Cliffs, N.J., 1969.
13. CAMAC, a Modular Instrumentation System for Data Handling, *Rept. EUR* 4100e, EURATOM, Ispra, Italy, March 1969.
14. Meng, J. D.: A Serial Input/Output Scheme for Small Computers, *Comput. Des.*, March 1970.
15. Holland, E.: Minicomputer I/O and Peripherals, *IEEE Comput. Group News*, July–August 1970.
16. Coury, F. F.: A Systems Approach to Minicomputer I/O, *Proc. SJCC*, 1970.
17. Babiloni, L., et al.: On-line Tradeoff: Hardware versus Software, *Control Eng.*, October 1970.
18. Korn, G. A., and T. M. Korn: *Electronic Analog and Hybrid Computers* (revised edition), McGraw-Hill, New York, 1972.
19. Huskey, H. D., and G. A. Korn: *Computer Handbook*, McGraw-Hill, New York, 1962.

Digital-circuit Noise

20. Jones, J. P.: *Causes and Cures of Noise in Digital Systems*, Computer Design Publication Company, West Concord, Mass., 1964.
21. Korn, G. A.: Reduction of Digital Noise in Hybrid Analog-digital Computers, *Simulation*, March 1966.
22. Printed-circuit Shielding in *AFAL-TR*-66-371, Bunker-Ramo Corporation, April 1967.
23. Walker, R. M., and R. A. Aldrich (Fairchild Semiconductor): Standard IC's for Digital Data Communication, *Electron. Eng.*, March 1968.
24. Saenz, R. G., and E. M. Fulcher (RCA): An Approach to Logic Circuit Noise, *Comput. Des.*, April 1969.
25. *Balun Applications*, Pulse Engineering, Inc., Santa Clara, Calif., 1969.
26. Heniford, B.: Noise in 54/74 TTL Systems, *Appl. Bull.* CA-108, Texas Instruments, Inc., Dallas, 1968.
27. Garrett, L. S.: Integrated-circuit Digital-logic Families, Part III, *IEEE Spectrum*, December 1970.

Shielding, Interconnections, and Grounding

28. Stewart, E. L. (Martin/Baltimore): Grounds, Grounds, and More Grounds, *Simulation*, August 1965.
29. ———: Noise Reduction in Interconnect Lines, *Simulation*, September 1965.
30. Sargent, R. S., and T. R. Kuchlewski: Reduction of Noise in Low-impedance (Ground) Lines, *Analog Rept.* 16, Martin Co., Baltimore, 1963.
31. Marsh, J. M., and V. P. Scott: Analog-facility Grounding Techniques, *WAPD-T*-1701, Bettis At. Power Lab., Westinghouse Electric Company, Pittsburgh, 1964.
32. Marimon, R. L. (NOTS/Pasadena): Ground Rules for Low-frequency High-gain Amplifiers, *Electron. Des.*, April 12, 1963.

33. Morrison, R. (Dynamics Instrument Company): Shielding Signal Circuits, *ISA J.*, March 1966.
34. EID Staff: Grounding Low-level Instrumentation Systems, *EID*, January 1966.
35. Ginn, D. (Data Control Systems, Inc.): Data-system Grounding Techniques, *Telemetry*, July 1966.
36. Burdi, A. J. (Interstate Electronics Corp.): Keep Sampled-data Systems Accurate, *Electron. Des.*, May 24, 1966.
37. McCullough, W. (Hewlett-Packard): How to Reduce Common-mode Effects, *EEE*, February 1967.
38. Bowers, W. J. (Scientific Data Systems): Minimizing Common-mode Noise, *Control Eng.*, July 1967.
39. *Dynamic Bridge Differential Amplifier 770-440*, Redcor Corporation, Canoga Park, Calif., 1967.
40. Klipec, B. (J. Moore and Company): Controlling Noise in Instrument Circuits, *Control Eng.*, March 1968.
41. Bailey, S. J.: Using Telephone Lines for Critical Signal Transmission, *Control Eng.*, March 1969.
42. Buntenbach, R. W.: On the Design of Ground Circuits, *STAR N*68-3573, Lawrence Radiat. Lab., Livermore, Calif., 1968.
43. Budzilovich, P. N.: Electrical Noise: Its Nature, Causes, Solutions, *Control Eng.*, May 1969.
44. Morrison, B.: *Grounding and Shielding Techniques in Instrumentation*, Wiley, New York, 1967.

CHAPTER 6

DEVELOPMENT AND EVALUATION OF IMPROVED MINICOMPUTER ARCHITECTURES

INTRODUCTION AND SURVEY

The progress of small-computer design, pushed forward by inexpensive logic circuits and fierce competition, is made more deliberate by the need to spread grievous software costs over as many machines as possible. Hardware and software, in any case, must be designed and evaluated together. Their development is the system designer's response to widely divergent markets, whose requirements are not always well defined for him. The enormous versatility of the quantity-produced miniprocessor is the key to its success, but consider just how wildly these applications differ:

1. *Logic-sequencing and timing operations* (as in simple process control). Sequences may be complex, but individual operations are simple and need not be very fast.
2. *Simple logic or character-string operations, but with a requirement for fast service and/or large volume* (communications handling, front-ending larger computers, supervision of time-critical operations or measurements). Such applications favor powerful interrupt systems, direct memory access, and fast processing—but simple instruction sets will do.
3. *More complicated on-line numerical computations* (data processing, digital filtering, simulation). Here one needs more advanced arithmetic—even accessory array or floating-point-arithmetic processors; or one tries to pass the load to a larger computer.

4. Applications combining data gathering (simple tallying, measurements, automatic testing, business-data acquisition) *and* the need to communicate with higher-level computers and programs.
5. *Sophisticated special-purpose applications* (e.g., display control, numerical control of machine tools, automated drafting, text editing).
6. *Small time-sharing systems for education or business.* These may use one minicomputer for arithmetic and one or two for communication and disk-access control (Sec. 7-15).
7. *"End users"* (as opposed to original-equipment manufacturers or OEMs) such as research groups whose not-so-secret desire is a private computer center, complete with advanced operating system and conversational input/output.

The simpler applications are nicely covered by 8-bit processors with simple instruction sets and memory-cycle times varying between 0.7 and 3 μsec (Sec. 6-1). If the memory required is small or if it is mostly read-only memory, the processor might as well be fast. A responsive interrupt system is desirable at least as an expansion option.

For increasingly more complex tasks, machines with 16-bit data words appear to cover the ground best. Some advanced features (hardware multiply/divide, floating-point arithmetic, extra interrupt levels) can be modular options (Sec. 2-15). As for the basic instructions, though, processor logic is cheap; a minicomputer system might comprise $10,000 worth of memory and $16,000 worth of peripheral equipment, with a processor costing less than $8,000 (Table 6-1a). In a competitive situation, it will pay to provide a very powerful instruction set, which should be versatile enough to allow for ever-new applications and ought to save memory (still fairly costly) as well as computing time. Note that, in this way, a knowledgeable end user, who may not require expensive printers and tape

TABLE 6-1a. Relative Cost of Typical Minicomputer Processors, Memory, and Some Peripheral Devices (1972 single-quantity prices; quantity discounts go up to 30 to 40 percent for 200 units).

	8-bit	16-bit
Processor with ASR-33, 4K memory	$4,000	$7,000
Hardware multiply/divide	. . . . .	1,500
Extra 4K memory	2,000	3,000
Additional 8K memory	4,000	5,000
Medium-speed paper-tape reader/punch, controller	$4,000	
Two tape cassette drives, controller	2,000	
IBM-compatible tape drive, controller	8,000	
Fixed-head disk (500K bytes), controller	10,000	
80-column line printer, controller	10,000	

TABLE 6-1*b*.   **Range of Minicomputer Specifications (1972).**
Surveys of commercially available minicomputers appear about once a year in journals such as *Computer Decisions, Control Engineering, Datamation, EEE*, etc., and in *Minicomputer Reports*, Auerbach Info, Inc., Philadelphia, Pa.   See also Tables 2-1, 3-3, 5-2, 6-1*a*, 6-2 to 6-7, and especially the checklist of Table 6-8.

Price (processor and 4K, unit quantity)	\$2,000–\$15,000
Word size (data-path width)	8–18 bits
Memory cycle time	0.3–4 μsec
Memory size	0.5K–256K
Fixed-point add time (from memory)	typically 2 cycles
Number of addressable registers	
(accumulators and/or index registers)	1–16
Number of hardware index registers	0–15
DMA transfer rate (maximum)	0.2–2 MHz
Number of external interrupts	1–256
Hardware multiply/divide	
Multiply time (unsigned)	3–25 μsec
Divide time (unsigned)	7–40 μsec
Typical options	Memory parity check
	Memory protection
	Real-time clock
	Power-failure restart
	Automatic bootstrap loader
	Floating-point hardware
Desirable software	FORTRAN IV and/or ALGOL, BASIC
	Relocatable assembler
	Macroassembler
	Disk operating system
	Real-time executive
	Editor
	Debugger

Some 16-bit machines permit *multilevel indirect addressing;* most 12-bit and 18-bit mini-computers do not.

drives, can benefit greatly from the inexpensive, advanced central-processor features.   We shall discuss several approaches for fitting sophisticated instruction sets to the short (16-bit) minicomputer instruction words.

MINI-MINICOMPUTERS

6-1.   Examples and Features of 8-bit Systems.   (a)   The Interdata Model 1 :[1] Input/Output Circuits.   8-bit machines are widely used as communications controllers and peripheral processors for larger computers (Secs. 7-13 and

---

[1] A slightly modified version of the Interdata Model 1 is sold by General Electric as GEPAC 30-CS.

7-14) as well as small logic controllers.   **The design of these small computers emphasizes fast input/output and 8-bit-character (byte) manipulation.**   The Interdata Model 1 (Fig. 3-10) has a 1-μsec memory cycle and permits **10^6 eight-bit DMA transfers/sec;** an optional block-transfer-channel card is available.   Programmed data transfers employ the flexible asynchronous ("hand-shaking") technique described in Sec. 5-6.   Special programmed I/O instructions can initiate non-DMA block transfers, which continue to the end of a 256-byte memory page.   The Model 1 has a built-in serial input/output interface, which transfers the accumulator carry bit to teletypewriters and communication devices.   **The interrupt system has up to eight true hardware automatic-priority-interrupt inputs with preassigned trap addresses; 8-bit request and mask registers are built right into the processor** (see also Secs. 5-12 to 5-15).   256 extra interrupts with wired-priority-chain assignments (Sec. 5-14) can be recognized semiautomatically through a READ INTERRUPT ADDRESS instruction (Sec. 5-15a).

(b) Interdata Model 1: The Instruction Set.   Model 1 has *a single 8-bit accumulator* and no index register.   The 14-bit program counter is combined with an interrupt-enable bit and the carry-flag bit into a 16-bit *status register*, which is stored in two successive core bytes during interrupts and subroutines.

There are 13 types of two-byte (i.e., 16-bit) *memory-reference instructions:* LOAD, STORE, ADD, SUBTRACT, AND, OR, XOR, INCREMENT/SKIP ON ZERO, INCREMENT/SKIP ON NOT ZERO; JUMP, JUMP/SAVE with and without various conditions; and two special bit-logic operations useful, for example, for parity checking.   Addressing modes set by instruction bits include page-0, current-page, immediate (second byte is data), and one-level indirect addressing (Sec. 2-7b).   Each indirect address (pointer) is a two-byte word including a 14-bit address and 2 command bits: the first command bit causes *incrementing* (*autoindexing*) of the pointer unless the second command bit is also set; in the latter case, the program skips unless the page address (second byte of pointer address) is $111\ 111\ 11_2$ (page-boundary detection).

As a powerful new feature, instruction bits in the LOAD, ADD, SUBTRACT, AND, OR, and XOR instructions cause a skip test of the result (on NOT ZERO, NOT MINUS, or NO CARRY) which does not require extra execution time.   **By setting another opcode bit we can, moreover, skip-test the result without loading it into the accumulator** (as in the Data General NOVA/SUPERNOVA, Table 6-3).   **Accumulator contents, then, are not destroyed by** such tests, which replace the important SKIP IF ACCUMULATOR BYTE DIFFERS instruction (Sec. 2-13) needed, for example, to test for an end-of-record character.

The non-memory-reference instructions for the Model 1 are conventional one-byte/one-cycle register/flag-logic, skip-test, and shift-left instructions, plus *two-byte multiple shift-rotate instructions which can also be combined with skip tests.*

(c) Varian Data Machines 520/i: Multiple Environments and Multiple Precision. More elaborate and expensive than the small Model 1, the 520/i has a 1.5-μsec 8-bit memory and 8-bit arithmetic and data paths, but it has 16-bit accumulators, which can be concatenated for 24-bit and 32-bit operations. Such operations are of interest for front-ending larger digital computers. Basic input/output, including DMA data transfers at up to 660,000 bytes/sec, is 8-bit, but parallel 16-bit I/O through programmed instructions is possible.

The 520/i's most interesting feature is that it has **two sets of programmable 16-bit registers;** each set has two accumulators and an index register. **This feature permits extra-fast interrupt service and return for critical interrupts** by eliminating the time-consuming register-saving/restoring operations described in Secs. 5-9 and 5-11 (a similar scheme with four "environments" is, incidentally, employed in the International Business Machines System/7). Multiple interrupts can, of course, still require register saving/restoring. The 520/i has a four-level, true-hardware, automatic priority-interrupt system with built-in mask register, which can be set *and read* by processor instructions. More external interrupts would have to be recognized through a READ INTERRUPT ADDRESS sequence (Sec. 5-15a).

The 520/i instruction set is conventional, except that a special instruction sets an **operand-precision register** (there are two, one for each "environment") to 8-, 16-, 24-, or 32-bit precision; the LOAD, STORE, ADD, SUBTRACT, AND, and SHIFT instructions then become multiple-precision, multicycle instructions. The register "environment" can also be changed by a programmed instruction, so the programmer has all six 16-bit registers at his disposition.

6-2. 12-bit Systems. (a) The Digital Equipment Corporation PDP-8/e. The pioneering and enormously successful PDP-8 series was 7 years old and had sold over 10,000 copies even before PDP-8/e production had hit its stride in late 1970. A massive amount of general-purpose and application software is supplied not only by the manufacturer but also through a very large organization of users engaged in every conceivable minicomputer application (see also Sec. 7-2). As with larger digital computers, such a large and valuable software inventory was a powerful incentive to preserve the instruction set of earlier PDP-8-series models without serious changes. If we consider that the original PDP-8 architecture was conditioned by expensive discrete-logic circuits on small cards, the PDP-8/e—which must compete in a medium-scale integrated-circuit era, and still preserves the old software—is a remarkable design compromise.

PDP-8/e (Figs. 3-1 and 6-1) is a simple 12-bit minicomputer of the "basic" type described in detail in Chap. 2, with a memory-cycle time of 1.2 μsec. The *instruction format* is shown in Fig. 2-2a. There are only five two-cycle memory-reference instructions (**STORE, ADD, AND, ISZ, JUMP AND SAVE**). One level of indirect addressing is possible, and eight memory locations on page 0 serve as autoindex registers (Sec. 2-7c). Like its predecessors, PDP-8/e has only a single accumulator, but the PDP-8/e adds a temporary-storage register (*MQ register*) whose contents can be transferred to and from, or swapped with, the accumulator by one-cycle instructions. The MQ is available even without the hardware multiply/divide option. If the latter is installed, MQ serves as an extended accumulator (multiplier/quotient register, hence MQ, Sec. 1-9) and admits new double-precision **STORE** and **ADD** instructions (5.2 μsec) as well as double-precision **NEGATE** (1.8 μsec), **INCREMENT** (1.8 μsec), and **SKIP IF ZERO** (1.2 μsec).

PDP-8/e has up to 512 I/O instructions (64 I/O instructions with up to three IO pulses, Sec. 5-2), a single-level interrupt system (see also Secs. 5-9 to 5-15a), and direct memory access within one memory cycle, or within three cycles with memory-implemented current-address and word counters (Sec. 5-23). The latter scheme permits automatic block transfers with a minimum of interface hardware. The DMA interface also permits memory-increment statistics computation (Sec. 5-21) and, unlike earlier PDP-8's, has a one-cycle or three-cycle add-to-memory facility useful for periodic-signal averaging (Sec. 5-22).

Many special PDP-8 options are available from the manufacturer and from other firms. *The Digital Equipment Corporation PDP-12 combines a PDP-8-type processor, a simple cathode-ray-tube display, tape storage, and a variety of analog, relay, and logic interfacing circuits in a neat package especially suitable for biological laboratory work.* A large amount of useful applications software exists for this machine, as for its predecessor LINC-8. The Digital Equipment Corporation FPP-12, costing about $7,000, is an *accessory floating-point arithmetic unit* for the PDP-8 series using the three 12-bit-word, floating-point format shown in Fig. 1-17. While PDP-8/e has no index register, FPP-12 implements floating-point-array indexing with core-register pointers and comes with a FORTRAN compiler making use of this facility. The PDP-8/e–FPP-12 combination permits fast floating-point operations (31-μsec addition and 37-μsec multiplication are typical) at a low price if the precision afforded by its short (23-bit plus sign) mantissa is sufficient for the application.

While the PDP-8/e instruction set is constrained by the need to preserve software, hardware layout and packaging are completely new and, like the PDP-11 design (Sec. 6-6), steer a very neat midcourse between expensive, small logic cards and awkward single-card processors. Medium-sized logic cards, including cards for various options, simply plug into available slots of an etched-circuit motherboard, which replaces a wire-wrapped backplane. This PDP-8/e "OMNIBUS" (Fig. 6-1) physically resembles the PDP-11 UNIBUS in Fig. 6-4a (but, unlike the latter, is *not* a true, single interconnection bus, Sec. 6-6).

In view of the excellent package design, large-scale manufacture, and pre-existing software, the small-quantity price of the PDP-8/e (about $5,000 with a 4K-word memory) would seem to leave a comfortable margin for quantity discounts and competitive bidding. Thus, although PDP-8/e is

Fig. 6-1. PDP-8/e motherboard (OMNIBUS) packaging. The single motherboard shown can accommodate the processor and 32K words of memory, plus up to nine device-controller or option cards. Additional OMNIBUS boards may be added. (*Digital Equipment Corporation.*)

less sophisticated than the 8-bit machines described in Sec. 6-1, it is a very serious competitor not only for 8-bit minicomputers but even for some 16-bit machines.

(b) A Different Approach: The General Automation, Inc. SPC-12/ Motorola Data Processor. The General Automation, Inc. SPC-12 and the essentially similar Motorola Data Processor (MDP) combine an 8-*bit* 2.16-μsec memory and a 12-*bit* processor with an interesting instruction set.

The SPC-12 has a special 12-bit register (B register) with two-word LOAD and STORE instructions capable of addressing up to 4,096 memory locations directly or indexed, but not indirectly. Either a 12-bit word or an 8-bit byte can be loaded in three or four memory cycles, respectively.

Two-word LOAD, STORE, ADD, SUBTRACT, AND, OR, and XOR instructions for each of *four* 12-*bit accumulators* can address only *four* memory locations and the B register directly. But a two-byte indirect address can be stored in each of the four addressable page-0 locations, and indexing is possible. Moreover, indirect-address-word bits can specify postindexing (which can be *combined* with preindexing) and/or automatic incrementing of the indirect address. Three of the four accumulators can serve as index registers.

The SPC-12/MDP represents an attempt to utilize an inexpensive memory efficiently. Its instruction code is more sophisticated than that of the PDP-8 series, but efficient general-purpose programming will be more difficult to learn. The SPC-12/MDP has been successful in dedicated manufacturing-control applications.

DEVELOPMENT OF 16/18-BIT ARCHITECTURES

6-3. 16/18-bit Design Considerations.   (a) Central-processor Packaging and Bus Connections.   Central-processor design, subject to strong competitive pressures, will employ medium-scale integrated (MSI) circuits and try to minimize interconnections, both *between* circuit cards and *on* circuit cards. This involves compromises. Processors designed before MSI circuits were widely available (e.g., the neatly packaged Honeywell 516) have many small plug-in circuit cards. This is excellent for maintenance—troubleshooting might simply involve plug-in replacement of a card identified by a diagnostic program.

But connectors and wiring are expensive. Thus several newer processors (e.g., NOVA, Varian 620/f and L) are complete on a single circuit card, with memory modules, interrupt systems, etc., on two to five extra cards (Fig. 1-1). On the other hand, improved processors have multiple general-purpose registers, which require extra etched-circuit interconnections and more space on the card. But large cards have a tendency to bend, breaking solder joints. Multilayer cards, which can alleviate the register-connection problem, are rather expensive for minicomputers. Large cards are also more difficult to troubleshoot and maintain.

Simplified maintenance is especially valuable to many "end users," but original-equipment manufacturers (who buy quantities of processors) are quite sensitive to unit costs. The maintenance of single-card processors becomes easier if we employ plug-in MSI packages. But integrated-circuit sockets are not cheap, and the possibility of thousands of unsoldered plug-in connections is a little uncomfortable. Perhaps the best way is to plug in *some* critical MSI circuits and to solder the others.

A different and significant way to attack the processor-interconnection problem is to time-share a single set of bus lines among several data paths between processor registers, memory, and external devices. This approach is taken, for instance, in the Digital Equipment Corporation PDP-11 (Sec. 6-9). It is then possible to divide the processor into several modular cards plugging into common bus connections on a motherboard (Figs. 6-1 and 6-2). This again simplifies maintenance and may also permit convenient addition of expansion or option modules. The price paid for these advantages is reduced computing speed, which is compromised by the time-shared bus.

(b) The Short-instruction-word Problem. The instruction format of Fig. 2-2*b*, typical of many "basic" 16-bit minicomputers, can directly address

Fig. 6-2. PDP-11 UNIBUS slices with medium-sized plug-in cards can be interconnected with flexible printed-circuit cable. The maximum bus length is 50 ft (counting stub connections), but it is possible to extend the bus through buffer amplifiers at the expense of extra time delay. (*Digital Equipment Corporation.*)

up to 528 memory locations (page 0 or current page). Indexing or (single-level) indirect addressing can reach up to $2^{16} = 65,536$ words or bytes, but note that either addressing mode requires an extra instruction to load the index register or pointer location.

It is fairly obvious that random addressing in so large a memory *necessarily* requires multiple 16-bit instruction words, no matter what addressing scheme is available. Paged, relative, indexed, and autoindex addressing (Sec. 2-7) can save instruction words because, in many programs, several instructions address clustered, consecutive, or evenly spaced memory locations. The choice of addressing modes is not merely a hardware problem but affects the assembler design. Relative and two-word immediate addresses are easy to relocate (Sec. 4-18). Index registers are very efficient for accessing arrays, but minicomputer programmers always run out of index registers, especially when multiple interrupts must be serviced; and multiple index registers require extra selection bits. With multiple registers and more sophisticated logic available at lower cost, the trend is to use *fewer* address bits and *more* opcode bits in 16-bit memory-reference instructions. We will, in the following sections, exhibit how different minicomputer architectures deal with the short-instruction-word problem; more discussion will be found in Sec. 6-14.

6-4. Improved "Basic" 16-bit and 18-bit Machines. The better 16-bit machines of the "basic" type described in Chap. 2 have two accumulators (which can be concatenated for double-precision operations) and at least one index register. "Basic" minicomputers in this class include the Honeywell 316/416/516 series, Varian Data Machines 620/f and L, and Westinghouse 2500. Lockheed MAC/MAC JR, Raytheon Computer 704/6, and several others have only two programmable 16-bit registers.

There are relatively few 18-bit minicomputers (see also Sec. 1-5). The extra precision of 18 bits versus 16 bits is not particularly useful; multiterm sums still require double-precision accumulation and a three-word floating-point format, and 16-bit ASCII-character packing is more efficient. But *the 18-bit format has a striking advantage in applications requiring graphic displays or plots* since 9-bit X and Y coordinates can be combined in a single computer word (Sec. 7-9).

The most popular 18-bit minicomputer is the **Digital Equipment Corporation PDP-15,** a fairly fast (800-nsec cycle time) TTL machine having one accumulator (plus an MQ register with the hardware multiply/divide option) and one index register. PDP-15 has 4,096 two-cycle and four-cycle I/O instructions, a true hardware automatic priority-interrupt system (with four levels assigned to wired chains of up to eight devices each, plus four program levels, Secs. 5-14 to 5-16), and excellent direct memory access. The DMA system has memory-increment and add-to-memory features (Secs. 5-22 and 5-23) and permits automatic block transfers with either hardware- or memory-implemented address and word counters (Sec. 5-23); an extra-cost option even permits access to one memory bank while the processor uses the other one.

PDP-15 also has good software, including a powerful macroassembler and a convenient disk operating system, plus FORTRAN, ALGOL, and SNOBOL compilers. There is also an elaborate graphic-display accessory and the possibility of adding a hardware floating-point unit (see also Secs. 5-6 and 7-10). On the debit side, processor hardware and instruction sets rely on memory-cycle speed rather than sophistication, presumably in order to preserve design features and especially software of the predecessor machine (PDP-9). There is only one accumulator; the index register and the limit register (designed to hold the index limit for program loops) must be loaded and read through the accumulator; and each such transfer takes *two* cycles. With its relatively small instruction set, PDP-15 can access 4K words directly when the index register is in the circuit or 8K words in a NO INDEX mode emulating the PDP-9, which has no index register (both

PDP-15 and PDP-9 permit autoindexing, Sec. 2-7c). The PDP-15 hardware multiply/divide option basically implements unsigned multiplication and division and requires awkward and time-consuming instruction sequences for 2s-complement arithmetic. Finally, the three-word floating-point format used with PDP-9 and PDP-15 commits a full 18-bit word to the exponent and thus sacrifices precision or memory to simplify programming. There is also a two-word floating-point format with less precision and *longer* software execution times. Floating-point operations can be speeded up dramatically with an *accessory floating-point processor*, which can also do single-precision and double-precision fixed-point operations (see also Sec. 6-12 and Table 6-7).

While PDP-15's most interesting features are its I/O system, software, and optional floating-point hardware, the *Varian Data Machines* 620/f (an improved and faster version of the earlier 629/i) has an especially powerful instruction set and processor hardware (see also Sec. 6-14). Memory-cycle time is 750 nsec (550 nsec with read-only memory modules). 620/f is basically a 16-bit machine, but it is available with 18-bit memory, arithmetic, and I/O, still using 16-bit instructions. *The* 18-*bit version is, again, especially suitable for use with cathode-ray-tube displays.*

620/f has two 16/18-bit accumulators *and* a 16-bit index register. The second accumulator extends the first for double-precision operations and can serve as a second index register. *Postindexing*, as well as preindexing, *multilevel* indirect addressing, relative addressing, and two-word direct and immediate addressing is possible. Two-word two-cycle conditional-jump instructions are available. The hardware multiply/divide option permits fast signed multiplication (8 to 9 μsec) and has a special instruction for *accumulation of double-precision products* (double-accumulator contents C are replaced by $C + AB$), which is very useful for digital integration, averaging, and filtering operations. The machine lacks autoindexing and special byte-manipulation instructions, but it can swap accumulator bytes through a two-cycle **ROTATE** instruction. A full range of software is provided.

NOTE: In many programs, 620/f may save memory and time compared to multiregister machines, such as the NOVA/SUPERNOVA (Sec. 6-5) and the PDP-11/20 (Secs. 6-6 to 6-11), which lack the 620/f's straightforward one-word and two-word memory-reference instructions.

620/f has a 1.3 × 10^6 word/sec DMA facility and an automatic priority-interrupt system. A slower (0.95 μsec) version of the machine, the 620/L/100, available only with 16 bits, offers almost the same instruction set as 620/f at a remarkably low price (Fig. 1-1d).

General Automation SPC-16 is an interesting *multiregister*, 16-bit computer with 960-nsec core-memory-cycle time and 480-nsec ROM access time. The machine permits one-word and two-word addressing in all addressing modes (direct, relative, single-level indirect, indexed, *post-indexed*, and relative to a *base register* which permits *double* indexing). There are *two sets* of eight general-purpose registers, eight each for foreground and background programs as in Sec. 6-1c.   Three registers in each set of eight can be used as index registers, and one can be used as a base register (essentially an extra index register permitting double indexing); two registers are simply accumulators, and one serves as a linkage register

TABLE 6-2.   NOVA/SUPERNOVA Instruction Execution Times (in microseconds).

Instruction	NOVA	NOVA 1200	NOVA 800	SUPERNOVA Core	SUPERNOVA Solid-state memory or ROM
LOAD, STORE INCREMENT (or DECREMENT),	5.2	2.6	1.6	1.6	1.2
SKIP IF ZERO	5.2	3.2	1.8	1.8	1.4
JUMP	2.6	1.4	0.8	0.8	0.6
JUMP AND SAVE	3.5	1.4	0.8	1.4	1.2
Extra time for indirect address	2.6	1.2	0.8	0.8	0.6
Indirect address and autoindexing	2.6	1.8	1.0	1.0	0.8
Arithmetic/logic instructions	5.6–5.9	1.4 2.7 if skip occurs	0.8 1.0 if skip occurs	0.8 1.6 if skip occurs	0.3 0.6–0.9 if skip occurs
MULTIPLY (unsigned)	11.1	3.9	8.8	5.4 (maximum)	5.3 (maximum)
DIVIDE (unsigned)	11.9	4.1	8.8	6.9	6.8
I/O (read or sense)	4.4	2.6	1.4–2.2	2.9	2.8
I/O (write)	4.7	3.2	2.2–2.8	3.3	3.2

holding subroutine and interrupt return addresses.   A single 10-cycle instruction will save or restore all eight registers and some flag bits through a transfer to or from core memory, a very useful feature for interrupt programming.

SPC-16 has 1.04-MHz DMA with memory-increment and add-to memory options and can implement eight 340-kHz memory-counter block-transfer channels (Secs. 5-21 to 5-23).   There is a full set of software, including a macroassembler and a disk operating system.

6-5.   The Data General NOVA/SUPERNOVA Systems.   (a) Design Features.   The various NOVAs and SUPERNOVAs are 16-bit minicomputers distinguishable by different memory speeds (Table 6-2) and by the fact that the less expensive members of the series (NOVA, NOVA 1200) cleverly execute 16-bit operations via successive 4-bit "nibbles" to trade computing time for hardware complexity. All NOVAs and SUPERNOVAs share the same instruction set and employ the same software. Our discussion will center on the faster NOVA 800 and SUPERNOVA SC.

Each of these machines has a compact one-card or two-card processor (Fig. 1-1) with **four accumulators,** two of which can also serve as **index registers.** NOVA/SUPERNOVA architecture, which implies Data General's approach to the short-instruction-word problem, has the following important features:

1. **There are only six simple types of memory-reference instructions—they do not implement arithmetic/logic operations:**

LOAD ACCUMULATOR	STORE ACCUMULATOR
(NO. 1, 2, 3, or 4)	(NO. 1, 2, 3, or 4)
INCREMENT, SKIP IF ZERO	DECREMENT, SKIP IF ZERO
JUMP	JUMP AND SAVE RETURN ADDRESS
	IN ACCUMULATOR 3

Each of these instructions can address 256 locations *directly* (on memory page 0), relative to the program counter (*relative addressing*), or relative to the contents of one of two accumulators, which thus serve as *index registers*. *Repeated indirect addressing* is permitted, and *preindexing* is possible. There are also 16 memory locations which *autoincrement* or *autodecrement* upon indirect addressing (see also Sec. 2-7).

2. **All arithmetic/logic instructions are one-cycle register-to-register instructions—they do not address memory. This frees instruction-word bits to make each such instruction quite powerful.**

Each of these instructions can **combine** an arithmetic or logic operation, an operation on the processor carry flag, a rotation of the resulting register-word-and-carry, *and* a skip test (Table 6-3).

3. **In the SUPERNOVAs, non-memory-reference, nonskip instructions fetched from a nondestructive-readout memory (i.e., read-only memory or semiconductor memory) can overlap the following instruction fetch.** Such instructions effectively require only 300 nsec rather than a complete 800-nsec memory cycle.

NOVA/SUPERNOVA users can buy most common options (Sec. 2-15), including *memory protection* and a *hardware multiply/divide unit* which implements only unsigned operations directly. Signed multiplication takes between 16 and 23 cycles, some of which can be overlapped in the SUPERNOVA SC. The *interrupt system* has ORed lines with individual trap

TABLE 6-3.   NOVA/SUPERNOVA Register-to-register Instructions.

Bit	
0	1 identifies this class of instructions
1 2	Specifies **source register**
3 4	Specifies **destination register**
5 6 7	**Operation code :** ADD, ADD COMPLEMENT, SUBTRACT, AND, MOVE; NEGATE, COMPLEMENT, INCREMENT
8 9	**Rotate** result and carry bit as specified below: LEFT, RIGHT, NOT AT ALL; or SWAP 8-BIT BYTES
10 11	**Select carry** (before rotation): 0, 1, OLD CARRY, COMPLEMENT
12	**Do not actually disturb destination register** if this bit is 1 (skip test only)
13 14 15	**Skip** next instruction*: NEVER, ALWAYS; IF RESULT = 0, ≠ 0; IF CARRY = 0, ≠ 0; IF RESULT OR CARRY = 0, IF RESULT AND CARRY = 0

* Note that skip tests are made on the rotated 16-bit result-and-carry. Thus, if the result of an addition is shifted left, SKIP ON ZERO CARRY actually tests the sign of the sum. Note also that skip tests can be made without loading the result into the destination register, thus preserving its current content.

addresses read into an accumulator after an ACKNOWLEDGE INTERRUPT instruction (Sec. 5-15a). Mask flip-flops can be implemented on interface cards. *Direct-memory-access operations* can effect single-cycle data transfers, memory-increment, and add-to-memory (Secs. 5-17 to 5-22). An accessory *multiprocessor communications adapter* provides simple, economical means of connecting several NOVA/SUPERNOVA computers to form multiprocessor systems. High-speed *data-channel cards* are also available.

Software includes an assembler (with double-precision and floating-point constants and conditional assembly—but no macros), FORTRAN IV, ALGOL, time-shared BASIC, and a disk-based operating system.

(b) Discussion. SUPERNOVA's instruction overlap is ingenious, especially since it anticipated the advent of reasonably priced semiconductor memories by a year or two. The powerful—and possibly overlapping—non-memory-reference instructions on Table 6-3 make for elegant and fast double-precision and floating-point subroutines, which can be stored in read-only memory if desired.

The NOVA/SUPERNOVA architecture has, on the other hand, a serious drawback in applications requiring mainly arithmetic or logic operations on words in memory, as in array or matrix processing. A conventional "basic" minicomputer requires a single instruction,

    ADD INTO ACCUMULATOR 2   X   / (2 machine cycles)

to add the number in memory location X to a number currently in accumulator 2. But NOVA/SUPERNOVA needs **two** instructions,

LOAD ACCUMULATOR 1   **X**   / (2 machine cycles)
ADD ACCUMULATOR 1 TO ACCUMULATOR 2   / (1 cycle, can be
                                    /   partially overlapped)

This takes extra time even with overlapping and thus wastes SUPERNOVA's high-speed hardware. Worse, the slower NOVA/SUPERNOVA program also uses twice as much memory as the "basic" minicomputer.

Data General minicomputers might make up for this deficiency in programs which really utilize their combination arithmetic/rotate/skip instructions. Multiple general-purpose registers can save time-consuming memory references by serving as temporary-storage locations; NOVA/SUPERNOVAs have four suitable registers, which should be compared, for instance, with three in the Varian 620/f and 620/L and with six or seven in the PDP-11. Data General's compact processor design may give them a price advantage, which should be checked against possible extra memory costs.

THE DIGITAL EQUIPMENT CORPORATION PDP-11 SYSTEM

6-6. Introduction. DEC's entry into the 16-bit minicomputer field combines a neat and inexpensive packaging scheme with **a new system design quite different from the "basic" small computer described in Chap. 2.** The architecture of the PDP-11 system, which will surely rival the PDP-8 series in importance, bears not simply on the processor design but on the operation and applications of complete systems involving multiple peripherals and, in fact, multiple processors.

PDP-11 has **eight programmable registers,** R0 through R7. R7 is the *program counter*, and R6 is the *processor-stack pointer* (Sec. 6-10). This means that various instructions will automatically change the contents of R6 and R7—they cannot really be used as general-purpose registers even though they are addressed like the other registers. Each register can serve as an accumulator, but their most important application is to hold operand and result *addresses*. Operands can be fetched from such addresses (and arithmetic/logic results can be deposited) without themselves passing

TABLE 6-4. PDP-11 Instruction-execution Times.

The total time required to execute a PDP-11 instruction is the **instruction time** plus **destination time** (for one-address instructions other than JUMP instructions with built-in relative addresses), plus the **source time** for two-address instructions (in microseconds). PDP-11/45 times are for 300-nsec memory *with fast internal bus*.

1. Two-address Instructions (add source time *and* destination time).

	11/20 System	11/45 System
MOVE, ADD, SUBTRACT, AND,*		
OR, COMPLEMENT SOURCE/AND	2.3	0.3
COMPARE*	2.3	0.3

2. One-address Instructions (add destination time).

	11/20 System	11/45 System
CLEAR, INCREMENT, DECREMENT,		
NEGATE, COMPLEMENT, ADD (or SUBTRACT)		
CARRY, TEST,* ROTATE/SHIFT, SWAP BYTES	2.3	0.3–0.75
JUMP (with destination field)	1.2	0.3–0.75
JUMP TO SUBROUTINE	4.4	1.5

3. Instructions without Address, or with Relative-address Field Only (nothing to add).

	11/20 System	11/45 System
JUMP (with relative-address field)	2.6	0.6
JUMP ON CONDITION: if condition is true	2.6	0.6
if not	1.5	0.3
SET (or CLEAR) FLAGS	1.5	0.6
RETURN FROM SUBROUTINE	3.5	1.2
RETURN FROM INTERRUPT	4.8	1.5

4. Source and Destination Times (add 0.6 μsec to PDP-11/20 source and/or destination time for odd-byte addresses).

	11/20 System		11/45 System	
	Source Time	Destination Time	Source Time	Destination Time
Register	0	0	0	0.15
Deferred register (with				
or without autoindexing)	1.5	1.4	0.37–1.0	0.3–0.5
Indirect (with and				
without autoindexing)	2.7	2.6	1.1	0.8–1.1
Two-word Indexed	2.7	2.6	0.82	0.5–0.9
Two-word Indexed and Indirect	3.9	3.8	1.4	0.9–1.4

* Subtract 0.4 μsec from PDP-11/20 destination time if destination is *not* a register.

through processor registers. **PDP-11, moreover, treats peripheral-device addresses exactly like (nonrelocatable) memory addresses.** It is possible, for instance, to add an analog-to-digital-converter output into a memory location or directly into a digital-to-analog-converter register. 8-bit bytes as well as 16-bit words can be addressed and transferred.

In each 16-bit PDP-11 system, **all data transfers among memory, processor, and peripheral devices are asynchronous transfers** (i.e., request/grant transfers, as in Secs. 5-6 and 5-13) **using a single bus** in the PDP-11/20 (more advanced systems can have multiple buses, Sec. 6-9). This **UNIBUS** is the key to the simplicity of PDP-11 packaging, but the asynchronous single-bus operations also constrain execution speed. Instruction execution times are listed in Table 6-4 and will be further discussed in Sec. 6-9.

6-7. Instructions and Addresses. (a) Two-address Instructions. PDP-11 has *no* direct-addressing memory-reference instructions like **LOAD INTO**

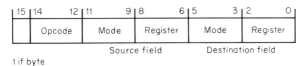

(*a*) **Two-address Instructions** (add extra address word or words, if any).

(*b*) **One-address Instructions** (add extra address word, if any).

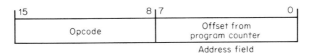

(*c*) **JUMP ON CONDITION** **Instructions.**

(*d*) **Subroutine Linkage.**

Fig. 6-3. PDP-11 instruction formats. (NOTE: PDP-11 manuals number bits from right to left.)

ACCUMULATOR although, as we shall see, the assembler can simulate direct addressing. Instead, the instructions **MOVE, ADD, SUBTRACT, AND, OR,** and **COMPLEMENT SOURCE/AND** are **two-address instructions:** the 16-bit instruction-word format (Fig. 6-3) comprises a 4-bit operation code and *two* 6-bit **address fields,** which determine the effective addresses of operands and result. Consider, for example,

ADD (effective source address), (effective destination address)

The first address field specifies the location of the first operand (first term of the sum). The second address field locates the second operand, which will be replaced by the result; the first operand remains undisturbed.

The *first operand* of the **MOVE** instruction and the result of **ADD**, **SUBTRACT, AND, OR**, and **COMPLEMENT SOURCE/AND** determine the subsequent state of **four processor flag flip-flops**: Z ($= 0$), N (<0, *sign bit*), C (*carry* for **ADD, SUBTRACT**), and V (2s-complement *overflow* for **ADD, SUBTRACT**). **AND, OR**, and **COMPLEMENT SOURCE/AND** clear V and leave C unaffected. A sixth two-address instruction,

COMPARE (effective source address), (effective destination address)

sets or clears the flags like **SUBTRACT** *but does not destroy the second operand* by depositing a result.

(b) One-address Instructions and Flag Operations. CLEAR, INCREMENT, DECREMENT, NEGATE, COMPLEMENT, ADD CARRY, SUBTRACT CARRY, SWAP BYTES, and **ROTATE/SHIFT** instructions have a single address field (Fig. 6-3) which can refer to a register, memory location, or peripheral-device address, as explained in Sec. 6-7c. **TEST** is a one-address instruction which sets the Z ($= 0$) and N (<0, *sign bit*) flags in accordance with the effectively addressed operand. **JUMP** is a one-address instruction whose destination may not be a processor register.

On the other hand, **JUMP ON CONDITION** instructions permit *only* relative addressing—the entire 8-bit address field is interpreted as an offset relative to the program counter. The **JUMP TO SUBROUTINE** instruction will be described in Sec. 6-10.

PDP-11 also has instructions for *setting* and for *clearing* combinations of the processor flags Z, N, C, and V.

(c) Addressing Modes. Three bits (one octal digit) of each 6-bit address field reference one of the eight programmable registers. The remaining 3 bits specify one of eight addressing modes (a two-address instruction could have up to 64 combinations of addressing modes for source and destination):

1. **Register addressing:** The referenced register contains the operand. For example,

    ADD R0, R3

    adds the contents of registers 0 and 3 and places the sum into register 3.
2. **"Deferred" addressing via registers:** The referenced register contains the *address* of the operand. Thus,

    MOVE R1, (R3)

moves the *contents* of register 1 to the memory location *addressed by* register 3.

3. **Autoincrement addressing:** The operand address is taken from the referenced register, which is *afterward* incremented.

CLEAR (R6) +

clears the memory location addressed by register 6 and *then* increments register 6.

4. **Autodecrement addressing:** The specified register is *first* decremented and *then* used as an address pointer.

ADD R1, −(R2)

adds the contents of register 1 into the memory location addressed by the decremented contents of register 2.

5. **Multiword indexed addressing:** The effective address is the sum of the word in the specified register (used here as an index register) and a 16-bit word following the current instruction. Two such address words follow if *both* address fields of a two-address instruction are indexed.

In addition, an address-field bit can be set to redefine the address found by deferred register addressing, autoincrementing, autodecrementing, or indexing as an **indirect address** (i.e., as a pointer to the actual effective address). We thus have eight addressing modes.

Noting that register 7 is the program counter, we can implement the following addressing modes as special cases (see also Sec. 2-7):

1. **Multiword immediate addressing:** Specify autoincrement addressing through the program counter, and store the operand immediately following the current instruction.
2. **Multiword direct addressing:** Specify indirect autoincrement addressing through the program counter, with the operand *address* immediately following the current instruction.
3. **Multiword relative addressing:** indexed addressing using the program counter and an address word following the current instruction.

Multiword immediate addressing conveniently produces operations on *literals* (Sec. 4-4). *PDP-11 assemblers normally use multiword relative addressing to implement memory-reference instructions with symbolic addresses, like*

ADD   X, Y

CLEAR   TEMP

Both these addressing modes make it easy to relocate programs (Sec. 4-18; note that all PDP-11 conditional-branching instructions *always* use relative addressing).

(d) Byte Addressing and Byte Operations. The 16-bit effective addresses generated by the various addressing modes can address up to 65,536 individual 8-bit bytes (32K words; the least significant address bit denotes the low-order or high-order byte). A **BYTE MODE** instruction bit (Fig. 6-3) can be set to make the instructions

MOVE	CLEAR	TEST
AND	INCREMENT	ADD CARRY
OR	DECREMENT	SUBTRACT CARRY
COMPLEMENT SOURCE/AND	NEGATE	ROTATE/SHIFT
COMPARE	COMPLEMENT	

operate only on the low-order byte(s) of their operand(s) so that PDP-11 can simulate an 8-bit machine. **SWAP BYTES** was already mentioned.

NOTE: Autoincrementing and autodecrementing are automatically done by *byte* addresses in BYTE mode and by *word* addresses otherwise. Register 6 (because it is used as the processor-stack pointer) permits only whole-word autoincrementing and autodecrementing. The same is true of register 7 (the program counter).

6-8. Stack Operations (see also Sec. 4-10). The *postincrementing* and *predecrementing* of register contents defined in Sec. 6-7c is especially suitable for *stack operations*. In the following example, register 2 serves as a *stack pointer*, which always points at the top of a stack of memory addresses which *increase* consecutively toward the bottom of the stack (Sec. 4-10). Typical stack operations will be implemented by

MOVE	A, − (R2)	/ *Pushes* **A** onto top of stack
MOVE	(R2) +, B	/ *Pops* **B** off the top
ADD	(R2) +, (R2)	/ Pops top element off
		/ and adds it to the new
		/ top element

It might be necessary to compare the stack pointer with the largest and/or smallest address allowed for the stack. Note also that *we can address any element of the stack by using the stack pointer as the index register for two-word indexed addressing.*

6-9. UNIBUS Operation and Instruction-execution Times. The PDP-11/45 System. PDP-11 system design is based on a simple and inexpensive packaging scheme, which facilitates modular expansion. Medium-sized circuit cards plug into etched-circuit motherboards (Fig. 6-2; see also Sec. 6-3a), which bear power and ground connections and **a single set of bus lines (UNIBUS,** Fig. 6-4a), viz.,

1. 16 **bidirectional data lines,** which carry *all* data transfers among processor (registers and arithmetic/logic), memory, and peripheral devices.

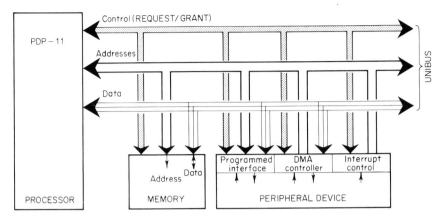

Fig. 6-4a. A PDP-11 UNIBUS system, showing a processor, a memory, and a peripheral device interfaced (like, for example, a disk) for programmed instructions (e.g., control-register setting), direct memory access, and interrupt.

2. 18 **address lines.** The same addressing scheme is used for programmed processor/memory intercourse, programmed I/O, direct memory access, and for transmitting interrupt trap addresses (Sec. 5-15*b*).

3. 22 **control-logic and parity-check lines.**

We have already noted that **peripheral-device registers** (data and control registers, Secs. 5-3 and 5-4) **and processor registers are addressed just like**

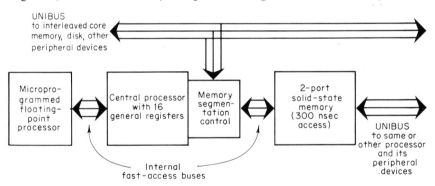

Fig. 6-4b. A PDP-11/45 system with (optional) fast solid-state memory and (optional) microprogrammed floating-point processor. The fast (Schottky-clamped TTL) PDP-11/45 hardware fits especially well into multiprocessor and time-sharing systems, which may comprise other PDP-11/45's or simpler PDP-11 processors. Fast-access buses to the optional solid-state memory and/or floating-point arithmetic avoid the ordinary UNIBUS access time. The solid-state memory has two ports for especially elegant multiprocessor interconnections (see also Secs. 6-12 and 7-15). For time-sharing/multiprogramming applications, the processor can access up to 124K words of segment-protected interleaved-core or solid-state memory and has *two* sets of eight general registers (for two "environments," Sec. 6-1*c*). Three of these registers can serve as hardware-incremented stack pointers for subroutine or interrupt-service-routine stacks (Secs. 6-8 and 6-10). See also Tables 6-4 and 6-7.

memory locations. This means that PDP-11 needs no special I/O instructions, but uses memory-reference instructions with device addresses. Device-requested direct-memory-access data transfers use the UNIBUS lines in the manner described in Secs. 5-17 and 5-18. Not only DMA data transfers, but also **all processor-requested information transfers (including each instruction-fetching operation) are asynchronous transfers; each such transfer employs request/grant logic similar to Figs. 5-11 and 5-13,** just like a DMA transfer.

Since a single UNIBUS serves processor-requested operations, DMA transfers, and interrupt trap-address transfers, **priority-arbitration logic** (similar to Fig. 5-11) assigns the highest priority to DMA requests and successively lower priorities to four hardware interrupt levels and four program levels. Interrupt levels can be masked by simplified masking instructions in the manner of Sec. 5-15b, and any number of devices can be chain-wired on each interrupt level (Sec. 5-14).

Asynchronous data-transfer operations make PDP-11 systems less sensitive to delays caused by peripheral devices or accessory processors, permit the use of faster and slower memories in the same system, and make it unnecessary to precede data transfers with a SKIP IF DEVICE NOT READY instruction (Secs. 5-6 and 5-8). On the other hand, **the time required for a UNIBUS request/grant cycle** (0.7 μsec for the 11/20 system and 0.35 μsec for the 11/45) **is necessarily added to the time required for every UNIBUS memory access.**

In the more advanced PDP-11/45 system (Fig. 6-4b), the central processor can request faster access to a semiconductor memory and to a *floating-point-arithmetic unit* via extra *internal buses*. This, together with faster (Schottky-diode-clamped TTL) processor logic, greatly speeds instruction execution. Optional address-computing logic (*memory-segmentation control*, Fig. 6-4b) can utilize all 18 UNIBUS address lines to address up to 124K words (248K bytes) of memory, with dynamic (program-controlled) allocation and protection of memory segments assigned to different programs or users.

Table 6-4 shows the various components of **PDP-11 instruction-execution times.** The instruction time includes the time needed to fetch the instruction, i.e., one bus request/grant time plus one memory cycle (between 0.3 and 2 μsec, depending on the memory used), and some execution time, which may be overlapped with the rewrite half-cycle. To this one must add the **destination time** for one-address instructions, plus the **source time** for two-address instructions (Sec. 6-7). Source or destination times are 0 if a processor register is the source or destination. Otherwise, each source and/or destination time involves a memory (or peripheral-device) access via the UNIBUS or internal bus, plus any extra memory cycle required for indirect addressing and/or two-word addressing.

6-10.   Automatic Stacking of Interrupt-service Routines and Subroutines.
PDP-11 interrupt and subroutine handling provides for **automatic nesting of routines and reentrant coding;** so one copy of a routine can serve multiple calls, and subroutines can call themselves (see also Sec. 4-16). As one result, PDP-11 FORTRAN, unlike conventional FORTRAN systems, permits reentrant real-time interrupt servicing and recursive subroutines.

1. PDP-11 has a **true hardware automatic priority-interrupt system** with four hardware priority levels and four priority levels for program segments, corresponding to mask flip-flops built into the processor. Any number of priority sublevels can be chain-wired within each level, and individual interrupt trap addresses are transmitted over UNIBUS address lines. Device-level mask flip-flops could be added as desired.

   Upon leaving an interrupt-service routine to enter a new one, we must store the *return address* (incremented program-counter reading) and a 16-bit **processor status word** comprising the Z, N, C, and V flag bits (Sec. 6-7) and the interrupt-mask status; we must also preserve all *temporary-storage words* (including words saving processor-register contents, if any) needed by the old routine (see also Secs. 4-16 and 5-15). PDP-11 programs save all these items in a **processor stack** maintained in core memory. A typical processor stack is built up (from *bottom to top*, i.e., with addresses *decreasing*) as follows:

. . . etc.	Top of stack
Temporary storage for routine 2	(*lowest* address)
Return address (to routine 1)	
Status word (at time of 2d jump)	
Temporary storage for routine 1	
Return address (to main program)	
Status word (at time of 1st jump)	

Some or all temporary-storage items for a routine may not get stored before the next interrupt occurs.

   Register 6, the **processor-stack pointer,** will be used to access the processor stack in the manner of Sec. 6-8. The programmer must set register 6 initially to the stack-bottom location, push temporary-storage items onto the stack with

$$\text{MOVE} \ldots, - \text{(R6)}$$

as needed, and pop them off the stack as they are used by the routine. This is all he needs to do because register 6 hardware has the special property that **every interrupt recognized by the computer automatically pushes the current status word and the return address onto the processor stack.** At the end of each interrupt-service routine, **the instruction**

RETURN FROM INTERRUPT automatically restores the program counter and status bits and increments register 6 twice to pop these items off the stack. These automatic features permit very efficient interrupt service.

2. A slightly different procedure is used for **subroutine stacking.** The instruction

    JUMP TO SUBROUTINE   (register), (effective destination address)

produces a jump to the effectively addressed destination and stores the return address in the specified register ("linkage register"), just like the **JUMP AND SAVE IN INDEX** instruction in Secs. 2-11 and 4-14. In addition, the PDP-11 **automatically pushes the previous linkage-register contents onto the processor stack** to preserve earlier return addresses in nested subroutines.

When a subroutine is completed, the special return-jump instruction

    RETURN FROM SUBROUTINE   (register)

resets the program counter to the address stored in the specified register and *pops the top element off the processor stack and into the register.* This top element should be the preceding return address; temporary-storage items will again be pushed onto the stack and will be popped off as the subroutine uses them up. Note that **JUMP TO SUBROUTINE** and **RETURN FROM SUBROUTINE** do *not* automatically save and restore the processor status word.

When data for a subroutine are supplied through a calling sequence (Sec. 4-14) like

    JUMP TO SUBROUTINE   R4, A
    DATA 1
    DATA 2
    . . .

we can access the data (or data address) by autoincrementing the linkage register (R4 in this case). If the data words are needed in random order, we can use two-word indexed addressing via R4, but we must make sure that R4 contains the correct return address when the subroutine is finished.

6-11. Discussion. Expansion and Combination of PDP-11 Systems. The PDP-11 addressing system simplifies many I/O operations, makes it easy to write relocatable code, and is at its best when it can access consecutive memory addresses (either words or bytes) by autoindexing, as in arrays and stacks. In most other situations, each two-address operation requires at least one extra instruction to load a register, and many memory-reference instructions will involve two-word or three-word relative, indexed, or immediate addressing. Note also that binary operations like **ADD A, B** *destroy the second operand;* a longer program is needed if we want to save **B**. In the PDP-11/20 system, the extra memory references take up not only memory but also rather substantial time because of the relatively slow asynchronous transfers through the UNIBUS.   The latter acts as a sort of bottleneck even when very fast semiconductor memories are available. Thus, a fast conventional minicomputer with at least a little one-word relative-addressing capability and *good index-manipulation instructions* may beat the PDP-11/20 even in array and loop routines (see also Secs. 6-4 and 6-9).

UNIBUS I/O operations, however, can be quite fast.   PDP-11 has a true hardware automatic priority-interrupt system and offers not only fast initial interrupt response (<7 μsec if no DMA requests have occurred) but also efficient stacking of reentrant interrupt-service routines (Sec. 6-10). DMA requests can gain access to the processor within 3.5 μsec (11/20) or 2 μsec (11/45), and up to 10^6 DMA data transfers/sec are possible.

The real strength of the UNIBUS design is as an inexpensive, flexible, and versatile packaging scheme, which permits convenient expansion of PDP-11 systems.   Device-controller cards, different kinds of memory modules, and even multiple processors can be simply plugged into free UNIBUS connector slots.

Multiple processors could, in principle, utilize a UNIBUS with little change in the standard hardware; it would only be necessary to establish appropriate priorities for requests from different processors.   In such a multiprocessor system, however, the single bus could stop the operation

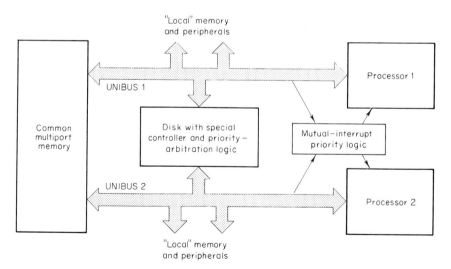

Fig. 6-5. A PDP-11 multiprocessor system.   Each processor communicates with its "local" memory and peripherals through its own UNIBUS and with the other processor via interrupt logic and a common multiport memory.   A special disk controller, started by programmed instructions from either processor (via priority-arbitration logic), can access either UNIBUS.

of all but the one processor currently using the bus. Proper PDP-11 multiprocessor systems will, therefore, utilize **multiple UNIBUSes** (as well as internal buses in the PDP-11/45) to join each processor to its "local" peripherals and memory and also to **common multiport memories** shared by two or more processors. Interprocessor communication through interrupts and programmed instructions will also be possible (Fig. 6-5).

As another interesting possibility, Ref. 7 outlines PDP-11 systems employing **multiple parallel UNIBUSes** with 32-bit and 48-bit memories and processors for double-precision and floating-point arithmetic. The concurrence afforded by multiple UNIBUSes then again helps to match the relatively slow UNIBUS operation to fast memories and processor logic.

FURTHER DEVELOPMENT OF
MINICOMPUTER SYSTEMS

6-12. I/O-bus-connected Accessory Arithmetic/Logic Circuits. **(a) Accessory Computing Modules.** Minicomputer input/output facilities (programmed I/O, direct memory access, and interrupt systems) are so convenient and flexible that it can be attractive to employ I/O buses for **field-installable modular expansion** of the processor itself (Fig. 6-6). Extra registers, special memory modules, table-lookup function generators, and even complete arithmetic units can be added in this way. This is not surprising, because many existing peripheral controllers (disk controllers, display controllers) can be fairly regarded as small accessory processors, with a program-loaded control register functioning as an instruction register.

Whenever possible, one attempts to utilize I/O instruction codes for accessory-module instructions since this does not interfere with existing instruction codes. There are usually plenty of spare I/O instructions, and it is easy to enter suitable mnemonics into the assembler symbol table. The main processor can command simple accessory-processor operations simply through various combinations of address bits, subdevice bits, and IO pulses in programmed I/O instructions (Sec. 5-2). More complex operations (in particular, operations requiring memory addresses) can be ordered through I/O instructions transferring an accumulator word from the main computer to the accessory module.

Unfortunately, many minicomputers require three or four machine cycles for every I/O instruction. This may waste time with some fast accessory-unit operations, and few users will want to alter the processor control logic. Another way to get (many) extra instruction codes is to set and clear an extra status-flag bit with two special instructions ENTER ACCESSORY-PROCESSOR MODE and LEAVE ACCESSORY-PROCESSOR MODE, but this also requires some modification of the control logic.

An accessory processor can receive and transmit data most quickly via the minicomputer DMA system, which connects to both the memory data register and the memory address register. When the accessory processor has finished a task, it can interrupt the main computer to advise it accordingly and perhaps to request new instructions; the accessory processor can transmit different interrupt trap addresses as needed. For example, the Digital Equipment Corporation FPP-12 and FPP-15 accessory floating-point arithmetic units steal memory cycles to transfer three-word floating-point numbers from and to the PDP-8 series and PDP-15 computers, respectively. Floating-point arithmetic execution times of such accessory processors are listed in Table 6-7.

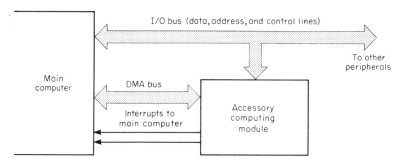

Fig. 6-6. An accessory computing module using programmed I/O instructions and DMA data transfers.

When you buy an accessory floating-point processor, be sure to check that it can really be used with the available software. Can the assembler reserve storage for floating-point (i.e., multiword) variables and arrays? How efficiently can the FORTRAN compiler and the BASIC interpreter use the floating-point instructions? How does one index floating-point arrays? To do *really* well, the floating-point processor will probably need a new compiler!

A true multiprocessor system involves at least one general-purpose digital computer as an accessory processor. Multiple processors communicate through a common memory, through mutual interrupts (including trap-address transmission), and via interprocessor buffer registers, which are loaded and read by I/O instructions from the various processors. Disk and tape units transfer data directly to and from the shared memory and can be controlled by programmed instructions from different processors on a time-division or priority-arbitration basis. We have met one such multiprocessor system in Sec. 6-11 (Fig. 6-5); we will return to this topic in Secs. 7-10 and 7-15.

(b) The GRI-909 System. Some minicomputer systems are specifically packaged for modular expansion through external buses, like the PDP-11

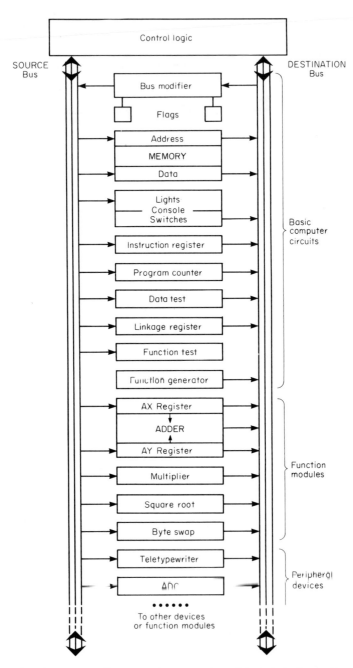

Fig. 6-7. GRI-909 system. Bus connections to each module include data, address, and/or control-signal lines.

UNIBUS system of Sec. 6-9. An even more striking example is the GRI Computer Corporation **GRI-909 "direct function processor,"** which is intended mainly as a process or system controller. Since some GRI-909 installations may not do much computing in the usual sense, even arithmetic circuits are made available as modular peripheral devices.

The GRI system is built around a dual bus ("source" and "destination" buses, Fig. 6-7). Processor elements, such as the program counter, instruction register, and adder, as well as memory modules and peripheral devices, are connected across these buses. If we refer to Fig. 6-7, we see that the vestigial processor comprises control logic and a one-input arithmetic/logic unit, the *bus modifier*, which can be programmed to increment, shift, complement, or negate a 16-bit word from the destination bus before placing it on the source bus. *Carry and overflow flags* are also associated with the bus-modifier block. Table 6-5 shows the GRI-909 instruction format. Each instruction contains a *source-device-address field*, a *destination-device-address field*, and some extra operation-code bits in a *modifier field*. There are five types of instructions:

1. *Register-to-register operations* fetch a 16-bit word from the source register (via the *destination bus*), modify it in the bus modifier, and place the result into the destination register via the *source bus*.
2. *Memory-reference instructions* are two-word instructions which specify "memory" as either the source or the destination device (not both). The second instruction word is the direct, indirect, or immediate address, depending on modifier bits.

Note that the adder is permanently connected to two input registers (AX and AY). One performs addition by loading AX and AY and then reading the adder output. For subtraction, the bus modifier inverts the subtrahend before loading.

3. *Data-test instructions* are two-word branching instructions which test the sign of a source-device word by specifying "data test" as the destination address. The second instruction word is the direct or indirect jump address. An addressable linkage register stores subroutine return addresses.
4. *Flag-test instructions* test flags in the source device by specifying "function test" in the destination-device field. The specific test logic is defined by the modifier bits; the program skips if the condition is true.
5. *Device-function instructions* address the "function generator" as the source device and send combinations of up to four IO pulses to the destination device (e.g., to start an ADC conversion).

These instructions can be programmed in a special simple assembly language, which is easily learned by control-system designers.

Some function modules (e.g., the multiplier) are "firmware operators" capable of issuing instruction sequences utilizing other modules (via the program counter). New function modules (which could be user-designed) can be connected to the data, address, and control lines of the GRI-909 bus system just like extra peripheral devices. Each module adds one or more instructions to the computer instruction set. Interrupt and DMA facilities are also available; the maximum DMA transfer rate is 568,000 sixteen-bit words/sec.

TABLE 6-5.   GRI-909 Instruction Format.

(GRI numbers bits from right to left.)

Bit	
15 14 13 12 11 10	**SOURCE-DEVICE-ADDRESS FIELD** $2^6 = 64$ possible addresses, including "memory" and "function generator"
9 8 7 6	**MODIFIER FIELD** 4 bits specify bus-modifier operations, memory-addressing mode, IO pulses, or test conditions
5 4 3 2 1 0	**DESTINATION-DEVICE-ADDRESS FIELD** $2^6 = 64$ possible addresses, including "memory," "data test," and "function test"

6-13.   The Microprogramming Approach.   As we saw in Sec. 2-4, a minicomputer decodes each instruction word into a sequence of control-bit combinations for various *microoperations*. A **microprogrammed** control unit obtains these control-bit combinations as successive **microinstruction words** looked up in a read-only memory (**control memory,** see also Sec. 1-14). Each complete computer instruction is, then, produced as a **microprogram.** The control unit actually functions as an "inner" stored-program computer (**microprocessor**) which addresses, fetches, and executes a sequence of microinstructions from the control memory.

Instruction-code bits of the "outer" or "virtual" computer set the microprocessor program counter ("microprogram counter") to a starting address in control memory. The microprogram counter is usually incremented after each microinstruction is executed, but unconditional and conditional branching are also possible. With a well-chosen microinstruction set, **one** can change the outer-computer instructions at will by plugging in a different read-only control memory or by using an electrically or mechanically alterable read-only memory. To add a new instruction, one simply requires enough extra read-only memory words to implement the new microprogram, without any change in the processor hardware.

The *microinstruction word length* need not be the same as the "outer-computer" word length. Long microinstruction words (up to 90 bits have been used in large digital computers) permit more complicated micro-operations with more overlapping (concurrence) of data transfers, bit tests, etc.; while short and simpler microinstructions simplify the processor but require longer microprograms with more control-memory references. The earlier microprogrammed minicomputers (Interdata Models 3, 4, 5, and 70 and Microdata 810) used 16-bit control memories. In the Interdata Model 70, the "outer-computer" instruction ADD REGISTER 1 INTO REGISTER 2 is implemented by three microinstructions. Interdata Model 80 has a 32-bit control memory, and Varian Data Machines Model 73 has 64 bits.

Microprogram execution times depend on ROM access time, which ought to be shorter than one-fifth to one-third of the main-memory cycle time. First-generation microprogrammed minicomputers employed magnetic ROMs (Fig. 1-15) with access times between 220 nsec and 400 nsec. Although magnetic ROMs are rugged and reliable, they have been replaced by semiconductor ROMs with shorter access times (40 to 200 nsec). Even this is still slow compared to logic speeds, so it will not pay to microprogram a minicomputer requiring a fixed simple instruction set. **Microprogramming comes into its own when one would like to:**

1. **Implement a large, sophisticated instruction set with a relatively simple processor**
2. **Permit the user to change instruction sets or to emulate different "outer" computers for use with different applications or software**

Microprogramming, moreover, becomes increasingly efficient when we microprogram increasingly complex operations (which would require subroutines in conventional minicomputers) because such programs tend to replace core-memory references with faster control-memory references. Examples are:

1. Efficient microprogramming not only of **floating-point arithmetic** but of **complete routines for trigonometric functions, fast Fourier transforms, integration, etc.**
2. **Microprogrammed I/O routines,** which can automate complex interrupt-service routines, buffer management, and/or formatting (Sec. 5-27)
3. **Microprogrammed** JUMP TO SUBROUTINE, RETURN FROM SUBROUTINE, **and** RETURN FROM INTERRUPT **instructions which implement automatic stacking of nested routines** (Secs. 4-16 and 6-10)

Some of these possibilities, though, can also be approached through ROM-stored subroutines with conventional processors.

To simplify the **development of new microprograms** by computer designers or users, the computer manufacturer usually has a "microassembly language" with mnemonics for the microinstructions, and two translation programs. The first translation program translates microprograms, possibly imbedded

---

(*a*) **RR FORMAT (one word).**

Register - to - register operations

(*b*) **RX FORMAT (two words).**

Memory – reference instructions involving register R1 or its floating-point counterpart in memory, indexed by register X2

(*c*) **RS FORMAT (two words).**

Immediate – address instructions involving register R1, indexed by register X2; also branching, index manipulation, and shifting instructions

---

Fig. 6-8. Interdata Models 3, 4, 5, and 70; instruction formats.

in "outer-computer" programs, for execution on a computer substituting core memory for the control memory so that the simulated microprograms can be run and debugged. Then the second translator makes a paper tape suitable for loading the actual ROM in the manufacturer's plant. The best way to implement and change new microprograms is to use semiconductor control memories which permit (possibly relatively slow) writing as well as reading (*writable control store*).

6-14. Microprogrammed Minicomputers. A microprogrammed minicomputer can have a very large instruction set. Some two-word instructions (or three-byte instructions, as in the Micro 810) will be required. Figure 6-8 shows instruction formats for the microprogrammed Interdata Models 3 to 80 (Models 3 and 4 were also sold with General Electric front panels as GEPAC 30-1 and 30-2). Table 6-6 lists their microinstructions, commonly supplied user instructions, and execution times. Each of these machines emulates a rather powerful "outer" computer having 16 programmable 16-bit registers, of which 15 can serve as index registers; operations on 8-bit bytes, 16-bit words, and 32-bit words are possible. **STORE MULTIPLE** (m) and **LOAD MULTIPLE** (m) *permit storing and loading of up to* $m = 16$ *registers in one microprogrammed instruction*, and special *stack-processing instructions* are available.

The microprogrammed Model 3 was interesting in that its processor was so very simple—this is actually an 8-bit processor handling consecutive 8-bit bytes, and its 16 general registers are really memory locations. Model 3 thus implemented its large user-instruction set at rather low speed (Table 6-6). Models 4, 5, 70, and 80 are faster; each has 16 *hardware* registers and can emulate a complete set of *floating-point-arithmetic instructions*. These employ a two-word floating-point format, but double-precision floating-point operations can be added as extra microprograms. In general, micro-programmed floating-point operations are faster than software-implemented operations but slower than true hardware floating-point arithmetic (Table 6-7). Very sophisticated "firmware" packages (microprograms for special applications) and a time-sharing firmware/software package are available.

Models 4 and 5 have 1-μsec core memories and permit up to 500,000 DMA byte transfers/sec. 300-nsec semiconductor memories are available with Models 70 and 80. Programmed data transfers are asynchronous (Sec. 5-6), and the optional eight-level interrupt system (up to 256 levels can be chain-wired, Sec. 5-14) employs a **READ INTERRUPT ADDRESS** instruction. Automatic interrupt and subroutine stacking can be microprogrammed.

The Varian Data Systems 620/i, similar to the 620/L mentioned in Sec. 6-4, is not a micro-programmed machine, but it permits some microprogramming *as an external option*. Processor clock and logic lines controlling individual microoperations for the 620/i instruction set are brought out to terminations accessible to knowledgeable users (MICRO-EXEC bus). Such users have, therefore, the option of controlling the execution of microinstruction combinations not only with an external control memory *but also with logic signals from suitable peripheral devices or accessory processors*. The possibilities of such a facility are limitless, although admittedly not easy to implement; there are critical requirements both on logic-level timing and on the user's know-how.

New 16-bit minicomputers implement sophisticated instruction sets, including floating-point arithmetic, through microprogramming with 24-bit, 32-bit, and even 64-bit microinstructions. This is fast enough to work even with 300-nsec solid-state main memories. A further trend is to incorporate such microprogrammed processors into asynchronous-bus architectures much like that of the PDP-11 system (Secs. 6-6 to 6-11), which can readily accommodate different memories, peripherals, and multiple processors. With the aid of bus switches, multiport memories, and memory-address computation in special **"memory mappers"** or **memory-segmentation units,** one can build 16-bit multiprocessor systems capable of addressing over 200,000 words of memory.

Table 6-6. Interdata Models, 3, 4, 5, 70, and 80 Instructions and Microinstructions.

These machines are 16-bit microprogrammed minicomputers. Model 70 has a solid-state control memory with 80-nsec access time; Models 3, 4, and 5 have magnetic control memories. Model 3, with magnetic control memory and an 8-bit (rather than 16-bit) microprocessor is 10 to 20 times slower than Model 70. Model 80 achieves its high speed by using 32-bit microinstructions. See Table 6-7 for floating-point execution times.

(a) User Instructions

Instruction (see Fig. 6-8 for instruction formats used)		Approximate EXECUTION TIMES, μsec			
		Model 3	Models 4, 5	Model 70	Model 80
LOAD/STORE (MOVE)	Register-to-register (RR)	22–30	2.8–4.8	1.25	0.45
ADD/SUBTRACT · ADD/SUBTRACT WITH CARRY · AND, OR, XOR · COMPARE	Two-word memory reference (RX)	32–38	4.8–6	4	0.90
LOAD/STORE/COMPARE BYTE	Two-word immediate (RS)	32–38	3.2–6	2.5	0.45
LOAD/STORE MULTIPLE	(n 16-bit words)	......	$8 + 3.5n$	$5 + 1.25n$	$1.25 + 0.4n$
ADD TO MEMORY		......	......	5	1.35
SWAP BYTES				1.25	0.45
MULTIPLY	Register-to-register (RR)	107–146	23–35	8.5 (average)	2.1
	Two-word memory reference (RX)	141–154	24–40	11 (average)	2.1
DIVIDE	Register-to-register (RR)	98–180	38–44	10.5 (average)	2.75
	Two-word memory reference (RX)	102–195	38–45	13 (average)	2.75
SHIFT (SINGLE)	n BITS	$39 + 3n$ to $39 + 4n$	$4 + 0.4n$ to $5 + 0.4n$	$3.25 + 0.25(n - 1)$	$0.5 + 0.1n$
SHIFT (DOUBLE)	n BITS	......	......	$4 + 0.25(n - 1)$	$0.7 + 0.1n$
ROTATE (DOUBLE)	n BITS			$3 + n$	$0.7 + 0.1n$
JUMP ON CONDITION	(RR)	28	4.8	1.5	0.45
	(RS)	34	5–6	3–5	0.45

(b) Microinstructions

OPERATION	MNEMONIC	EXECUTION TIMES, nsec			
		Model 3 (8-bits)	Models 4, 5, 7 (16-bits)	Model 70 (16 bits)	Model 80 (32-bit microinstructions)
Add	A	760	800	250	200
Add, immediate					
Subtract	⋯				
Subtract, immediate					
EXCLUSIVE OR	X	380	400	250	200
EXCLUSIVE OR, immediate					
AND	N				
AND, immediate	⋮ O				
OR					
OR, immediate	L				
Load					
Load, immediate					
Load I/O	L	⋯	1,200	750 (average)	400
Command	C	380	400	250	200
Test	T	380	400	250	200
Branch on Condition	B	760	800	250	200
Branch on Counter	⋯	⋯	800	250	200
Do; decode	D	Special	Special	Special	200

TABLE 6-7.   Examples of Minicomputer Floating-point-arithmetic Execution Times.
(*Average* times are in microseconds; note that examples refer to different word lengths and floating-point formats and can, thus, not be compared directly.)

	Add	Multiply	Divide	Sine
Subroutine 620/f (*two* 16-bit words, 0.75-μsec cycle)	168	177	245	980
PDP-11/20* (effective 1.5-μsec cycle, *three* 16-bit words)	275	810	1,770	9,700
PDP-11/20 (effective 1.5-μsec cycle, *two* 16-bit words)	160	204	205	2,400
ROM Subroutine SUPERNOVA SC (*two* 16-bit words, 0.3- to 0.8-μsec cycle)	34	46	56	200–500 (estimated)
Microprogram Interdata Model 5	56	157	213	640
Interdata Model 70	27	76	111	390 (estimated)
Interdata Model 80 (all *two* 16-bit words, 1-μsec cycle)	12	19	35	100 (estimated)
Hardware FPP-12 (*three* 12-bit words, 1.2-μsec cycle)	31	37	38	880
FPP-15 (*three* 18-bit words, 0.8-μsec cycle)	19	28	28	600 (estimated)
PDP-11/45 (effective 0.6-μsec cycle) *Two* 16-bit words	6–8	6–10	7–13	<300 (estimated)
Four 16-bit words	9–11	11–17	11–24	<500 (estimated)

* Without hardware multiply/divide option.

The most important example of this type of architecture is the PDP-11/45 (Sec. 6-9 and Fig. 6-4*b*), which has a separate microprogrammed floating-point processor, memory segmentation, and dual foreground/background register sets (Sec. 6-1*c*) and is especially suitable for multiprogramming applications.   A slightly later development is the Lockheed Electronics SUE, a microprogrammed 16-bit machine with a single-memory input/output bus for asynchronous transfers, registers, and instructions very much like the PDP-11, except that either the source or destination of any two-address instruction *must* be a register.   There are, thus, no three-word instructions (Sec. 6-7).   On the other hand, SUE (unlike PDP-11) admits multiple indirect addressing.

Varian Data Machines Model 73 is a microprogrammed, ultrafast 16-bit machine with 64-bit microinstructions matched nicely to 330-nsec solid-state memories as well as to 660-nsec core memories.   An asynchronous-bus architecture and two-port memories make Model 73 very suitable for multiprocessor systems.

Because of the formidable cost of providing full software to go with the large instruction sets possible with microprogramming, new microprogrammed minicomputers are frequently first marketed with software systems emulating a more primitive predecessor computer.   Thus, the Hewlett-Packard Type 2100, with its 24-bit microinstructions and eight registers, emulates the earlier 2114/2116 computers (which had only two programmable registers) and adds some floating-point instructions.   Similarly, the new Varian Data Machines Model 73 (64-bit microinstructions, 16 free registers) was originally marketed with software emulating the 620 series (Sec. 6-4), which has only three programmable registers.   The assembly language is, however, expanded to accept new user-defined instructions from writable control store.

6-15.   Future System Development.   Second-generation minicomputer design is based on medium-scale, integrated transistor/transistor logic, which permits multiregister processors, small multiprocessor systems, and much accessory logic to be built compactly and at reasonable cost.   As it turns out, central-processor logic constitutes a decreasing percentage (depending on the installation) of total system cost, which includes peripherals and software.   As shown in Secs. 6-2 and 6-3, investments in software can produce a drag on minicomputer hardware development, just as in the case of larger digital computers.   This is true especially since an important class of OEM customers is more interested in cost than in computing speed.

Aside from much work on miniperipherals (most of which, unfortunately, cannot be grown on silicon chips), the next generation of minicomputer hardware will be dependent on *the system-design aspects of semiconductor memories*.   This is not simply a matter of replacing core with solid-state

TABLE 6-8. A Checklist of Desirable Minicomputer Features.

It is clear that not all features are needed in all applications. It is assumed that machines under discussion have the most common instructions, and hardware and peripheral options as needed.

A. INSTRUCTION SET/ARCHITECTURE

1. **How many general-purpose registers?** Or is there a fast scratchpad memory? What memory-to-register operations are available? What **addressing modes** are available? Note that relative addressing and two-word immediate addressing (for literals) simplify program relocation.
2. **Is there an index register or registers?** How efficient are indexing operations for array-accessing program loops? Is there any autoindexing? Postindexing?
3. Can skip tests be combined with arithmetic/logic instructions? Can a result be tested without disturbing register contents?
4. What **byte-manipulation instructions** are available?
5. Are there any double-precision instructions?
6. How fast are signed multiply/divide operations (hardware or software)?
7. How does the system handle nested subroutines and interrupts? Is there an automatic stack pointer?

B. INPUT/OUTPUT

1. How many **programmed I/O instructions** are available? How many machine cycles are needed for such an instruction?
2. Is there a **hardware automatic priority-interrupt system?** If so, how many levels can it handle? Is there a way to read interrupt addresses for additional interrupts? **How fast are these interrupt-servicing schemes?**
3. How easy is it to modify interrupt priorities? To save and restore processor register and interrupt masks?
4. **How fast are DMA transfers?** Is hardware for automatic block transfers readily available? How critical is the wiring and timing of external DMA circuits? Does the system permit memory-increment and add-to-memory techniques?
5. **How expensive are interface cards and cables available for this machine?** If many devices are interfaced, these items can cost more than the processor (see also Chap. 5).

C. SOFTWARE

1. **Does the assembler permit:**
   (*a*) **Automatic crossing of page boundaries?**
   (*b*) **Relocation and linking with external programs** (especially FORTRAN I/O)?
   (*c*) Double-precision and/or floating-point operations?
   (*d*) **Macros?**
   (*e*) **Conditional assembly?** (See also Secs. 4-22 to 4-24.)
2. **Is there a convenient executive program** (sometimes referred to as a monitor) **which permits:**
   (*a*) **Calling I/O driver routines,** without any need to write or copy interrupt-service routines?
   (*b*) **Calling system programs?**
   (*c*) **Storing, copying, and retrieving files?**
3. Do the I/O routines furnished permit the use of double buffers in memory (Secs. 3-12 and 5-27)?
4. Does the FORTRAN compiler admit logical variables? Complex variables? Are there any reentrant subroutines for multiple-interrupt servicing? How fast are typical floating-point operations?
5. Is there a convenient BASIC system?
6. **Is there a convenient editing program?** Can it be used with a cathode-ray-tube display?
7. Is there an interpreter system for conversational programming of instrumentation and/or process-control systems?

---

memory circuits. *Faster semiconductor memories will close the gap between memory speed and processor-logic speed, which now so profoundly affects the design of hardware and software systems.* Quickly accessible integrated-circuit memory/selection-logic arrays can implement multiple registers with a minimum of interconnections and assembly. Again, new, very fast solid-state read-only memories permit one to use microprogramming with a 200- to 600-nsec main memory without any sacrifice in computing speed. Microprogramming, which, as we have noted, becomes more cost-effective as the firmware implements more complex operations (Sec. 6-13), is, then, another way to utilize array-type integrated circuits (i.e., many similar circuits repeated on each chip) in a minicomputer. Microprogramming can, of course, also ease the software problem through emulation of different instruction sets with plug-in or electrically alterable ROMs.

REFERENCES AND BIBLIOGRAPHY

(See also the reference, interface, and software manuals for the mini-computers discussed in each section.)

1. *Small Computer (PDP-8/e) Handbook*, Digital Equipment Corporation, Maynard, Mass. (current edition).
2. *PDP-11 Handbooks*, Digital Equipment Corporation, Maynard, Mass. (current edition).
3. *PDP-11 Paper-tape-software Programming Handbook*, Digital Equipment Corporation, Maynard, Mass., 1970.
4. *PDP-11 UNIBUS Interface Manual*, Digital Equipment Corporation, Maynard, Mass., 1970.
5. Flores, I.: *Computer Organization*, Prentice-Hall, Englewood Cliffs, N.J., 1969.
6. Bell, C. G., and A. Newell: *Computer Structures*, McGraw-Hill, New York, 1971.
7. ——— et al.: A New Architecture for Minicomputers: The DEC PDP-11, *Proc. SJCC*, 1970.
8. Chertkow, D., and R. Cady: Unified Bus Maximizes Minicomputer Flexibility, *Electronics*, December 21, 1970.
9. Husson, S. S.: *Microprogramming Principles and Practices*, Prentice-Hall, Englewood Cliffs, N.J., 1970.
10. Roberts, W.: Microprogramming Concepts and Advantages as Applied to Small Digital Computers, *Comput. Des.*, November 1969.
11. Ramamoorthy, C. V., and M. Tsuchiya: A Study of User-microprogrammable Computers, *Proc. SJCC*, 1970.
12. Langley, F. J.: Small-computer Design Using Microprogramming and Multifunction LSI Arrays, *Comput. Des.*, April 1970.
13. Hornbuckle, G. D., and E. I. Ancona: The LX-1 Microprocessor, *IEEETC*, August 1970.
14. House, D. L., and R. A. Henzel: The Effect of Low-cost Logic on Minicomputer Organization, *Comput. Des.*, January 1971.
15. Hauber, V. P.: Computer Simulators—Something for Nothing?, *Data Process.*, March 1971.

CHAPTER 7

A SURVEY OF
MINICOMPUTER APPLICATIONS

INTRODUCTION

In this chapter, we will try to outline the most important categories of mini-computer applications. The list in Table 7-1 is just a starter. There are literally thousands of applications, and more new applications develop every day. A detailed, useful exposition of each major application area would fill a book in its own right. This is true not because of the computer hardware and programs but because fairly sophisticated knowledge of the applications is required. If minicomputer applications were completely simple, they might not need the computer.

CONTROL, INSTRUMENTATION, TESTING, AND SUPERVISORY APPLICATIONS

7-1. Sequencing, Timing, and Logic. Process-control applications of minicomputers rely on their ability to communicate inexpensively and flexibly with external devices. In the important class of sequencing, timing, and logic applications needed to control material-handling systems, counting operations, banks of elevators, psychological experiments, etc., a mini-computer controls discrete outputs, such as relay closures, solenoid valves, stepping motors, lights, etc., usually through program-loaded control registers (Sec. 5-4). The computer accepts discrete inputs from limit switches, push buttons, and assorted temperature, pressure, and voltage sensors through sense and interrupt lines (Secs. 5-8 and 5-9).

TABLE 7-1. Examples of Minicomputer Applications.
This list of minicomputer applications—by no means an exhaustive list—was compiled
by General Automation, Inc., Anaheim, California.

MANUFACTURING

PRODUCTION MACHINES

Controls and monitors automatic and manually operated production machines at a higher sustained efficiency rate. Monitors the actual piece-count production and machine status and signals out-of-limit conditions as they occur. Enables corrective action to be taken immediately.

PACKAGE PROCESSING

Controls high-speed packaging equipment and prevents inaccurate operation and breakdowns. Controls the speed of the filling device and the amount of product in the package to be filled, and weighs each package accurately.

SHOP-FLOOR CONTROL DATA

Provides an economical data collection system for shop-floor control validation of shipments, monitoring and testing of goods, and the staging of goods for production monitoring of plant facilities; monitoring of the attendance, productivity, and the efficiency of production personnel; and direct dispatching of jobs in a predetermined priority sequence.

INDUSTRIAL TESTING SYSTEMS

Monitors and controls complex testing sequences in an industrial testing system. Operations include: product identification, selection of test sequence, calibration check of test equipment, automatic handling of units during testing, source collection and analysis of test data, accept/reject determination of testing units, and printout of test results.

AUTOMOTIVE

INTERNAL COMBUSTION ENGINES

Acquires data recorded from sensors attached to the internal combustion engine. Measures water temperature, oil temperature, RPM speed, torque, oil pressure, exhaust temperature, manifold pressure, and timing.

AUTOMOTIVE EXHAUST EMISSION

Identifies vehicle for record purposes. Analyzes samples of exhaust gas components during the test cycle. Computes the concentration and/or volume of each monitored gaseous constituent and compiles a test record.

PRODUCTION TESTING

Provides on-line analysis of automotive carburetors in a high-volume production assembly line. Significantly reduces the test time required while providing a greater yield of better quality carburetors.

RUBBER

RUBBER PRODUCTION

Controls in-process inventories and maximizes utilization of machine tools in the production of rubber products. Substantially reduces the time and personnel required to summarize and review the stripcharts of production activity and the manually produced shift-end reports.

ELECTRONICS

PERIPHERAL TEST

Computer interfacing and multiunit control of input/output peripherals for large-scale computer installation. I/O units include a line printer, card reader, card punch, and magnetic tapes.

COIL WINDING PRODUCTION

Control of automatic winding machines for the mass production of small coils for magnetic-latching reed switches. Eight winding patterns are stored in the computer's memory. All eight of the patterns can be run on up to 16 machines. Coils are wound on plastic inserts in a steel plate on an 8 in by 8 in matrix. Inserts extend from both plate surfaces and provide 64 winding cores on each side.

PC BOARD PRODUCTION

Used for the automatic development, formatting, and conversion of instruction programs for numerically controlled printed circuit board drilling machines. Complete patterns are stored in the computer memory to perform step-and-repeat operations accurately. Frequently repeated patterns for standard devices are entered into memory that will completely define all points in the pattern after only two points have been located by the operator.

ELECTRONIC TESTING

Tests each of electric/electronic component in a high volume production line. Executes tests at a predetermined maximum rate; variations in manual operator rates are eliminated.

TABLE 7-1. Examples of Minicomputer Applications (*Continued*).

TESTING AND ANALYSIS OF CIRCUITS

Controls circuit testing and analysis systems. Coordinates the testing operations, specifications, signals, and the test sequence at electronic speeds, including: continuity, impedance, test stimuli, and measurement of the circuit output.

AEROSPACE

AIRCRAFT WING PRODUCTION

Controls and monitors automatic riveting machines for manufacturing aircraft wings. Riveting patterns are stored in the computer's memory to perform step-and-repeat operations accurately and quickly.

FATIGUE TESTING

Acquires, processes, and analyzes fatigue stress data for a variety of metals as well as bonded joined materials. Prints out data for corrective action, thereby preventing potential accidents and malfunction due to fatigue stress.

METALS AND WOODWORKING

STEELMAKING

Controls and operates steel furnaces, and produces the metal in exact accordance with preset specifications. Calculates oxygen requirements, alloy additions, and power requirements.

METAL ANALYSIS

Monitors and controls optical emission and x-ray spectrometers widely used in the metals industry for high-speed determination of the chemical composition of metal.

TENSILE TESTING

Provides quality control, production techniques evaluation, product classification, and customer certification. Calculates the product's strength and other characteristics, records and calculates vital material properties, and measures and computes tensile strength.

TRANSFER LINE

Monitors and controls transfer lines producing high production parts, and consisting of many machining stations mechanically connected by work-piece transfer mechanisms and closely interlocked with electrical controls. Receives input from operator or sensors, then concurrently checks the operating condition of line-mounted controls, takes protective action when required, prints out a report of the malfunction, and generates production reports.

MATERIALS HANDLING

AUTOMATED WAREHOUSING

Provides optimum space utilization, significant manpower savings, and high turnaround for material requests in an automated "high cube" vertical storage warehouse. Keeps track of numerous units of merchandise and optimizes the movement of stacker cranes. Provides real-time inventory control and warehousing applications to be integrated into a plant-wide information system.

MATERIAL-HANDLING SYSTEM

Controls complex material-handling system including storage and retrieval equipment. Processes orders, prepares shipping documents and invoices, provides operator guidance, maintains accurate inventories, and provides direct control of transport facilities and stacker units.

PAPER

PAPER-MILL PRODUCTION

Regulates the average basis weight and moisture variables in each paper grade. Manipulates the steam flow valve, adjusts the stock valve to the regulated basis weight, and monitors and/or controls total flow and digital filtering of instruments' signals.

TRANSPORTATION

RAILROAD

Counts and identifies railroad cars transporting materials and goods. Provides accurate weighing of each railroad car as it passes through the scale weighing system without stopping.

AUTOMOBILE

Provides centralized computer control of an electronic traffic control system. Records, analyzes, and prints out traffic count and flow at various time periods, accident control and notification, control of traffic lights, etc.

AIRLINE

Monitors and displays airline flight arrivals and departures. Provides accurate up-to-date information on air flights to numerous air terminals and airline offices.

COMMERCIAL

BANKING

Reads, analyzes, and tabulates check data and monetary transactions in real-time applications at branch offices. Central computer at the main-bank processing center provides fast analyses and totals for management control.

TABLE 7-1.   Examples of Minicomputer Applications (*Continued*).

ACCOUNTING
Acquires, processes, and prints out man-hours on-the-job for job/function/time evaluation.

ENVIRONMENTAL CONTROL
Controls and monitors environmental conditions throughout a large office building. Evaluates and monitors temperature, humidity, pollen, airborne dirt and irritants, etc., within the controlled environment.

PRINTING

PRINTING PRESSES
Monitors and controls the operation of large multicolor printing presses. Preset ink fountain and compensator positions are maintained during running, taking into consideration temperature, humidity, ink absorption, etc.

TYPESETTING
Automation of formatting and typesetting in a high-volume newspaper operation.

RETAIL

MERCHANDISE
Automates check-out-stand operations in large retail stores. Computes transactions for accounting and inventory control.

FOOD
Computes transactions quickly and accurately in a fast-food service. Maintains "instant" inventory control throughout the food chain's operation.

DISPLAY SYSTEMS

EXTERNAL
Monitors and controls scoreboard displays located in sports stadiums providing score information, animation displays, and audience messages. Stores repetitive messages and animation programs of all types.

INTERNAL
Provides generation and control of architectural display, light, sound, and temperature effects of remote-site data from microphones and CCTV sets.

COMMUNICATIONS

SYNCHRONOUS DATA EXCHANGE
The synchronous exchange of information on medium-speed to high-speed data links involves multiprocessor or multidevice complexes. Remote computers perform process control or data-gathering distribution tasks, and provide a supervisory computer with information and data for process and/or management decisions and commands.

TELEMETRY DATA ACQUISITION
Monitors remotely the physical status of objects, animals, people, or the environment in space flights. Evaluates incoming data for relative importance and validity. Isolates useful data from "noise" and other spurious signals.

BROADCASTING
Provides automatic timing control of audio/visual processes for radio and television stationbreak advertising. Maintains time-of-day synchronization with the national networks.

EDUCATION
Provides audio/visual control of the teacher's presentation and real-time data acquisition. Processes and tabulates student responses.

TELEVISION
Provides real-time data acquisition and processing of audience-viewer responses in audience participation shows. Tabulates and prints out responses for "instant" results while still on the air.

POWER

SUBSTATION MONITORING AND CONTROL
Monitors and controls high voltage and extra high voltage substations from centralized dispatching offices.

PLANT POWER SYSTEM
Assures proper distribution of available electricity, gas, or steam in utility systems. Monitors powerhouse facilities, schedules distribution of the energy, and produces operating distribution logs.

LABORATORY/MEDICAL

PHYSIOLOGICAL MONITORING
Monitors the patient's disorder, including his blood pressure, respiration, temperature, appearance, urine output, blood and fluid loss, fluid and electrolyte intake, blood chemistry, weight, and electrocardiogram.

SPECTROMETER OPERATION
Provides the computational, functional, and communication capabilities for optimum use of a spectrometer used in industrial applications. This includes checking, sequencing, calculating percentage composition of each element, outputting results, and calculating interelement effect.

TABLE 7-1.   **Examples of Minicomputer Applications** (*Continued*).

GAS CHROMATOGRAPHS
Accurately measures chromatograph signal output and controls instrument functions amenable to external control, such as temperature programming, column switching.

AMINO ACID ANALYSIS
Controls instrumentation obtaining amino acid analysis data. Evaluates, acquires, and processes data for meaningful information and displays information for laboratory personnel.

CHEMICAL
AMMONIA AND ETHYLENE PROCESSING
Identifies mechanical problems in large compressors used to manufacture ammonia, ethylene, etc. Monitors bearing temperatures, operation of clearance pockets, compressor speed, power consumption, vibration, discharge temperatures, pressures, suction flow, and gas compositions.

PLASTICS
Acquires, processes, and provides stress analysis for a wide range of plastic materials. Calculates the product's strength, records and calculates material properties, measures and computes elasticity and hardness.

EXPLOSIVES
Provides data acquisition and analysis of explosive shock waves. Measures and calculates explosive force and duration.

DYES
Monitors and controls the processing of dyes used in the textile industry. Provides accurate processing of color blending and matching to predetermined values.

PETROLEUM
GAS TRANSMISSION AND DISTRIBUTION
Monitors and controls pressures and flows of gas transmission and distribution systems. Data is gathered, measured in the field, and transmitted to the System 18/30.

OIL FIELD
Provides on-site acquisition and processing of data received from drilling rigs on depth, density, etc.

In typical applications of this kind, the processor steps through a program of instructions in response to a real-time clock (Table 5-2). Sequencing logic is readily added through tests of sense lines, which produce sense/skip loops (Sec. 5-8) until some external condition is satisfied. The computer program can implement any desired logical relationship involving clock signals, external conditions, and results of computer operations. Examples of such applications are production-line control, counting parts, limit tests of production tolerances, and actions responding to various alarm conditions. In the preminicomputer era, such operations were commonly performed by banks of relays and stepping switches connected to produce the desired logical relationships. Relay circuits were later replaced by solid-state logic. The present trend is to minicomputers, which may be minimum-cost "stripped" processors without front panels or options. Quite often, programs or parts of programs can be implemented in read-only memory, using plug-in ROM cards for program changes. Many timing, sequencing, and logic operations in automated factories are relatively slow. Many jobs may be able to share a small computer, which could still have time for some data logging and report generation.

Interface logic required for such operations is available from many manufacturers in the form of plug-in cards with wire-wrapped interconnections, much like those shown in Fig. 5-18*b*. This logic may have to function in electrically noisy factory environments, but need not be overly fast. Special logic families with large logic levels and slowed-down flip-flop inputs have been designed for this purpose, and many compatible accessories, such as timers, indicators, thumb-wheel-switch encoders, power-line control relays, and special racks and cabinets, are available (Ref. 81).

7-2. Digital Control of Machine Tools and Processes. (a) Numerical-control Systems (see Refs. 12 to 16). Numerical-control systems position and feed cutting tools in terms of digital coordinate values. Control may involve a single dimension or axis (e.g., a simple lathe), two axes (plate drilling, simple milling), or three, four, and up to twelve axes in complex machines permitting angular positioning of multiple tools. Numerical control may require $\frac{1}{10,000}$-in precision throughout a 100-in positioning range, which requires double precision with 12- and 16-bit words; such accurate positioning cannot be achieved with stepping motors, but requires **incremental digital servomechanisms.** These adjust tool positions through position feedback from shaft encoders or pulse generators which produce pulses corresponding to small tool-displacement increments. The incremental servo counts these pulses, compares the total count with a specified or computed desired count value, and positions a servomotor as needed. **Point-to-point** numerical control simply positions the tool (or the work, say by moving a drill-press table) on successive points of a programmed pattern. **Contouring** controllers, on the other hand, *interpolate* many intermediate points between specified positions to move a cutting or grinding tool continuously along a programmed contour; both *straight-line* and *circular-arc* interpolation can be obtained. In addition, feed rate, drilling depth, etc., can be preset or feedback-controlled, and sequences of different tools (e.g., on a turret lathe) may be specified by digital commands.

Computer-controlled drafting systems have quite similar requirements.

There are *two basic ways of utilizing digital computers in numerical-control systems:*

1. The computer is used **to prepare a punched tape** containing the coordinate values specifying a desired pattern. The tape is read by a separate dedicated machine-tool controller, which positions the tool and performs the desired straight-line or circular-arc interpolation for contouring with the aid of hard-wired digital logic (operational digital-computing elements, digital-differential-analyzer circuits, Refs. 15 and 16).

2. In **direct numerical control,** a minicomputer, as an integral part of the machine-tool controller, is used to program and edit the control program, to perform the desired interpolation, and to supervise and log the performance of the cutting operations. This information can be communicated to an operator and/or to a supervisory digital computer, which may also store patterns and programs on a disk or tape (see also Sec. 7-6).

Elaborate multitool systems may even employ one minicomputer for coarse interpolation and a second minicomputer for fine interpolation and tool acceleration/
deceleration.

The future probably belongs to *direct numerical control*.   While this still
requires high-quality servomotors and feedback transducers, the computer
replaces an expensive and potentially troublesome paper-tape reader and the
dedicated interpolation logic.   A single PDP-8/e can control two multiaxis
machines, and more elaborate minicomputers may control up to twelve
machines.   Only "stripped" minicomputers with few options are needed,

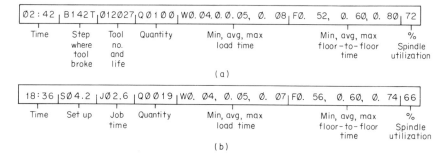

Fig. 7-1. Example of a trouble report (*a*) and of a summary report (*b*) prepared by a minicomputer
implementing direct numerical control.   Such reports can be typed out on the operator's
teleprinter, or they can go to a supervisory computer.   (*Digital Equipment Corporation.*)

and as their price is reduced by more and more large-scale integration, they
will not cost too much more than dedicated interpolation logic.   Convenient
generation and logging of production reports (time required per job, times
and rates of tool failures, etc., Fig. 7-1) are of importance in plant operation
with supervisory computers (Sec. 7-6); while small job shops can use suitable
minicomputer systems to prepare the numerical-control programs on line,
with the minicomputer simultaneously controlling its machine tools on
another job.

   (b) A Simple Numerical-control Language (see Ref. 81).   Simple and
convenient languages for specifying numerical-control programs permit
either remote-computer preparation of paper tapes or direct numerical
control.   The Digital Equipment Corporation's QUICKPOINT language,
designed mainly for preparation of point-to-point tapes, is a fine example of
what can be achieved with a very small computer (PDP-8/e, Sec. 6-2*a*).   In
addition to its positioning chores, the program can handle 32 to 256 *discrete
inputs*, say from limit switches or operator push buttons, plus a similar
number of *discrete outputs* (motor starters, solenoids, parts-handling
devices, etc.).

A sequence of points can be specified by their *coordinate values*, such as

> X 3.91   Y 7.30   Z 1.01
> X 3.99   Z 2.00   / Repeats Y = 7.30

or in terms of *coordinate increments* (designated by the prefix D), which are referred to the last-specified point position:

> X 4.12   DY 2.14   DZ −3.05

The command OFFSET, followed by a set of coordinate values, will automatically offset all subsequent coordinates by the values entered. This helps with machines having fixed-positioning coordinate origins.

Examples of **pattern commands** are:

1. INC m/(R, L, U, or D) S n

    generates n points separated from the preceding point by successive distances S to the right, left, up, or down.

2. LAA m/(angle in degrees) S n

    (*line at angle*) generates n points separated from the preceding point by successive distances S along a line at the specified angle from a reference line.

3. GRD m/(R or L) $S1$, $n1$ (V or D) $S2$, $n2$

    generates an $n1 \times n2$ *grid* right or left, up or down, from the last point, with increments S1, S2 in the X and Y directions.

4. MOV/ X 0.51   Y 7.32
    BHC m/(radius) (starting angle) (number of holes)

    generates a *bolt-hole circle* with center coordinates 0.51, 7.32 and a specified radius, number of holes, and a starting angle (angle of first hole with respect to X axis). MOV can also specify *increments* DX, DY instead of X and/or Y.

5. MOV/ X 0.51   Y 7.32
    ARC m/(radius) (starting angle) (angular increment) (number of holes)

    generates *points along a circular arc*, as specified.

The machine remembers each pattern, which can be *recalled* by its pattern number m during the current program, e.g.,

> GRD   22
> MOV/ X 5.34   DY 0.11
> BHC 19

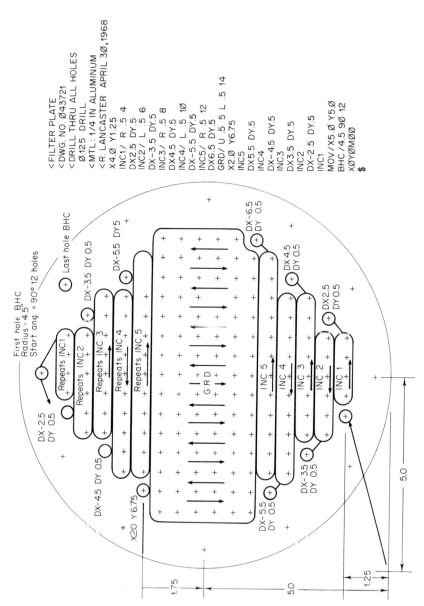

Fig. 7-2. The QUICKPOINT program for generating the numerical-control tape used to drill this 192-hole pattern requires only 25 statements and eliminates all trigonometric computations for bolt-hole circles. The symbol < is used as a comment delimiter. *(Digital Equipment Corporation.)*

The operator can also *preserve his own patterns* through a sort of macro generation (Sec. 4-21). The desired pattern, delimited by **PAT** $m/$ and **END**, must specify only *increments* and can be called at will with **PAT** m. Thus,

> **PAT 7/**
> **DX 2.11 DY** −0.33
> **BHC 2/0.55**   0.00   8
> **DY 9.12**
> **END**

can be started from the reference location 5.00, 6.00 with

> **X 5.00**   **Y 6.00**
> **PAT 7**

It is also possible to preserve patterns, such as **BHC 22**, **GRD 9**, or **PAT 7**, for other programs by writing any number of them within the delimiters **LPM** (*load permanent memory*) and **END**.

Figure 7-2 shows an example of a real QUICK POINT program.

An example of a more elaborate language permitting straight-line and circular-arc interpolation for contouring as well as point-to-point numerical control is the UNIAPT language designed by General Automation, Inc. for its 18/30 minicomputer numerical-control system.

(c) Direct Digital Process Control. A digital process-control system may simply present and convert digital **setpoint values** for valve displacements, temperatures, pressures, etc., to multiple analog controllers (servos, thermostats, pressure controllers, voltage regulators, etc.), which do the actual adjusting and control. In **direct digital control** (which we have already encountered in the example of direct numerical control of machine tools, Sec. 7-2a), the digital computer is itself part of a servo feedback loop; i.e., it supplies corrections for the actual controller *outputs* as well as the desired setpoint values. The computer evaluates *sampled data errors* and employs them in suitable *control algorithms* to produce the desired response (Ref. 80). Many process-control systems have relatively long time constants (minutes or hours), so a digital computer can be time-shared among multiple controllers. The computer may also perform all kinds of sequencing, timing, logic, data acquisition, and data logging between sampled-data control operations. Extra (redundant) processors can improve the otherwise possibly precarious reliability of sych systems. The low prices of the new minicomputers facilitate such redundancy.

There are also instances of much faster direct digital-control systems, in which an entire minicomputer is dedicated to one possibly complicated multidimensional control operation. Reference 80 is a good starting point for the computer algorithms needed in direct digital control.

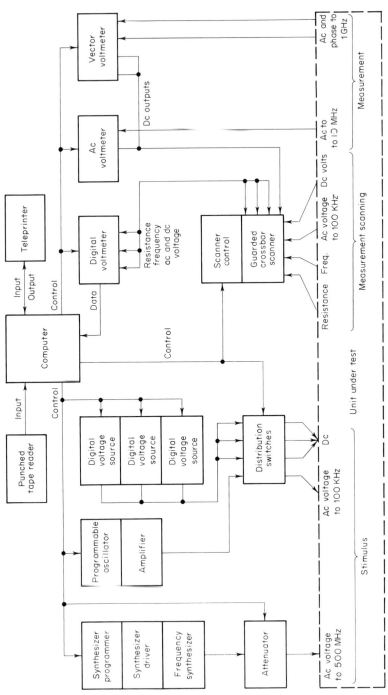

Fig. 7-3a. An automatic test system employing a minicomputer and computer-compatible test instruments. This system is suitable for experimentation and tests with many electronic circuits such as amplifiers, receivers, and modulators. (*Hewlett-Packard Corporation*, expanded Model 9500A test system.)

7-3. Instrumentation Systems and Control of Experiments. (a) Problem Statement. Computer-automated instrumentation is rapidly transforming experimental techniques in physics, chemistry, biomedical science, the earth sciences, and psychology as well as in engineering design, testing, and quality control (see also Sec. 7-4). Computer operation of instruments requires measuring devices designed or modified so that they are **computer-compatible**: measured outputs must be available as binary or binary-coded decimal words with suitable logic levels, and it must be possible to switch measurement modes and measurement ranges with digital logic levels. Many optical and mechanical instruments also require mechanical positioning (translation, rotation, focusing).

Computer-controlled experimentation involves automation of the following procedures:

1. **Program experiment or test timing and logic** (switch system configuration, signal sources, measuring instrument modes and ranges, position measuring devices). This encompasses a range of operations similar to those discussed in Sec. 7-1. A real-time-clock-controlled

Fig. 7-3b. Photograph of the automatic test system of Fig. 7-3a. (*Hewlett-Packard Corporation.*)

operation sequence may well take place without human-operator intervention, say over a weekend.

2. **Program test signals or signal sequences.**

3. **Acquire, process, and/or record instrument data. Data-acquisition systems** most frequently involve analog-to-digital converters preceded by multichannel multiplexers set up by a program-loaded control register (Table 5-2), plus signal-conditioning filters and sample-hold circuits needed for acquiring fast voltage waveforms. Depending on the computing time available, the minicomputer may also perform computations or formatting operations on the acquired data (**data processing**). Data may be passed to a supervisory computer, or they may be printed out or recorded on magnetic tape (**data logging**).

4. **Make decisions** (accept, reject, change test conditions; note and act on alarm conditions).

5. **Document results.** This is not restricted to printing out the results of data-logging operations, but may include complete reports on the history of each experiment, special conditions encountered, equipment failures, etc.

Even more sophisticated systems may also involve direct digital control, say for accurate positioning of probes or catheters.

As we pointed out in Chap. 5, the design of computer interfaces for a wide variety of instruments and other devices is not difficult with prepackaged components and logic cards. The user must, however, face the costs not only of this (relatively simple) hardware design but also the possibly larger costs of writing device drivers and other input/output software for his system. Some instrument manufacturers (notably the Hewlett-Packard Corporation), as well as minicomputer manufacturers, have placed special emphasis on making a wide variety of instruments computer-compatible by developing special interface cards and associated device-driver software. You should realize that these very substantial conveniences are not free but are reflected in the price of instruments and prepackaged interface cards.

The ESONE committee of the Commission of the European Communities has established interface-hardware, enclosure, and bus-signal standards for instrumentation (mainly in nuclear physics). A number of manufacturers build components for this CAMAC system (Refs. 5 and 6).

(b) Programming Languages and Operating Systems for Computer-controlled Instrumentation. Once the necessary device-driver routines have been written (or made available with standard instruments), instrumentation programs for timing and sequencing measurements, for data processing, and for report preparation can be written in *assembly language* if maximum execution speed is of the essence. Since the progress of a computer-controlled experiment will depend on many real-time-clock and instrument interrupts, a *real-time executive program* is almost mandatory in order to free the programmer from the details of interrupt servicing (Sec. 3-13).

In many experiments, however, time intervals between experiments are measured in minutes rather than in milliseconds, and the instruments themselves have similarly long time constants. We can then safely avail ourselves of the convenience of *interpreter or compiler languages*, which are closer to ordinary English-cum-mathematics and permit scale-factor-free floating-point computations.

Conversational programming with interpreter languages (Sec. 3-8) is particularly convenient when an *operator* works with the instrumentation system to do switching and plug-in operations and to enter some data upon typed or CRT-displayed commands *from the computer*. A neat example of such an interpreter language is Hewlett-Packard Corporation's extension of the BASIC language for instrumentation control (Refs. 21 and 22). The programmer can define variables and program computations in BASIC (Table 3-2), which is extended to call for input/output operations serving many standard instruments through library subroutines. Figure 7-4 shows an example of such a program; the statement

220 CALL (10, 2, 0.1, I)

uses a digital voltmeter (instrument 10) to make an ac measurement (mode 2) on the 0.1-volt range and to label the result as I. The statement

WAIT (30)

delays the program for 30 msec to allow an instrument to settle. Such programs permit *branching* through additional statements, such as

IF G LESS THAN 5 THEN   320

(Fig. 7-4). Such programs are widely used for automated testing operations (Sec. 7-5). Timed measurements can be performed through IF statements tied to real-time-clock operation, but the simple BASIC programming system is not suitable for foreground/background operation with multiple interrupts.

A more powerful—and still easily learned—programming system is INDAC, jointly developed by Digital Equipment Corporation and the Bell Telephone Laboratories Power-System Development Group (Refs. 4 and 80). The syntax of the INDAC language is similar to that of BASIC, but INDAC is used as a compiler language in conjunction with a disk-based real-time executive program, which is astonishingly powerful and simple to use if one considers that the system works with the small (12-bit) PDP-8/e.

INDAC program segments consist of BASIC-like statements, plus special I/O routines called by statements like **GET** and **SEND** (Fig. 7-5).

The executive program is informed of the I/O devices to be used through a

Program	Comment
100 CALL (8, 1, 0, 1)	Sets power supply 1 to zero
110 CALL (8, 2, 0, 1)	Sets power supply 2 to zero
120 PRINT "PLUG IN AMPLIFIER"	Instructs operator
125 PRINT "SERIAL NUMBER IS"	Asks operator for information
130 INPUT S	Operator types in serial number
140 CALL (6, 4, 3, 0, 0)	Connects supply #1 to output 4, supply #2 to output 3
150 CALL (8, 1, −12, 100)	Sets supply #1 to −12, 100 mA max
160 CALL (8, 2, 12, 100)	Sets supply #2 to +12, 100 mA max
170 FOR F = 1000 TO 5000 STEP 1000	Establishes loop for changing frequency
180 CALL (5, F, .10)	Sets oscillator to 1,000 (then 2,000, 3,000, 4,000, 5,000) Hz, 0.1 volt
190 CALL (7, 7, 0, 0, 0)	Connects oscillator to output 7
200 CALL (9, 5)	Connects oscillator output to DVM
210 WAIT (30)	Delays 30 msec to allow settling
220 CALL (10, 2, .1, I)	Measures input ac voltage on 0.1 range
230 CALL (9, 23)	Connects amplifier output to DVM
240 WAIT (30)	Delays 30 msec to allow settling
250 CALL (10, 2, 10, V)	Measures amplifier output
260 LET G = V/I	Calculates gain
270 IF G < 5 THEN 320	Checks for low gain
280 IF G > 10 THEN 340	Checks for high gain
290 NEXT F	Return to 170 for next frequency
300 PRINT "AMPLIFIER SERIAL" S "GAIN OK, GAIN =" G "AT 5000 HZ"	
310 GO TO 290	
320 PRINT "AMPL SERIAL" S "GAIN LOW, GAIN =" G "AT" F "HZ"	
330 GO TO 290	
340 PRINT "AMPL SERIAL" S "GAIN HIGH, GAIN =" G "AT" F "HZ"	
350 GO TO 290	
360 END	

Fig. 7-4. Program for testing an audio amplifier, written in Hewlett-Packard extended BASIC. The test itself is automatic, but the computer types requests to plug in the amplifier and to enter its serial number. (*R. H. Grimm, Hewlett-Packard J., August* 1969. See also Ref. 21.)

system-generator program (Sec. 3-12*b*) at the time the instrumentation system is configured or changed. The executive will then service all interrupts as needed, using standard I/O routines loaded only when the user program contains references to the I/O devices in question.

Figure 7-5 illustrates a typical INDAC program. All executable tasks are organized routines (usually interrupt-service routines) called SNAPS. A SNAP may involve I/O operations and/or data processing, conditioning, or logging; *timed operations* are called by statements involving **AT** . . . and **EVERY** . . . (Fig. 7-5). Corresponding to typical system requirements, these

PROGRAM LISTING	STATEMENT FUNCTION

Equipment Specification Statements

.EQUIPMENT	Indicates that the following statements (up to next statement) comprise a description of the total equipment complement needed to execute the program.
↑ *AF04	Device identification (ADC Subsystem).
↑ CHAN(1) TEMPA	Identifies the input variable wired to the first channel of the AF04 as TEMPA,
↑ CHAN(2) TEMPB	second channel input as TEMPB, and
↑ CHAN(3) TEMPC	third channel input as TEMPC.
↑ #101 DC,100MV,.01 DO TCONV	This statement specifies that an operation identified as TCONV is to be performed for each channel input. The identified operation is normally a plug-in subprogram used to perform a standard conversion, scaling, or other signal conditioning operation.

Phase Statements

#1 .PHASE	Introduces a program PHASE segment.
.ACTION	Indicates that all of the following statements up to the next (.) statement are concerned with the scheduling operations performed within this PHASE.
#10 DO SNAP #2 EVERY 10 SEC	Specifies that the SNAP tagged #2 is to be performed every 10 sec.
TIMER(START,#10)	Begins the timing operation specified in the statement tagged #10.

Snap Statements

#2 .SNAP	Identifies a SNAP program segment which is tagged #2.
.PROCESS	Indicates that all of the statements up to the next (.) statement are to be executed to carry out the process assigned to this SNAP.
GET (AF04,#101) TEMPA,TEMPB,TEMPC	This statement directs the system to get from device AF04 inputs TEMPA, B and C and to perform on each input the operation described in control statement #101 (i.e., TCONV).
SEND (TTY) TEMPA,TEMPB,TEMPC	This statement directs the system to send the data processed in the preceding statement (TEMPA, etc.) to the teletypewriter I/O device for printout.
EXIT	Indicates the end of the current SNAP program segment; command returns control to the operating system.
.END	Indicates the end of the program.

Fig. 7-5a. Sample INDAC data-acquisition program. (*Digital Equipment Corporation.*)

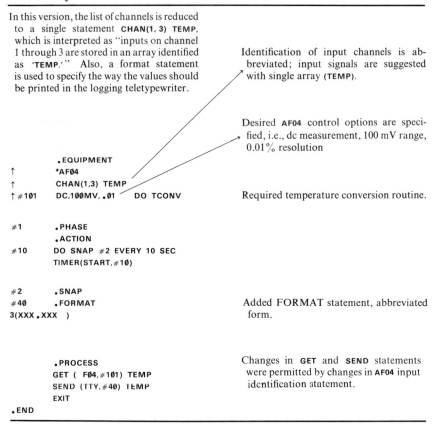

In this version, the list of channels is reduced to a single statement CHAN(1, 3) TEMP, which is interpreted as "inputs on channel 1 through 3 are stored in an array identified as 'TEMP.'" Also, a format statement is used to specify the way the values should be printed in the logging teletypewriter.

Identification of input channels is abbreviated; input signals are suggested with single array (TEMP).

Desired AF04 control options are specified, i.e., dc measurement, 100 mV range, 0.01% resolution

```
        .EQUIPMENT
↑       *AF04
↑       CHAN(1,3) TEMP
↑ #101  DC,100MV,.01    DO TCONV
```

Required temperature conversion routine.

```
#1      .PHASE
        .ACTION
#10     DO SNAP #2 EVERY 10 SEC
        TIMER(START,#10)

#2      .SNAP
#40     .FORMAT
3(XXX.XXX   )
```

Added FORMAT statement, abbreviated form.

```
        .PROCESS
        GET ( F04,#101) TEMP
        SEND (TTY,#40) TEMP
        EXIT
.END
```

Changes in GET and SEND statements were permitted by changes in AF04 input identification statement.

Fig. 7-5b. Condensed version of INDAC data-acquisition program shown in Fig. 7-5a. (*Digital Equipment Corporation.*)

routines are organized into three types of so-called **phases,** viz.,

1. **Foreground phases** include tasks called for by real-time-clock interrupts, e.g., periodic measurements and data-processing operations. There can be several such foreground phases, corresponding to different clock-timed operations.
2. **The priority phase,** which includes operations in response to instrument or process interrupts other than ordinary clock interrupts. INDAC admits only a single priority phase.
3. **The background phase** can be any background computing operation, such as routine data processing, used to occupy idle time between interrupts. INDAC admits only one background phase.

The INDAC executive permits the various phases to time-share the available core (which may be as small as 8K words) by swapping program segments between core and disk as needed. It is also possible to chain (overlay) segments of long programs (Sec. 3-10). Such core swapping will, of course, require time; INDAC programs are intended for the relatively slow operations (involving seconds or minutes rather than microseconds) typical of most instrumentation requirements.

As an example of a still more powerful operating system useful for both instrumentation and process control, we mention Honeywell Information Systems' OLERT (on-line executive for real time), a FORTRAN IV-based software system providing real-time multiprogramming for the DDP-516 computer. The OLERT executive again handles all interrupts, sorts out the relative priorities of different computing and instrumentation-control tasks, permits FORTRAN programming and linkage of new subprograms, and optionally contains a library of reentrant utility routines (Sec. 4-16).

(c) Laboratory-computer Packages. Special **laboratory-computer packages** consisting of a minicomputer, selected peripherals and instruments, and much software, have been developed for general-purpose experimentation, especially in university laboratories. An important example is the Digital Equipment Corporation PDP-12 (Fig. 7-6) which, like its predecessor LINC-8, combines a 12-bit PDP-8-class minicomputer, a simple graphic-display oscilloscope, a small disk and/or unformatted magnetic tape, a real-time clock, analog-to-digital and digital-to-analog converters, discrete-logic input and output lines, and a pulse generator which can be triggered by external inputs to generate interrupts or DMA request pulses. The central processor has all the capabilities of a PDP-8. In addition, a special instruction (LINC) places the PDP-12 into its *LINC mode;* a new instruction set comprising both one-word and two-word instructions is now in force and permits autoincrementing of indirect memory addresses, addition of accumulator contents into a memory location, two-word direct addressing, 6-bit byte manipulation, and various multiplication and shifting instructions. A large number of standard I/O instructions operate the peripherals supplied with the PDP-12. The entire instruction set is designed to emulate that of the LINC laboratory computer project sponsored by the United States government at Washington University during the 1960s; therefore a substantial amount of useful instrumentation control software is added to the already large software system available for the PDP-8.

For experimenters who like to program in assembly language, the LINC instruction set may be more powerful and convenient than that of the PDP-8 class alone, although LINC instruction execution is not especially fast. *The power of the PDP-12 can, however, be radically improved at relatively low cost by adding the FPP-12 floating-point processor* (Sec. 6-12) which, together with a new FORTRAN compiler, permits much laboratory work to be done in the FORTRAN language using scale-factor-free floating-point notation.

PDP-12 software includes a complete keyboard operating system (Sec. 3-11) and a large number of application programs including programs for

Fig. 7-6. PDP-12 laboratory computer. The PDP-12 control panel is more elaborate than that of a PDP-8 (Fig. 3-1); the operator can, for instance, load the processor instruction register from a separate switch register and then execute the instruction just loaded. (*Digital Equipment Corporation.*)

signal averaging, time-interval histograms, signal editing and frequency analysis, software to service chemical-analysis instrumentation, multi-instrument data acquisition, BASIC, FORTRAN, and FOCAL, and even a business-oriented data-processing language called DIBOL. The PDP-12 and selected applications are described in detail in Ref. 1.

For researchers less interested in the LINC instruction set, LAB 8/e is a lower-cost modular laboratory package combining a PDP-8/e (Sec. 6-2a), a display oscilloscope, a real-time clock, and a wide variety of peripheral options. While, as we have noted in Sec. 5-24, it is not difficult for a knowledgeable researcher to interface instruments, displays, etc., with a minicomputer himself, the main advantage of prepackaged laboratory computers is the standard I/O software and data-processing subroutines provided by the manufacturers of such systems.

(d) Special Instrumentation Packages. For important instrumentation applications, full-time-dedicated minicomputers have been combined with instruments, special control panels, and special-purpose software into complete **instrumentation packages.** For operator convenience, special instructions, commands, and subroutines can be called through *interrupts from control-panel keys* rather than by conventional programming. A teletypewriter may still be available, and extended BASIC or FORTRAN programs can contain special measurement and data-processing routines.

As an interesting example, the Hewlett-Packard Type 5450A Fourier Analyzer shown in Fig. 7-7 illustrates the use of accessory modules to transform a minicomputer into a keyboard-controlled special-purpose instrument which performs very complex operations easily and simply. With a "canned" paper-tape program loaded, the operator need not know any computer programming at all. He merely operates front-panel keys and switches to produce oscilloscope or plotter graphs showing the power spectrum, magnitude, phase, complex components, Nyquist, or Bode diagrams for the Fourier transform of a voltage input. A digital display (dark area at the right of CRT) automatically indicates the scale and type of plot. Other keyboard commands control data acquisition and storage and produce transfer functions, coherence functions, amplitude distributions,

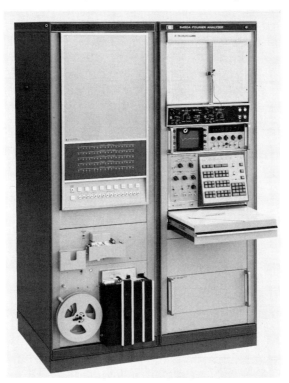

Fig. 7-7. Fourier analyzer using a dedicated minicomputer. (*Hewlett-Packard Corporation.*)

and correlation functions, all without computer programming. But the full power of the digital computer is still available to more knowledgeable operators.

7-4. Data-processing Operations. The most frequently encountered minicomputer **data-processing operations** include **code conversion** and **data formatting, signal conditioning by digital filtering,** and **computation of statistics,** such as **averages, mean squares, variances, correlation functions, spectra,** and **amplitude distributions. Processing of graphic data** from digital-scanner outputs and **pattern recognition** also belong in this category. Data-processing operations may take place *on line* as part of an automatic instrumentation system, or *off line*, frequently with data read from magnetic-tape storage in analog or digital form.

Reference 77 is a good introduction to digital filtering and contains a large bibliography. The vast field of statistical data processing will not fit into this volume, but we would like to remind the reader that *the cumulative additions involved in statistical averaging with minicomputers usually require double-precision accumulation in order to avoid successive truncation errors* (see also Sec. 1-5a).

The **fast-Fourier-transform technique,** which has revolutionized the computation not only of Fourier transforms and spectra but also of correlation functions and digital-filter outputs, is introduced neatly in Ref. 79; Ref. 78 is a comprehensive bibliography. While fast Fourier transforms for large digital computers are naturally in floating-point format, minicomputers with as little as 8K of memory can do very fast *fixed*-point Fourier transformations; a 1,024-point transformation will take in the order of 1 sec. A number of manufacturers supply special accessory processors to speed up minicomputer fast Fourier transformation.

Measurement of pulse-amplitude distributions is of the greatest importance to nuclear physicists. Typical pulses to be analyzed are generated by charged-particle or gamma-ray detectors, whose output pulses are proportional to nuclear-particle energies. The neatest instrumentation packages for pulse-height analysis are built around the **direct-memory-access/memory-increment technique** described in Sec. 5-21. A very small minicomputer can readily accumulate amplitude-distribution statistics for several thousand class intervals. Joint distributions of two or more variables—say, three variables with 100 class intervals each—will, however, require more event-class "counters" than are available in ordinary minicomputer memories. Note, though, that since the total number of pulses measured may be much fewer than $100 \times 100 \times 100$ or 10^6, most of the possible events will never take place. Very elegant scatter-storage techniques using both core and disk memories have been developed to utilize this fact (Refs. 7 to 9).

Another minicomputer direct-memory-access technique, viz., the **add-to-memory signal-averaging method** of Sec. 5-22, is of the greatest importance for **evoked-response studies** in biomedical research, as well as in other situations requiring recovery of small periodic signals submerged in noise. A number of special minicomputer instrument packages have been developed for such measurements.

7-5.   Automatic Test Systems.   Automated component and system testing achieve more than direct test-cost reduction.   Automation makes it possible to perform much more complete testing or inspection (e.g., 100 percent inspection of incoming or outgoing parts, or of system functions) and in this way can radically improve safety, reliability and/or loss rates.

Automated test systems are special instrumentation-control systems which, in addition to the experiment-controlling procedures listed in Sec. 7-4, may involve:

Parts handling with conveyor belts, turntables, mechanical component feeders
Automated decisions accepting, rejecting, or *grading* tested items
Documentation of test results or test statistics to provide management information

A test program can be entirely computer-controlled, or a computer may display messages such as "DEPRESS SWITCH 7" for the operator to determine the further progress of a test procedure.   Results can be displayed on meters, digital indicators, or oscilloscopes.   Hard copy and/or tape output for off-line data processing can be provided.   As in other automation systems, substitution of computers for hard-wired controllers saves logic design, improves flexibility with a view toward possible test-prodecure changes, and permits test-related data processing.   An automatic test station can be self-contained (portable, if desired) with its own minicomputer, or it can time-share a larger computer.

References 21 to 29 highlight a number of minicomputer-based systems for testing *electrical components* and *networks*, such as cables, wiring harnesses, circuit cards, and integrated circuits (Fig. 7-3).   Automated *integrated-circuit tests* are especially important because of the very large numbers of parts (and of different tests) involved.   A tester can:

Verify interconnections and/or digital logic with a computer-programmed test-signal pattern by checking the output-signal sequence against a computer program (or against a comparison module)
Check electrical circuits with computer-programmed dc and ac test signals by reading digital voltmeters, automatic bridge circuits, frequency counters, etc., all with computer-compatible mode switching and outputs

Check circuit or system tolerances under worst-case power-supply, signal, and environmental conditions

Wheeled or truck-mounted automatic test systems, which may use standard or ruggedized versions of commercially available minicomputers, perform complete checks of entire aircraft or missile avionics systems.

With suitable transducers, a wide variety of *nonelectrical* apparatus is similarly tested. Internal-combustion engines and gas compressors can be automatically checked for pressures, temperatures, fuel flow, exhaust components, efficiency, etc. Reference 23 further discusses automatic testing.

7-6. Multicomputer Control of Manufacturing Operations. Minicomputer sequencing logic, numerical control, and automatic testing (Secs. 7-1 to 7-5) may be said to implement automation at the "worker" level on the factory floor. Computers used in these operations can be "stripped" minicomputers, each comprising little more than a basic processor, interface logic, and read-only memory, plus a little core memory if frequent program changes are anticipated. More advanced plant-automation systems will link these "worker" minicomputers into a larger "supervisor" digital computer—this can still be a 16-bit minicomputer—which can:

Transmit new parameter values and/or stored programs to the "worker" computers

Schedule operations of individual fabricating machines and test stations with respect to one another

Reschedule operations in case of equipment failures or other emergencies

Provide operating statistics and system status as management information

Each "worker level" minicomputer will, then, not only control a test station or one to a dozen fabricating machines, but will communicate test results or status to a "supervisor" computer, which might also transmit new programs. The supervisory minicomputer may further communicate with a large central digital computer, which need not be located in the manufacturing plant. The design of such systems requires careful attention to graceful degradation in case of computer failures; this, indeed, is the reason why the use of multiple "worker" and "supervisor" minicomputers at the plant location seems preferable to more centralized systems time-sharing a single large digital computer. It is fair to say that multicomputer plant-automation system design is still in its infancy.

Some of the most striking applications of multicomputer control have been designed by the International Business Machines Corporation for use in its own plants, linking IBM 1130, 1800, and System/7 computers into larger central machines. Practically all minicomputer manufacturers are attempting to break into this field, which requires much system-engineering and manufacturing know-how in addition to computer development. An especially strong proponent of multicomputer automation has been General Automation, Inc., whose SPC-12 and SPC-16 minicomputers (Secs. 6-2*b* and 6-4) will communicate with the company's larger 18/30 supervisory minicomputer, a 16-bit machine frankly designed to accept software written for the IBM 1130 and 1800 (these machines are also 16-bit minicomputers in all but price).

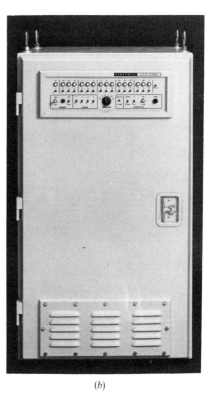

(*a*)   (*b*)

Fig. 7-8. Rack-mounted Honeywell 316 minicomputer for use in permissive industrial environments (*a*) and ruggedized minicomputer in a heavy-duty industrial enclosure (*b*). (*Honeywell Information Systems.*)

Ruggedized minicomputers for factory, mobile, or military environments (Fig. 7-8*b*) may have circuit-card hold-downs to reduce vibration, especially stiffened circuit cards, heavy-duty fans, rugged metal cabinets designed to protect the computer from spilled liquids as well as from shock, electromagnetic-interference protection, moisture-sealed switches and cabinets, military-type connectors, and, if necessary, antifungus coating of electronic components (Fig. 7-8).

7-7. Minicomputers in Business-data Acquisition Systems.   The vast field of *business-data processing* is outside the scientific/engineering applications area treated in this book, but the burgeoning use of minicomputers in on-line business-data acquisition systems promises to provide so large a market that we should at least mention it here. A typical and especially important application is *minicomputer automation of supermarket check-out stands*, as developed by Honeywell Information Systems. As individual sales items are checked out, the operator either manually keys a code number printed

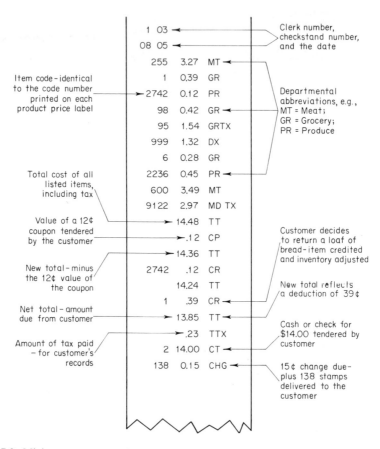

Fig. 7-9. Minicomputer-prepared supermarket sales receipt, indicating the amount of information handled by the computer system. (*Honeywell Information Systems.*)

on the individual can or cereal package into a local minicomputer, or the code is read automatically with a mark-reading sensing probe.

The check-out terminal displays the item's price (and, if relevant, its weight) to the customer and computes the total purchase price and sales tax, and prints a sales tape (Fig. 7-9). The checker need not read, compute, or enter prices or sales totals. A computer-compatible scale next to the terminal is used to weigh produce.

The store manager has a counterpart of the check-out terminal ("manager's interrogation device," MID). Since the minicomputer keeps track of the sale of each individual item, the manager can use his terminal to ascertain his inventory of any product, to determine sales up to the moment in any department or at any check-out stand, to know total sales, to change prices, to see whether any purchases have been paid for with coupons or food stamps, and to determine what taxes have been paid. In addition, all bookkeeping concerned with sales and inventories is taken care of by the small computer; books are balanced more accurately because automatic computation has replaced human arithmetic errors. The minicomputer will prepare daily sales reports of the entire store, showing the number of customers handled by each checker at each check-out stand, to permit management to schedule and rate store personnel and thus to reduce costs. A daily sales report by stores and with total transactions permits management to evaluate store operation, the effect of special promotions, and to handle its own inventory problem. These reports can be printed out and sent through the mail, or the local minicomputer may be connected to a supervisory computer at a central location through a communication link.

CATHODE-RAY-TUBE GRAPHIC DISPLAYS
AND SERVO PLOTTERS

7-8. Cathode-ray-tube Displays. A cathode-ray-tube graphic display positions and brightens a CRT beam to plot a sequence of points (and/or brightens the beam *between* points to draw line segments or "vectors"). Small displays (up to 11-in diameter) employ *electrostatic deflection* in the X and Y directions and can plot up to 10^6 distinct points/sec. Larger displays use *electromagnetic deflection* for better focusing and resolution, but such displays are slower (up to 100,000 points/sec). High-quality electromagnetic-deflection displays may add fast electrostatic deflection for small beam displacements (e.g., to display characters labeling a picture).

Figure 7-10 shows how the X and Y deflection amplifiers of a CRT display are driven by X **and** Y **digital-to-analog converters** (DACs). A digitally controlled **brightening voltage (Z-axis voltage)** is also indicated. 9-bit X and Y resolution is quite satisfactory for most CRT displays, but many displays have 10-bit DACs.

Very elaborate displays can use full 16-bit resolution to specify points in a picture much larger than actually displayed on the CRT screen. 10-bit portions of the 16-bit X- and Y-coordinate words are then shifted into position to display small or large portions of the overall picture at different scales (*scissoring*).

Displayed pictures range from simple 256-point graphs with coordinate axes to elaborate design drawings with several thousands of points, plus alphanumeric characters. A *storage-tube CRT display* (Fig. 7-11) permits

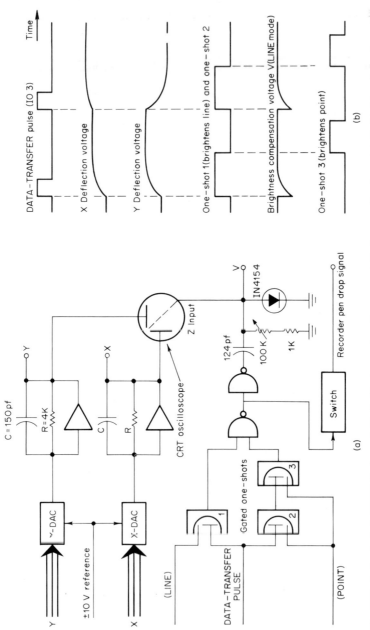

Fig. 7-10. A simple digital CRT display suitable for Dertouzos-type line-segment display as well as for point display (*a*) and waveforms (*b*). The low-pass-filter capacitors *C* establish equal *X* and *Y* time constants *RC* and also reduce transients ("glitches") due to switching spikes and different DAC bit-switching times. The line-brightness-compensation-voltage waveform also has the time constant *RC* to brighten the beam most when it moves most quickly. But perfect compensation is not possible (Fig. 7-11*a*). The *X* and *Y* display outputs can operate at a slow rate with an *xy* servo recorder, in which case the brightening logic drops the recorder pen on the paper. (*University of Arizona*; see also **Ref** 39.)

you to view the displayed points after they have been written only once—
the display remains visible until a manually controlled or computer-
controlled voltage pulse is applied to an erasing electrode in the storage tube.
Storage CRTs have excellent resolution and greatly simplify display
operation. But they cannot display *moving* pictures and require complete
erasure and rewriting for *display editing.* Most digital displays, therefore,
use short-persistence cathode-ray tubes (P7 phosphor) and must **rewrite
(refresh) the entire display periodically** 30 to 60 times/sec. This requires not

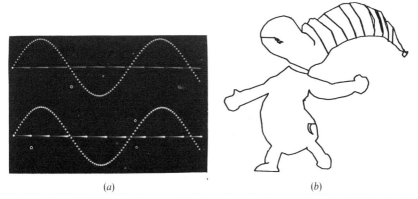

(*a*)   (*b*)

Fig. 7-11. CRT displays (*a*) and servo plot (*b*) produced by the simple display/plotter circuit of
Fig. 7-10. Both POINT and LINE modes are used in Fig. 7-11*a*; note the effect of adjusting the
line-brightness-compensation time constant. Perfect compensation for the exponential
change in the writing rate was not possible because the compensation voltage tends to defocus
the beam. (*University of Arizona.*)

only many fast writing operations but a **display-refreshing memory** capable
of storing coordinate and brightness information for 1,000 to 6,000 points
and/or vectors. *Alphanumeric characters* are generated and refreshed as
sets of points or vectors (strokes) usually stored in special read-only memories
(**character generators**) and called out by special character-code display-
instruction words.

Each display point will require 18 to 20 bits of refresher storage for X
and Y plus, possibly, some extra bits to specify brightness or special display
operations. Some CRT displays, especially the more elaborate displays
used with larger digital computers, have their own 16- to 24-bit refresher
memories, perhaps 4K to 16K words. **A minicomputer display can conveniently share the minicomputer memory.** This simplifies computer
operations on display words and makes the extra memory available to the
computer when the display is not used; although the time needed for display-
refreshing operations will necessarily slow concurrent computations.

7-9. Display Operations and Interfaces. (a) Simple Point Display. To display a point, we transfer its X- and Y-coordinate words from a processor register or from memory into the X and Y DAC registers (Fig. 7-12) and then brighten the beam.   This can be done through programmed I/O instructions with different control bits and IO pulses (Sec. 5-2), but **it is much more**

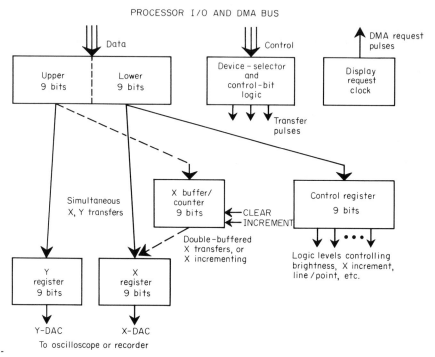

Fig. 7-12. Design of a graphic-display interface for an 18-bit minicomputer.   Programmed or DMA data transfers can transmit packed X, Y words or load a buffer with X and then transfer X from the buffer and Y from the data bus.   It is also possible to simply *increment* the X buffer for graph plotting while transferring only Y-coordinate words from the bus.   The 9-bit control register is loaded with the last 9 bits of any DMA data word starting with 100 000 000. (*University of Arizona;* see also Ref. 39 and Sec. 7-10.)

efficient to employ direct-memory-access block transfers (Sec. 5-19).   A DMA display interface can readily request and transfer alternate X and Y words (from one array or two arrays in memory), but **an especially neat scheme is to use an 18-bit minicomputer with 9-bit X and Y bytes packed into a single word;** this *halves* the refresh memory needed *and* the computer time needed to refresh the display, and simplifies the interface.   Figure 4-8*d* shows a suitable word-packing program.   In Fig. 7-12, a brightness control bit gates the transfer pulse loading the X and/or Y DAC into a pair of monostable multivibrators to brighten the beam.   One usually controls brightness by changing the *duration* of the brightening waveform (e.g., by

ORing outputs of different logic-controlled monostable multivibrators). Beam *current* changes will also control brightness, but may defocus the beam.

(b) Simple Line-segment Generation. Figure 7-10 also illustrates the Dertouzos technique of displaying *line segments* between display points. *The X and Y DACs shown drive operational-amplifier low-pass filters with equal time constants RC so that the beam will move from point to point along a straight line after the X and Y DACs have been loaded simultaneously* (Fig. 7-10b). This line is brightened if a control bit gates the DAC transfer pulse into monostable multivibrator 1. Unfortunately, the beam speed varies exponentially along each line segment, so the beam becomes progressively brighter. This is partially compensated in Fig. 7-11 by a differentiating network in the brightness control circuit, but beam defocusing makes perfect compensation impossible (Fig. 7-11a). *The simple Dertouzos line-segment generation technique is, however, excellent for producing hard copy with a simple servo plotter.* Figure 7-11b shows a drawing produced by feeding the X and Y inputs of a servo recorder with the display circuit of Fig. 7-11a; the brightness voltage lowers the pen to plot line segments. The transfer rate was about 10 points/sec, and the monostable-multivibrator time constant was appropriately longer (Refs. 39 and 40).

(c) Improved Line-segment Generation and Incremental Display Techniques. More elaborate line-segment generators employ operational-amplifier integrators for *straight-line* interpolation between successive coordinate voltages so that line brightness will remain constant between successive display points. If the time interval between successive display points remains constant, though, short line segments will necessarily be brighter than long ones. For this reason, elaborate displays employ *digital interpolation* (hardware or software similar to numerical-control methods, Sec. 7-2) to place extra display points between widely separated points; analog interpolation may still be used. Electromagnetically deflected CRT beams can, in general, follow short displacements more quickly than long ones.

In many of the better graphic displays, DAC registers (or DAC buffers) are implemented as *reversible binary counters*, which can be incremented or decremented by IO pulses to produce small beam displacements. The incrementing pulse may be gated to higher-order or lower-order bits to produce increments of a few different sizes, but many displays only permit

$$\Delta X = -2^{-10}, 0, \text{ or } 2^{-10} \qquad \Delta Y = -2^{-10}, 0, \text{ or } 2^{-10}$$

so increment/decrement operations can move a display point only in one of eight directions separated by 45° angles. *Incrementing-mode* display programs can generate any reasonable curve from such displacements.

In display pictures containing continuous curves or small detail, incrementing-mode instructions can save refresh memory and memory accesses at the expense of extra display-logic hardware. For example, the 10-bit X and Y coordinates of a single point require *two* 16-bit words. But a *single* 16-bit word could specify up to 2^{16} different combinations of X and Y *increments* (usually the hardware will not permit all possible combinations). With still more elaborate hardware, a display can be instructed, say, to *repeat* the same beam displacement n times to generate a straight line from n line segments.

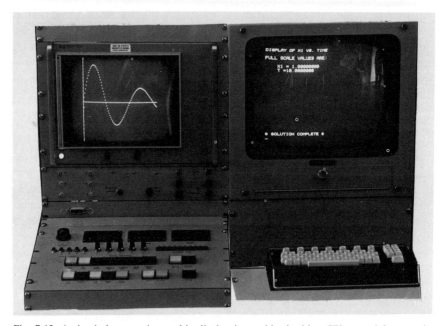

Fig. 7-13. A simple homemade graphic display is combined with a TV-scan alphanumeric display in this minicomputer system for on-line solution of ordinary differential equations. Reading coordinate labels and scales off the alphanumeric display is much like reading a figure legend and imposes no hardship. (*University of Arizona.*)

Even simple CRT displays may permit incrementing the X coordinate to permit graph plotting (Y versus X in equal increments) without any need to fetch X-coordinate words (Fig. 7-12).

(d) A Suggestion for Do-it-yourself Displays. Addition of alphanumerics to graphs and pictures (e.g., labels on coordinate axes) complicates display hardware and software, because:

1. The display of characters adds much fine detail and many display points
2. Characters are generated from points (five by seven dot matrix) or strokes by reference to a fair-size table, which must be stored either in the computer memory or in display-controller hardware (MOSFET read-only memory)

3. The need for character spacing and line feed requires still more software and/or hardware

An excellent way to simplify this situation is to provide two displays side by side, viz., a simple graphic display (refreshed or storage-tube display) *and* an inexpensive TV-scan alphanumeric display with MOSFET character generation and refresher shift registers (Fig. 7-13), which permits convenient text editing and can work with only slight modification of teletypewriter software (Sec. 3-14).

7-10. From Display Control Registers to Display Processors. The simplest graphic displays have only a simple point mode with a single brightness level. Such a display can be operated with only *two* I/O instructions, viz., TRANSFER X and TRANSFER Y AND BRIGHTEN. If we use packed 18-bit X, Y words, a *single* I/O instruction will do (TRANSFER AND BRIGHTEN).

As we noted, though, it is *by far* more efficient to fetch alternate X- and Y-coordinate words, or packed X, Y words, *by direct memory access*. For example, the points of a simple picture may be represented as packed 18-bit X, Y words stored in an N-word block starting at the memory location PICT.

To display the picture (i.e., its N successive points), the program first places the addresses of PICT and N into two pointer locations in memory. The program then enables interrupts from a real-time clock in the display or processor to refresh the display 30 to 60 times/sec through the following interrupt-service routine:

1. Programmed I/O instructions preset a *current-address counter* and a *word counter* (Sec. 5-19) in the display (or in the computer memory, Sec. 5-23) to PICT and to N, respectively.
2. Another programmed instruction enables a **DMA request-pulse oscillator** in the display to produce successive cycle-stealing co-ordinate-data transfers and to display successive points.
3. The word counter counts down from N with each DMA transfer and *stops the request oscillator* when the count reaches 0, presumably before the next clock interrupt repeats the process.

More complicated display programs will display multiple blocks of points, corresponding to different portions of an overall picture (Sec. 7-11).

Display options associated with individual display points, such as different brightnesses, line brightening, and X incrementing for plotting graphs, are controlled with logic levels from a **display control register** (Sec. 5-4), which may have between 1 and 18 flip-flops. Programmed display instructions can include a few control bits, and there may be special instructions to load the control register. To obtain the control-register information through *direct memory access:*

1. Control bits may be packed into data words (e.g., a 16-bit word could contain a 10-bit Y coordinate and 6 control bits).
2. The display may always request X words, Y words, and control-register words in succession. This can waste a good deal of time.
3. The display may recognize certain codes as data words and some as control words.

As an example of the last possibility, packed 18-bit X, Y words need not represent $X = -1$ and $Y = -1$, since $X = 1$ and $Y = 1$ are not available in 2s-complement code either. Thus, data words *beginning* or *ending* with 100 000 000 can be used to load two 9-bit control registers; such control words can be freely inserted into the display file, as needed. Figure 7-13 illustrates the design of a simple graphic-display interface with a control register (Ref. 40).

Our direct-memory-access display interface can be regarded as an accessory processor (display processor) which shares the computer memory, accepts programmed instructions from the central processor, and can respond with interrupts (see also Sec. 6-12a). The accessory processor has:

A *program counter* (the DMA word counter)
A *memory address register* (the DMA current-address counter)
A *memory data register* (DAC register or buffer)
An *instruction register* (the display control register)

The simple "instructions" executed by the display processor are **DISPLAY A POINT** (using X- and Y-coordinate information), **CHANGE BRIGHTNESS**, etc. With more elaborate display operations, the display processor looks more and more like a small stored-program computer; it might implement:

Coordinate-incrementing instructions (Sec. 7-9b)
Display subroutine jumps and returns, using a display linkage register to store return addresses
Hard-wired subroutines (ROM-implemented character generation called by suitable control words)
Output to multiple CRT consoles

Display operations involving actual *arithmetic*, e.g.,

$$X = aX' + b \qquad\qquad Y = aY' + c \qquad (TRANSLATION\ AND$$
$$SCALING\ OF\ PICTURE$$
$$OR\ SUBPICTURE)$$
$$X = X' \cos \vartheta + Y' \sin \vartheta \qquad Y = -X' \sin \vartheta + Y' \cos \vartheta \qquad (ROTATION)$$

can be implemented either in the main processor or in the display processor; a few display processors incorporate fast multiplying digital-to-analog converters for rotation operations. The display processor can be a complete minicomputer.

7-11. The Display File and Display Software. The display file for a simple picture is a block of words containing display-point-coordinate and display-control information.   There must also be "header" words specifying the block starting address and the block size (**PICT** and **N** in Sec. 7-10). It will be expedient to structure display files for more complicated pictures as *linked lists* (Sec. 4-10c): each item in the list is a subpicture file ending with a pointer to the start of the next subpicture file and its block size.   Display requests can then fetch each subpicture in turn, and it will still be possible to perform operations such as erasure, scaling, or rotation only on selected subpictures.

Suitable header or label words can further structure subpictures into hierarchies of sub-subpictures; so operations can be performed on sets of sub-subpictures which in some sense "belong together."   Display-structuring and display-modifying operations can be called as assembly-language subroutines or macros and as FORTRAN subroutines, with symbolic names for display files and subpictures.

7-12. Operator/Display Interaction.   Joy sticks, various **tablet-stylus combinations,** and the **"mouse"** rolling on a table surface all contain dual analog-to-digital conversion devices which enter X and Y coordinates into a computer display file so that the operator can "draw" points and lines on the CRT screen.

A light pen contains a photocell, which is held against a CRT display screen and which responds to the flash of a display point with an interrupt or sense-line response.   The computer can then mark the X and Y coordinates of the point in question to *erase* or further brighten the point.   The computer can generate a dimly lighted raster or random-scan pattern and brighten points touched by the light pen (which contains a button switch to disable this action, if desired), so the operator can draw pictures on the CRT screen. The computer can also generate a *tracking pattern* with a program designed to move this pattern in order to center it on the light pen; this can also be used for drawing on the screen and for moving subpictures (e.g., circuit or block-diagram symbols) into desired screen positions with the light pen.

Finally, the computer may display a "menu" of possible decisions or commands on the CRT screen, each with a "light-button" pattern which is touched by the light pen to implement the command.

FRONT-ENDING, DATA-COMMUNICATIONS, AND MULTIPROCESSOR TIME-SHARING SYSTEMS

7-13. Minicomputers as Input/Output Processors. An ever-increasing number of minicomputers are employed as **front ends** intended to relieve a larger digital computer of input/output operations and its memory of multiple input/output routines. We discussed in Sec. 7-10 how a data channel designed to implement block transfers of input and output data (and to perform a few extra device-control chores) acquires many of the features of a small digital processor. A minicomputer transferring data blocks by direct memory access and communicating with a larger digital computer through programmed instructions and interrupts (see also Sec. 6-12) can perform data-transfer and control operations equivalent to those of several data channels; like a data channel, it accepts programmed instructions to preset address counters, word counters, and control registers and, in turn, speaks to the larger digital computer through processor interrupts.

But a minicomputer can do much more than transfer data blocks and control device functions. The minicomputer memory *buffers* external devices, which can thus operate at their optimal speed without waiting for the main digital-computer program, and vice versa. If there is the time, moreover, the minicomputer peripheral processor can perform formatting, scaling, and code-changing operations, sense and announce error conditions, and perform parity and syntax checks. What is more, many input/output programs, interrupt-service routines, etc., can be stored in the minicomputer memory at substantially lower cost than is possible in the more expensive large-computer memory with its greater word length. Tens of thousands of bytes of main-computer core storage may be saved in this manner. Minicomputers have been used as **peripheral processors** for practically all types of peripherals, such as multiple teletypewriters, CRT displays, line printers, disks, multiple tape units, and communication interfaces (Sec. 7-14). Such applications favor minicomputer instruction sets which permit 8-bit byte handling and operations on multibyte data words. In particular, microprogrammed minicomputers may be furnished with instruction sets especially adapted to those of an associated large digital computer. As an example, the microprogrammed Interdata Models 70 and 80 have instruction sets conveniently related to those of IBM System/360 and 370 machines.

7-14. Minicomputers and Data Communications (see Refs. 48 to 58). For data communication over distances greater than a few hundred feet, digital words are transmitted serially (bit by bit, Sec. 1-3) and *modulate a carrier* on a communication line or wireless data link. Amplitude, phase, frequency modulation, or combination amplitude and phase modulation is used. Communication links specially designed for digital data transmission may employ radio-frequency carriers, but audio frequencies are used on telephone lines (which are not primarily designed for data transmission). At each end of any carrier link, one requires a **modulator/ demodulator (modem).**

Simplex transmission is one direction only; **half-duplex** permits communication in both directions, but only one at a time; **full-duplex** permits simultaneous transmission and reception (e.g., on two two-wire lines).

Conversion between parallel computer input/output lines and serial bit streams is usually achieved with *shift registers* having parallel input/serial output and/or serial input/parallel output (Table 1-5*b*; see also Sec. 5-1). Most digital data transmission is in terms of 8-bit ASCII-character bytes, 1 bit being a parity bit (Sec. 1-4). It is necessary to mark the start and/or

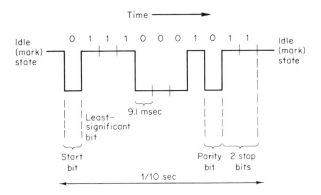

Fig. 7-14. Serial representation for an ASCII 7-bit-and-parity character. Start and stop bits "delimit" the serial character representation for asynchronous transmission. Timing is for an ASR-33 teletypewriter operating at 110 baud (bits/sec) or 10 characters/sec.

end of each byte or word unequivocally. In **asynchronous** data transmission, this is done through **start/stop bits** inserted between data words by the transmitting shift-register interface (Fig. 7-14). Since 3 start/stop bits transmitted with each 8-bit byte waste a good deal of time, asynchronous transmission is used only with low-cost, slow data-transmission systems (up to 1,400 bits/sec). Faster data-communication systems justify the cost of **synchronous** transmission, which transmits a continuous stream of true data bits and marks the start of a *message* (not the start of a word or byte) with a synchronizing signal (or the *end* of a LINE IDLE signal) transmitted *over an extra link or carrier frequency*. In any case, the interface between a parallel computer I/O bus and the serial input/output of a modem requires, besides a shift register, a bit-rate-determining clock, a bit counter, and some logic which generates or recognizes start/stop bits or synchronizing signals. This interface, which is usually designed for a specific computer, is called a **data-set coupler (data-set controller)** and connects to a general-purpose **data set** combining the functions of a modem and various options, such as automatic telephone dialing.

TABLE 7-2. Some Commercially Available Data Sets. *(Table compiled by Interdata, Inc.)*

Data set	Baud rate	Two-wire	Four-wire	Unattended	Attended	Private line	Public line	Synchronous	Asynchronous	Approximate rental per month	Remarks
103A	200	Yes	No	Yes	Yes	No	Yes	No	Yes	$27	
103B	300	Yes	No	No	Yes	Yes	Yes	No	Yes	27	Discontinued
103F	300	Yes	No	Yes	Yes	Yes	Yes	No	Yes	27	Replaces 103B
201A	2,000	Yes	Yes	Yes	Yes	Yes	Yes	Yes	No	80	Requires line conditioning
201B	2,400	Yes	Yes	Yes	Yes	Yes	No	Yes	No	80	Requires line conditioning
202A	1,800	Yes	No	Yes	Yes	Yes	Yes	No	Yes	40	1,800-baud transmission requires line conditioning
202B	1,800	Yes	Yes	Yes	Yes	Yes	Yes	No	Yes	40	Discontinued
202C	1,200 or 1,800	Yes	Yes	Yes	Yes	Yes	Yes	No	Yes	40	1,800-baud transmission requires line conditioning
202D	1,800	No	Yes	No	Yes	Yes	No	No	Yes	40	Replaces 202B/C

Table 7-2 lists typical data sets. Wires and signals between a data-set coupler include:

1. **Ring indicator:** Data set to terminal—it indicates that a caller requests local connection of the data set to the line. The terminal responds with data terminal RDY.
2. **Data terminal RDY:** This requests the data set to connect to the telephone line.
3. **Data set RDY:** This informs the terminal that the data set is connected to the line and is ready to exchange data.
4. **RCV signal detect:** This is used for status.
5. **Request send:** From terminal to data set—it is used to start transmission.
6. **Ready to send:** This indicates that the line amplifiers are stabilized and that the remote terminal is able to receive. The terminal may pass data to the modem.
7. **Send data:** Data path from terminal to data set.
8. **Receive data:** Data path from data set to terminal.
9. **Present next digit:** ACU[1] has dialed one digit and is ready for the next.
10. **Digit present:** The adapter has the next digit available.
11. **Abandon call:** ACU has reached the end of its time out and since there was no answer, it invites a disconnect.

Ordinary ASR-33/35 teletypewriter links (Sec. 3-3) operate at 110 bits/sec (bauds) using the 11-bit character format illustrated in Fig. 7-14. *Dial-up telephone lines*, which involve telephone-exchange switching, can have data rates up to 2,400 bits/sec, but special line conditioning is needed to get more than 1,800 bits/sec. *High-quality private lines*, line conditioning, and special modems permit rates above 40,000 bits/sec.

Since many data streams—say, to and from teletypewriters—are slower than a line will admit, several data streams may share the line bandwidth (**frequency multiplexing**); or we can interleave bits or (preferably) characters in time (**time-division multiplexing**). A **time-division multiplexer/demultiplexer** (or **data concentrator/deconcentrator**) involves a *buffer memory* which transfers parallel data bytes to and from a digital computer as needed, while it attempts to transmit or receive a serial data stream over the communication link at its optimal bit rate (Fig. 7-15).

A minicomputer with special communication-link and computer-to-computer interfaces can neatly perform data concentration/deconcentration, using its core memory for buffering. In addition, such a minicomputer **communications controller** acts as an extremely flexible peripheral processor (Sec. 7-13) which combines multiplexing/demultiplexing with many useful functions,

[1] Automatic control unit for dialing.

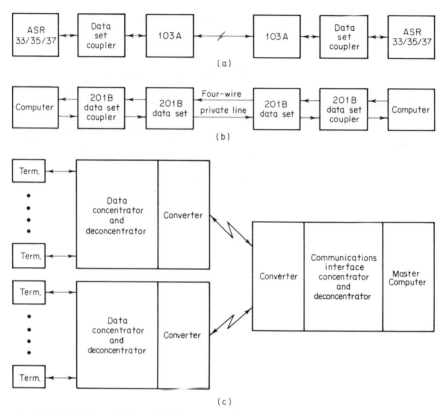

Fig. 7-15. A 110- to 150-baud link between teletypewriters (*a*) a 2,400-baud computer-to-computer link (*b*) and a multiterminal system with time-division multiplexing (*c*). (*Interdata, Inc.*)

such as:

Error checks
Checking for spurious echoes
Formatting and code conversion
Logic-controlled line selection
Automatic dialing
Accumulation of traffic statistics
Computation of charges
Message storage during system failures

The minicomputer can, again, greatly relieve the burdens on large and expensive digital computers connected into communication networks. Once again, *microprogramming* is an especially flexible way to adapt a minicomputer intended as a communications controller to different master computers and communications systems.

7-15. Minicomputer Time-sharing Systems (see Refs. 69 to 74). The simplest minicomputer time-sharing systems are foreground/background systems (Sec. 3-15), which share the available core memory among a *background program*, an interrupt-driven *foreground program*, and a simple *time-sharing-executive program*, relying on memory-protection interrupts to prevent overwriting (Sec. 2-15). Such systems are severely limited by the available core memory.

More powerful time-sharing systems *swap user programs in and out of a disk or disks* in response to user-terminal interrupts. Each user can program his work as though he had sole access to a set of core-memory pages all his own, although these pages are really disk-resident when he is not looking.

Besides doing a great deal of computing for different users, a time-sharing system must service multiple teletypewriters and/or CRT terminals, and it will have a formidable executive program to handle the disk swapping and file manipulation for several users. To relieve the job processor which does the actual computing, one employs an extra minicomputer (or even two minicomputers, Fig. 7-16) for peripheral processing (Sec. 7-13) and for holding most of the executive program. The time-sharing system thus becomes a *multiprocessor system*. The minicomputer holding the resident executive program takes the role of the *master processor*. It recognizes interrupts from user-terminal commands and processor job-completion interrupts, and it issues programmed instructions to initiate direct-memory-access block transfers of programs and data between processors and disks (see also Sec. 6-12). A minicomputer job processor, thus relieved of I/O and executive operations, can do respectable BASIC and FORTRAN time sharing for up to 32 users, with typical access times below 2 sec. Time-sharing file-manipulation commands permit each user to protect his files.

It is a good idea to have an extra processor for redundancy in case of processor failures. An elaborate time-sharing system might have two or more job processors, but their simultaneous operation will saturate a single direct-memory-access bus between processors. At this point, one needs multiport memories and multiple DMA buses, and the multiprocessor system becomes more complicated and expensive; but with quantity-produced modular interface components this will be the direction of future development (see also Fig. 6-5, Refs. 71 and 73). Two minicomputer job processors will, in all probability, rarely work *together* on the same job, so they may not need to communicate *with each other* during computation.

MISCELLANEOUS APPLICATIONS

7-16. Minicomputers versus Electronic Desk Calculators (see Ref. 76). Modern electronic desk calculators can perform fairly complicated

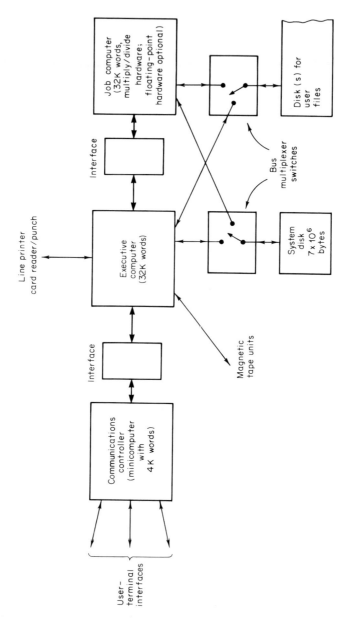

Fig. 7-16. A multi-minicomputer time-sharing system using three 16-bit minicomputers (similar to Honeywell H1648 system).

calculations, which can involve trigonometric and exponential functions. Such machines have multiple registers for storing intermediate results and can store small programs on magnetic cards. The more advanced desk calculators can even accept instrument inputs and may be used for automatic oscilloscope display and plotting of graphs.

Nevertheless, the simplest minicomputer programmed in conversational BASIC is incomparably more powerful and flexible. Even users quite averse to real computer programming can use calculator-mode commands (Table 3-2), e.g.,

$$\text{LET A} = 1.573 - \text{SIN (0.35)}$$
$$\text{PRINT B} = A - 0.333$$

If you still prefer to punch keys instead of typing, it is easy to construct keyboards which call arithmetic operations through keyboard interrupts; since the human operator is relatively slow, the most primitive interrupt system will do. Desk calculators have only one real advantage over most currently available BASIC systems, and that is their 10-digit (decimal) or better precision. Minicomputer BASIC is usually designed for only five-digit or six-digit precision, and few minicomputer BASIC systems provide for double-precision operation, although this could be readily added with a little effort.

7-17. Continuous-system Simulation. Digital **continuous-system simulation** employs a digital computer for "experimentation" with the model of a physical system (e.g., an aircraft or chemical process) represented by a set of **ordinary differential equations**

$$\frac{dX_i}{dt} = F_i(X_1, X_2, \ldots, X_n; t) \qquad i = 1, 2, \ldots, n$$

(**system state equations**). The computer solves these differential equations with various **initial conditions** and **system parameters** to produce time histories of the state variables (or of functions of these state variables); one can then study the effects of parameter variations on the system performance. If the computer is fast enough to permit synchronization of its time-history output with a real-time clock, then the simulated system operation can be experienced in *real time*. Real-time simulation is of the greatest importance in training-type simulators such as flight simulators, aerospace-mission simulators, and process-control trainers, which permit on-line modification of the digital simulation through external-device inputs from control sticks, switches, etc., as well as on-line instrument-output displays and tilt-table or cockpit motion.

A **training-type flight simulator,** which may support multiple crew positions and an instructor's console, may have to solve over 20 highly nonlinear differential equations and service of the order of 1,000 instrument displays and cockpit-control inputs (the latter mostly in the form of discrete-switch settings). These formidable input/output requirements are readily handled with a direct-memory-access system, which can transfer discrete inputs and outputs as multibit-register words (Sec. 5-20). Small digital computers have replaced analog computation in practically all commercially available flight simulators. Some 24-bit machines are used in large simulators, but minicomputers will usually do. As a rule of thumb, an 18-bit 1-μsec machine (PDP-15, 620/f, Sec. 6-4) will readily simulate a twin-engined aircraft in real time, using fixed-point arithmetic. Training-type flight simulators need not simulate high-speed subsystems such as hydraulic servos.

General-purpose continuous-system simulation, most frequently slower than real time, is so important for engineering design that several special **continuous-system-simulation languages** have been written for this purpose. Such languages do away with the need to program complicated integration formulas and to plot routines in FORTRAN. One merely types or cardpunches the system's differential equations in a form like

$$X1' = -A * X2 + B * SIN (W * T)$$
$$X2' = A * X1 - C * X2$$

One adds a number of statements which specify *parameter values* (e.g., **A = 0.332**), *initial values* (e.g., **X1** = 0., **X2** = −1.5), and, if desired, *iteration programs for consecutive solution runs,* plus *output requests* like

PLOT X1, X2, VS T

Most continuous-system-simulation languages are batch-processed on large digital computers. It is, however, possible to do a respectable simulation (involving 20 to 30 nonlinear differential equations and considerable control programs) on minicomputers, especially if floating-point hardware options are available. The accessibility of the minicomputer makes it possible to obtain solutions *on line* by typing differential equations directly on an alphanumeric CRT and to obtain solutions on an adjacent simple graphic display (Fig. 7-13), *so the user can immediately assess the effect of varying parameters and other program changes,* a very useful feature. The first on-line minicomputer simulation system of this type was developed at the University of Arizona under U.S. government sponsorship, using a 16K PDP-9 or PDP-15 with 16K and a small disk (Project DARE, for differential analyzer replacement).

DARE-type simulation can replace conventional analog computation in many applications. On a minicomputer, though, scale-factor-free floating-point computations are too slow to permit, say, three-dimensional flight simulation in real time; a simple 12-equation aerospace simulation involving a few function generations and trigonometrical transformations may not admit state-variable changes with frequency components faster than 0.1 Hz (Ref. 61). For this reason, Project DARE also developed a *fixed-point simulation system* employing the macro-block technique outlined in Sec. 4-22b to generate assembly-language programs capable of very fast execution. DARE II permits real-time flight simulation using a PDP-15; the fixed-point variables must be scaled in the manner of Sec. 1-8, just as in analog-computer simulation (Ref. 63). DARE II integration steps can be synchronized with a real-time clock, so DARE II can be used with analog inputs and outputs (e.g., flight simulation with a human pilot in the loop, partial-system test of autopilot components on a tilt table).

7-18. Hybrid Analog/Digital Computation. Hybrid computers, widely employed for fast continuous-system simulation (especially in the aerospace, chemical, and nuclear-reactor design areas), combine digital computers with analog computers (electronic differential analyzers) where ordinary differential equations must be solved more quickly than is possible with digital computers alone. Such computing techniques are described in detail in Refs. 66 and 67. **Hybrid-computer applications fall into three broad classes:**

1. **Digital-computer control of** (one hopes fast) **analog computation.** The analog computer solves a differential-equation system many times with different system parameters or initial conditions supplied by a digital-computer program, which also evaluates the analog-simulated-system performance after each differential-equation solving run. Principal applications involve **iterative optimization** of some system performance measure (e.g., control-system error) by the digital-computer program, and **digital accumulation of statistics** from a sample of analog-computer runs with random inputs (**Monte Carlo simulation**).

2. **Combined analog/digital simulation,** where the digital computer and interface actually convert and process simulated-system variables and return computed outputs through digital-to-analog converters into the simulated system. An especially important application is **digital storage and table lookup of empirical functions** needed by the analog computer.

3. **Simulation of actual digital computing equipment** in simulated analog/digital control, guidance, and communication systems.

Each hybrid-computer system requires an **analog/digital interface** or **linkage** comprising multiplexed analog-to-digital converters, multiple digital-to-analog converters, logic-level interfacing for switching analog-computer components (possibly even including digital control of analog-computer patching), and sense and interrupt lines.

Digital control of analog computation is a natural application for mini-computers, so much so that even medium-size analog/hybrid computers often incorporate a minicomputer as an integral part of the analog-computer console. *Closed-loop, combined analog/digital simulation*, which is subject to severe sampled-data frequency-response errors, is a by far more difficult and cumbersome technique and applies mainly to real-time or fast-time simulation of large systems where all-digital simulation may still be too slow or too expensive. Because such problems are usually large ones, a mini-computer may lack sufficient computing power unless fixed-point arithmetic is satisfactory; but this excludes FORTRAN programming. The simulation-software systems of Refs. 63 and 68 (see also Sec. 7-18) replace or simplify assembly-language programming for fixed-point computations. Another possible application of minicomputers in combined analog/digital simulation is in *special-purpose hybrid function generators* (Ref. 67).

7-19. Editing and Typesetting. Minicomputer editing software (Sec. 3-16*b*) was originally designed mainly for editing *computer programs*. Similar programs are directly useful for editing many types of *reference lists* which require frequent updating, e.g., catalogs, inventories, directories, and time tables. As noted in Sec. 3-16*b*, the best way to perform such editing operations is with the aid of an alphanumeric CRT terminal.

With the expansion of the character set to incorporate lowercase as well as uppercase letters, on-line minicomputer editing becomes applicable to *general text material* in letters, reports, and books. An early application was on-line computer insertion of different names, addresses, prices, and account numbers in *form letters* stored on magnetic tape; a single tape unit can control multiple electric typewriters.

Typesetting machines for both hot-metal and photocomposition type (and, in particular, machines for setting newspaper type) usually accept inputs from punched paper tape as well as from keyboards. Tapes are now commonly prepared with the aid of minicomputer programs which accept unjustified and unhyphenated paper-tape or keyboard input and convert it to justified, hyphenated form. These programs take account of the different character widths and thus save space automatically. Such systems produce text, advertisements, and headings in various formats; they can set upward of 10,000 lines/hr; newspaper items or headings which reoccur daily can be stored on the computer disk or magnetic tape.

Combination of minicomputer programs for on-line text editing and type preparation offers especially intriguing possibilities for ultrafast preparation and updating of news bulletins and reports.

REFERENCES AND BIBLIOGRAPHY

See also the literature published by minicomputer manufacturers' users' groups. The largest of these is the Digital Equipment Corporation Users

Group (DECUS), Maynard, Massachusetts, which publishes a newsletter and two yearly symposium proceedings.

Data Acquisition and Supervision of Experiments

1. *Laboratory Computer Handbook*, Digital Equipment Corporation, Maynard, Mass. (current edition). This book contains chapters on PDP-12 applications in physics, chemistry, biomedical, clinical, industrial, and educational laboratories.
2. Bevington, P. R.: *Data Reduction and Error Analysis for the Physical Sciences*, McGraw-Hill, New York, 1970.
3. Computer-controlled Data-acquisition Systems (Survey), *Mod. Data*, January 1970.
4. Torpey, P. J.: Minicomputerizing Analog Data Collection, *Control Eng.*, June 1970.
5. *CAMAC, a Modular Instrumentation System for Data Handling*, A.E.C. Comm. Nucl. Instrum. Modules; request from Natl. Bur. Stand., Washington, D.C.
6. CAMAC Final Specification, *Rept. EUR* 4600e, EURATOM, Brussels, 1970.
7. Soucek, B., et al.: Million-channel Pulse-height Analyzer, *Nucl. Instrum. Method*, **66**: 202 (1968).
8. ———: Pseudo-random Digital Transformation, *Nucl. Instrum. Method*, **66**: 213 (1968).
9. Soucek, B.: New Trends in Multi-channel Pulse Data Analysis, *Rept. BNL* 14442, Brookhaven Natl. Lab., New York, 1969.
10. *Computers in the Psychology Laboratory*, Digital Equipment Corporation, Maynard, Mass., 1969.

Process Control and Numerical Control

11. Clough, J. E., and A. W. Westerberg: FORTRAN for On-line Control, *Control Eng.*, March 1968.
12. Williams, T. J., and F. M. Ryan: *Progress in Direct Digital Control*, Instrument Society of America, Pittsburgh, 1970.
13. Lapidus, G.: A Look at Minicomputer Applications, *Control Eng.*, November 1969.
14. Rosenblatt, A.: Minicomputers Penetrate N/C Field, *Electronics*, August 31, 1970.
15. Mesniaeff, P. G.: The Technical Ins and Outs of Computerized Numerical Control, *Control Eng.*, March 1971.
16. Leslie, W. H. P.: *Numerical Control User's Handbook*, McGraw-Hill, New York, 1971.
17. Broekhuis, H., and M. S. Jongkine: Planning and Managing Process-computer Projects, *Control Eng.*, February 1971.
18. Aronson, R. L.: Machine Monitoring in Appliance Manufacture, *Control Eng.*, February 1971.
19. Bader, F. P.: How to Interface Pneumatic Controls with Computers, *Control Eng.*, April 1971.
20. Lapidus, G.: Programmable Logic Controllers, *Control Eng.*, April 1971.

Automated Testing

(See also *Hewlett-Packard J.*, August 1969 and September 1970.)

21. Grimm, R. A.: Using Standard Instruments and an Abbreviated English-language Program in a Computer-based Automatic Test System, *Electron. Instrum. Dig.*, May 1969.
22. Mactaggart, D.: Computer . . . in an Automatic Test System, *Electronics*, July 6, 1970.
23. Fichtenbaum, M.: Computer-controlled Testing, *Electronics*, January 19, 1970.
24. Bobroff, D. A.: Avoid Pitfalls in Computerized Testing, *Electron. Des.*, August 1969.
25. Smith, K. D.: A Minicomputer-aided MOS Array Tester, *Comput. Des.*, December 1970.
26. McAleer, H. T.: A Look at Automatic Testing, *IEEE Spectrum*, May 1971.
27. Survey of Automated-test Instrumentation, *Electron. Instrum. Dig.*, May 1971.
28. Heffner, A. B.: Automatic Test Equipment for Electronic Components, *NASA Contractor Rept.* CR-1755, March 1971.
29. Curran, L.: Meeting the MOS/LSI Challenge: A Special Report on Testers, *Electronics*, May 10, 1971.

Multicomputer Manufacturing-plant Supervision

30. Young, N. F.: Distributed Computer Systems, *Automation*, October 1969.
31. Abramson, E.: The Minicomputer—Does It Figure in Large-scale Process Control?, *Datamation*, February 1970.

32. Fryer, S. J.: Minicomputers Speed Automation on the Factory Floor, *Comput. Decis.*, September 1970.
33. Tulles, R., and S. Reese: Computer-controlled System Automatically Tests Magnetic-tape Transports, *Comput. Des.*, October 1970.
34. Harrison, T. J., et al.: IBM System/7 and Plant Automation, *IBM J. Res. Dev.*, November 1970.
35. Kinberg, C., and B. W. Landeck: Integrated Manufacturing Systems, *IBM J. Res. Dev.*, November 1970.
36. Thoburn, F. W.: A Transmission-control Unit for High-speed Computer-to-computer Communication, *IBM J. Res. Dev.*, November 1970.
37. Hippert, R. O.: IBM 2790 Digital Transmission Loop, *IBM J. Res. Dev.*, November 1970.
38. Aronson, R. L.: Line-sharing Systems for Plant Monitoring and Control, *Control Eng.*, January 1971.

Display/Plotter Systems

39. Dertouzos, M. L.: PHASEPLOT, an On-line Graphical Display Technique, *IEEE Tech.*, April 1967.
40. Korn, G. A., et al.: Graphic Display/Plotter for Small Computers, *Proc. SJCC*, 1969.
41. Davis, S.: *Computer Data Displays*, Prentice-Hall, Englewood Cliffs, N.J., 1969.
42. Sherr, S.: *Display-system Design*, Wiley, New York, 1970.
43. *VT 15 Graphic Processor Manual*, Digital Equipment Corporation, Maynard, Mass., 1971.

Display Software

44. Sutherland, I. E.: Sketchpad, a Man-Machine Graphical Communication System, *Proc. SJCC*, 1963.
45. Coggan, B. B.: "The Design of a Graphic Display System," M.S. thesis, Dept. of Eng., University of California, Los Angeles, 1967.
46. Henderson, D. A.: "A Graphics Display Language," M.S. thesis, Dept. of Comput. Sci., University of Illinois, Urbana, Ill., 1967.
47. Chase, E. N., and D. A. Westlake: Development of Hierarchical Graphical Logical-entity Capabilities, *Rept. AFCRL-68-0129/30/31*, Adams Assoc., Inc., Bedford, Mass., 1968.

Communication-system Applications

48. *Introduction to Data Communication*, Digital Equipment Corporation, Maynard, Mass., 1967.
49. Data Communication Systems, *Publ.* 38-029 Rol, Interdata, Oceanport, N.J., 1968.
50. Stimler, S.: *Real-time Processing Systems*, McGraw-Hill, New York, 1969.
51. Stifle, J., and M. Johnson: Design Pruning Trims Costs of Data Modem, *Electronics*, July 20, 1970.
52. Brening, R. L.: External Control, *Datamation*, September 1, 1970.
53. Barth, J.: Using Minicomputers in Teleprocessing Systems, *Data Process.*, November 1970.
54. Crisis in Data Communications (Special Report), *Comput. Decis.*, November 1970.
55. O'Hare, R. A.: Modems and Multiplexers, *Mod. Data*, December 1970.
56. Jones, W. S.: System Aspects of Data Modems, *Electron. Prod.*, February 15, 1971.
57. Harper, W. L.: The Remote World of Digital Switching, *Datamation*, March 15, 1971.
58. *Varian 620/DC Data-communication System*, Varian Data Machines, Irvine, Calif., 1971.

Education

59. Robinson, D. M.: A Computer Engineering Laboratory, *Proc. FJCC*, 1969.
60. Woodfill, M. C.: Teaching Digital-system Design with a Minicomputer, *Proc. FJCC*, 1970.

Continuous-system Simulation

61. Korn, G. A.: Project DARE: Differential Analyzer REplacement by On-line Digital Simulation, *Proc. FJCC*, 1969.
62. Goltz, J. R.: The DARE-I Systems, *Proc. SWIEEECO*, Dallas, 1970.
63. Liebert, T. A.: DARE II: Fast On-line Digital Simulation on a Small Computer, *Proc. SCSC*, Denver, 1970.

64. Benham, R. D.: Interactive Simulation Language ISL-8, *DECUS Symp.*, Houston, 1970.
65. Aus, H. M., and G. A. Korn: The Future of On-line Digital Simulation, *Proc. FJCC*, 1971.

Hybrid Analog/Digital Computation

66. Bekey, G. A., and W. J. Karplus: *Hybrid Computation*, Wiley, New York, 1968.
67. Korn, G. A., and T. M. Korn: *Electronic Analog and Hybrid Computers*, 2d ed., McGraw-Hill, New York, 1972.
68. Benham, R. D., et al.: SIMPL-1, a Simple Approach to Simulation, *Simulation*, September 1969.

Time Sharing and Multiprocessor Systems

69. Taylor, M. M., et al.: PDP-9T: Compatible Time Sharing for the Real-time Laboratory, *Tech. Pap.* 688, Defense Research Establishment, Toronto, 1968.
70. Two Computers Are Cheaper than One, *Electron Des. News*, September 1970.
71. Wolfe, R. E.: Multiple Minicomputers Go to Work for Large Time-sharing Applications, *Data Process.*, September 1970.
72. Christensen, C., and A. D. Hause: A Multiprogramming Virtual Memory System for a Small Computer, *Proc. SJCC*, 1970.
73. Riley, W. B.: Minicomputer Networks—a Challenge to Maxicomputers?, *Electronics*, March 29, 1971.
74. Pearlman, J.: Put Your Input/Output Cares in the Hands of a Mini, *Comput. Decis.*, April 1971.

Business Applications

75. *Program Description*, Computing Corporation International, Englewood, Colo., 1970.

Miscellaneous

76. Howard, H. T.: Programmable Calculators, *Electron Des. News*, May 1970.
77. Wait, J. V.: Digital Filters; in L. P. Huelsman: *Active Filters*, McGraw-Hill, New York, 1970.
78. Singleton, R. C.: A Short Bibliography on the Fast Fourier Transform, *IEEE Trans. Audio Electroacoust.*, June 1969.
79. Bergland, G. D.: A Guided Tour of the Fast Fourier Transform, *IEEE Spectrum*, July 1969.
80. Cadzow, J. A., and H. R. Martens: *Discrete-time and Computer Control Systems*, Prentice-Hall, Englewood Cliffs, N.J., 1970.
81. *Control Handbook*, Digital Equipment Corporation, Maynard, Mass. (current edition).
82. *DDP-516 OLERT Programmer's Reference Manual*, Honeywell Information Systems, Framingham, Mass. (current edition).
83. *Discrete-signal Analysis*, Hewlett-Packard Corporation, Cupertino, Calif., 1970.
84. Special issue on computer-controlled printing, *Datamation*, December 1, 1970.
85. Krasny, L.: A Special-purpose Digital Computer for Real-time Flight Simulation, *M.I.T. Electron. Syst. Lab. Rept.* ESL-R-118, 1961.
86. Chew, S. P.: Multivariable Function Generation for Simulation, *Proc. FJCC*, 1971.

APPENDIX: REFERENCE TABLES

TABLE A-1. Powers of Two.

2^N					N
				1	0
				2	1
				4	2
				8	3
				16	4
				32	5
				64	6
				128	7
				256	8
				512	9
			1	024	10
			2	048	11
			4	096	12
			8	192	13
			16	384	14
			32	768	15
			65	536	16
			131	072	17
			262	144	18
			524	288	19
		1	048	576	20
		2	097	152	21
		4	194	304	22
		8	388	608	23
		16	777	216	24
		33	554	432	25
		67	108	864	26
		134	217	728	27
		268	435	456	28
		536	870	912	29
	1	073	741	824	30
	2	147	483	648	31
	4	294	967	296	32
	8	589	934	592	33
	17	179	869	184	34
	34	359	738	368	35
	68	719	476	736	36
	137	438	953	472	37
	274	877	906	944	38
	549	755	813	888	39
1	099	511	627	776	40
2	199	023	255	552	41
4	308	046	511	104	42
8	796	093	022	208	43
17	592	186	044	416	44
35	184	372	088	832	45
70	368	744	177	664	46
140	737	488	355	328	47
281	474	976	710	656	48
562	949	953	421	312	49

				2^N						N
			1	125	899	906	842	624		50
			2	251	799	813	685	248		51
			4	503	599	627	370	496		52
			9	007	199	254	740	992		53
			18	014	398	509	481	984		54
			36	028	797	018	963	968		55
			72	057	594	037	927	936		56
			144	115	188	075	855	872		57
			288	230	376	151	711	744		58
			576	460	752	303	423	488		59
		1	152	921	504	606	846	976		60
		2	305	843	009	213	693	952		61
		4	611	686	018	427	387	904		62
		9	223	372	036	854	775	808		63
		18	446	744	073	709	551	616		64
		36	893	488	147	419	103	232		65
		73	786	976	294	838	206	464		66
		147	573	952	589	676	412	928		67
		295	147	905	179	352	825	856		68
		590	295	810	358	705	651	712		69
	1	180	591	620	717	411	303	424		70
	2	361	183	241	434	822	606	848		71
	4	722	366	482	869	645	213	696		72
	9	444	732	965	739	290	427	392		73
	18	889	465	931	478	580	854	784		74
	37	778	931	862	957	161	709	568		75
	75	557	863	725	914	323	419	136		76
	151	115	727	451	828	646	838	272		77
	302	231	454	903	657	293	676	544		78
	604	462	909	807	314	587	353	088		79
1	208	925	819	614	629	174	706	176		80
2	417	851	639	229	258	349	412	352		81
4	835	703	278	458	516	698	824	704		82
9	671	406	556	917	033	397	649	408		83
19	342	813	113	834	066	795	298	816		84
38	685	626	227	668	133	590	597	632		85
77	371	252	455	336	267	181	195	264		86
154	742	504	910	672	534	362	390	528		87
309	485	009	821	345	068	724	781	056		88
618	970	019	642	690	137	449	562	112		89
1	237	940	039	285	380	274	899	124	224	90
2	475	880	078	570	760	549	798	248	448	91
4	951	760	157	141	521	099	596	496	896	92
9	903	520	314	283	042	199	192	993	792	93
19	807	040	628	566	084	398	385	987	584	94
39	614	081	257	132	168	796	771	975	168	95
79	228	162	514	264	337	593	543	950	336	96
158	456	325	028	528	675	187	087	900	672	97
316	912	650	057	057	350	374	175	801	344	98
633	825	300	114	114	700	748	351	602	688	99
1 267	650	600	228	229	401	496	703	205	376	100

TABLE A-2. Miscellaneous Tables.

2^x IN DECIMAL

x	2^x	x	2^x	x	2^x
0.001	1.00069 33874 62581	0.01	1.00695 55500 56719	0.1	1.07177 34625 36293
0.002	1.00138 72557 11335	0.02	1.01395 94797 90029	0.2	1.14869 83549 97035
0.003	1.00208 16050 79633	0.03	1.02101 21257 07193	0.3	1.23114 44133 44916
0.004	1.00277 64359 01078	0.04	1.02811 38266 56067	0.4	1.31950 79107 72894
0.005	1.00347 17485 09503	0.05	1.03526 49238 41377	0.5	1.41421 35623 73095
0.006	1.00416 75432 38973	0.06	1.04246 57608 41121	0.6	1.51571 65665 10398
0.007	1.00486 38204 23785	0.07	1.04971 66836 23067	0.7	1.62450 47927 12471
0.008	1.00556 05803 98468	0.08	1.05701 80405 61380	0.8	1.74110 11265 92248
0.009	1.00625 78234 97782	0.09	1.06437 01824 53360	0.9	1.86606 59830 73615

$10^{\pm n}$ IN OCTAL

10^n	n	10^{-n}	10^n	n	10^{-n}
1	0	1.000 000 000 000 000 000 00	112 402 762 000	10	0.000 000 000 006 676 337 66
12	1	0.063 146 314 631 463 146 31	1 351 035 564 000	11	0.000 000 000 000 537 657 77
144	2	0.005 075 341 217 270 243 66	16 432 451 210 000	12	0.000 000 000 000 043 136 32
1 750	3	0.000 406 111 564 570 651 77	221 411 634 520 000	13	0.000 000 000 000 003 411 35
23 420	4	0.000 032 155 613 530 704 15	2 657 142 036 440 000	14	0.000 000 000 000 000 264 11
303 240	5	0.000 002 476 132 610 706 64	34 327 724 461 500 000	15	0.000 000 000 000 000 022 01
3 641 100	6	0.000 000 206 157 364 055 37	434 157 115 760 200 000	16	0.000 000 000 000 000 001 63
46 113 200	7	0.000 000 015 327 745 152 75	5 432 127 413 542 400 000	17	0.000 000 000 000 000 000 14
575 360 400	8	0.000 000 001 257 143 561 06	67 405 553 164 731 000 000	18	0.000 000 000 000 000 000 01
7 346 545 000	9	0.000 000 000 104 560 276 41			

$n \log_{10} 2$, $n \log_2 10$ IN DECIMAL

n	$n \log_{10} 2$	$n \log_2 10$	n	$n \log_{10} 2$	$n \log_2 10$
1	0.30102 99957	3.32192 80949	6	1.80617 99740	19.93156 85693
2	0.60205 99913	6.64385 61898	7	2.10720 99696	23.25349 66642
3	0.90308 99870	9.96578 42847	8	2.40823 99653	26.57542 47591
4	1.20411 99827	13.28771 23795	9	2.70926 99610	29.89735 28540
5	1.50514 99783	16.60964 04744	10	3.01029 99566	33.21928 09489

ADDITION AND MULTIPLICATION TABLES

Addition   Multiplication

Binary Scale

$0 + 0 = 0$ $0 \times 0 = 0$

$0 + 1 = 1 + 0 = 1$ $0 \times 1 = 1 \times 0 = 0$

$1 + 1 = 10$ $1 \times 1 = 1$

Octal Scale

0	01	02	03	04	05	06	07		1	02	03	04	05	06	07
1	02	03	04	05	06	07	10		2	04	06	10	12	14	16
2	03	04	05	06	07	10	11		3	06	11	14	17	22	25
3	04	05	06	07	10	11	12		4	10	14	20	24	30	34
4	05	06	07	10	11	12	13		5	12	17	24	31	36	43
5	06	07	10	11	12	13	14		6	14	22	30	36	44	52
6	07	10	11	12	13	14	15		7	16	25	34	43	52	61
7	10	11	12	13	14	15	16								

MATHEMATICAL CONSTANTS IN OCTAL SCALE

$\pi = 3.11037\ 552421_8$	$e = 2.55760\ 521305_8$	$\gamma = 0.44742\ 147707_8$
$\pi^{-1} = 0.24276\ 301556_8$	$e^{-1} = 0.27426\ 530661_8$	$\ln \gamma = -0.43127\ 233602_8$
$\sqrt{\pi} = 1.61337\ 611067_8$	$\sqrt{e} = 1.51411\ 230704_8$	$\log_2 \gamma = -0.62573\ 030645_8$
$\ln \pi = 1.11206\ 404435_8$	$\log_{10} e = 0.33626\ 754251_8$	$\sqrt{2} = 1.32404\ 746320_8$
$\log_2 \pi = 1.51544\ 163223_8$	$\log_2 e = 1.34252\ 166245_8$	$\ln 2 = 0.54271\ 027760_8$
$\sqrt{10} = 3.12305\ 407267_8$	$\log_2 10 = 3.24464\ 741136_8$	$\ln 10 = 2.23273\ 067355_8$

TABLE A-3. Octal-Decimal Integer Conversion Table.

$X =$	0	1	2	3	4	5	6	7
0X	0	1	2	3	4	5	6	7
1X	8	9	10	11	12	13	14	15
2X	16	17	18	19	20	21	22	23
3X	24	25	26	27	28	29	30	31
4X	32	33	34	35	36	37	38	39
5X	40	41	42	43	44	45	46	47
6X	48	49	50	51	52	53	54	55
7X	56	57	58	59	60	61	62	63
10X	64	65	66	67	68	69	70	71
11X	72	73	74	75	76	77	78	79
12X	80	81	82	83	84	85	86	87
13X	88	89	90	91	92	93	94	95
14X	96	97	98	99	100	101	102	103
15X	104	105	106	107	108	109	110	111
16X	112	113	114	115	116	117	118	119
17X	120	121	122	123	124	125	126	127
20X	128	129	130	131	132	133	134	135
21X	136	137	138	139	140	141	142	143
22X	144	145	146	147	148	149	150	151
23X	152	153	154	155	156	157	158	159
24X	160	161	162	163	164	165	166	167
25X	168	169	170	171	172	173	174	175
26X	176	177	178	179	180	181	182	183
27X	184	185	186	187	188	189	190	191
30X	192	193	194	195	196	197	198	199
31X	200	201	202	203	204	205	206	207
32X	208	209	210	211	212	213	214	215
33X	216	217	218	219	220	221	222	223
34X	224	225	226	227	228	229	230	231
35X	232	233	234	235	236	237	238	239
36X	240	241	242	243	244	245	246	247
37X	248	249	250	251	252	253	254	255
40X	256	257	258	259	260	261	262	263
41X	264	265	266	267	268	269	270	271
42X	272	273	274	275	276	277	278	279
43X	280	281	282	283	284	285	286	287
44X	288	289	290	291	292	293	294	295
45X	296	297	298	299	300	301	302	303
46X	304	305	306	307	308	309	310	311
47X	312	313	314	315	316	317	318	319
50X	320	321	322	323	324	325	326	327
51X	328	329	330	331	332	333	334	335
52X	336	337	338	339	340	341	342	343
53X	344	345	346	347	348	349	350	351

Octal	Decimal
10000 =	4096
20000 =	8192
30000 =	12288
40000 =	16384
50000 =	20480
60000 =	24576
70000 =	28672

TABLE A-3.   Octal-Decimal Integer Conversion Table (*Continued*).

$X =$	0	1	2	3	4	5	6	7
54X	352	353	354	355	356	357	358	359
55X	360	361	362	363	364	365	366	367
56X	368	369	370	371	372	373	374	375
57X	376	377	378	379	380	381	382	383
60X	384	385	386	387	388	389	390	391
61X	392	393	394	395	396	397	398	399
62X	400	401	402	403	404	405	406	407
63X	408	409	410	411	412	413	414	415
64X	416	417	418	419	420	421	422	423
65X	424	425	426	427	428	429	430	431
66X	432	433	434	435	436	437	438	439
67X	440	441	442	443	444	445	446	447
70X	448	449	450	451	452	453	454	455
71X	456	457	458	459	460	461	462	463
72X	464	465	466	467	468	469	470	471
73X	472	473	474	475	476	477	478	479
74X	480	481	482	483	484	485	486	487
75X	488	489	490	491	492	493	494	495
76X	496	497	498	499	500	501	502	503
77X	504	505	506	507	508	509	510	511
100X	512	513	514	515	516	517	518	519
101X	520	521	522	523	524	525	526	527
102X	528	529	530	531	532	533	534	535
103X	536	537	538	539	540	541	542	543
104X	544	545	546	547	548	549	550	551
105X	552	553	554	555	556	557	558	559
106X	560	561	562	563	564	565	566	567
107X	568	569	570	571	572	573	574	575
110X	576	577	578	579	580	581	582	583
111X	584	585	586	587	588	589	590	591
112X	592	593	594	595	596	597	598	599
113X	600	601	602	603	604	605	606	607
114X	608	609	610	611	612	613	614	615
115X	616	617	618	619	620	621	622	623
116X	624	625	626	627	628	629	630	631
117X	632	633	634	635	636	637	638	630
120X	640	641	642	643	644	645	646	647
121X	648	649	650	651	652	653	654	655
122X	656	657	658	659	660	661	662	663
123X	664	665	666	667	668	669	670	671
124X	672	673	674	675	676	677	678	679
125X	680	681	682	683	684	685	686	687
126X	688	689	690	691	692	693	694	695
127X	696	697	698	699	700	701	702	703

Octal	Decimal
100000 =	32768
200000 =	65536
300000 =	98304
400000 =	131072
500000 =	163840
600000 =	196608
700000 =	229376

$X =$	0	1	2	3	4	5	6	7
130X	704	705	706	707	708	709	710	711
131X	712	713	714	715	716	717	718	719
132X	720	721	722	723	724	725	726	727
133X	728	729	730	731	732	733	734	735
134X	736	737	738	739	740	741	742	743
135X	744	745	746	747	748	749	750	751
136X	752	753	754	755	756	757	758	759
137X	760	761	762	763	764	765	766	767
140X	768	769	770	771	772	773	774	775
141X	776	777	778	779	780	781	782	783
142X	784	785	786	787	788	789	790	791
143X	792	793	794	795	796	797	798	799
144X	800	801	802	803	804	805	806	807
145X	808	809	810	811	812	813	814	815
146X	816	817	818	819	820	821	822	823
147X	824	825	826	827	828	829	830	831
150X	832	833	834	835	836	837	838	839
151X	840	841	842	843	844	845	846	847
152X	848	849	850	851	852	853	854	855
153X	856	857	858	859	860	861	862	863
154X	864	865	866	867	868	869	870	871
155X	872	873	874	875	876	877	878	879
156X	880	881	882	883	884	885	886	887
157X	888	889	890	891	892	893	894	895
160X	896	897	898	899	900	901	902	903
161X	904	905	906	907	908	909	910	911
162X	912	913	914	915	916	917	918	919
163X	920	921	922	923	924	925	926	927
164X	928	929	930	931	932	933	934	935
165X	936	937	938	939	940	941	942	943
166X	944	945	946	947	948	949	950	951
167X	952	953	954	955	956	957	958	959
170X	960	961	962	963	964	965	966	967
171X	968	969	970	971	972	973	974	975
172X	976	977	978	979	980	981	982	983
173X	984	985	986	987	988	989	990	991
174X	992	993	994	995	996	997	998	999
175X	1000	1001	1002	1003	1004	1005	1006	1007
176X	1008	1009	1010	1011	1012	1013	1014	1015
177X	1016	1017	1018	1019	1020	1021	1022	1023
200X	1024	1025	1026	1027	1028	1029	1030	1031
201X	1032	1033	1034	1035	1036	1037	1038	1039
202X	1040	1041	1042	1043	1044	1045	1046	1047
203X	1048	1049	1050	1051	1052	1053	1054	1055
204X	1056	1057	1058	1059	1060	1061	1062	1063
205X	1064	1065	1066	1067	1068	1069	1070	1071

Octal	Decimal
1000000 =	262144
2000000 =	524288
3000000 =	786432
4000000 =	1048576
5000000 =	1310720
6000000 =	1572864
7000000 =	1835008

$X =$	0	1	2	3	4	5	6	7
206X	1072	1073	1074	1075	1076	1077	1078	1079
207X	1080	1081	1082	1083	1084	1085	1086	1087
210X	1088	1089	1090	1091	1092	1093	1094	1095
211X	1096	1097	1098	1099	1100	1101	1102	1103
212X	1104	1105	1106	1107	1108	1109	1110	1111
213X	1112	1113	1114	1115	1116	1117	1118	1119
214X	1120	1121	1122	1123	1124	1125	1126	1127
215X	1128	1129	1130	1131	1132	1133	1134	1135
216X	1136	1137	1138	1139	1140	1141	1142	1143
217X	1144	1145	1146	1147	1148	1149	1150	1151
220X	1152	1153	1154	1155	1156	1157	1158	1159
221X	1160	1161	1162	1163	1164	1165	1166	1167
222X	1168	1169	1170	1171	1172	1173	1174	1175
223X	1176	1177	1178	1179	1180	1181	1182	1183
224X	1184	1185	1186	1187	1188	1189	1190	1191
225X	1192	1193	1194	1195	1196	1197	1198	1199
226X	1200	1201	1202	1203	1204	1205	1206	1207
227X	1208	1209	1210	1211	1212	1213	1214	1215
230X	1216	1217	1218	1219	1220	1221	1222	1223
231X	1224	1225	1226	1227	1228	1229	1230	1231
232X	1232	1233	1234	1235	1236	1237	1238	1239
233X	1240	1241	1242	1243	1244	1245	1246	1247
234X	1248	1249	1250	1251	1252	1253	1254	1255
235X	1256	1257	1258	1259	1260	1261	1262	1263
236X	1264	1265	1266	1267	1268	1269	1270	1271
237X	1272	1273	1274	1275	1276	1277	1278	1279
240X	1280	1281	1282	1283	1284	1285	1286	1287
241X	1288	1289	1290	1291	1292	1293	1294	1295
242X	1296	1297	1298	1299	1300	1301	1302	1303
243X	1304	1305	1306	1307	1308	1309	1310	1311
244X	1312	1313	1314	1315	1316	1317	1318	1319
245X	1320	1321	1322	1323	1324	1325	1326	1327
246X	1328	1329	1330	1331	1332	1333	1334	1335
247X	1336	1337	1338	1339	1340	1241	1342	1343
250X	1344	1345	1346	1347	1348	1349	1350	1351
251X	1352	1353	1354	1355	1356	1357	1358	1359
252X	1360	1361	1362	1363	1364	1365	1366	1367
253X	1368	1009	1370	1371	1372	1373	1374	1375
254X	1376	1377	1378	1379	1380	1381	1382	1383
255X	1384	1385	1386	1387	1388	1389	1390	1391
256X	1392	1393	1394	1395	1396	1397	1398	1399
257X	1400	1401	1402	1403	1404	1405	1406	1407
260X	1408	1409	1410	1411	1412	1413	1414	1415
261X	1416	1417	1418	1419	1420	1421	1422	1423
262X	1424	1425	1426	1427	1428	1429	1430	1431

Octal	Decimal
10000000 =	2097152
20000000 =	4194304
30000000 =	6291456
40000000 =	8388608
50000000 =	10485760
60000000 =	12582912
70000000 =	14680064

$X =$	0	1	2	3	4	5	6	7
$263X$	1432	1433	1434	1435	1436	1437	1438	1439
$264X$	1440	1441	1442	1443	1444	1445	1446	1447
$265X$	1448	1449	1450	1451	1452	1453	1454	1455
$266X$	1456	1457	1458	1459	1460	1461	1462	1463
$267X$	1464	1465	1466	1467	1468	1469	1470	1471
$270X$	1472	1473	1474	1475	1476	1477	1478	1479
$271X$	1480	1481	1482	1483	1484	1485	1486	1487
$272X$	1488	1489	1490	1491	1492	1493	1494	1495
$273X$	1496	1497	1498	1499	1500	1501	1502	1503
$274X$	1504	1505	1506	1507	1508	1509	1510	1511
$275X$	1512	1513	1514	1515	1516	1517	1518	1519
$276X$	1520	1521	1522	1523	1524	1525	1526	1527
$277X$	1528	1529	1530	1531	1532	1533	1534	1535
$300X$	1536	1537	1538	1539	1540	1541	1542	1543
$301X$	1544	1545	1546	1547	1548	1549	1550	1551
$302X$	1552	1553	1554	1555	1556	1557	1558	1559
$303X$	1560	1561	1562	1563	1564	1565	1566	1567
$304X$	1568	1569	1570	1571	1572	1573	1574	1575
$305X$	1576	1577	1578	1579	1580	1581	1582	1583
$306X$	1584	1585	1586	1587	1588	1589	1590	1591
$307X$	1592	1593	1594	1595	1596	1597	1598	1599
$310X$	1600	1601	1602	1603	1604	1605	1606	1607
$311X$	1608	1609	1610	1611	1612	1613	1614	1615
$312X$	1616	1617	1618	1619	1620	1621	1622	1623
$313X$	1624	1625	1626	1627	1628	1629	1630	1631
$314X$	1632	1633	1634	1635	1636	1637	1638	1639
$315X$	1640	1641	1642	1643	1644	1645	1646	1647
$316X$	1648	1649	1650	1651	1652	1653	1654	1655
$317X$	1656	1657	1658	1659	1660	1661	1662	1663
$320X$	1664	1665	1666	1667	1668	1669	1670	1671
$321X$	1672	1673	1674	1675	1676	1677	1678	1679
$322X$	1680	1681	1682	1683	1684	1685	1686	1687
$323X$	1688	1689	1690	1691	1692	1693	1694	1695
$324X$	1696	1697	1698	1699	1700	1701	1702	1703
$325X$	1704	1705	1706	1707	1708	1709	1710	1711
$326X$	1712	1713	1714	1715	1716	1717	1718	1719
$327X$	1720	1721	1722	1723	1724	1725	1726	1727
$330X$	1728	1729	1730	1731	1732	1733	1734	1735
$331X$	1736	1737	1738	1739	1740	1741	1742	1743
$332X$	1744	1745	1746	1747	1748	1749	1750	1751
$333X$	1752	1753	1754	1755	1756	1757	1758	1759
$334X$	1760	1761	1762	1763	1764	1765	1766	1767
$335X$	1768	1769	1770	1771	1772	1773	1774	1775
$336X$	1776	1777	1778	1779	1780	1781	1782	1783
$337X$	1784	1785	1786	1787	1788	1789	1790	1791

Octal	Decimal
100000000 =	16777216
200000000 =	33554432
300000000 =	50331648
400000000 =	67108864
500000000 =	83886080
600000000 =	100663296
700000000 =	117440512

$X =$	0	1	2	3	4	5	6	7
340X	1792	1793	1794	1795	1796	1797	1798	1799
341X	1800	1801	1802	1803	1804	1805	1806	1807
342X	1808	1809	1810	1811	1812	1813	1814	1815
343X	1816	1817	1818	1819	1820	1821	1822	1823
344X	1824	1825	1826	1827	1828	1829	1830	1831
345X	1832	1833	1834	1835	1836	1837	1838	1839
346X	1840	1841	1842	1843	1844	1845	1846	1847
347X	1848	1849	1850	1851	1852	1853	1854	1855
350X	1856	1857	1858	1859	1860	1861	1862	1863
351X	1864	1865	1866	1867	1868	1869	1870	1871
352X	1872	1873	1874	1875	1876	1877	1878	1879
353X	1880	1881	1882	1883	1884	1885	1886	1887
354X	1888	1889	1890	1891	1892	1893	1894	1895
355X	1896	1897	1898	1899	1900	1901	1902	1903
356X	1904	1905	1906	1907	1908	1909	1910	1911
357X	1912	1913	1914	1915	1916	1917	1918	1919
360X	1920	1921	1922	1923	1924	1925	1926	1927
361X	1928	1929	1930	1931	1932	1933	1934	1935
362X	1936	1937	1938	1939	1940	1941	1942	1943
363X	1944	1945	1946	1947	1948	1949	1950	1951
364X	1952	1953	1954	1955	1956	1957	1958	1959
365X	1960	1961	1962	1963	1964	1965	1966	1967
366X	1968	1969	1970	1971	1972	1973	1974	1975
367X	1976	1977	1978	1979	1980	1981	1982	1983
370X	1984	1985	1986	1987	1988	1989	1990	1991
371X	1992	1993	1994	1995	1996	1997	1998	1999
372X	2000	2001	2002	2003	2004	2005	2006	2007
373X	2008	2009	2010	2011	2012	2013	2014	2015
374X	2016	2017	2018	2019	2020	2021	2022	2023
375X	2024	2025	2026	2027	2028	2029	2030	2031
376X	2032	2033	2034	2035	2036	2037	2038	2039
377X	2040	2041	2042	2043	2044	2045	2046	2047
400X	2048	2049	2050	2051	2052	2053	2054	2055
401X	2056	2057	2058	2059	2060	2061	2062	2063
402X	2064	2065	2066	2067	2068	2069	2070	2071
403X	2072	2073	2074	2075	2076	2077	2078	2079
404X	2080	2081	2082	2083	2084	2085	2086	2087
405X	2088	2089	2090	2091	2092	2093	2094	2095
406X	2096	2097	2098	2099	2100	2101	2102	2103
407X	2104	2105	2106	2107	2108	2109	2110	2111
410X	2112	2113	2114	2115	2116	2117	2118	2119
411X	2120	2121	2122	2123	2124	2125	2126	2127
412X	2128	2129	2130	2131	2132	2133	2134	2135
413X	2136	2137	2138	2139	2140	2141	2142	2143
414X	2144	2145	2146	2147	2148	2149	2150	2151
415X	2152	2153	2154	2155	2156	2157	2158	2159

$X =$	0	1	2	3	4	5	6	7
$416X$	2160	2161	2162	2163	2164	2165	2166	2167
$417X$	2168	2169	2170	2171	2172	2173	2174	2175
$420X$	2176	2177	2178	2179	2180	2181	2182	2183
$421X$	2184	2185	2186	2187	2188	2189	2190	2191
$422X$	2192	2193	2194	2195	2196	2197	2198	2199
$423X$	2200	2201	2202	2203	2204	2205	2206	2207
$424X$	2208	2209	2210	2211	2212	2213	2214	2215
$425X$	2216	2217	2218	2219	2220	2221	2222	2223
$426X$	2224	2225	2226	2227	2228	2229	2230	2231
$427X$	2232	2233	2234	2235	2236	2237	2238	2239
$430X$	2240	2241	2242	2243	2244	2245	2246	2247
$431X$	2248	2249	2250	2251	2252	2253	2254	2255
$432X$	2256	2257	2258	2259	2260	2261	2262	2263
$433X$	2264	2265	2266	2267	2268	2269	2270	2271
$434X$	2272	2273	2274	2275	2276	2277	2278	2279
$435X$	2280	2281	2282	2283	2284	2285	2286	2287
$436X$	2288	2289	2290	2291	2292	2293	2294	2295
$437X$	2296	2297	2298	2299	2300	2301	2302	2303
$440X$	2304	2305	2306	2307	2308	2309	2310	2311
$441X$	2312	2313	2314	2315	2316	2317	2318	2319
$442X$	2320	2321	2322	2323	2324	2325	2326	2327
$443X$	2328	2329	2330	2331	2332	2333	2334	2335
$444X$	2336	2337	2338	2339	2340	2341	2342	2343
$445X$	2344	2345	2346	2347	2348	2349	2350	2351
$446X$	2352	2353	2354	2355	2356	2357	2358	2359
$447X$	2360	2361	2362	2363	2364	2365	2366	2367
$450X$	2368	2369	2370	2371	2372	2373	2374	2375
$451X$	2376	2377	2378	2379	2380	2381	2382	2383
$452X$	2384	2385	2386	2387	2388	2389	2390	2391
$453X$	2392	2393	2394	2395	2396	2397	2398	2399
$454X$	2400	2401	2402	2403	2404	2405	2406	2407
$455X$	2408	2409	2410	2411	2412	2413	2414	2415
$456X$	2416	2417	2418	2419	2420	2421	2422	2423
$457X$	2424	2425	2426	2427	2428	2429	2430	2431
$460X$	2432	2433	2434	2435	2436	2437	2438	2439
$461X$	2440	2441	2442	2443	2444	2445	2446	2447
$462X$	2448	2449	2450	2451	2452	2453	2454	2455
$463X$	2456	2457	2458	2459	2460	2461	2462	2463
$464X$	2464	2465	2466	2467	2468	2469	2470	2471
$465X$	2472	2473	2474	2475	2476	2477	2478	2479
$466X$	2480	2481	2482	2483	2484	2485	2486	2487
$467X$	2488	2489	2490	2491	2492	2493	2494	2495
$470X$	2496	2497	2498	2499	2500	2501	2502	2503
$471X$	2504	2505	2506	2507	2508	2509	2510	2511
$472X$	2512	2513	2514	2515	2516	2517	2518	2519

X =	0	1	2	3	4	5	6	7
473X	2520	2521	2522	2523	2524	2525	2526	2527
474X	2528	2529	2530	2531	2532	2533	2534	2535
475X	2536	2537	2538	2539	2540	2541	2542	2543
476X	2544	2545	2546	2547	2548	2549	2550	2551
477X	2552	2553	2554	2555	2556	2557	2558	2559
500X	2560	2561	2562	2563	2564	2565	2566	2567
501X	2568	2569	2570	2571	2572	2573	2574	2575
502X	2576	2577	2578	2579	2580	2581	2582	2583
503X	2584	2585	2586	2587	2588	2589	2590	2591
504X	2592	2593	2594	2595	2596	2597	2598	2599
505X	2600	2601	2602	2603	2604	2605	2606	2607
506X	2608	2609	2610	2611	2612	2613	2614	2615
507X	2616	2617	2618	2619	2620	2621	2622	2623
510X	2624	2625	2626	2627	2628	2629	2630	2631
511X	2632	2633	2634	2635	2636	2637	2638	2639
512X	2640	2641	2642	2643	2644	2645	2646	2647
513X	2648	2649	2650	2651	2652	2653	2654	2655
514X	2656	2657	2658	2659	2660	2661	2662	2663
515X	2664	2665	2666	2667	2668	2669	2670	2671
516X	2672	2673	2674	2675	2676	2677	2678	2679
517X	2680	2681	2682	2683	2684	2685	2686	2687
520X	2688	2689	2690	2691	2692	2693	2694	2695
521X	2696	2697	2698	2699	2700	2701	2702	2703
522X	2704	2705	2706	2707	2708	2709	2710	2711
523X	2712	2713	2714	2715	2716	2717	2718	2719
524X	2720	2721	2722	2723	2724	2725	2726	2727
525X	2728	2729	2730	2731	2732	2733	2734	2735
526X	2736	2737	2738	2739	2740	2741	2742	2743
527X	2744	2745	2746	2747	2748	2749	2750	2751
530X	2752	2753	2754	2755	2756	2757	2758	2759
531X	2760	2761	2762	2763	2764	2765	2766	2767
532X	2768	2769	2770	2771	2772	2773	2774	2775
533X	2776	2777	2778	2779	2780	2781	2782	2783
534X	2784	2785	2786	2787	2788	2789	2790	2791
535X	2792	2793	2794	2795	2796	2797	2798	2799
536X	2800	2801	2802	2803	2804	2805	2806	2807
537X	2808	2809	2810	2811	2812	2813	2814	2815
540X	2816	2817	2818	2819	2820	2821	2822	2823
541X	2824	2825	2826	2827	2828	2829	2830	2831
542X	2832	2833	2834	2835	2836	2837	2838	2839
543X	2840	2841	2842	2843	2844	2845	2846	2847
544X	2848	2849	2850	2851	2852	2853	2854	2855
545X	2856	2857	2858	2859	2860	2861	2862	2863
546X	2864	2865	2866	2867	2868	2869	2870	2871
547X	2872	2873	2874	2875	2876	2877	2878	2879

$X =$	0	1	2	3	4	5	6	7
550X	2880	2881	2882	2883	2884	2885	2886	2887
551X	2888	2889	2890	2891	2892	2893	2894	2895
552X	2896	2897	2898	2899	2900	2901	2902	2903
553X	2904	2905	2906	2907	2908	2909	2910	2911
554X	2912	2913	2914	2915	2916	2917	2918	2919
555X	2920	2921	2922	2923	2924	2925	2926	2927
556X	2928	2929	2930	2931	2932	2933	2934	2935
557X	2936	2937	2938	2939	2940	2941	2942	2943
560X	2944	2945	2946	2947	2948	2949	2950	2951
561X	2952	2953	2954	2955	2956	2957	2958	2959
562X	2960	2961	2962	2963	2964	2965	2966	2967
563X	2968	2969	2970	2971	2972	2973	2974	2975
564X	2976	2977	2978	2979	2980	2981	2982	2983
565X	2984	2985	2986	2987	2988	2989	2990	2991
566X	2992	2993	2994	2995	2996	2997	2998	2999
567X	3000	3001	3002	3003	3004	3005	3006	3007
570X	3008	3009	3010	3011	3012	3013	3014	3015
571X	3016	3017	3018	3019	3020	3021	3022	3023
572X	3024	3025	3026	3027	3028	3029	3030	3031
573X	3032	3033	3034	3035	3036	3037	3038	3039
574X	3040	3041	3042	3043	3044	3045	3046	3047
575X	3048	3049	3050	3051	3052	3053	3054	3055
576X	3056	3057	3058	3059	3060	3061	3062	3063
577X	3064	3065	3066	3067	3068	3069	3070	3071
600X	3072	3073	3074	3075	3076	3077	3078	3079
601X	3080	3081	3082	3083	3084	3085	3086	3087
602X	3088	3089	3090	3091	3092	3093	3094	3095
603X	3096	3097	3098	3099	3100	3101	3102	3103
604X	3104	3105	3106	3107	3108	3109	3110	3111
605X	3112	3113	3114	3115	3116	3117	3118	3119
606X	3120	3121	3122	3123	3124	3125	3126	3127
607X	3128	3129	3130	3131	3132	3133	3134	3135
610X	3136	3137	3138	3139	3140	3141	3142	3143
611X	3144	3145	3146	3147	3148	3149	3150	3151
612X	3152	3153	3154	3155	3156	3157	3158	3159
613X	3160	3161	3162	3163	3164	3165	3166	3167
614X	3168	3169	3170	3171	3172	3173	3174	3175
615X	3176	3177	3178	3179	3180	3181	3182	3183
616X	3184	3185	3186	3187	3188	3189	3190	3191
617X	3192	3193	3194	3195	3196	3197	3198	3199
620X	3200	3201	3202	3203	3204	3205	3206	3207
621X	3208	3209	3210	3211	3212	3213	3214	3215
622X	3216	3217	3218	3219	3220	3221	3222	3223
623X	3224	3225	3226	3227	3228	3229	3230	3231
624X	3232	3233	3234	3235	3236	3237	3238	3239
625X	3240	3241	3242	3243	3244	3245	3246	3247

$X =$	0	1	2	3	4	5	6	7
626X	3248	3249	3250	3251	3252	3253	3254	3255
627X	3256	3257	3258	3259	3260	3261	3262	3263
630X	3264	3265	3266	3267	3268	3269	3270	3271
631X	3272	3273	3274	3275	3276	3277	3278	3279
632X	3280	3281	3282	3283	3284	3285	3286	3287
633X	3288	3289	3290	3291	3292	3293	3294	3295
634X	3296	3297	3298	3299	3300	3301	3302	3303
635X	3304	3305	3306	3307	3308	3309	3310	3311
636X	3312	3313	3314	3315	3316	3317	3318	3319
637X	3320	3321	3322	3323	3324	3325	3326	3327
640X	3328	3329	3330	3331	3332	3333	3334	3335
641X	3336	3337	3338	3339	3340	3341	3342	3343
642X	3344	3345	3346	3347	3348	3349	3350	3351
643X	3352	3353	3354	3355	3356	3357	3358	3359
644X	3360	3361	3362	3363	3364	3365	3366	3367
645X	3368	3369	3370	3371	3372	3373	3374	3375
646X	3376	3377	3378	3379	3380	3381	3382	3383
647X	3384	3385	3386	3387	3388	3389	3390	3391
650X	3392	3393	3394	3395	3396	3397	3398	3399
651X	3400	3401	3402	3403	3404	3405	3406	3407
652X	3408	3409	3410	3411	3412	3413	3414	3415
653X	3416	3417	3418	3419	3420	3421	3422	3423
654X	3424	3425	3426	3427	3428	3429	3430	3431
655X	3432	3433	3434	3435	3436	3437	3438	3439
656X	3440	3441	3442	3443	3444	3445	3446	3447
657X	3448	3449	3450	3451	3452	3453	3454	3455
660X	3456	3457	3458	3459	3460	3461	3462	3463
661X	3464	3465	3466	3467	3468	3469	3470	3471
662X	3472	3473	3474	3475	3476	3477	3478	3479
663X	3480	3481	3482	3483	3484	3485	3486	3487
664X	3488	3489	3490	3491	3492	3493	3494	3495
665X	3496	3497	3498	3499	3500	3501	3502	3503
666X	3504	3505	3506	3507	3508	3509	3510	3511
667X	3512	3513	3514	3515	3516	3517	3518	3519
670X	3520	3521	3522	3523	3524	3525	3526	3527
671X	3528	3529	3530	3531	3532	3533	3534	3535
672X	3536	3537	3538	3539	3540	3541	3542	3543
673X	3544	3545	3546	3547	3548	3549	3550	3551
674X	3552	3553	3554	3555	3556	3557	3558	3559
675X	3560	3561	3562	3563	3564	3565	3566	3567
676X	3568	3569	3570	3571	3572	3573	3574	3575
677X	3576	3577	3578	3579	3580	3581	3582	3583
700X	3584	3585	3586	3587	3588	3589	3590	3591
701X	3592	3593	3594	3595	3596	3597	3598	3599
702X	3600	3601	3602	3603	3604	3605	3606	3607

$X =$	0	1	2	3	4	5	6	7
703X	3608	3609	3610	3611	3612	3613	3614	3615
704X	3616	3617	3618	3619	3620	3621	3622	3623
705X	3624	3625	3626	3627	3628	3629	3630	3631
706X	3632	3633	3634	3635	3636	3637	3638	3639
707X	3640	3641	3642	3643	3644	3645	3646	3647
710X	3648	3649	3650	3651	3652	3653	3654	3655
711X	3656	3657	3658	3659	3660	3661	3662	3663
712X	3664	3665	3666	3667	3668	3669	3670	3671
713X	3672	3673	3674	3675	3676	3677	3678	3679
714X	3680	3681	3682	3683	3684	3685	3686	3687
715X	3688	3689	3690	3691	3692	3693	3694	3695
716X	3696	3697	3698	3699	3700	3701	3702	3703
717X	3704	3705	3706	3707	3708	3709	3710	3711
720X	3712	3713	3714	3715	3716	3717	3718	3719
721X	3720	3721	3722	3723	3724	3725	3726	3727
722X	3728	3729	3730	3731	3732	3733	3734	3735
723X	3736	3737	3738	3739	3740	3741	3742	3743
724X	3744	3745	3746	3747	3748	3749	3750	3751
725X	3752	3753	3754	3755	3756	3757	3758	3759
726X	3760	3761	3762	3763	3764	3765	3766	3767
727X	3768	3769	3770	3771	3772	3773	3774	3775
730X	3776	3777	3778	3779	3780	3781	3782	3783
731X	3784	3785	3786	3787	3788	3789	3790	3791
732X	3792	3793	3794	3795	3796	3797	3798	3799
733X	3800	3801	3802	3803	3804	3805	3806	3807
734X	3808	3809	3810	3811	3812	3813	3814	3815
735X	3816	3817	3818	3819	3820	3821	3822	3823
736X	3824	3825	3826	3927	3828	3829	3830	3831
737X	3832	3833	3834	3835	3836	3837	3838	3839
740X	3840	3841	3842	3843	3844	3845	3846	3847
741X	3848	3849	3850	3851	3852	3853	3854	3855
742X	3856	3857	3858	3859	3860	3861	3862	3863
743X	3864	3865	3866	3867	3868	3869	3870	3871
744X	3872	3873	3874	3875	3876	3877	3878	3879
745X	3880	3881	3882	3883	3884	3885	3886	3887
746X	3888	3889	3890	3891	3892	3893	3894	3895
747X	3896	3897	3898	3899	3900	3901	3902	3903
750X	3904	3905	3906	3907	3908	3909	3910	3911
751X	3912	3913	3914	3915	3916	3917	3918	3919
752X	3920	3921	3922	3923	3924	3925	3926	3927
753X	3928	3929	3930	3931	3932	3933	3934	3935
754X	3936	3937	3938	3939	3940	3941	3942	3943
755X	3944	3945	3946	3947	3948	3949	3950	3951
756X	3952	3953	3954	3955	3956	3957	3958	3959
757X	3960	3961	3962	3963	3964	3965	3966	3967

TABLE A-3. **Octal-Decimal Integer Conversion Table** (*Continued*).

X =	0	1	2	3	4	5	6	7
760X	3968	3969	3970	3971	3972	3973	3974	3975
761X	3976	3977	3978	3979	3980	3981	3982	3983
762X	3984	3985	3986	3987	3988	3989	3990	3991
763X	3992	3993	3994	3995	3996	3997	3998	3999
764X	4000	4001	4002	4003	4004	4005	4006	4007
765X	4008	4009	4010	4011	4012	4013	4014	4015
766X	4016	4017	4018	4019	4020	4021	4022	4023
767X	4024	4025	4026	4027	4028	4029	4030	4031
770X	4032	4033	4034	4035	4036	4037	4038	4039
771X	4040	4041	4042	4043	4044	4045	4046	4047
772X	4048	4049	4050	4051	4052	4053	4054	4055
773X	4056	4057	4058	4059	4060	4061	4062	4063
774X	4064	4065	4066	4067	4068	4069	4070	4071
775X	4072	4073	4074	4075	4076	4077	4078	4079
776X	4080	4081	4082	4083	4084	4085	4086	4087
777X	4088	4089	4090	4091	4092	4093	4094	4095

TABLE A-4. **Powers of Sixteen.**

16^n						n
					1	0
					16	1
					256	2
				4	096	3
				65	536	4
			1	048	576	5
			16	777	216	6
			268	435	456	7
		4	294	967	296	8
		68	719	476	736	9
	1	099	511	627	776	10
	17	592	186	044	416	11
	281	474	976	710	656	12
	4 503	599	627	370	496	13
	72 057	594	037	927	936	14
1	152 921	504	606	846	976	15

Decimal Values

TABLE A-5. Octal-Decimal Fraction Conversion Table.

Octal	Decimal	Octal	Decimal	Octal	Decimal	Octal	Decimal
.000	.00000000	.061	.09570313	.142	.19140625	.223	.28710938
.001	.00195313	.062	.09765625	.143	.19335938	.224	.28906250
.002	.00390625	.063	.09960938	.144	.19531250	.225	.29101563
.003	.00585938	.064	.10156250	.145	.19726563	.226	.29296875
.004	.00781250	.065	.10351563	.146	.19921875	.227	.29492188
.005	.00976563	.066	.10546875	.147	.20117188	.230	.29687500
.006	.01171875	.067	.10742188	.150	.20312500	.231	.29882813
.007	.01367188	.070	.10937500	.151	.20507813	.232	.30078125
.010	.01562500	.071	.11132813	.152	.20703125	.233	.30273438
.011	.01757813	.072	.11328125	.153	.20898438	.234	.30468750
.012	.01953125	.073	.11523438	.154	.21093750	.235	.30664063
.013	.02148438	.074	.11718750	.155	.21289063	.236	.30859375
.014	.02343750	.075	.11914063	.156	.21484375	.237	.31054688
.015	.02539063	.076	.12109375	.157	.21679688	.240	.31250000
.016	.02734375	.077	.12304688	.160	.21875000	.241	.31445313
.017	.02929688	.100	.12500000	.161	.22070313	.242	.31640625
.020	.03125000	.101	.12695313	.162	.22265625	.243	.31835938
.021	.03320313	.102	.12890625	.163	.22460938	.244	.32031250
.022	.03515625	.103	.13085938	.164	.22656250	.245	.32226563
.023	.03710938	.104	.13281250	.165	.22851563	.246	.32421875
.024	.03906250	.105	.13476563	.166	.23046875	.247	.32617188
.025	.04101563	.106	.13671875	.167	.23242188	.250	.32812500
.026	.04296875	.107	.13867188	.170	.23437500	.251	.33007813
.027	.04492188	.110	.14062500	.171	.23632813	.252	.33203125
.030	.04687500	.111	.14257813	.172	.23828125	.253	.33398438
.031	.04882813	.112	.14453125	.173	.24023438	.254	.33593750
.032	.05078125	.113	.14648438	.174	.24218750	.255	.33789063
.033	.05273438	.114	.14843750	.175	.24414063	.256	.33984375
.034	.05468750	.115	.15039063	.176	.24609375	.257	.34179688
.035	.05664063	.116	.15234375	.177	.24804688	.260	.34375000
.036	.05859375	.117	.15429688	.200	.25000000	.261	.34570313
.037	.06054688	.120	.15625000	.201	.25195313	.262	.34765625
.040	.06250000	.121	.15820313	.202	.25390625	.263	.34960938
.041	.06445313	.122	.16015625	.203	.25585938	.264	.35156250
.042	.06640625	.123	.16210938	204	.25781250	.265	.35351563
.043	.06835938	.124	.16406250	.205	.25976563	.266	.35546875
.044	.07031250	.125	.16601563	.206	.26171875	.267	.35742188
.045	.07226563	.126	.16796875	.207	.26367188	.270	.35937500
.046	.07421875	.127	.16992188	.210	.26562500	.271	.36132813
.047	.07617188	.130	.17187500	.211	.26757813	.272	.36328125
.050	.07812500	.131	.17382813	.212	.26953125	.273	.36523438
.051	.08007813	.132	.17578125	.213	.27148438	.274	.36718750
.052	.08203125	.133	.17773438	.214	.27343750	.275	.36914063
.053	.08398438	.134	.17968750	.215	.27539063	.276	.37109375
.054	.08593750	.135	.18164063	.216	.27734375	.277	.37304688
.055	.08789063	.136	.18359375	.217	.27929688	.300	.37500000
.056	.08984375	.137	.18554688	.220	.28125000	.301	.37695313
.057	.09179688	.140	.18750000	.221	.28320313	.302	.37890625
.060	.09375000	.141	.18945313	.222	.28515625	.303	.38085938

TABLE A-5. **Octal-Decimal Fraction Conversion Table** (*Continued*).

Octal	Decimal	Octal	Decimal	Octal	Decimal	Octal	Decimal
.304	.38281250	.323	.41210938	.342	.44140625	.361	.47070313
.305	.38476563	.324	.41406250	.343	.44335938	.362	.47265625
.306	.38671875	.325	.41601563	.344	.44531250	.363	.47460938
.307	.38867188	.326	.41796875	.345	.44726563	.364	.47656250
.310	.39062500	.327	.41992188	.346	.44921875	.365	.47851563
.311	.39257813	.330	.42187500	.347	.45117188	.366	.48046875
.312	.39453125	.331	.42382813	.350	.45312500	.367	.48242188
.313	.39648438	.332	.42578125	.351	.45507813	.370	.48437500
.314	.39843750	.333	.42773438	.352	.45703125	.371	.48632813
.315	.40039063	.334	.42968750	.353	.45898438	.372	.48828125
.316	.40234375	.335	.43164063	.354	.46093750	.373	.49023438
.317	.40429688	.336	.43359375	.355	.46289063	.374	.49218750
.320	.40625000	.337	.43554688	.356	.46484375	.375	.49414063
.321	.40820313	.340	.43750000	.357	.46679688	.376	.49609375
.322	.41015625	.341	.43945313	.360	.46875000	.377	.49804688

Note: $(0.4)_8 = (0.5)_{10}$
therefore, for example,

$$(0.652)_8 = (0.252)_8 + (0.5)_{10}$$
$$= (0.33203125)_{10} + (0.5)_{10}$$

TABLE A-5. Octal-Decimal Fraction Conversion Table (*Continued*).

Octal	Decimal	Octal	Decimal	Octal	Decimal
.000000	.00000000	.000060	.00018311	.000140	.00036621
.000001	.00000381	.000061	.00018692	.000141	.00037003
.000002	.00000763	.000062	.00019073	.000142	.00037384
.000003	.00001144	.000063	.00019455	.000143	.00037766
.000004	.00001526	.000064	.00019836	.000144	.00038147
.000005	.00001907	.000065	.00020218	.000145	.00038528
.000006	.00002289	.000066	.00020599	.000146	.00038910
.000007	.00002670	.000067	.00020981	.000147	.00039291
.000010	.00003052	.000070	.00021362	.000150	.00039673
.000011	.00003433	.000071	.00021744	.000151	.00040054
.000012	.00003815	.000072	.00022125	.000152	.00040436
.000013	.00004196	.000073	.00022507	.000153	.00040817
.000014	.00004578	.000074	.00022888	.000154	.00041199
.000015	.00004959	.000075	.00023270	.000155	.00041580
.000016	.00005341	.000076	.00023651	.000156	.00041962
.000017	.00005722	.000077	.00024033	.000157	.00042343
.000020	.00006104	.000100	.00024414	.000160	.00042725
.000021	.00006485	.000101	.00024796	.000161	.00043106
.000022	.00006866	.000102	.00025177	.000162	.00043488
.000023	.00007248	.000103	.00025558	.000163	.00043869
.000024	.00007629	.000104	.00025940	.000164	.00044250
.000025	.00008011	.000105	.00026321	.000165	.00044632
.000026	.00008392	.000106	.00026703	.000166	.00045013
.000027	.00008774	.000107	.00027084	.000167	.00045395
.000030	.00009155	.000110	.00027466	.000170	.00045776
.000031	.00009537	.000111	.00027847	.000171	.00046158
.000032	.00009918	.000112	.00028229	.000172	.00046539
.000033	.00010300	.000113	.00028610	.000173	.00046921
.000034	.00010681	.000114	.00028992	.000174	.00047302
.000035	.00011063	.000115	.00029373	.000175	.00047684
.000036	.00011444	.000116	.00029755	.000176	.00048065
.000037	.00011826	.000117	.00030136	.000177	.00048447
.000040	.00012207	.000120	.00030519	.000200	.00048828
.000041	.00012589	.000121	.00030899	.000201	.00049210
.000042	.00012970	.000122	.00031281	.000202	.00049591
.000043	.00013351	.000123	.00031662	.000203	.00049973
.000044	.00013733	.000124	.00032043	.000204	.00050354
.000045	.00014114	.000125	.00032425	.000205	.00050735
.000046	.00014496	.000126	.00032806	.000206	.00051117
.000047	.00014877	.000127	.00033188	.000207	.00051498
.000050	.00015259	.000130	.00033569	.000210	.00051880
.000051	.00015640	.000131	.00033951	.000211	.00052261
.000052	.00016022	.000132	.00034332	.000212	.00052643
.000053	.00016403	.000133	.00034714	.000213	.00053024
.000054	.00016785	.000134	.00035095	.000214	.00053406
.000055	.00017166	.000135	.00035477	.000215	.00053787
.000056	.00017548	.000136	.00035858	.000216	.00054169
.000057	.00017929	.000137	.00036240	.000217	.00054550

TABLE A-5. Octal-Decimal Fraction Conversion Table (*Continued*).

Octal	Decimal	Octal	Decimal	Octal	Decimal
.000220	.00054932	.000302	.00074005	.000364	.00093079
.000221	.00055313	.000303	.00074387	.000365	.00093460
.000222	.00055695	.000304	.00074768	.000366	.00093842
.000223	.00056076	.000305	.00075150	.000367	.00094223
.000224	.00056458	.000306	.00075531	.000370	.00094604
.000225	.00056839	.000307	.00075912	.000371	.00094986
.000226	.00057220	.000310	.00076294	.000372	.00095367
.000227	.00057602	.000311	.00076675	.000373	.00095749
.000230	.00057983	.000312	.00077057	.000374	.00096130
.000231	.00058365	.000313	.00077438	.000375	.00096512
.000232	.00058746	.000314	.00077820	.000376	.00096893
.000233	.00059128	.000315	.00078201	.000377	.00097275
.000234	.00059509	.000316	.00078583	.000400	.00097656
.000235	.00059891	.000317	.00078964	.000401	.00098038
.000236	.00060272	.000320	.00079346	.000402	.00098419
.000237	.00060654	.000321	.00079727	.000403	.00098801
.000240	.00061035	.000322	.00080109	.000404	.00099182
.000241	.00061417	.000323	.00080490	.000405	.00099564
.000242	.00061798	.000324	.00080872	.000406	.00099945
.000243	.00062180	.000325	.00081253	.000407	.00100327
.000244	.00062561	.000326	.00081635	.000410	.00100708
.000245	.00062943	.000327	.00082016	.000411	.00101089
.000246	.00063324	.000330	.00082397	.000412	.00101471
.000247	.00063705	.000331	.00082779	.000413	.00101852
.000250	.00064087	.000332	.00083160	.000414	.00102234
.000251	.00064468	.000333	.00083542	.000415	.00102615
.000252	.00064850	.000334	.00083923	.000416	.00102997
.000253	.00065231	.000335	.00084305	.000417	.00103378
.000254	.00065613	.000336	.00084686	.000420	.00103760
.000255	.00065994	.000337	.00085068	.000421	.00104141
.000256	.00066376	.000340	.00085449	.000422	.00104523
.000257	.00066757	.000341	.00085831	.000423	.00104904
.000260	.00067139	.000342	.00086212	.000424	.00105286
.000261	.00067520	.000343	.00086594	.000425	.00105667
.000262	.00067902	.000344	.00086975	.000426	.00106049
.000263	.00068283	.000345	.00087357	.000427	.00106430
.000264	.00068665	.000346	.00087738	.000430	.00106812
.000265	.00069046	.000347	.00088120	.000431	.00107193
.000266	.00069427	.000350	.00088501	.000432	.00107574
.000267	.00069809	.000351	.00088882	.000433	.00107956
.000270	.00070190	.000352	.00089264	.000434	.00108337
.000271	.00070572	.000353	.00089645	.000435	.00108719
.000272	.00070953	.000354	.00090027	.000436	.00109100
.000273	.00071335	.000355	.00090408	.000437	.00109482
.000274	.00071716	.000356	.00090790	.000440	.00109863
.000275	.00072098	.000357	.00091171	.000441	.00110245
.000276	.00072479	.000360	.00091553	.000442	.00110626
.000277	.00072861	.000361	.00091934	.000443	.00111008
.000300	.00073242	.000362	.00092316	.000444	.00111389
.000301	.00073624	.000363	.00092697	.000445	.00111771

Octal	Decimal	Octal	Decimal	Octal	Decimal
.000446	.00112152	.000530	.00131226	.000612	.00150299
.000447	.00112534	.000531	.00131607	.000613	.00150681
.000450	.00112915	.000532	.00131989	.000614	.00151062
.000451	.00113297	.000533	.00132370	.000615	.00151443
.000452	.00113678	.000534	.00132751	.000616	.00151825
.000453	.00114059	.000535	.00133133	.000617	.00152206
.000454	.00114441	.000536	.00133514	.000620	.00152588
.000455	.00114822	.000537	.00133896	.000621	.00152969
.000456	.00115204	.000540	.00134277	.000622	.00153351
.000457	.00115585	.000541	.00134659	.000623	.00153732
.000460	.00115967	.000542	.00135040	.000624	.00154114
.000461	.00116348	.000543	.00135422	.000625	.00154495
.000462	.00116730	.000544	.00135803	.000626	.00154877
.000463	.00117111	.000545	.00136185	.000627	.00155258
.000464	.00117493	.000546	.00136566	.000630	.00155640
.000465	.00117874	.000547	.00136948	.000631	.00156021
.000466	.00118256	.000550	.00137329	.000632	.00156403
.000467	.00118637	.000551	.00137711	.000633	.00156784
.000470	.00119019	.000552	.00138092	.000634	.00157166
.000471	.00119400	.000553	.00138474	.000635	.00157547
.000472	.00119781	.000554	.00138855	.000636	.00157928
.000473	.00120163	.000555	.00139236	.000637	.00158310
.000474	.00120544	.000556	.00139618	.000640	.00158691
.000475	.00120926	.000557	.00139999	.000641	.00159073
.000476	.00121307	.000560	.00140381	.000642	.00159454
.000477	.00121689	.000561	.00140762	.000643	.00159836
.000500	.00122070	.000562	.00141144	.000644	.00160217
.000501	.00122452	.000563	.00141525	.000645	.00160599
.000502	.00122833	.000564	.00141907	.000646	.00160980
.000503	.00123215	.000565	.00142288	.000647	.00161362
.000504	.00123596	.000566	.00142670	.000650	.00161743
.000505	.00123978	.000567	.00143051	.000651	.00162125
.000506	.00124359	.000570	.00143433	.000652	.00162506
.000507	.00124741	.000571	.00143814	.000653	.00162888
.000510	.00125122	.000572	.00144196	.000654	.00163269
.000511	.00125504	.000573	.00144577	.000655	.00163651
.000512	.00125885	.000574	.00144958	.000656	.00164032
.000513	.00126266	.000575	.00145340	.000657	.00164413
.000514	.00126648	.000576	.00145721	.000660	.00164795
.000515	.00127029	.000577	.00146103	.000661	.00165176
.000516	.00127411	.000600	.00146484	.000662	.00165558
.000517	.00127792	.000601	.00146866	.000663	.00165939
.000520	.00128174	.000602	.00147247	.000664	.00166321
.000521	.00128555	.000603	.00147629	.000665	.00166702
.000522	.00128937	.000604	.00148010	.000666	.00167084
.000523	.00129318	.000605	.00148392	.000667	.00167465
.000524	.00129700	.000606	.00148773	.000670	.00167847
.000525	.00130081	.000607	.00149155	.000671	.00168228
.000526	.00130463	.000610	.00149536	.000672	.00168610
.000527	.00130844	.000611	.00149918	.000673	.00168991

TABLE A-5. Octal-Decimal Fraction Conversion Table (*Continued*).

Octal	Decimal	Octal	Decimal	Octal	Decimal
.000674	.00169373	.000723	.00178146	.000752	.00186920
.000675	.00169754	.000724	.00178528	.000753	.00187302
.000676	.00170135	.000725	.00178909	.000754	.00187683
.000677	.00170517	.000726	.00179291	.000755	.00188065
.000700	.00170898	.000727	.00179672	.000756	.00188446
.000701	.00171280	.000730	.00180054	.000757	.00188828
.000702	.00171661	.000731	.00180435	.000760	.00189209
.000703	.00172043	.000732	.00180817	.000761	.00189590
.000704	.00172424	.000733	.00181198	.000762	.00189972
.000705	.00172806	.000734	.00181580	.000763	.00190353
.000706	.00173187	.000735	.00181961	.000764	.00190735
.000707	.00173569	.000736	.00182343	.000765	.00191116
.000710	.00173950	.000737	.00182724	.000766	.00191498
.000711	.00174332	.000740	.00183105	.000767	.00191879
.000712	.00174713	.000741	.00183487	.000770	.00192261
.000713	.00175095	.000742	.00183868	.000771	.00192642
.000714	.00175476	.000743	.00184250	.000772	.00193024
.000715	.00175858	.000744	.00184631	.000773	.00193405
.000716	.00176239	.000745	.00185013	.000774	.00193787
.000717	.00176620	.000746	.00185394	.000775	.00194168
.000720	.00177002	.000747	.00185776	.000776	.00194550
.000721	.00177383	.000750	.00186157	.000777	.00194931
000722	.00177765	.000751	.00186539		

TABLE A-6a.   Hexadecimal Addition Table.

	1	2	3	4	5	6	7	8	9	A	B	C	D	E	F	
1	2	3	4	5	6	7	8	9	A	B	C	D	E	F	10	1
2	3	4	5	6	7	8	9	A	B	C	D	E	F	10	11	2
3	4	5	6	7	8	9	A	B	C	D	E	F	10	11	12	3
4	5	6	7	8	9	A	B	C	D	E	F	10	11	12	13	4
5	6	7	8	9	A	B	C	D	E	F	10	11	12	13	14	5
6	7	8	9	A	B	C	D	E	F	10	11	12	13	14	15	6
7	8	9	A	B	C	D	E	F	10	11	12	13	14	15	16	7
8	9	A	B	C	D	E	F	10	11	12	13	14	15	16	17	8
9	A	B	C	D	E	F	10	11	12	13	14	15	16	17	18	9
A	B	C	D	E	F	10	11	12	13	14	15	16	17	18	19	A
B	C	D	E	F	10	11	12	13	14	15	16	17	18	19	1A	B
C	D	E	F	10	11	12	13	14	15	16	17	18	19	1A	1B	C
D	E	F	10	11	12	13	14	15	16	17	18	19	1A	1B	1C	D
E	F	10	11	12	13	14	15	16	17	18	19	1A	1B	1C	1D	E
F	10	11	12	13	14	15	16	17	18	19	1A	1B	1C	1D	1E	F
	1	2	3	4	5	6	7	8	9	A	B	C	D	E	F	

TABLE A-6b. Hexadecimal Multiplication Table.

	1	2	3	4	5	6	7	8	9	A	B	C	D	E	F	
1	1	2	3	4	5	6	7	8	9	A	B	C	D	E	F	1
2	2	4	6	8	A	C	E	10	12	14	16	18	1A	1C	1E	2
3	3	6	9	C	F	12	15	18	1B	1E	21	24	27	2A	2D	3
4	4	8	C	10	14	18	1C	20	24	28	2C	30	34	38	3C	4
5	5	A	F	14	19	1E	23	28	2D	32	37	3C	41	46	4B	5
6	6	C	12	18	1E	24	2A	30	36	3C	42	48	4E	54	5A	6
7	7	E	15	1C	23	2A	31	38	3F	46	4D	54	5B	62	69	7
8	8	10	18	20	28	30	38	40	48	50	58	60	68	70	78	8
9	9	12	1B	24	2D	36	3F	48	51	5A	63	6C	75	7E	87	9
A	A	14	1E	28	32	3C	46	50	5A	64	6E	78	82	8C	96	A
B	B	16	21	2C	37	42	4D	58	63	6E	79	84	8F	9A	A5	B
C	C	18	24	30	3C	48	54	60	6C	78	84	90	9C	A8	B4	C
D	D	1A	27	34	41	4E	5B	68	75	82	8F	9C	A9	B6	C3	D
E	E	1C	2A	38	46	54	62	70	7E	8C	9A	A8	B6	C4	D2	E
F	F	1E	2D	3C	4B	5A	69	78	87	96	A5	B4	C3	D2	E1	F
	1	2	3	4	5	6	7	8	9	A	B	C	D	E	F	

TABLE A-7. Teletype* Code.

Even parity bit	7-bit octal code	Character	Remarks
0	000	NUL	Null, tape feed. Repeats on Model 37. Control shift P on Model 33 and 35.
1	001	SOH	Start of heading; also SOM, start of message. Control A.
1	002	STX	Start of text; also EOA, end of address. Control B.
0	003	ETX	End of text; also EOM, end of message. Control C.
1	004	EOT	End of transmission (END); shuts off TWX machines. Control D.
0	005	ENQ	Enquiry (ENQRY); also WRU, "Who are you?" Triggers identification ("Here is . . . ") at remote station if so equipped. Control E.
0	006	ACK	Acknowledge; also RU, "Are you . . . ?" Control F.
1	007	BEL	Rings the bell. Control G.
1	010	BS	Backspace; also FEO, format effector. Backspaces some machines. Repeats on Model 37. Control H on Model 33 and 35.
0	011	HT	Horizontal tab. Control I on Model 33 and 35.
0	012	LF	Line feed or line space (NEW LINE); advances paper to next line. Repeats on Model 37. Duplicated by control J on Model 33 and 35.
1	013	VT	Vertical tab (VTAB). Control K on Model 33 and 35.
0	014	FF	Form feed to top of next page (PAGE). Control L.
1	015	CR	Carriage return to beginning of line. Control M on Model 33 and 35.
1	016	SO	Shift out; changes ribbon color to red. Control N.
0	017	SI	Shift in; changes ribbon color to black. Control O.
1	020	DLE	Data link escape. Control P (DCO).
0	021	DC1	Device control 1, turns transmitter (reader) on. Control Q (X ON).
0	022	DC2	Device control 2, turns punch or auxiliary on. Control R (TAPE, AUX ON).
1	023	DC3	Device control 3, turns transmitter (reader) off. Control S (X OFF).
0	024	DC4	Device control 4, turns punch or auxiliary off. Control T (AUX OFF).
1	025	NAK	Negative acknowledge; also ERR, error. Control U.
1	026	SYN	Synchronous idle (SYNC). Control V.
0	027	ETB	End of transmission block; also LEM, logical end of medium. Control W.
0	030	CAN	Cancel (CANCL). Control X.
1	031	EM	End of medium. Control Y.
1	032	SUB	Substitute. Control Z.
0	033	ESC	Escape, prefix. This code is also generated by control shift K on Model 33 and 35.
1	034	FS	File separator. Control shift L on Model 33 and 35.
0	035	GS	Group separator. Control shift M on Model 33 and 35.
0	036	RS	Record separator. Control shift N on Model 33 and 35.
1	037	US	Unit separator. Control shift O on Model 33 and 35.
1	040	SP	Space.
0	041	!	
0	042	"	

* Teletype is a registered trademark of the Teletype Corporation.

TABLE A-7.   Teletype Code (*Continued*).

Even parity bit	7-bit octal code	Character	Even parity bit	7-bit octal code	Character
1	043	#	0	116	N
0	044	$	1	117	O
1	045	%	0	120	P
1	046	&	1	121	Q
0	047	'	1	122	R
0	050	(	0	123	S
1	051	)	1	124	T
1	052	*	0	125	U
0	053	+	0	126	V
1	054	,	1	127	W
0	055	−	1	130	X
0	056	.	0	131	Y
1	057	/	0	132	Z
0	060	Ø	1	133	[Shift K on Model 33 and 35.
1	061	1	0	134	\ Shift L on Model 33 and 35.
1	062	2	1	135	] Shift M on Model 33 and 35.
0	063	3	1	136	↑
1	064	4	0	137	←
0	065	5	0	140	'
0	066	6	1	141	a
1	067	7	1	142	b
1	070	8	0	143	c
0	071	9	1	144	d
0	072	:	0	145	e
1	073	;	0	146	f
0	074	<	1	147	g
1	075	=	1	150	h
1	076	>	0	151	i
0	077	?	0	152	j
1	100	@	1	153	k
0	101	A	0	154	l
0	102	B	1	155	m
1	103	C	1	156	n
0	104	D	0	157	o
1	105	E	1	160	p
1	106	F	0	161	q
0	107	G	0	162	r
0	110	H	1	163	s
1	111	I	0	164	t
1	112	J	1	165	u
0	113	K	1	166	v
1	114	L	0	167	w
0	115	M	0	170	x

TABLE A-7.   Teletype Code (*Continued*).

Even parity bit	7-bit octal code	Character	Remarks
1	171	y	
1	172	z	
0	173	{	
1	174			
0	175	}	
0	176	~	On early versions of the Model 33 and 35, this code may be generated by either the ALT MODE or ESC key.
1	177	DEL	Delete, rub out. Repeats on Model 37.

	Keys that generate no codes
REPT	Model 33 and 35 only: causes any other key that is struck to repeat continuously until REPT is released.
PAPER ADVANCE	Model 37 local line feed.
LOCAL RETURN	Model 37 local carriage return.
LOC LF	Model 33 and 35 local line feed.
LOC CR	Model 33 and 35 local carriage return.
INTERRUPT, BREAK	Opens the line (machine sends a continuous string of null characters).
PROCEED, BRK RLS	Break release (not applicable).
HERE IS	Transmits predetermined 20-character message.

$\rightarrow$, $-$, . , $=$, X, x, also repeat on Model 37.

TABLE A-8. Teletype*/Paper-tape Code.

● = HOLE PUNCHED = MARK = 1 BIT
O = NO HOLE PUNCHED = SPACE = O BIT

MOST SIGNIFICANT BIT
LEAST SIGNIFICANT BIT

	(letter)		(punct)		Control	8	7	6	5	4	S	3	2	1
	@	*	SPACE		NULL (IDLE)			O	O	O		O	O	O
	A		!	*	START OF MESSAGE			O	O	O		O	O	●
	B		"	*	END OF ADDRESS (EOA)			O	O	O		O	●	O
	C		#	*	END OF MESSAGE (EOM)			O	O	O		O	●	●
	D		$	*	END OF TRANSMISSION (EOT)			O	O	O		●	O	O
	E		%	*	WHO ARE YOU (WRU)			O	O	O		●	O	●
	F		&	*	ARE YOU (RU)			O	O	O		●	●	O
	G		'	*	BELL			O	O	O		●	●	●
	H		(	*	FORMAT EFFECTOR			O	O	●		O	O	O
	I		)	*	HORIZONTAL TAB			O	O	●		O	O	●
	J		*	*	LINE FEED			O	O	●		O	●	O
	K		+	*	VERTICAL TAB			O	O	●		O	●	●
	L		,		FORM FEED			O	O	●		●	O	O
	M		–		CARRIAGE RETURN			O	O	●		●	O	●
	N		.		SHIFT OUT			O	O	●		●	●	O
	O		/		SHIFT IN			O	O	●		●	●	●
	P		0		DC0			O	●	O		O	O	O
	Q		1		READER ON			O	●	O		O	O	●
	R		2		TAPE (AUX ON)			O	●	O		O	●	O
	S		3		READER OFF			O	●	O		O	●	●
	T		4		(AUX OFF)			O	●	O		●	O	O
	U		5		ERROR			O	●	O		●	O	●
	V		6		SYNCHRONOUS IDLE			O	●	O		●	●	O
	W		7		LOGICAL END OF MEDIA			O	●	O		●	●	●
	X		8		S0			O	●	●		O	O	O
	Y		9		S1			O	●	●		O	O	●
	Z		:		S2			O	●	●		O	●	O
	[	*	;		S3			O	●	●		O	●	●
ACK	\	*	<	*	S4			O	●	●		●	O	O
ALT MODE	]	*	=	*	S5			O	●	●		●	O	●
	↑	*	>	*	S6			O	●	●		●	●	O
RUB OUT	←	*	?	*	S7			O	●	●		●	●	●

NON-TYPING

NON-TYPING

●	O	O	SAME
●	O	●	SAME
●	●	O	SAME
●	●	●	SAME

* OBTAINED WITH SHIFT KEY

---

* Teletype is a registered trademark of the Teletype Corporation.

TABLE A-9.   ASCII/Teletypewriter/Hexadecimal Conversion Table.

Teletypewriter-tape channels 1, 2, . . . , 7 correspond to bits 0 (LSB), 1, 2, . . . , 6 of a character byte; channel 8 or bit 7 represents the parity bit.   The unassigned codes are used optionally for lowercase letters.

HEX (MSD) →					8	9	A	B	C	D	E	F
(LSD)				8	DEPENDS	UPON	PARITY					
Teletypewriter Tape Channels →				7	0	0	0	0	1	1	1	1
				6	0	0	1	1	0	0	1	1
				5	0	1	0	1	0	1	0	1
	4	3	2	1								
0	0	0	0	0	NULL	DC_0	SPACE	0	@	P		
1	0	0	0	1	SUM	X-ON	!	1	A	Q		
2	0	0	1	0	EOA	TAPE ON	"	2	B	R		
3	0	0	1	1	EOM	X-OFF	#	3	C	S		
4	0	1	0	0	EOT	TAPE OFF	$	4	D	T		
5	0	1	0	1	WRU	ERR	%	5	E	U		
6	0	1	1	0	RU	SYNC	&	6	F	V		
7	0	1	1	1	BELL	LEM	'	7	G	W		
8	1	0	0	0	FE_0	S_0	(	8	H	X		
9	1	0	0	1	HT/SK	S_1	)	9	I	Y		
A	1	0	1	0	LF	S_2	*	:	J	Z		
B	1	0	1	1	VT	S_3	+	;	K	[		
C	1	1	0	0	FF	S_4	,	<	L	\		ACK
D	1	1	0	1	CR	S_5	−	=	M	]		ALT. MODE
E	1	1	1	0	SO	S_6	.	>	N	↑		ESC
F	1	1	1	1	SI	S_7	/	?	O	←		DEL

TABLE A-10. ASCII/Card-Code Conversion Table.

Graphic	8-bit ASCII code	7-bit ASCII code	Card code	Graphic	8-bit ASCII code	7-bit ASCII code	Card code
SPACE	A0	20	0-8-2	@	C0	40	8-4
!	A1	21	12-8-7	A	C1	41	12-1
"	A2	22	8-7	B	C2	42	12-2
#	A3	23	8-3	C	C3	43	12-3
$	A4	24	11-8-3	D	C4	44	12-4
%	A5	25	0-8-4	E	C5	45	12-5
&	A6	26	12	F	C6	46	12-6
'	A7	27	8-5	G	C7	47	12-7
(	A8	28	12-8-5	H	C8	48	12-8
)	A9	29	11-8-5	I	C9	49	12-9
*	AA	2A	11-8-4	J	CA	4A	11-1
+	AB	2B	12-8-6	K	CB	4B	11-2
,	AC	2C	0-8-3	L	CC	4C	11-3
−	AD	2D	11	M	CD	4D	11-4
.	AE	2E	12-8-3	N	CE	4E	11-5
/	AF	2F	0-1	O	CF	4F	11-6
0	B0	30	0	P	D0	50	11-7
1	B1	31	1	Q	D1	51	11-8
2	B2	32	2	R	D2	52	11-9
3	B3	33	3	S	D3	53	0-2
4	B4	34	4	T	D4	54	0-3
5	B5	35	5	U	D5	55	0-4
6	B6	36	6	V	D6	56	0-5
7	B7	37	7	W	D7	57	0-6
8	B8	38	8	X	D8	58	0-7
9	B9	39	9	Y	D9	59	0-8
:	BA	3A	8-2	Z	DA	5A	0-9
;	BB	3B	11-8-6	[	DB	5B	12-8-2
<	BC	3C	12-8-4	\	DC	5C	11-8-1
=	BD	3D	8-6	]	DD	5D	11-8-2
>	BE	3E	0-8-6	↑	DE	5E	11-8-7
?	BF	3F	0-8-7	←	DF	5F	0-8-5

TABLE A-11.   7-bit and 6-bit "Trimmed" ASCII Codes.

Printing character	7-bit ASCII	6-bit trimmed ASCII	Printing character	7-bit ASCII	6-bit trimmed ASCII
@	100	00	(Space)	040	40
A	101	01	!	041	41
B	102	02	"	042	42
C	103	03	#	043	43
D	104	04	$	044	44
E	105	05	%	045	45
F	106	06	&	046	46
G	107	07	'	047	47
H	110	10	(	050	50
I	111	11	)	051	51
J	112	12	*	052	52
K	113	13	+	053	53
L	114	14	'	054	54
M	115	15	−	055	55
N	116	16	.	056	56
O	117	17	/	057	57
P	120	20	0	060	60
Q	121	21	1	061	61
R	122	22	2	062	62
S	123	23	3	063	63
T	124	24	4	064	64
U	125	25	5	065	65
V	126	26	6	066	66
W	127	27	7	067	67
X	130	30	8	070	70
Y	131	31	9	071	71
Z	132	32	:*	072	72
[*	133	33	;	073	73
\	134	34	<	074	74
]*	135	35	=	075	75
↑*	136	36	>	076	76
← *	137	37	?	077	77
Null	000				
Horizontal Tab	011				
Line Feed	012				
Vertical Tab	013				
Form Feed	014				
Carriage Return	015				
Rubout	177				

INDEX

References in the index are to section numbers, not page numbers. Note that section numbers are displayed at the top of text pages for convenient reference.